DEMOCRATIC DIALOGUE AND THE CONSTITUTION

Democratic Dialogue and the Constitution

ALISON L YOUNG

OXFORD
UNIVERSITY PRESS

OXFORD
UNIVERSITY PRESS

Great Clarendon Street, Oxford, OX2 6DP,
United Kingdom

Oxford University Press is a department of the University of Oxford.
It furthers the University's objective of excellence in research, scholarship,
and education by publishing worldwide. Oxford is a registered trade mark of
Oxford University Press in the UK and in certain other countries

First Edition published in 2017

Published in the United States of America by Oxford University Press
198 Madison Avenue, New York, NY 10016, United States of America

British Library Cataloguing in Publication Data
Data available

Library of Congress Control Number: 2016953194

ISBN 978–0–19–878374–9

For Mycroft, Muse, and Mornington Crescent

Acknowledgements

The research for this book was most generously funded by The Leverhulme Trust, to whom I owe my largest debt of gratitude. Without their Research Fellowship award, this book may never have come to fruition. I was able to use their funding to teach part-time for two years from 2013 to 2015, which enabled me to complete a first draft of the book. The fact that it took me a further year to finalize this draft, whilst teaching full-time, provides a clear exemplification of how this book would have taken considerably longer to complete without their generosity. Being able to take part-time leave would also not have been possible without the support of my colleagues at Hertford College. I owe particular thanks to Stephen Dimelow, who tirelessly took over my undergraduate tutorial teaching in both constitutional and administrative law for two years. I also owe special thanks to my esteemed colleague Alan Bogg for his unceasing support, especially in the second year of my part-time leave. He was, is, and I'm sure will ever remain the epitome of civic virtues.

I have been extremely fortunate to benefit from a supportive academic community, who have listened to my vague ramblings, encouraged my search for new ideas, and read many a badly written draft. Foremost in this regard, I owe an extremely large debt of gratitude to Paul Craig. Space really does preclude a proportionate expression of my thanks, so I'm afraid that Paul will have to make do, for now, with words that barely scrape through an application of the *Wednesbury* unreasonableness standard of scrutiny. I will limit myself to two points. Not only did he read the entire book in draft form, graciously pointing out errors and hostages to fortune, but also he has been a constant source of support and encouragement. I am also grateful to Graham Gee, Hayley Hooper, and Menelaos Markakis for their comments on earlier drafts. It is always problematic to provide a list of all who have listened to arguments or acted as a sounding board for my, often strange, ideas on public law which then somehow made their way into this book, or were rightly rejected. I can only endeavour to try my best (and hope anyone I miss off the list realizes that this is due to exhaustion and my own forgetfulness). With that note of disclaimer, I would like to thank: Farrah Ahmed, Trevor Allan, Merris Amos, Nicholas Bamforth, Nick Barber, Sophie Boyron, Paul Craig, Richard Danbury, Stephen Dimelow, Mark Elliott, Carolyn Evans, Liz Fisher, Stephen Gardbaum, Andrew Geddis, Graham Gee, Les Green, Carol Harlow, Janet Hiebert, Hayley Hooper, Grant Huscroft, Aileen Kavanagh, Tarunabh Khaitan, Jeff King, Roger Masterman, Danny Nicol, Jane Norton, Sebastian Payne, Adam Perry, Gavin Phillipson, Rick Rawlings, Kent Roach, Ewan Smith, Adrienne Stone, Stephen Tierney, and Grégoire Webber.

I am also fortunate to benefit from working with extremely bright and enthusiastic students, many of whom have suffered these ideas sneaking into tutorials and BCL seminars. To that extent, I would like simultaneously to thank, and apologize to, the undergraduate law students at Hertford, Merton, Balliol, and Keble, in addition to anyone attending the comparative public law seminars. Whenever I mentioned 'it's all about the dialogue …', or muttered darkly about being a 'dialogue theorist', this is what I meant.

There are also those who have supplied tea, coffee, and a friendly face to help me through what have been some dark and difficult times whilst writing this book. Without their support, I'd not have made it to the end of the book. My thanks go to Alan Bogg, Oliver Butler, Richard Danbury, Stephen Dimelow, Hayley Hooper, Jieun

Kiaer, James Lazarus, Graham May, Dana Mills, Rebecca Sitsapesan, and Felix Wardle. I would also like to thank 'the mothership'—Grace, Jill, Laura, Shelly, and Tina—Hannah, and the rest of my Springboard group. I also need to thank my family—Duncan, Imogen, Bagheera, and Roo.

Alison L Young

Oxford
July 2016

Table of Contents

Table of Authorities

UNITED KINGDOM

AUSTRALIA

CANADA

EUROPEAN COURT OF HUMAN RIGHTS

EUROPEAN UNION

GERMANY

NEW ZEALAND

SOUTH AFRICA

UNITED STATES

Introduction

Dialogue has become an increasingly popular term in constitutional theory. Although dialogue had previously been referred to in American scholarship in political science,[1] and in the legal literature,[2] its gain in popularity appears to have been triggered by the seminal article of Hogg and Bushell (now Thornton) in relation to the Canadian Charter of Fundamental Rights and Freedoms.[3] This is particularly true of the use of dialogue in the UK literature on human rights. Given the similarities between the protection of rights found in the Canadian *Charter* and in the UK's Human Rights Act 1998, scholarship on the Act referred to the Canadian literature, drawing in turn on theories of democratic dialogue.

Dialogue's influence, however, is not confined to the Human Rights Act or other commonwealth or midway protections of human rights. It has grown in two different, yet converging directions. First, dialogue has been adopted as a means of resolving perceived tensions between different courts as well as those between the legislature and the courts. Second, dialogue has been elevated as a proposed new model of the constitution, capable of providing a midway position between legal and political constitutionalism. These developments converge in EU law and in the UK. With regard to the European Union, there is a growing tendency to regard the Union as an example of constitutional or legal pluralism. As such, an account of dialogue between the national constitutional courts and the Court of Justice of the European Union begins to take on a new dimension. It is no longer a descriptive account of how two judicial institutions interact, but has been elevated to a normative account of how these institutions should interact in a post-sovereign world.[4] In the UK, convergence occurs due to the way in which arguments as to the role of the Human Rights Act relate to legal and political constitutionalism.[5] Those advocating a stronger protection of human rights draw on legal constitutionalism, with those advocating a weaker protection of rights drawing on political constitutionalism. Dialogue is presented as a means of squaring the circle, providing a protection of human rights that draws on the strengths of both legal and political protections of human rights. This can be regarded either as providing a midway position between extreme versions of legal and political constitutionalism, or as providing a new, independent theory of constitutionalism which draws on, but is nevertheless distinct from, more moderate forms of legal and political constitutionalism

[1] See, for example, L Fisher, *Constitutional Dialogues: Interpretation as Political Process* (Princeton University Press 1988) and RA Burt, *The Constitution in Conflict* (Belknap, Harvard University Press 1992).

[2] See, for example, B Friedman, 'Dialogue and Judicial Review' (1993) 91 Michigan Law Review 577.

[3] P Hogg and A Bushell, 'The *Charter* Dialogue between Courts and Legislatures (Or Perhaps *The Charter of Rights* Isn't Such a Bad Thing After All)' (1997) 35 Osgoode Hall Law Journal 75.

[4] See, for example, N MacCormick, *Questioning Sovereignty* (Oxford University Press 1999) and MP Maduro, 'Contrapunctual Law: Europe's Constitutional Pluralism in Action' in N Walker (ed), *Sovereignty in Transition* (Oxford, Hart 2003) 532.

[5] See S Gardbaum, *The New Commonwealth Model of Constitutionalism: Theory and Practice* (Cambridge University Press 2013) 32–35.

which also recognize the need for the legislature and the judiciary to work together to protect human rights and control the executive.

As with every popular phrase, however, the more it is used, the more we begin to doubt its utility. In particular, there are concerns as to what dialogue actually means and whether it can deliver on its promises. What does it mean for courts and legislatures to talk to each other about human rights? How can national, supranational, and international courts interact with each other when it comes to protecting human rights? Is it possible to provide a theory that can combine the strengths of legal and political protections of human rights whilst negating their weaknesses? Can you provide an account of a midway theory of constitutional law without this collapsing into a more refined theory of either legal or political constitutionalism?

This book is concerned with answering these questions. To do so it needs to first define dialogue before assessing its claims to provide a better account of constitutional law and of the manner in which we should protect human rights. The purpose of this introduction is to provide a guide to the reader coming across these claims for the first time, and to provide a context within which to assess this theory. To define and defend dialogue is no easy task. It is easy to dismiss the theory as making overly general claims that cannot be defended, or of providing an account of constitutional law that it is impossible to define or to distinguish from other accounts of the constitution or other means of protecting human rights. This book aims to answer these criticisms.

I. A Brief Introduction to Democratic Dialogue: Panacea or Placebo?

It is difficult to start any account of democratic dialogue without referring to the seminal account of constitutional dialogue found in Hogg and Bushell's account of human rights protections under the Canadian Charter of Fundamental Rights and Freedoms. Their account was so influential as it promised to provide a means of defending strong judicial protections of human rights from the criticism that such protections were anti-democratic. Strong protections of human rights empower courts to strike down legislation that is incompatible with human rights. Yet, legislation is usually enacted by democratically elected and democratically accountable institutions. The judiciary, however, is neither democratically elected nor democratically accountable. Hogg and Bushell argued that this criticism did not apply to the Canadian *Charter* because it facilitated dialogue between the legislature and the courts. Dialogue occurs whenever the legislature has the ability to respond to a decision of the court. In the context of the Canadian *Charter*, Hogg and Bushell argued that this could occur in four ways:[6] (i) through the 'override clause' where legislatures could enact legislation 'notwithstanding' the provisions of the *Charter*;[7] (ii) through the use of the general restrictions clause, where legislatures can place restrictions on rights as justified in a democratic and free society;[8] (iii) the qualified rights which also allow for reasonable restrictions as justified in a democratic and free society;[9] and (iv) the equality clause.[10]

[6] Hogg and Bushell (n 3) 82–92.

[7] The *Charter* is found in the Constitution Act (1982) (Canada) and the Canada Act 1982 (UK). For ease of reference, this book will refer to the provisions of the *Charter* by referring to the Canadian Charter of Fundamental Rights and Freedoms. The notwithstanding provision is found in section 33 of the *Charter*.

[8] ibid, section 1.

[9] ibid, sections 7, 8, 9, and 12.

[10] ibid, section 15.

Each of these provisions empowers the legislature to respond to decisions of the courts. The override clause empowers the legislature to enact measures notwithstanding the *Charter* protections, effectively allowing for derogation from the *Charter*. Such legislation effectively has a five-year sunset clause, the notwithstanding provision needing to be renewed after five years. Legislatures could respond to court decisions striking down legislation by re-enacting the legislation with a notwithstanding clause. The general restrictions clause and qualified rights facilitate dialogue in a different manner. These provisions allow the legislation to impose restrictions on *Charter* rights, with the court checking to ensure that such restrictions are reasonable and justified in a democratic and free society. When making this assessment, the court can grant a larger or a smaller discretionary area of judgment to the legislature, depending on how precisely the court determines whether restrictions are reasonable. This enables legislatures to respond to court decisions by exercising a choice from a range of possible restrictions. The equality clause facilitates dialogue as all the law requires is that like situations are treated alike. The law does not dictate whether, to achieve equality, those in a worse position need to be given the advantage given to those in a better position or vice versa. The law may require that women are given the same pay as men performing the same job. However, it does not dictate whether this is achieved through raising the women's salary, or lowering the men's salary, or both. The legislature can respond to court decisions by determining the means through which equality is achieved. These possibilities of legislative response mitigate, if not remove, the criticism that protecting rights is anti-democratic.

Hogg and Bushell's account of democratic dialogue influenced constitutional design. Their work suggested that States no longer needed to choose between a strong protection of human rights, with its potential problems of overriding democracy, and a weak parliamentary protection of human rights with its preservation of democracy, but the ever-present worry that democratic majorities will harm the human rights of minority groups. Rather, there is the possibility of combining the advantages of a strong protection of human rights and of the preservation of democracy. This led to the emergence of midway, partial, or commonwealth models of human rights protections designed to protect human rights in a manner that facilitates democratic dialogue between the legislature and the courts.[11] These models can be found in Canada,[12] New Zealand,[13] the United Kingdom,[14] and in Australia, albeit not at a Federal level.[15] In his work on the commonwealth model, Stephen Gardbaum concludes that this model of human rights protections can enable constitutions to have the best of both worlds. States can obtain the advantages and minimize the disadvantages of a strong legal protection of human rights and also of a purely parliamentary protection of human rights.

However, in addition to recognizing the value of democratic dialogue models of human rights protections, his work also draws attention to one of the main problems of democratic dialogue; how do we define dialogue and how is it different from other theories or means of protecting human rights? Gardbaum's original work referred to a democratic dialogue model of human rights protections. However, he later changed his mind, referring, instead, to the commonwealth model of rights protections. Gardbaum believes that democratic dialogue is too vague to serve as a label for this new model

[11] For the most comprehensive account of this model of constitutionalism, see Gardbaum (n 5).

[12] Canadian Charter of Fundamental Rights and Freedoms (n 7).

[13] New Zealand Bill of Rights Act 1992.

[14] The Human Rights Act 1998.

[15] The Australian Capital Territories Human Rights Act 2004 and the Victorian Charter of Human Rights and Responsibilities Act 2006.

of human rights protections. In particular, it is over-inclusive given that dialogue can occur between the legislature and the judiciary in legal systems that have a strong protection of human rights, for example in the United States.[16] Nevertheless, Gardbaum is convinced that the commonwealth model can provide a better form of protection for human rights by incorporating the strengths of both legal and political protections of rights, whilst also alleviating some of the weaknesses found in a purely legal or purely political protection of rights. To ensure the distinct nature of these claims, Gardbaum focuses on constitutional design. The commonwealth model is distinct as it is designed to facilitate dialogue through the different legal powers it gives to the legislature and the judiciary.

The problem of determining what is meant by democratic dialogue explains one way in which democratic dialogue models of human rights protections appear to be a panacea, but may be a mere placebo. The model promises to provide a protection of human rights that maximizes the advantages and minimizes the dangers of purely legal or purely political protections of human rights. However, it has been questioned whether this really does provide a novel solution to the anti-democratic criticism of strong legal protections of human rights, particularly as legal systems with strong protections of human rights often use tools such as judicial minimalism or deference, designed to show respect for democratic decision-making, in order to avoid striking down legislation. Gardbaum recognizes this criticism of dialogue, but argues that, nevertheless, democratic dialogue can provide a distinct means of protecting human rights, provided that we recognize it is advocating a novel form of constitutional design. Is this enough to rescue democratic dialogue from claims that it is meaningless and incapable of providing a distinct theory?

Mark Tushnet would argue that this is insufficient because we need to examine not just different forms of legal rights, but also the manner in which these legal rights are exercised. He argues that democratic dialogue, or commonwealth models, are both inherently unstable. In practice these models collapse either into legal or parliamentary protections of human rights.[17] Tushnet argues that this collapse occurs because constitutional provisions that are designed to protect democratic dialogue need not be exercised in a manner that facilitates dialogue. For example, due to criticism of its initial use, the notwithstanding clause has almost fallen into desuetude.[18] This has led some commentators to argue that Canada has, in reality, a strong legal protection of rights[19] and for others to argue that it is the general restrictions clause found in section 1 of the *Charter* that provides the strongest justification for classifying the Canadian constitution as providing a democratic dialogue model of human rights.[20] This criticism is not confined to the Canadian model. In his assessment of the commonwealth model, Gardbaum recognized not only that different models gave different powers to the legislature and the judiciary when protecting human rights, but that these powers had been exercised differently in each country and over time.[21]

This potential for collapse is also illustrated in different academic accounts of how democratic dialogue should apply in practice. Academic commentators advocate different forms of democratic dialogue, placing more or less emphasis on the advantages

[16] See Gardbaum (n 5) 16–17.

[17] M Tushnet, 'New Forms of Judicial Review and the Persistence of Rights and Democracy-based worries' (2003) 38 Wake Forest Law Review 813.

[18] See Gardbaum (n 5) 121–28.

[19] G Huscroft, 'Constitutionalism from the Top Down' (2007) 45 Osgoode Hall Law Journal 91.

[20] See Hogg and Bushell (n 3).

[21] See Gardbaum (n 5).

of judicial or parliamentary protections of human rights. This can be illustrated by the academic commentary in UK law concerning whether courts should prefer section 3 or section 4 of the Human Rights Act 1998. Section 3 requires courts to read and give effect to legislation so as to ensure its compatibility with Convention rights, so far as it is possible to do so. It therefore gives more power to the courts. Courts provide a remedy for the individual through reading the law so as to protect their human rights. Section 4 empowers courts of the level of the high court or above to issue a declaration of incompatibility. These declarations of incompatibility have no impact on the legal force, validity or effect of legislation. No remedy is given to the individual and it is left to the legislature to respond to this declaration of incompatibility through enacting legislation, or for the executive to respond through enacting secondary legislation, subject to parliamentary approval. Section 4, therefore, gives more power to the legislature.

Danny Nicol's account of democratic dialogue places more emphasis on the advantages of a parliamentary protection of rights.[22] He argues that Parliament should possess the final authority to make determinative conclusions as to the definition of rights. He argues that courts should employ section 4 more frequently than section 3, advocating that courts should provide a robust interpretation of rights when making a declaration of incompatibility. Parliament, in turn, should provide an equally robust response when determining whether to modify legislation following a section 4 declaration of incompatibility. In making its response, Parliament should be free to disagree with judicial conceptions of rights and should also reiterate 'the compelling reasons of principle why Parliament, not the courts, remains sovereign'.[23] Tom Hickman, on the other hand, advocates a theory of dialogue favouring the use of section 3 over section 4, based upon the argument that courts should be the dominant institution when protecting rights.[24] This is because courts are better suited to protecting long-standing fundamental rights than the legislature.[25] Rather than being the main means through which rights are protected, Hickman argues that section 4 declarations of incompatibility should be used either to vent scorn against the legislature when faced with legislation that cannot be read or given effect in a manner compatible with Convention rights, or where, given the institutional features of the courts, it would not be possible for the court to provide the specific remedy needed to provide an adequate protection of Convention rights.[26]

Our discussion so far has touched on both the potential strengths and weaknesses of democratic dialogue models of human rights protections. Democratic dialogue promises to provide a better means of protecting human rights through combining the advantages of both judicial and legislative protections of rights. However, as might be suspected for a theory that makes such big claims, there is criticism as to whether the theory offers anything novel at all and, if so, whether it is able to make good on its promises. We argued that it may be possible to regard democratic dialogue as distinct as it provides a unique constitutional model. It advocates a constitutional structure that avoids giving either the legislature or the court the ability to make final, authoritative determinations of human rights. However, as different examples of this model provide different ways of combining legal and political protections of human rights,

[22] D Nicol, 'Law and Politics after the Human Rights Act' [2006] Public Law 722.

[23] ibid, 746.

[24] T Hickman, 'Constitutional Dialogue, Constitutional Theories and the Human Rights Act 1998' [2005] Public Law 306, 327.

[25] ibid, 322–26.

[26] ibid, 327.

democratic dialogue models of human rights protections would appear be, at best, a broad church and, at worst, no different from traditional models of rights protections. These fears are exacerbated by concerns that these models, in practice, will inevitably collapse into legal or parliamentary protections of rights and would appear to be realized in the range of commonwealth models of human rights protections analysed in Gardbaum's work. They are also replicated in academic commentary advocating different ways in which constitutional powers given to the courts and the legislature should be exercised. The more we realize these problems, the more difficult it is to determine whether democratic dialogue can deliver its proposed resolution of the democratic deficit problem.

These concerns escalate when we examine the other areas in which democratic dialogue has developed. Hogg and Bushell's seminal work gave rise to a plethora of articles advocating the values of democratic dialogue. However, it is important to recognize that Hogg and Bushell's analysis did not purport to provide a normative justification for a novel mechanism of protecting human rights. It was descriptive, analysing decisions of the Canadian Supreme Court and responses to these decisions by the Canadian legislature. Hogg and Bushell concluded that this evidence of legislative responses to judicial decisions weakened the democratic deficit criticism of strong legal protections of human rights. They did not advocate democratic dialogue as a better means of protecting human rights. Nor did they provide a theory as to how dialogue should operate under the Canadian *Charter* to ensure that the *Charter* provides the best protection of human rights. To provide this normative justification, theorists draw on the traditional arguments used to justify why either the courts or the legislature should play a predominant role in the protection of human rights. In drawing on these theories, the claims of democratic dialogue are escalated. Not only can democratic dialogue provide for a better way of protecting human rights, it also provides a better account of constitutions as a whole, advocating a middle way between accounts of legal and political constitutionalism.

Democratic dialogue appears to advocate a midway position between a legal and a parliamentary protection of human rights, or a position which aims to combine the relative strengths and weaknesses of legal and political protections of rights, giving the legislature and the courts a more equal role than might be found in theories of legal or political constitutionalism. However, arguments for legal or parliamentary protections of rights are not made in a vacuum. They derive from normative theories which justify why human rights are better protected by the legislature or by the courts. These theories, in turn, rely on different understandings of rights and on perceived institutional and constitutional differences between the legislature and the courts. Those advocating a strong legal protection of human rights do so because of normative arguments supporting the claim that the judiciary is best-placed to decide these issues. Some advocate that rights are considered to be objective principles discernible through a process of moral reasoning and that the judiciary is better suited to carrying out this task, legal reasoning being closely related to the moral reasoning used to discern the content of human rights. The judiciary are also regarded as better at protecting human rights because they can discern when general provisions inadvertently harm human rights. By focusing on the individual, the judiciary can check whether legislation that provides a good protection of human rights in general also provides a good protection of human rights when applied to specific individuals. It is also argued courts are the best institution to regulate human rights disputes as such disputes normally occur between the state and the individual. The judiciary, as an independent arbitrator, is best suited to resolving these complaints, being able to hear both sides and discern the right answer from a neutral perspective. It is also argued that human rights are those principles that emerge from judicial decision. As such, by definition they can only be defined by the judiciary.

Those who propose a parliamentary protection of rights may argue that rights are best determined by democratically accountable bodies as rights are not objective, but are merely another example of a policy argument to protect a particular interest. If the resolution of rights does not require moral reasoning, but the balancing of competing interest groups and the negotiation of an acceptable compromise, this is best performed by a democratically accountable legislative body than by a court. In a similar manner, others argue that human rights are contestable. It can be reasonable to disagree about the range of human rights a society should protect, the way in which rights should be defined, or how rights should be applied to a particular situation. This contestability also means that moral reasoning about rights is insufficient. If it is reasonable to disagree about rights, then it may be reasonable to disagree with the conclusions reached by courts when applying legal or moral reasoning in a particular human rights decision. Legislatures are better at solving these issues; not because they are more likely to reach the right conclusion but because they will reach the conclusion in a more legitimate manner. More groups and individuals will be able to contribute to the debate, either directly or indirectly. In addition, the democratic accountability of the legislature enables legislatures to be better held to account for their decisions than the judiciary. It is also argued that legislatures are better at protecting individual rights. To see the legislature as formed of large majorities empowered to restrict the rights of minorities is to misunderstand its composition. Rather, the legislature is made up of groups representing divergent minority interests who need to group together to form a majority. As such, legislatures are just as likely, if not more likely, to protect the rights of minority groups than the judiciary.

These arguments are connected to a broader tension between legal and political constitutionalism. Those advocating a strong legal protection of human rights rely on arguments similar to those underpinning legal constitutionalism whereas those advocating a parliamentary protection of rights, in turn, rely on arguments similar to those underpinning political constitutionalism. Advocates of legal constitutionalism argue for the need for a strong legal protection of rights, but also for a larger role for the judiciary in other areas of the constitution. Legal constitutionalists, for example, are likely to advocate a written constitution, with the judiciary possessing the final say on the interpretation of all constitutional provisions, not just those protecting human rights—courts for example would be called in to resolve issues concerning the legal powers of the Queen when enacting legislation, the powers of the executive to declare war, form Treaties, or even to form a government and dissolve Parliament. Advocates of political constitutionalism do not merely advocate a greater role for the legislature in the protection of human rights, but also with regard to other areas of the constitution. They would argue that it is for the legislature and not the courts to govern ministerial misconduct, the dissolution of Parliament, and the exercise of prerogative powers by the Queen or by Ministers acting on her behalf. Broadly speaking, legal constitutionalism advocates legal regulation of the constitution, regarding this as the best means of ensuring the protection of the rule of law and the separation of powers. Political constitutionalism advocates greater political regulation of the constitution, motivated by concerns of the anti-democratic nature of legal regulation by a non-democratically accountable and non-democratically representative judiciary.

Although not expressed in terms of a tension between legal and political constitutionalism, similar arguments are found in legal systems that have an entrenched

Constitution. As we saw in our brief account of two competing views as to the application of the Human Rights Act 1998, constitutional provisions can be interpreted differently. The more constitutional provisions are interpreted according to the original intentions of the authors, the smaller the relative power given to the courts to interpret constitutional provisions. The same argument operates in the opposite direction. The less attention courts pay to the original intentions of the author, the greater the power of the court to develop its own interpretation of constitutional provisions. This is not to argue that those advocating a form of originalism, where greater attention is to be paid to the intention of the authors of constitutional documents, are drawing on the same arguments as political constitutionalists. However, the effect of different theories of constitutional interpretation is similar to the consequences of political and legal constitutionalism. It redistributes relative power between the legislature and the judiciary to authoritatively determine the content of constitutional provisions, including constitutional provisions including human rights.

Democratic dialogue, therefore, can lay claims not only to provide a different model of human rights protections, but also to pave the way for a novel theory of constitutionalism. It aims to combine the advantages of legal and political constitutionalism, whilst minimizing the weaknesses of these protections. However, with this broadening of the normative claims of democratic dialogue come even greater difficulties of defining a clear, stable account of democratic dialogue that does not collapse into a theory of legal or political constitutionalism in practice. The difficulty of defining and defending dialogue as a new theory of constitutionalism may explain the second, more modest development of democratic dialogue when applied to protections of human rights. Democratic dialogue advocates dialogue as opposed to conflict. Instead of granting powers to the legislature or the judiciary to provide the final authoritative determination of the content of human or constitutional rights, the two institutions are encouraged to interact and work together to provide a solution.

This preference for interaction and discussion is also suggested as a possible solution to other tensions that arise in the protection of rights. Tensions can arise in particular between domestic and international protections of human rights. This is particularly true in the United Kingdom, where the Human Rights Act 1998 does not provide a separate domestic list of British human rights incorporating instead the provisions of the European Convention of Human Rights. In addition, directly effective European Union law may also protect human rights, applying to UK legal provisions which are in the scope of European Union law.[27] This tension often takes place between domestic and international or supranational constitutional courts designed to protect human rights. Democratic dialogue, therefore, may appear to go beyond resolving tensions between legislatures and courts, being capable of providing a framework of relieving potential tensions between different courts, albeit one where the focus is more on dialogue and the purpose is no longer one of providing a remedy for the potential democratic deficit which occurs when courts strike down legislative provisions.

[27] Although the United Kingdom voted on 23 June 2016 in favour of leaving the European Union, European Union law will continue to apply in the United Kingdom unless and until a withdrawal agreement between the United Kingdom and the rest of the EU is concluded, or until the negotiation period (two years, with the possibility of agreed extensions) has passed and no agreement has been reached (article 50 TFEU). At the time of writing, the United Kingdom had still not triggered article 50 by notifying the European Council of its intention to leave the European Union. This book will discuss the law is it currently stands, drawing attention to the possible future repercussions of the Referendum decision.

With regard to European Union law, tensions arise when the Court of Justice of the European Union and national constitutional courts reach divergent conclusions over human rights issues. One recent example of this conflict arose in *Melloni*, concerning the application of the European Arrest Warrant.[28] The Spanish Constitutional Court concluded that it would be contrary to its constitutional protection of rights to execute the arrest warrant for Mr Melloni. Mr Melloni had been tried *in absentia*. The Spanish constitution, as interpreted by the court, required that those tried *in absentia* should be able to demand a retrial. However, Italian law precluded a retrial. Moreover, the Framework Directive regulating the European Arrest Warrant did not require a retrial as, although Mr Melloni had been tried *in absentia* he had been represented by legal counsel at the trial.[29] Difficulties arise in this case given different conclusions reached on the same issue by two constitutional courts. The Spanish Constitutional Court provided Mr Melloni with a stronger protection of rights than that found in the European Arrest Warrant as interpreted by the Court of Justice of the European Union.

In *Melloni*, the Court of Justice resolved this conflict by focusing on the supremacy of European Union law, with the provisions of the European Arrest Warrant overriding the procedural protections found in the Spanish Constitution.[30] However, to resolve the case in this manner may create potential problems. First, problems arise for the legitimacy of European Union law which appears to prefer the weaker protection of rights found in the Framework Decision establishing the European Arrest Warrant as opposed to the stronger human rights protections found in the Spanish Constitution. Second, problems arise with regard to the relationships between the Court of Justice of the European Union and national constitutional courts. The European Union relies on national courts to implement directly effective provisions of European Union law. However, difficulties arise for national constitutional courts when directly effective European Union law clashes with the constitutional protection of rights found in their national constitutions. Is it legitimate for a national constitutional court to have its stronger protection of human rights overridden by the weaker protection of human rights found in European Union law?

Dialogue between the national constitutional courts and the Court of Justice of the European Union is seen as a potential resolution to this conflict. National constitutional courts can alert the Court of Justice of the European Union to potential conflicts, empowering the court to determine whether European Union law can be re-interpreted so as to avoid these potential clashes. Dialogue between the courts can help to reduce instances of potential conflicts as well as enhancing the legitimacy of European Union law, helping it to provide a protection of human rights that respects the strong protection of human rights found in national constitutions. Clashes and conflicts are replaced with dialogue and compromise. This need not mean, however, that dialogue will resolve all problems. *Melloni* itself can be interpreted as a situation where the Court of Justice of the European Union ignored dialogue, refusing to respond to the concerns raised by the Spanish Constitutional Court by allowing for a compromise, enabling the Spanish to provide a stronger protection of rights than that found in European Union law.[31] Alternatively, it could be argued that dialogue had taken place earlier, with a series of criticisms of the European Arrest Warrant

[28] C-399/11 *Stefano Melloni v Ministerio Fiscal* [2013] QB 1067.

[29] Article 4a(1) of Framework Decision 2002/584.

[30] C-399/11 *Stefano Melloni v Ministerio Fiscal* (n 28) paras 59–64.

[31] See, for example, A Torres Pérez, '*Melloni* in Three Acts: From Dialogue to Monologue' (2014) 10 European Constitutional Law Review 308.

from academic commentators and constitutional courts having led to a modification of the European Arrest Warrant by the enactment of a new Framework Directive, this Directive being an example of a democratic resolution to these tensions agreed to by the member states.

A similar argument is made with regard to the potential conflicts between decisions of the European Court of Human Rights and national constitutional protections of human rights. Difficulties arise here not when national constitutional protections are higher than those found in the European Court of Human Rights, but when the European Court of Human Rights concludes that the Convention has been breached when the national constitutional courts would reach the opposite conclusion. An example here is the case of *Horncastle*, concerning the use of hearsay evidence.[32] English law would allow convictions on the basis of hearsay evidence, albeit in limited circumstances with these limits designed to protect the rights of the defendant. However, a decision of the European Court of Human Rights in *Al Khawaja*, concluded that article 6 ECHR would be breached when convictions were based solely or decisively on hearsay evidence. The Supreme Court concluded that, as *Al Khawaja* was on appeal to the Grand Chamber and may not have taken account of the other protections of procedural rights in criminal cases where hearsay evidence was used, it would depart from the decision of the European Court of Human Rights. When *Al Khawaja* was heard before the Grand Chamber, the European Court of Human Rights took account of the arguments of the UK Supreme Court in *Horncastle*, recognizing that there could be circumstances in which article 6 would not be breached where criminal convictions relied on hearsay evidence. This evidence of dialogue between the UK Supreme Court and the European Court of Human Rights is seen as a better solution than the conflict that arose in *Melloni* between the Spanish Constitutional Court and the European Court of Human Rights.

Dialogue is not merely advocated because it promotes mediation over conflict. It is also argued that this dialogue gives rise to a better protection of human rights. By allowing international and national courts to interact, national courts are able to protect rights in a manner that takes account of specific legal cultures, whilst international and supranational courts are able to ensure that these national protections of human rights do not transgress an accepted minimal protection of human rights. *Horncastle* and *Al-Khawaja* are not merely examples of a less confrontational solution to a human rights issue than that found in *Melloni*. The European Court of Human Rights was able to be better informed, enabling it to realize that it could be possible for article 6 rights to be protected and allow for hearsay evidence to be relied upon in some convictions. Its analysis of the situation also enabled UK courts to think more carefully about how the balance is struck between ensuring criminal trials are fair for the defendant, whilst also being able to achieve justice. The recognition of how dialogue can lead to better human rights protections also weakens some of the criticisms of *Melloni*. The case is criticized because EU law provided a lower protection of human rights than that found in the Spanish constitution, yet the Court of Justice concluded that, nevertheless, EU law should override national law. However, this criticism is weakened when we understand the context of the *Melloni* case. National constitutional courts had criticized earlier forms of the European Arrest Warrant because it failed to provide sufficient protection for those tried *in absentia*. The Framework Decision establishing the European Arrest Warrant was modified to take account of these concerns, reaching

[32] *R v Horncastle* [2009] UKSC 14, [2010] 2 AC 373.

a democratically agreed compromise. Interaction between national and supranational and international courts can potentially enhance rights protections in a similar manner to dialogue between the legislature and the judiciary. Each institution brings its own specialist knowledge and expertise, maximizing the strengths and minimizing the weaknesses that can occur if human rights protections are only protected by national or international and supranational courts.

Our brief overview of democratic dialogue appears to have come full circle. We are left with a theory that promises to provide a better protection of human rights, both in terms of domestic and supranational or international protections of human rights, as well as offering a better account of constitutional law writ large. The democratic deficit argument is challenged and a better way is found of protecting human rights and constitutional principles, as well as providing for a better means through which states interact in a post-sovereign world. Democratic dialogue does indeed appear to be a panacea for all constitutional ills. However, we have also argued that democratic dialogue is hard to define, both in terms of constitutional design, constitutional practice, and its normative claims to provide an alternative account of constitutions to that found in legal or political constitutionalism. Whenever we try to clarify what dialogue means, what it requires, or how it provides a better normative account, the theory appears to collapse. Democratic dialogue may be nothing more than the weak claim that it is better to talk than it is to fight. It is no panacea but a mere placebo, designed to reassure that all is well. To investigate these arguments further, it helps to place them in context. The next section aims to do this by looking at these arguments through the lens of prisoner voting. The next section will first explain why prisoner voting provides such a good context from which to assess the claims of democratic dialogue, before assessing how far this contextualization can help resolve the tension between the claims of democratic dialogue and its ability to achieve them.

II. Prisoner Voting: A Franchise too Far?

We have argued that democratic dialogue aims to provide a better protection of human rights. Its claims have the most impact in the area of contestable rights-issues. A rights-issue is a question about how human rights should apply in a particular situation. Asking whether prisoners should be allowed to vote is a rights-issue. It questions how we should apply the right to vote in a particular situation—whether it should be granted to prisoners and, if so, whether this should be granted to all prisoners and, if not, which prisoners should be entitled to vote. A rights-issue is contestable when it is reasonable to disagree about its resolution. A prima facie case can be made that the issue of prisoner voting is contestable given the range of answers that can be found to this question. Arguments for democratic dialogue models of human rights protections are at their most persuasive with regard to contestable rights. If a rights-issue is contestable, then we would expect legislatures and the judiciary, and national, international, and supranational courts, to disagree as to its resolution. Democratic dialogue aims to facilitate a solution to this disagreement without it having to be resolved through conflict or assertions of relative authority. Contestable rights-issues are difficult to resolve. They therefore provide a good example from which to determine whether democratic dialogue can make good on its promise to provide a better protection of human rights, maximizing the advantages and minimizing the disadvantages of a purely legal or purely political protection of rights.

An overview of the law relating to prison voting in the United Kingdom, Ireland, Canada, the United States, Australia, New Zealand, and South Africa easily demonstrates that prisoner voting rights is a contestable rights-issue. Not only is there a range of solutions to this rights-issue across the spectrum, but, particularly in the United Kingdom and in New Zealand, the law has either recently changed or is currently in the process of change. The strongest protection of prisoner voting rights is found in Canada, Ireland, and South Africa, where all prisoners are entitled to vote. The opposite extreme is found in the United Kingdom and New Zealand, which currently have a blanket ban on prisoner voting. The middle ground is exemplified by the United States and Australia. The US Constitution allows states to remove the franchise from prisoners, empowering each state to determine whether it wishes to remove the vote from prisoners. Australia delineates between categories of prisoners who are allowed to vote and those removed from the franchise.

The blanket ban on prisoner voting in the United Kingdom is found in section 3(1) of the Representation of the People Act 1983. This provides that '[a] convicted person during the time that he is detained in a penal institution in pursuance of his sentence ... is legally incapable of voting at any parliamentary or local election'. However, this blanket ban has been subject to challenge before the European Court of Human Rights for contravening article 3 of the First Protocol of the European Convention on Human Rights, which provides that '[t]he High Contracting Parties undertake to hold free elections at reasonable intervals by secret ballot, under conditions which will ensure the free expression of the opinion of the people in the choice of the legislature'. In the joined cases of *R (Pearson and Martinez) v Secretary of State for the Home Department* and *Hirst v Attorney General*, the UK courts concluded that there was no breach of article 3 of the First Protocol, recognizing that the European Court of Human Rights provided for a wide margin of appreciation with regard to the interpretation of the right, as well as recognizing both that Parliament had continued to approve legislation that removed the franchise from prisoners and that this was a matter more suited for legislative as opposed to judicial resolution.[33] Hirst appealed to the European Court of Human Rights. In *Hirst v UK (No 2)* the fourth section of the European Court of Human Rights concluded that the absolute ban was a disproportionate restriction of article 3 of the First Protocol.[34] The court recognized that there was a wide margin of appreciation granted to the signatory states. In particular, states have a wide margin of appreciation to determine whether distinctions as to the categories of prisoners entitled to vote should depend upon the length of sentence served, or on the serious nature of the offence. States also had a wide margin of appreciation to determine whether voting rights should be determined by the court when sentencing is passed or by the executive either at the time of sentencing or at a later time. Nevertheless a blanket ban removing all prisoners from the franchise was a disproportionate restriction on the right to vote.[35]

The UK Government appealed the decision before the Grand Chamber of the European Court of Human Rights, which confirmed the breach of the Convention on 6 April 2005.[36] Again, the Court emphasized that although states had a large margin of appreciation, it was for the European Court of Human Rights to determine when a Convention right would be breached and the court concluded that it was contrary to the Convention for a prisoner to forfeit his or her right to vote merely because they

[33] [2001] EWHC Admin 239, [2001] HRLR 39.
[34] App No 74025/01, (2004) 38 EHRR 825. [35] ibid, para 51.
[36] *Hirst v UK (No 2)* App No 74025/01, (2005) 42 EHRR 849.

were detained following conviction. The blanket ban formed a 'general, automatic and indiscriminate restriction' on the right to vote and, as such, fell outside the margin of appreciation granted to the United Kingdom.[37] This has triggered a series of reactions from the then Labour and later Coalition and Conservative governments, the judiciary, and Parliament, as well as further decisions of the European Court of Human Rights. At the time of writing, prisoners are still removed from the franchise. However, a joint Committee of the House of Commons and the House of Lords on the Voting Eligibility (Prisoners) Draft Bill of November 2012 concluded that prisoners serving sentences of twelve months or less should be entitled to vote, with prisoners being entitled to apply to vote six months before their release.[38] The Draft Bill has yet to be enacted.

New Zealand also currently has a general prohibition on prisoner voting. However, unlike the United Kingdom, this is not a long-standing blanket ban that has been questioned by international human rights protection. Rather, New Zealand has recently moved in the opposite direction. Following a judicial challenge to earlier legislation imposing a blanket ban on prisoner voting, legislation was enacted to allow prisoners to vote. This was replaced by new legislation re-instating a blanket ban which was recently the subject of a declaration of inconsistency in the New Zealand High Court.[39]

The challenge to New Zealand's first legislation banning prisoner voting is found in *Re Bennett*.[40] The High Court of New Zealand concluded that the blanket ban on prisoner voting was contrary to section 12 of the New Zealand Bill of Rights Act 1990 (NZBORA). However, the court did not provide any analysis of whether the blanket ban could be justified under section 5 of the NZBORA which allows the human rights protected in the NZBORA to be subject to reasonable limitations which are necessary in a democratic society. Following *Re Bennett*, the New Zealand legislature enacted section 80(1) of the Electoral Act 1993, which enabled prisoners serving sentences of less than three years to vote. In 2010, the legislature reversed this policy, enacting the Electoral (Disqualification of Sentenced Prisoners) Amendment Act 2010, initially proposed as a private members Bill, which removed the right to vote for prisoners. The legislation was enacted despite the Attorney General providing notice to the House of Representatives that the proposed Bill was contrary to section 12 of the NZBORA and could not be justified under section 5.[41] In a ground-breaking decision, *Taylor v Attorney-General*, the New Zealand High Court confirmed that the New Zealand courts could issue declarations of inconsistency with the New Zealand Bill of Rights Act 1990, despite the fact that the legislation does not specifically empower the issuing of such declarations.[42] It then issued a declaration of inconsistency for the 2010 legislation. The High Court concluded that, given the important nature of the right and the severity of the restriction, a declaration should be issued, adding that 'if a declaration were not made in this case, it is difficult to conceive of one in which it would'.[43]

[37] ibid, para 82.

[38] Joint Committee on the Draft Voting Eligibility (Prisoners) Bill, First Report, 'Draft Voting Eligibility (Prisoners) Bill' HL Paper 103, HC 924, 2013–14 Session, 18 December 2013; http://www.publications.parliament.uk/pa/jt201314/jtselect/jtdraftvoting/103/10311.htm.

[39] *Taylor v Attorney-General of New Zealand* [2015] NZHC 1706.

[40] (1993) 2 HRNZ 358 (HC).

[41] Christopher Finlayson Report of the Attorney-General under the New Zealand Bill of Rights Act 1990 on the Electoral (Disqualification of Convicted Prisoners) Amendment Bill (J4, published by Order of the House of Representatives, 2010).

[42] See n 39.

[43] *Taylor v Attorney-General of New Zealand* (n 39) at para 69. See A Geddis, 'Prisoner Voting and Consistency with the New Zealand Bill of Rights Act' [2016] Public Law 352 and A Geddis 'Message

The New Zealand Government has announced that it has no plans to introduce new legislation to grant prisoners the right to vote in response to the decision of the New Zealand High Court.[44]

At the opposite end of the spectrum are Canada, Ireland, and South Africa. All of these states allow prisoners to vote. In Canada, the Canada Elections Act 1985 originally removed the right to vote from all prisoners. This was challenged in a series of federal decisions, culminating in a decision of the Supreme Court in *Sauvé v Canada (Attorney General) (Sauvé I)* in 1993, which concluded that the blanket ban on prisoner voting breached section 3 of the Canadian Charter of Rights and Freedoms.[45] The Canadian legislature responded by enacting section 51(e) of the Canada Elections Act RSC 1985, which removed the right to vote from prisoners serving a sentence of two years or more. This, in turn, was challenged before the Supreme Court in 2002 in *Sauvé v the Attorney General of Canada* (*Sauvé II*), which held by a majority of one that the new legislation was contrary to section 3 of the *Charter* and could not be justified under section 1 of the *Charter*.[46] The Supreme Court of Canada struck down section 51(e) and, following no further legislative interventions, all prisoners are now able to vote in Canada.

In Ireland, there has never been legislation removing the franchise from prisoners. However, the lack of a legislative provision enabling prisoners to exercise their vote made it impossible for prisoners to vote in practice. Although not removed from the franchise, prisoners were not allowed to leave prison to attend a polling station to vote and there was no provision to enable prisoners to obtain a postal vote, or any other means to enable them to participate in elections. Following the decision in *Hirst v United Kingdom*, the Irish government felt the need to change the law to ensure compatibility with the European Convention on Human Rights. As such it introduced legislation in 2006 to facilitate the right to vote for prisoners.[47] The Electoral (Amendment) Act 2006 provided a means for prisoners to exercise their right to vote through enabling them to register for a postal vote in the constituency in which they resided prior to their incarceration.

Similarly, South Africa, following the enactment of its Constitution in 1996, had no legislation prohibiting prisoners from voting. However, there were no mechanisms in place to facilitate prisoner voting. This was challenged in *August v The Electoral Commission*,[48] where prisoners challenged the refusal to place them upon the electoral register. The Supreme Court of South Africa concluded that, as there was no legislation removing the right to vote from prisoners, it should be assumed that prisoners had the right to vote. As such, article 19 of the Constitution, protecting the right to vote, had been breached. The decision in *August* effectively empowered the South African legislature to remove the power to vote from some, or all, prisoners should it wish to do so—subject to further constitutional challenges should such legislation be enacted. In 2004, the South African legislature passed legislation to remove the right to vote from all prisoners, with the exception of those imprisoned for the non-payment of a fine.[49] This was challenged in the Constitutional Court in *Minister for Home Affairs*

on Prisoner Voting Rights Unequivocal' *New Zealand Herald* 28 July 2015: http://www.nzherald.co.nz/opinion/news/article.cfm?c_id=466&objectid=11488139.

44 http://nzccl.org.nz/content/government-ignores-high-court-wont-change-prisoner-voting-law.

45 [1993] 2 SCR 438.

46 [2002] 3 SCR 519.

47 http://debates.oireachtas.ie/dail/2006/10/05/00008.asp.

48 (CCT8/99) [1999] ZACC 3 (South African Constitutional Court).

49 Electoral Laws Amendment Act 34 of 2003 amending the Electoral Act 73 of 1998.

v National Institute for Crime Prevention and the Re-integration of Offenders (NICRO), which struck down the legislation as unconstitutional, being a disproportionate restriction on the right to vote.[50] As no further legislative measures have been enacted, all prisoners currently have the right to vote in South Africa.

Australia provides a middle-ground solution, restricting voting rights for certain categories of prisoner. In Australia, prisoners serving a sentence of three years or more are excluded from voting, whereas those serving shorter sentences are allowed to vote. In a similar manner to New Zealand, the most recent legislation removed the right to vote for all prisoners. However, unlike New Zealand, this decision was struck down by the High Court of Australia as contrary to the structure and provisions of the Australian Constitution which protect representative government, including the right to vote. From 1902 to 1983, Australia removed the right to vote from prisoners sentenced to terms of one year or longer and those who had committed crimes that were subject to be sentenced to one year or longer. From 1983 to 1995, the law was changed to remove the franchise from those serving terms or subject to be sentenced to a term of five years or longer. The law was changed again such that from 1995 to 2004 only prisoners serving a sentence of five years or longer were removed from the franchise. This pattern of increasing prisoner voting rights was reversed, and from 2004–06 prisoners serving a sentence of three years or longer were unable to vote. In 2006, legislation was passed to enact section 93(8AA) of the Commonwealth Electoral Act 1918, which removed the right to vote from all prisoners. This was challenged in *Roach v Electoral Commissioner*.[51] By a vote of four judges to two, the High Court held that the complete ban on prisoner voting contravened the Australian Constitution. The court declared the 2006 legislation unconstitutional, but allowed the validity of the earlier 2004 amendments, such that prisoners serving sentences of three years or more are excluded from voting.

The United States also, arguably, falls in the middle of the spectrum on prisoner voting. Each state is free to enact its own legislation as to whether prisoners can vote, resulting in a range of solutions. However, this solution is reached because the US Supreme Court has concluded that state laws forbidding convicted felons or prisoners from voting are not, in and of themselves, contrary to the US Constitution. It was argued that rules preventing prisoners from voting could breach the Equal Protection Clause found in the Fourteenth Amendment to the Constitution. However, in *Richardson v Ramirez*, the Supreme Court held that, far from requiring that prisoners be allowed to vote, the Fourteenth Amendment contained express constitutional authority empowering the states to enact laws removing the vote from those convicted of crimes.[52] The second clause of the Fourteenth Amendment to the Constitution provides for a reduced congressional representation for those states that remove the right to vote from male citizens over the age of 21. However, the reduction in congressional representation is specifically exempted for states removing the right to vote from those who had participated in 'rebellion or other crime'. According to the reasoning of the Supreme Court, if the removal of the right to vote for those convicted of rebellion or other crimes is exempt from the punishment of a reduction in congressional representation found in the second clause of the Fourteenth Amendment, then it must also be exempt from the first clause of the Fourteenth Amendment providing for equal protection. Therefore, there is express constitutional approval for state laws removing the right to

[50] (CCT 03/04) [2004] ZACC 10.
[51] (2007) 233 CLR 162.
[52] 418 US 24 (1974).

vote from prisoners. The only exemption is for laws where there is an express intention to discriminate when enacting a prisoner disenfranchisement law.[53]

This overview of the laws on prisoner voting across a range of common law countries demonstrates that the issue of prisoner voting is, at least prima facie, contestable. A range of legal systems have reached different solutions, mostly following both judicial and legislative intervention. It also shows that all of the legal systems have regulated prisoner voting through a combination of measures taken by courts and legislatures. The law in the UK and Ireland also demonstrates the interaction between national and international courts, with measures taken in these countries in response to decisions of the European Court of Human Rights. It also demonstrates the difficulty of assessing whether different constitutional provisions provide a better protection of rights. Of the systems examined, the United States, Ireland, Canada, and South Africa have the strongest protection of rights, empowering courts to strike down legislation that contravenes constitutional rights. However, although Ireland, Canada, and South Africa provide the strongest protection of prisoner voting rights, the United States arguably provides one of the weakest protections.

Both South Africa and Canada provide an example of a strong protection of rights reached through dialogue between the legislature and the courts. Moreover, Ireland provides an example of legislative changes prompted by decisions of the European Court of Human Rights. This may suggest that democratic dialogue does provide a better protection of rights. However, both New Zealand and the United Kingdom are recognized as examples of the commonwealth model of human rights and yet provide the weakest protection of prisoner voting rights. Moreover, although both Canada and South Africa reached a conclusion on prisoner voting rights following input from both the legislature and the courts, Gardbaum recognizes Canada as an example of a commonwealth model of rights protections, but not South Africa. Moreover, the solution reached by the US Supreme Court could also be regarded as one which facilitates dialogue, providing greater discretion to state legislatures when determining whether to grant prisoners the right to vote. In addition, if the issue of prisoner voting rights, is contestable, then how can we determine which country has the best interpretation of the right? Should we criticize New Zealand for moving towards a blanket restriction of rights, or the United Kingdom for potentially moving away from a blanket ban towards providing prisoner voting rights to some prisoners? The legal system which provides for the strongest protection of rights need not be the one which provides the best protection of these rights. This seems to suggest that we should be more sceptical of the claims of democratic dialogue, both in terms of its assertion of a better protection of rights and of its ability to provide a distinct protection of human rights.

III. Defining Dialogue—A Distinct Constitutional Model?

We suggested earlier that it may be difficult to define democratic dialogue as a distinct account either of human rights protections or of constitutions more generally. We would expect to discover a binary separation between two models of human rights protections, with democratic dialogue models of human rights protections occupying the middle ground. At one extreme we should find legal systems with a strong

[53] *Hunter v Underwood* 417 US 222 (1985).

constitutional protection of human rights, where courts strike down legislation that is contrary to human rights and constitutional provisions. At the other extreme we should find parliamentary systems, where courts are unable to strike down legislation either for contravening human rights provisions or constitutional principles. Democratic dialogue theories should then occupy a middle ground, with both legislatures and the judiciary combining to protect human rights and enforce constitutional principles. However, when we examine the way in which the United Kingdom, Ireland, Canada, the United States, Australia, New Zealand, and South Africa protect human rights, it is hard to classify their protections in this manner. The difference between their protections of human rights appears to be more a matter of degree. This questions the distinct nature of democratic dialogue.

Legal constitutionalism would argue that, as prisoners have a right to vote, it should be for the court to decide the extent of the right. A simplified model of political constitutionalism would argue that it is for the legislature, as a democratically composed and democratically representative body, to determine the right to vote for prisoners. However, none of the legal systems could be described as a clear model of political constitutionalism when it comes to protecting human rights. The closest illustration of a pure parliamentary protection of rights would appear to be found in Australia. At the Federal level, Australia has no measure protecting human rights, although it does have a written Constitution to provide for its federal structure. Despite this lack of a Federal Bill of Rights, the Australian High Court concluded that legislation providing for a blanket ban on prisoner voting was unconstitutional because it was contrary to constitutional rights and the structure of the constitution. The constitution is based on principles of representative government, including rights to vote. This is an example of the way in which the Australian High Court has protected some human rights, despite their lack of express protection in the Constitution, by reading in these rights as implied rights in the Constitution. This use of implied rights makes it hard to determine whether Australia has a protection of human rights in line with political constitutionalism, or legal constitutionalism, or is best-described as a democratic dialogue model of rights at the federal level as well as its examples of democratic dialogue models of rights protections found in the Australian Capital Territory and Victoria.

The United States[54] and Ireland[55] are arguably clear examples of legal constitutionalism as regards the manner in which they protect human rights. Both of these legal systems provide for a strong constitutional protection of rights, enabling courts to strike down legislation that is contrary to the Constitution, including those provisions of human rights found in the Constitution. However, if the ability to strike down legislation as contrary to the Constitution is a sign of legal constitutionalism, then this would appear to include Australia, in part, Canada, and South Africa in our account of models of strong constitutional protections of human rights, incorporating the ideology of legal constitutionalism. Yet, Canada is regarded as providing for a democratic dialogue model of rights protections. It may empower courts to strike down legislative acts, but it also provides a means through which the legislature can respond. The picture becomes even more complicated when we examine how constitutions with a strong protection of rights protect rights in practice. For example, although the United States has a strong, legal protection of rights, by concluding that it was not unconstitutional to disenfranchise prisoners, the US Supreme Court effectively granted the

[54] Following the decision in *Marbury v Madison* 5 US 137 (1803) interpreting Article III of the US Constitution.

[55] Section 15:4 of the Irish Constitution.

legislature a right of response to its judgment through granting states the power to determine whether, and if so which, prisoners should be granted the right to vote. These complications can be illustrated more clearly when comparing the model of human rights protections in Canada and South Africa. It becomes difficult to pinpoint which, if any, of the four mechanisms mentioned by Hogg and Bushell are necessary or sufficient features of a democratic dialogue model of human rights protections. The more we try and separate out examples of legal constitutionalism, political constitutionalism, and democratic dialogue, the more blurred the picture becomes.

To return to Hogg and Bushell's account, democratic dialogue occurs whenever the legislature has the ability to respond to judicial determinations of human rights:

> [w]here a judicial decision is open to legislative reversal, modification, or avoidance, then it is meaningful to regard the relationship between the Court and the competent legislative body as a dialogue.[56]

However, legislative reversal, modification or avoidance of a judicial decision could occur in a legal system with a strong constitutional protection of rights as well as in legal systems that are categorized as having a democratic dialogue or commonwealth model of rights protections. Hogg and Bushell argue that dialogue is an apt description as allowing the judicial decision to be open to legislative response 'causes a public debate in which *Charter* values play a more prominent role than they would if there had been no judicial decision'.[57] However, this can occur in a legal system that has a strong constitutional protection of rights. If a court strikes down legislation that contravenes a constitutionally protected right, then it is open to the legislature to re-enact legislation to achieve the same policy goals as the earlier legislation, but to do so in a manner that does not contradict the earlier judicial decision holding the earlier legislation to be unconstitutional.

This ability of the legislature to respond to a court decision in this manner is illustrated by the changes in prisoner voting legislation in both Canada and South Africa. The Canadian legislature amended the Canada Elections Act RSC 1985 in response to the decision of the Canadian Supreme Court in *Sauvé I*. South Africa enacted legislation in 2004 following the decision of the Supreme Court of South Africa in *August v Electoral Commissioner* that it was not unconstitutional to remove the right to vote from some prisoners. Moreover, both of these legislative responses were subject to further court scrutiny—in Canada in *Sauvé II* and in South Africa in *NICRO*. After the courts scrutinized the original legislative responses, finding these contrary to the Constitution, the legislatures in both Canada and South Africa decided to respond no further, resulting in the existence of prisoner voting rights in both countries. Given these similarities, it becomes difficult to determine why Canada is regarded as a democratic dialogue model of rights protections, but South Africa is not.

Hogg and Bushell also provide a more detailed account of four features of the Canadian *Charter* that facilitate democratic dialogue: (i) the notwithstanding clause in section 33; (ii) the general restrictions clause in section 1; (iii) specific qualified rights; and (iv) equality rights.[58] However, it is not clear which of these features of the Canadian *Charter* are necessary or sufficient to give rise to its classification as a democratic dialogue model. Some of the features of the Canadian *Charter* are shared by other protections of human rights. The European Convention on Human Rights, for example, also contains qualified rights in articles 8–11. It also contains an equality protection in article 14. The US Constitution also provides for equality protections in

[56] Hogg and Bushell (n 3) 79. [57] ibid. [58] ibid, 82.

the equal protection clause found in the Fourteenth Amendment. The South African constitution also has a general restrictions clause, article 36, which is similar to article 1 of the Canadian *Charter*. The similarities between the South African and the Canadian account of prisoner voting rights could be explained by differences between these four features. However, the more we analyse the differences, the more they would appear to be a matter of degree.

Article 8 of the South African Constitution makes it clear that the Bill of Rights 'binds the legislature, the executive, the judiciary and all organs of State'.[59] There is no specific provision in the South African constitution that enables the legislature to respond to or overturn a decision of the court. As the legislature is itself bound to follow the Bill of Rights, any measure it did take would have to comply with the Bill of Rights. This contrasts with the notwithstanding clause found in the Canadian *Charter*. However, there are two difficulties that arise if we are to regard the existence of a notwithstanding clause as a necessary component of a democratic dialogue model of rights protection which also empowers the court to strike down legislation. First, the South African constitution contains a provision which could be argued to have a similar effect to the notwithstanding clause found in the Canadian *Charter*. Second, the notwithstanding clause is so rarely used that it has effectively fallen into desuetude.

Although not containing a broad notwithstanding clause, the South African constitution does empower the legislature to enact provisions that are immune from constitutional rights. Article 37 of the South African constitution empowers the legislature to declare a state of emergency through an Act of the South African Parliament. During a state of emergency, the legislature can enact legislation that contravenes the Bill of Rights.[60] Although different from the notwithstanding clause, it could be argued that these differences are matters of degree. The notwithstanding clause is more general than the emergency provisions clause and is longer in duration. The emergency provisions can only be used when there is a threat to the life of the nation.[61] There are no such provisions restricting the use of the notwithstanding clause. The notwithstanding clause empowers the legislature to legislate contrary to the Canadian *Charter* writ large. The South African Constitution restricts breaches of the Bill of Rights to those that are required by the state of emergency and which comply with South Africa's international obligations.[62] The Canadian notwithstanding clause can exempt legislation for a period of five years, which is renewable. The South African constitution restricts states of emergency to twenty-one days, subject to periods of renewal for three months, the first period of renewal requiring a 50 per cent and any subsequent renewals a vote of 60 per cent in favour.[63] Moreover, unlike the Canadian notwithstanding clause, the declaration of a state of emergency is subject to judicial review.[64]

Although presented above as differences in degree, the better understanding of the different clauses is that they are designed to serve distinct purposes. The South African clause is designed to suspend constitutional rights on a temporary basis in the face of emergency situations. The Canadian clause is interpreted as facilitating democratic dialogue. However, due to criticism of its initial use, the notwithstanding clause has almost fallen into desuetude through lack of use.[65] This has led some commentators to argue that Canada has, in reality, a strong legal protection of rights.[66] If the presence of

[59] Constitution of South Africa, arte 8.
[60] Constitution of South Africa, art 37(4).
[61] Constitution of South Africa, art 37(1).
[62] Constitution of South Africa, art 37(4).
[63] Constitution of South Africa, art 37(2).
[64] Constitution of South Africa, art 37(3).
[65] See Gardbaum (n 5) 121–28.
[66] Huscroft (n 19) 91.

a notwithstanding clause is the main distinguishing feature of the Canadian *Charter*, then the fact that it is never used, and its use has been criticized, also begins to challenge the distinction between the Canadian *Charter* as a democratic dialogue protection of rights and the South African constitution as an example of a strong legal protection of human rights. It may be that there is more of an opportunity for the South African legislature to suspend constitutional rights in an emergency than for the Canadian legislature to enact legislation notwithstanding the provisions of the Canadian *Charter*.

The presence, or otherwise, of a notwithstanding clause in a system which provides for a strong protection of constitutional rights could still be regarded as the distinguishing feature of a democratic dialogue model of rights protections. However, our assessment of the similarities between both the outcome on prisoner voting rights in Canada and South Africa and the way in which this outcome is reached casts further doubt on this conclusion. Dialogue occurred between the courts and the legislature in Canada and South Africa because both constitutions include a general restrictions clause. Is the presence or absence of this clause the distinguishing feature of a democratic dialogue model of rights protections?

Section 1 of the Canadian *Charter* 'guarantees the rights and freedoms set out in it subject only to such reasonable limits prescribed by law as can be demonstrably justified in a free and democratic society'.[67] The South African Constitution also has a general restrictions clause, found in section 36 of the Constitution which states:

> The rights in the Bill of Rights may be limited only in terms of law of general application to the extent that the limitation is reasonable and justifiable in an open and democratic society based on human dignity, equality and freedom, taking into account all relevant factors, including
> a. the nature of the right;
> b. the importance of the purpose of the limitation;
> c. the nature and extent of the limitation;
> d. the relation between the limitation and its purpose; and
> e. less restrictive means to achieve the purpose.

As with our examination of the notwithstanding clause, the South African restrictions clause is more specific than the Canadian clause. But, again, this can be understood merely as a matter of degree. Moreover, the factors required by the South African restrictions clause are similar to those used by the Canadian Supreme Court when applying section 1 of the *Charter*. In addition, as we saw in our overview of prisoner voting rules, the clauses were used in both Canada and South Africa to facilitate dialogue between the legislature and the courts, ultimately reaching the same conclusion in both legal systems. These similarities question the distinct nature of the democratic dialogue model of rights protections. The general restrictions clause appears to be a more effective means of facilitating dialogue in practice than the notwithstanding clause. Yet this clause is present in both the South African Constitution and the Canadian *Charter*. Consequently, we either have to question the classification of the Canadian *Charter* as providing for a democratic dialogue model of rights protections, or we have to question the conclusion that the South African constitution does not provide for a democratic dialogue model of rights protections.

Similar conclusions arise when we assess whether a specific clause restricting rights is a necessary or sufficient feature of democratic dialogue. The Canadian *Charter*

[67] Canadian Charter of Rights and Freedoms, s 1.

includes both a general restrictions clause and rights which list specific restrictions which may be placed on these rights. The European Convention of Human Rights also contains rights with specific restrictions, yet there are no suggestions that the European Convention of Human Rights is an example of a democratic dialogue model of rights protections. To require a general restrictions clause as a distinguishing feature of democratic dialogue models of rights protections is arbitrary and formulistic. However, if democratic dialogue models of rights protection were to include any legal system with examples of rights with specific restrictions, then the model is pushed to the point of collapse. Almost all legal systems with a constitutional or legal protection of rights will include examples of human rights which can be specifically restricted.[68] Moreover, it is hard to distinguish between those legal systems which allow for specific restrictions to be placed on rights and other legal systems where specific restrictions on rights are not permitted, but nevertheless the content of the right in question is interpreted in such a manner as to indirectly permit restrictions. Is there any real difference, for example, between a legal system with an absolute protection of the right to freedom of expression, but where speech is defined in such a manner so as not to include speech which incites racial hatred, and a legal system which specifically permits restrictions to be placed on the right to freedom of expression in order to protect the rights of others, including the right not to be subjected to racial hatred?

The search for the distinguishing features of a democratic dialogue model becomes more complicated when we examine the protection of rights found in the United Kingdom, New Zealand, and Australia. In the United Kingdom democratic dialogue is facilitated through sections 3 and 4 of the Human Rights Act 1998. Section 3 requires courts to read and give effect to legislation in a manner compatible with Convention rights, so far as it is possible to do so. Section 4 empowers courts of the level of the High Court or above to issue a declaration of incompatibility. Declarations of incompatibility do not affect the legal validity, force, or effect of legislation. These provisions enable the legislature to respond to decisions of the court in two ways. First, the legislature has a choice as to whether, and if so how, to respond to any declaration of incompatibility. There is no legal requirement in English law for the legislature to respond to a declaration of incompatibility by modifying legislation to ensure its compatibility with Convention rights. Second, the legislature can choose to respond to a Convention-compatible interpretation of legislation by re-enacting the legislation in question, modifying its provisions to reflect its interpretation of Convention rights in a manner that would make it impossible for the court to read and give effect to the legislation according to the court's interpretation of Convention rights.

In a similar manner to the United Kingdom, the courts in New Zealand have the ability to interpret legislation so as to comply with the provisions of the New Zealand Bill of Rights Act 1990 (NZBORA). A rights-compatible interpretation is 'preferred to any other meaning', whenever the enactment can be given that meaning.[69] Similar provisions are found in Australia's examples of a democratic dialogue model of rights protections in Victoria and the Australian Capital Territories. The NZBORA does not provide New Zealand courts with the power to declare legislation inconsistent with the rights found in the NZBORA. However, the High Court of New Zealand has recently

[68] I am grateful to Paul Craig for pointing out this argument.
[69] New Zealand Bill of Rights Act 1990, s 6.

issued a declaration of inconsistency for the first time, a judicial creation that appears to be similar to section 4 of the UK Human Rights Act.[70]

The more we analyse the similarities and differences between the democratic dialogue models of rights protections, the harder it is to determine the definitive feature of such a model. If we rely on the ability of the legislature to overturn judicial determinations of human rights, then the existence of emergency powers and their ability to suspend constitutional rights are, arguably, also means through which legislatures can respond to judicial determinations of human rights. Albeit more limited in scope and time and serving a different purpose, the distinction between democratic dialogue and other forms of human rights protections arguably becomes a matter of degree. If we focus on the existence, or otherwise, of general or specific clauses enabling restrictions to be placed on human rights, then it is hard not to recognize the South African constitution as a democratic dialogue model of rights protections. If we wished to stretch the point, an argument could be made that the US constitution also facilitates dialogue given the equal protection clause found in the Fourteenth Amendment.

These difficulties do not just challenge whether democratic dialogue models of rights protections exist as a distinct account of human rights protections. They also question the assertion that democratic dialogue can provide a novel account that takes a middle ground between legal and political constitutionalism. In all of the systems discussed so far, the law relating to prisoner voting has been influenced by both the legislature and the courts. The relative authoritative determinations of either institution, in reality, appear to depend more on how the courts have exercised their constitutional powers than on the nature of the power they possess. Again the suspicion is that the distinction between legal and political constitutionalism is really a matter of degree. If so, then we begin to doubt whether democratic dialogue can take a middle ground between the two theories.

IV. Inevitable Collapse?

The previous section suggested that it is hard to determine the necessary and sufficient criteria of democratic dialogue models. There is a range of mechanisms designed to enable the legislature to respond to decisions of the courts. This discovery casts doubt on the idea that democratic dialogue can provide a distinct model of human rights protections. It also questions the further claim that it can provide for a midway position between legal and political constitutionalism. At this stage, however, all we have done is cast doubt on these claims. Democratic dialogue theories may be a broad church. It may be that there is a range of possible mechanisms designed to facilitate dialogue. There is no need to find the precise necessary and sufficient criteria of a democratic dialogue model of rights protections. It is sufficient to recognize enough of a resemblance between these models, and how they differ, in general, from purely legal or purely political models of rights protections to establish a claim that they form a distinct model of rights protections. Whilst this may help to preserve a model of democratic dialogue as an aspect of constitutional design, there are further criticisms that democratic dialogue models of rights protections are unstable in practice. They tend to collapse into models of strong legal or weak parliamentary protections of rights. An investigation of prisoner voting rights lends credence to this suspicion. Moreover,

[70] *Taylor v Attorney-General of New Zealand* (n 39).

evidence can also be found of a blurring in the opposite direction, with dialogue occurring in constitutions that provide for a strong legal or a weak political protection of rights in their Constitutions.

A. Unstable democratic dialogue

Prisoner voting rights provides examples of instability of democratic dialogue in two directions. New Zealand provides an example of how democratic dialogue can collapse in practice into a weak parliamentary protection of rights, whereas Canada exemplifies how democratic dialogue can collapse into a strong legal protection of human rights.

As discussed above, New Zealand enacted legislation to re-instate the blanket ban on prisoner voting. A change in the legislative position is not, in and of itself, evidence of a shift towards a purely parliamentary protection of human rights. However, the way in which this legislation was enacted does provide evidence of a potential collapse, with Parliament enacting legislation it believes is in accordance with the wishes of the people, regardless of concerns raised as to its compatibility with human rights. The legislation was proposed by Paul Quinn as a private member's Bill. Quinn's argument in favour of the Bill rested primarily on his belief that he was representing the wishes of his constituents, as illustrated for example in his introduction to the Bill at first reading:

> The bill comes before the House because a large number of ordinary folk have asked me to introduce it. They have discussed this matter with me and believe that that should be the case. I have to say that since the bill has become public knowledge, the level of support for it has been overwhelming. I think that speaks volumes about the mood of the community in getting behind this bill. I acknowledge that there have been some muffled criticisms, but most of them have come from prisoner aid-type organisations.[71]

This fits strongly with the ideology of political constitutionalism. Rights are to be determined by the legislature, according to the wishes of the majority of the people. If the majority want to remove the right to vote from prisoners, then this is what the legislature should do. The Bill also appeared to be motivated purely by party-political grounds, with members of the coalition government voting for the Bill because of the arrangements of the coalition, not because of any strong support of the removal of prisoner voting rights.[72]

Further evidence of a collapse into a purely parliamentary protection of rights is found in the way in which mechanisms designed to facilitate dialogue appear to have been ignored. The NZBORA requires the Attorney General to 'bring to the attention of the House of Representatives any provision in the Bill that appears to be inconsistent with any of the rights and freedoms contained in this Bill of Rights'.[73] This provision aims to bring potential human rights breaches to the attention of the House of Representatives, enabling the House to explain clearly why it believes either that legislation is compatible with human rights, or why it wishes to enact legislation despite its incompatibility with human rights. However, the New Zealand Electoral (Disqualification of Convicted Prisoners) Amendment Act 2010 was enacted despite a

[71] New Zealand Hansard, House of Representatives, Debates 17 March 2010, vol 661 p 9610.

[72] See, for example, the statement of Hilary Calvert (ACT). 'I rise to take a call on the third reading of the Electoral (Disqualification of Sentenced Prisoners) Amendment Bill. I cannot pretend this bill is my favourite thing ... This bill is not my favourite thing. However, ACT is supporting National on this bill.' House of Representatives, Debates 8 December 2010, vol 669 p 15961.

[73] New Zealand Bill of Rights Act 1990, s 7.

statement from the Attorney General concluding that the blanket ban introduced by the legislation would be contrary to the provisions of the NZBORA 1990, providing a disproportionate restriction on the right to vote.[74] The Attorney General for New Zealand concluded that there was no rational link between the objective of the Bill and the blanket ban on prisoner voting. The Bill was stated as having the purpose of removing the right to vote for serious offenders. However, not all prisoners were serious offenders.[75] Moreover, the Attorney General concluded that the Bill was both over- and under-inclusive. Those convicted of a serious offence whose sentence would end before a general election would be able to vote, but those convicted of a less serious offence with a much shorter sentence, but which happened to occur during an election period, would lose their right to vote.[76] Although this was raised during the process of the Bill through the New Zealand Parliament,[77] the arguments were not discussed by Paul Quinn, who proposed the Bill, or others who spoke in support of the Bill, either at the first, second, or third reading stage,[78] or during the Bill's committee stage.[79] If the Attorney General's conclusions had been discussed, but reasons were given for disagreeing with his conclusions, or for enacting the Bill despite his conclusions, then it would be possible to conclude that democratic dialogue was working effectively with regard to prisoner voting issues in New Zealand. However, it is hard to reach this conclusion when Parliament appears to have enacted legislation by ignoring human rights concerns.

Even though the New Zealand High Court has now issued a declaration of inconsistency against this legislation, as Andrew Geddis argues, there are concerns as to whether this will prove to be effective.[80] First, the legitimacy of issuing a declaration of inconsistency is in doubt, given that the NZBORA does not provide for this remedy. The courts have determined that this remedy is needed. There is no certainty that the issuing of a declaration of inconsistency will survive on appeal to the New Zealand Court of Appeal or the New Zealand Supreme Court. Moreover, given the lack of statutory authority, there may be less weight given to this declaration of inconsistency by the New Zealand legislature than is given by the Westminster Parliament. Moreover, the Human Rights Act 1998 is tied in to the European Convention of Human Rights. A declaration of incompatibility under section 4 of the Human Rights Act may lead to a petition before the European Court of Human Rights and, should the Strasbourg court agree with the UK courts, pressure being applied under international law to modify legislation so as to comply with human rights. This additional pressure is not present in New Zealand. This, coupled with the lack of detailed scrutiny in the New Zealand Parliament when enacting the blanket ban in the first place, in addition to the lack of a specialist committee to scrutinize legislation for human rights compatibility,

[74] Report of the Attorney General under the New Zealand Bill of Rights Act 1990 on the Electoral (Disqualification of Convicted Prisoners) Amendment Bill, 2010.

[75] ibid, para 12. [76] ibid, para 14.

[77] See the statements of Hone Harawiwa at the second reading stage, New Zealand Hansard, House of Representatives, Debates 20 October 2010, vol 667 p 14679; Stuart Nash at the Committee stage, New Zealand Hansard, House of Representatives, Debates 10 November 2010, vol 668 page 15184 and Grant Robertson at the Third Reading Stage, New Zealand Hansard, House of Representatives, Debates 8 December 2010, vol 669 p 15961.

[78] New Zealand Hansard, House of Representatives, Debates 17 March 2010, vol 661 p 9610; 21 April 2010, vol 662 p 10339; 20 October 2010, vol 667 p 14679; 8 December 2010, vol 669 p 15961.

[79] New Zealand Hansard, House of Representatives, Debates 10 November 2010, vol 668 p 15184.

[80] A Geddis 'Prisoner Voting and Consistency with the New Zealand Bill of Rights Act' [2016] Public Law 352.

casts doubt on the extent to which the declaration of inconsistency challenges our earlier assessment of the danger that, as concerns prisoner voting rights, New Zealand's democratic dialogue model of rights protections has effectively collapsed into a parliamentary protection of rights.[81] Geddis' concerns appear to have been realized. In a recent letter to the New Zealand Council for Civil Liberties, the New Zealand Minister of Justice, Amy Adams, confirmed that the declaration of inconsistency had 'no impact' on Parliament's decision to remove the franchise from prisoners.[82]

The situation in Canada arguably provides evidence of collapse in the opposite direction with a democratic dialogue model of rights protections operating in practice in a manner similar to a constitutional system with a strong, legal protection of rights. Canada currently grants the franchise to all prisoners. This situation was reached through a combination of legislation and court decisions. As such, this would appear to provide support that democratic dialogue is working well in Canada. However, a closer analysis of the reasoning of the majority and minority judgments in *Sauvé II* casts doubt on this conclusion. In *Sauvé I* the Canadian Supreme Court concluded that an absolute ban on prisoner voting rights was contrary to the Canadian *Charter*. In *Sauvé II*, the court had to determine whether the legislature's response to its earlier judgment—enacting legislation entitling prisoners serving sentences of two years or less to vote—was compatible with the *Charter*. It is the reasoning of the minority, as opposed to the majority, that appears to be more in line with democratic dialogue. The reasoning of the majority appears to be much more compatible with a strong, legal protection of rights where courts have the final say over the content of a human right.

The democratic dialogue approach is most evident in Gonthier J's dissent. For Gonthier J, the role of the court is not to ensure that the legislature reaches the perfect answer when balancing competing rights, but that it is acting within the legal scope of the proportionality test.[83] He was motivated by his conclusion that the issue as to whether prisoners serving sentences of two years or more should be disenfranchised requires an assessment of competing social and political philosophies for which there is a lack of scientific proof.[84] For Gonthier J, 'the heart of the dialogue metaphor is that neither the courts nor Parliament hold a monopoly on the determination of values'[85] and 'when, after a full and rigorous s. 1 analysis, Parliament has satisfied the court that it has established a reasonable limit to a right that is demonstrably justified in a free and democratic society, the dialogue ends; the court lets Parliament have the last word and does not substitute Parliament's reasonable choices with its own'.[86] These statements exemplify the approach of democratic dialogue models of human rights protections, enabling courts and legislatures to work together to develop human rights. Courts can check that the social and political choices made by Parliament are not contrary to *Charter* rights, but they do not replace social and political choices of the legislature with their own social and political choices.[87]

[81] See A Geddis, 'Prisoner Voting and Rights Deliberation: How New Zealand's Parliament Failed' [2011] New Zealand Law Review 443, 452.

[82] The letter is reproduced on the website of the New Zealand Council for Civil Liberties: http://nzccl.org.nz/sites/default/files/20151202%20Amy%20Adams%20no%20change%20to%20prisoner%20voting%20letter.pdf.

[83] *Sauvé II* (n 46) para 68. [84] ibid, para 67. [85] ibid, para 75. [86] ibid.

[87] See also PW Hogg, AA Bushell Thornton, and WK Wright, '*Charter* Dialogue Revisited—or "Much Ado About Metaphors"' (2007) 45 Osgoode Hall Law Review 1; R Haigh and M Sobkin, 'Does the Observer Have an Effect?: An Analysis of the Use of Dialogue Metaphor in Canadian Courts' (2007) 45 Osgoode Hall Law Review 67; G Huscroft, 'Constitutionalism from the Top Down' (2007) 45 Osgoode Hall Law Review 91; C Manfredi, 'The Day the Dialogue Died: A Comment on *Sauvé v Canada*' (2007) 45 Osgoode Hall Law Review 105; Don Stuart: 'Zigzags No Rights of Accuse: Brittle

This approach contrasts with that of McLachlin CJ for the majority. McLachlin regards the right to vote as 'fundamental to our democracy and the rule of law' and, as such, it 'cannot be lightly set aside'.[88] The court should therefore define the right broadly and liberally,[89] without paying deference to Parliament as the matter is not an issue of 'social and political philosophy'.[90] For McLachlin:

> [t]he core democratic rights of Canadians do not fall within a 'range of acceptable alternatives' among which Parliament may pick and choose at its discretion ... This case ... represents a conflict between the rights of citizens to vote—one of the most fundamental rights guaranteed by the *Charter*—and Parliament's denial of that right ... It is for the courts, unaffected by the shifting winds of public opinion and electoral interests, to safeguard the right to vote guaranteed by s.3 of the *Charter*.[91]

McLachlin's approach gives the final, authoritative determination of prisoner voting rights to the court. Although the legislature had the ability to enact legislation following the first *Sauvé* case, that legislation is subject to final scrutiny by the courts. The only way in which the legislature can respond to this judicial decision would be to enact legislation that complies with the final authority of the Supreme Court of Canada.

The contrasting approaches of McLachlin and Gonthier illustrate how Canada's democratic dialogue model of human rights protections has arguably collapsed into a strong, legal protection of rights in practice. They also hint at a deeper issue, explaining why this collapse may be inevitable. Despite their disagreement as to the outcome on prisoner voting rights, both McLachlin and Gonthier agreed that, were prisoner voting to be an issue of 'social and political philosophy' then it is one that is better determined by the legislature than by the courts. Courts, on the other hand, should determine legal rights. This calls into question the stability of a democratic dialogue model in practice as it can be reasonable to disagree about whether an issue is one of social and political philosophy or a legal right. Therefore, it can be reasonable to argue both that an issue should be determinatively resolved by the courts or by the legislature. As these reasonable disagreements occur in the court, we can expect court decisions to either collapse into a strong legal protection of rights or a weak parliamentary protection of rights in practice, depending on whether a majority of the judiciary classify the rights-issue as a legal issue or an issue of social and political philosophy.

More fundamentally, it challenges the underpinning normative foundations of a democratic dialogue model. The disagreement between Gonthier and McLachlin merely replicates some of the arguments made by those advocating legal and political constitutionalism. Advocates of political constitutionalism argue for greater political protections of rights, in part, because they believe that many rights are merely issues of social and political philosophy that are better determined by the legislature. Advocates of legal constitutionalism argue, inter alia, that the determination of rights issues requires moral reasoning, a task better performed by the courts precisely because they will focus on rational arguments as opposed to balancing issues of social and political philosophy. Understood in this manner, collapse would appear to be inevitable. Democratic dialogue models of rights protection provide no distinct normative

Majorities Manipulate Weasel Words of Dialogue, Deference and Charter Values' (2003) 20 S CT L Rev 267; David M Brown, 'Sauvé and Prisoners' Voting Rights: The Death of the Good Citizen?' (2003) 20 S Ct L Rev 297; Richard Haigh, 'Between Here and There is Better Than Anything Over There: The Morass of *Sauvé v Canada*' (2003) 20 S Ct L Rev 353.

[88] *Sauvé II* (n 46) para 9. [89] ibid, para 11. [90] ibid, para 12.
[91] ibid, para 13.

justification for their preferred protection of rights. They merely replicate old arguments in a different arena.

B. Unstable legal and political constitutionalism

Similar conclusions as to potential instability can be made when we examine examples of strong legal protections of rights and parliamentary protections of rights. The United States is regarded as an archetypal example of a constitutional system that provides for a strong protection of human rights. Since the seminal decision of *Marbury v Madison*, the Supreme Court has recognized the ability of individuals to petition for legislation to be struck down as incompatible with the US Constitution.[92] The Constitution is designed to give the courts the final word in the definition of human rights. However, the conclusion reached on prisoner voting arguably reverses this assessment. *Richardson v Ramirez* does provide an example of the Supreme Court providing the final word on whether the US Constitution is breached by legislation removing prisoners from the electoral franchise. However, by reading the Fourteenth Amendment of the Constitution in a manner that permits legislation banning prisoners from voting, the Supreme Court's decision effectively gives the final word on prisoner voting to state legislatures. State legislatures may enact legislation restricting prisoners from voting, or enact legislative provisions that permit prisoner voting.[93]

The opposite conclusion is reached when we examine Australia's experience of prisoner voting laws. In terms of the protection of human rights, Australia can be regarded, at the Federal level, as preserving a purely parliamentary model of protection of human rights. The final word on human rights is given to the legislature. The Federal Constitution contains no list of constitutionally protected human rights. The restrictions placed on state and federal legislatures by the Constitution are restricted to those required to preserve the federal structure of Australia. However, in *Roach* the majority in the High Court concluded that legislation imposing a blanket ban on prisoners was contrary to articles 7 and 24 and the structure of the Constitution, which supported representative democracy.[94]

These apparent contradictions between constitutional structure and practice arise because of the flexibility inherent in interpreting constitutional provisions. If a court provides a detailed and precise reading of a constitutional provision, it restricts the range of decisions that can be taken by the legislature. If, however, the court provides a less detailed interpretation of the same provision, greater decision-making power is given to the legislature. The decision of the majority of the High Court of Australia effectively granted greater power to the courts than the legislature to determine whether prisoners should be allowed to vote by providing a more detailed account of a constitutional right, reading detail in to the Constitution so as to place greater restrictions on legislative choice. This was achieved in two ways: by reading constitutional provisions in a manner that respected the 'structure' of the constitution and through reading its provisions in a way that allows the Constitution to change over time, reflecting changes in the views of society.

The judgments of Gummow, Kirby, and Crennan JJ are examples of the first method. Their arguments start by paying close attention to the text of the Constitution, recognizing the power of the legislature to determine the electoral franchise in article 30 of the Australian Constitution. This power in turn was expressly made subject to

[92] See n 54. [93] See, for example, Maine and Vermont.
[94] (2007) 233 CLR 162.

other constitutional provisions—in particular articles 7 and 24, requiring, respectively, that senators and members of the House of Representatives be 'directly chosen by the people'. Gummow, Kirby, and Crennan JJ conclude that the phrase 'directly chosen by the people' should be interpreted according to the structure as well as the text of the Constitution.[95] The structure of the Constitution includes the system of representative Government established by the Constitution.[96] After interpreting the legislative history, which illustrates a steady broadening of the franchise over time,[97] they conclude that the constitutional restrictions on the power of the legislature found in article 30 of the Constitution mean that any restriction on the electoral franchise has to be reasonably appropriate to furthering representative government.[98] The measure restricting all prisoners from voting does not meet this requirement. To ensure compatibility with the requirement that the legislature be 'directly chosen by the people', prisoner disenfranchisement would need to be limited to those prisoners committing serious enough offences. This is not true of a blanket ban.

Gleeson CJ's judgment illustrates the second method of interpreting constitutional provisions in a way that increases the relative power of the court and reduces that of the legislature. He reasoned that the meaning of the phrase 'directly chosen by the people' could change over time as historical facts change. As universal adult suffrage is a long-established fact in Australia, the meaning of 'chosen by the people' is to be read as referring to universal adult suffrage. Any limitation placed by Parliament on universal adult suffrage must 'constitute a substantial reason for exclusion' from the right to vote.[99] Gleeson CJ concluded that there was no substantial reason to exclude all prisoners from voting, therefore concluding that a blanket ban on prisoner voting is unconstitutional.[100]

When courts restrict constitutional provisions in a less detailed manner, they grant greater discretion to the law-maker. One way in which this can be achieved is when courts interpret constitutional provisions narrowly in reliance on an interpretation of the intention of the authors of the constitution. For example, Haynes J, giving a dissenting judgment in *Roach*, focused more closely on the meaning of the phrase 'directly chosen by the people'. He regarded the phrase as requiring 'generality' as opposed to 'universality'—a less-exacting requirement. Consequently, the legislature had a greater ability to determine the extent of the electoral franchise. The legislature need only ensure that the right to vote was sufficiently general to satisfy the requirements of articles 7 and 24 of the Constitution. There was no need to ensure that any restriction on the right to vote was reasonably appropriate to furthering democratic government. Moreover, he was less willing to allow the meaning of constitutional provisions to evolve over time. He concluded that, as there were earlier examples of legislatures who had restricted the right to vote of prisoners, the legislature must clearly have the constitutional power to do so.[101] There was no need to allow the meaning of constitutional terms to evolve over time, reflecting contemporary standards. For Haynes J:

> The meaning of constitutional standards does not vary with the level of popular acceptance that particular applications of the power might enjoy.[102]

The meaning of 'chosen by the people', therefore, did not change over time.[103]

Heydon J's interpretation of the Australian Constitution is even more explicit in terms of its aim to grant greater authority to the legislature to determine the extent of

[95] ibid, paras 47–48. [96] ibid, para 53. [97] ibid, paras 80–81.
[98] ibid, paras 85–95. [99] ibid, para 7. [100] ibid, paras 11–26.
[101] ibid, paras 105–14. [102] ibid, para 159. [103] ibid, para 161.

the franchise. For Heydon to interpret the phrase 'directly chosen by the people' in the manner advocated by the majority would have the effect of ensuring that legislatures 'could not wind the clock back';[104] once widened the franchise could not be reduced. To interpret the Constitution in the manner advocated by the majority would remove one of the

> advantages of having a liberal democratic legislature, particularly when the legislators belong to political parties having different opinions on some issues … its capacity to experiment, to test what does or does not work, to make up for unsatisfactory 'advances' by carrying out prudent 'retreats'.[105]

Similarly, Rehnquist J's conclusion in the US Supreme Court decision of *Richardson v Ramirez*[106] rests on a very specific interpretation of the equal protection clause, looking to the history of the clause and trying to establish its specific historical purpose. Rehnquist read the first clause of the Fourteenth Amendment of the US Constitution in the light of the second clause of the Fourteenth Amendment. The US Constitution imposed penalties on states who enacted legislation that reduced the electoral franchise in their state. The second clause of the Fourteenth Amendment expressly exempted these penalties where the reduction in the franchise occurred as states disenfranchised felons. If removal of the right to vote from felons did not incur this penalty, then it could be inferred that it was not contrary to the equal protection clause to remove the right to vote from felons. This is not to argue that Rehnquist J interpreted the Constitution in order to empower state legislatures, so that legislatures as opposed to the courts authoritatively decide whether prisoners should be allowed to vote. However, it is clear that Rehnquist is aware of this consequence. Rehnquist notes that arguments for extending the franchise to prisoners should be addressed to legislatures 'which may properly weigh and balance' these arguments against those in favour of continuing felon disenfranchisement;[107] it is not for the court to 'choose one set of values over another'.[108] It may be, therefore, that similar concerns as to whether an issue should be resolved finally by the legislature or the courts could influence whether a narrow or broad interpretation is taken to constitutional provisions.

A detailed examination of the case law in Australia and the United States suggests that the way in which the law is applied in practice may be contrary to expectations given the constitutional model of protecting human rights. It also suggests that, rather than being understood as extremes, legal and political constitutionalism provide general arguments that are applied to varying degrees with regard to different decisions. This may appear to suggest that all systems are best understood as democratic dialogue models of human rights. The way in which courts exercise their powers of interpretation can have knock-on consequences as to the relative powers of the courts and the legislature to authoritatively determine the scope of a constitutionally protected human right. Moreover, as Rehnquist's comments illustrate, even courts that have the power to strike down legislation are sensitive to whether a particular issue is best determined by the court or by the legislature, with Rehnquist suggesting that the issue of prisoner disenfranchisement was one best left to the legislature. This conclusion would appear to be reinforced by the South African experience. In its first assessment of prisoner voting in *August*, Sachs J, giving the judgment of the South African Supreme Court, concluded that it was not necessary for the court to decide whether Parliament would have had the power to limit the right of prisoners to vote.[109] All the court was being asked was

[104] ibid, para 180. [105] ibid. [106] 418 US 24 (1974). [107] ibid, 55.
[108] ibid. [109] *August v The Electoral Commission* (n 48).

whether prisoners should have the right to vote, given that, at the time, there was no legislation disenfranchising prisoners.[110] Sachs J also noted that the legislative silence on this issue did not mean that the 'court should decide which prisoners may vote'.[111] The judgment of the court 'should not be read … as suggesting that Parliament is prevented from disenfranchising certain prisoners'.[112] These statements facilitate democratic dialogue in the manner suggested by a democratic dialogue model of rights, making it clear to Parliament that it has the ability to respond to the decision of the court by enacting legislation to disenfranchise some prisoners, should it wish to do so.

V. Outline of the Argument

Our overview of democratic dialogue theories, analysed through the lens of comparative provisions on prisoner voting rights, appears to paint a bleak picture. Far from providing a new theory that is capable of resolving complex rights-issues which can combine the advantages of legal and political constitutionalism whilst minimizing their disadvantages, we appear to have discovered that democratic dialogue appears to be more akin to a myth. First, it seems impossible to define what is meant by democratic dialogue. The suggestion, taken from the starting point of Hogg and Bushell's work, was to argue that democratic dialogue occurs when the legislature has the opportunity to respond to judicial determinations of human rights. This interaction between institutions helps to alleviate the democratic deficit criticism of strong, judicial protections of human rights. However, our discussion of prisoner voting cases demonstrated that this approach is too vague. All of the systems studied demonstrated examples of change in the law occurring through a combination of judicial decisions and legislative intervention. Second, we looked at whether democratic dialogue is distinct as providing for a novel model of rights protections. Drawing on Gardbaum's analysis of commonwealth models of rights protections, this suggested that democratic dialogue was best understood as an aspect of constitutional design. However, particularly as shown by our comparison of the constitutional protection of rights in South Africa and Canada, it is hard to determine either necessary or sufficient criteria to help distinguish between dialogue and other models of human rights protections. These difficulties were exacerbated when we used the experience of prisoner voting rights to assess how these constitutional provisions are applied in practice. We discovered inherent instability not only in democratic dialogue models of rights protections, but also in those models based on legal constitutionalism, with its strong legal protection of rights, and political constitutionalism with its preference for a parliamentary protection of rights. Far from providing an account of two diverse and distinct theories of constitutionalism, with democratic dialogue providing a mid-way position that can combine the strengths and minimize the weaknesses of both views, we appear to have a blurring of different theories. Our initial examination appears to suggest, therefore, that democratic dialogue is either ubiquitous or non-existent. There is no separate account of a democratic dialogue model of the constitution and democratic dialogue takes place in a range of different constitutional models.

It is the task of this book to challenge this perception. It will not argue that democratic dialogue theories are a panacea. However, it will argue that democratic dialogue is capable of providing a distinct model of constitutionalism. It will also explain that

[110] ibid, para 20. [111] ibid, para 30. [112] ibid, para 31.

democratic dialogue has distinct normative advantages. It can provide for a better protection of human rights. In addition, it can facilitate deliberation, both in the legislature and the courts and in the wider community, provide an effective set of checks and balances between institutions of the constitution and help to provide a more effective means of resolving potential constitutional crises which arise from the need for constitutions to be both rigid enough to provide stability and flexible enough to change as societies evolve. Nevertheless, it is important to recognize that democratic dialogue can occur through a number of different mechanisms. The advantages of democratic dialogue can be achieved to a greater or lesser degree in a range of constitutional structures and aiming to achieve these advantages often focuses less on issues of constitutional design and more on analyses of how institutions should exercise their powers.

Proposing a new way of analysing constitutions is complicated. To add to the complication, various aspects of the defence of democratic dialogue intertwine, making it hard to present each stage of the argument in isolation. The first part of the book will undertake the challenge of defining democratic dialogue. It will start by re-examining our initial suspicion that democratic dialogue is either ubiquitous or non-existent. Chapter 1 will revisit the distinction between legal and political constitutionalism. The distinction between these two theories is often referred to as one of control. Whilst legal constitutionalism advocates legal controls over human rights, political constitutionalism prefers political controls. Democratic dialogue is perceived as a distinct theory because it advocates a combination of legal and political protections of human rights. However, when we analyse accounts of both legal and political constitutionalism, these accounts blur. The difference between them appears to be one of degree as opposed to a bright line. The more we analyse legal and political constitutionalism, the more these theories appear to advocate a combination of legal and political controls. This poses problems for any account of democratic dialogue which aims to occupy a middle ground between these two theories.

Having rejected an understanding of democratic dialogue in terms of control, Chapter 2 analyses whether democratic dialogue is distinct because of its dynamic as opposed to static approach. Democratic dialogue examines interactions between institutions of the constitution. It analyses constitutions over time, as opposed to determining unchanging principles of the constitution, or analysing legal or political institutions in isolation. However, Chapter 2 will argue that although this dynamic component is a necessary criterion of democratic dialogue, it is not sufficient to distinguish democratic dialogue from legal and political constitutionalism. We can find dynamic accounts of both legal constitutionalism and political constitutionalism. In Chapter 2, for example, we will evaluate the dynamic component of Trevor Allan's account of legal constitutionalism and Griffith's account of political constitutionalism. Our search for the definitive account of a distinct theory of democratic dialogue does not reach its end through the recognition of the dynamic nature of democratic dialogue.

Chapter 3 moves on from this disappointing beginning to our search by re-examining accounts of political and legal constitutionalism and the dynamic nature of democratic dialogue. It provides a starting point for a workable and distinct account of democratic dialogue by recognizing that the distinction between legal and political constitutionalism is not best understood in terms of control, but in terms of how these theories rest on different constitutional foundational assumptions. By this I mean an assumption which is used as a starting point, or organizational principle, in any account of constitutionalism.[113] Accounts of political constitutionalism tend to be grounded

[113] See, for example, M Gordon, *Parliamentary Sovereignty in the UK Constitution: Process, Politics and Democracy* (Oxford, Hart 2015) 23–28.

in a preference for popular sovereignty and democracy over liberal, or other, principles of rights. Accounts of legal constitutionalism tend to be grounded in a preference for a protection of liberal rights or other constitutional principles over popular sovereignty and democracy. Accounts of democratic dialogue—or at least the account found in this book—are grounded in the importance of both democracy and the protection of rights, seeing neither as more foundational nor more important than the other.

However, even this possible means of distinguishing between legal and political constitutionalism, leaving a distinct middle ground to be occupied by democratic dialogue, is problematic. It runs the risk either of providing an artificial divide between extreme forms of legal and political constitutionalism, leaving a middle ground for democratic dialogue, or pushing all accounts of constitutionalism on to the middle ground, subsumed into accounts of democratic dialogue.[114] Legal and political constitutionalism will advocate a combination of both legal and political controls over the executive and protection of human rights. Any difference between them may merely be better expressed in terms of the starting point of their argument. Legal constitutionalism will start with an analysis of legal controls, or a presumption in favour of some form of legal control, using arguments to recognize when legal controls should be exercised less stringently in order to recognize the importance of showing respect for democratic deliberation and giving the legislature a wider area of discretionary judgment. Political constitutionalism starts with an analysis of democratic controls, moving on to assess how legal controls can supplement political controls.

The starting point of democratic dialogue is different. It starts by recognizing the existence of interactions between institutions of the constitution. It assumes that these interactions are better able to protect human rights and to provide a better control over the executive and examines the types of interaction needed in different areas to achieve this aim. Rather than aiming to forge a middle ground to be occupied by democratic dialogue, it is better to recognize the ways in which accounts of democratic dialogue can add to, and draw from, accounts of political and legal constitutionalism. There is no clear line between legal and political constitutionalism. However, we classify accounts of the constitution along these lines through drawing on the relative importance of protecting liberal principles and of democracy. Accounts of political and legal constitutionalism allocate different roles to the legislature and the judiciary, and also recognize how these roles may be complementary, or contradictory. However, these theories stop short of providing an account of how these institutions can interact with each other, or how these interactions can be used to facilitate the achievement of different normative values in the constitution. They do, however, provide accounts of the relative value of principles and of democracy, providing arguments that can be used to influence the relative power of the judiciary and the legislature when they interact.

This difference in focus distinguishes democratic dialogue from legal and political constitutionalism and is reflected in a distinct understanding of the nature of the interactions between the legislature and the judiciary—these will be referred to as inter-institutional interactions. Democratic dialogue advocates inter-institutional interactions which reflect the relative strength of the legislature and the judiciary when reasoning about rights. The extent to which the legislature and the courts reason differently about rights depends upon the powers they are provided with in different constitutions. In addition, the account of democratic dialogue found in this book

[114] I'm grateful to Paul Craig for pointing out this potential criticism to me.

will distinguish between two distinct forms of inter-institutional interaction: constitutional counter-balancing and constitutional collaboration. Constitutional counter-balancing mechanisms are required to ensure that both the legislature and the judiciary play a role in the determination of rights-issues, whilst ensuring that it is not the case that one institution is always able to authoritatively determine these issues, effectively overriding the contribution of the other. Constitutional collaboration mechanisms are designed to enable the legislature and the judiciary to work together drawing on their relative strengths and weaknesses when reasoning about rights. Having established these different mechanisms, the following chapter will explore both the normative values which can be facilitated by inter-institutional interactions, in addition to explaining the types of inter-institutional interaction that are best able to achieve these normative values, providing a framework for democratic dialogue.

Chapter 4 provides an account of different forms of inter-institutional interactions, examining how constitutional collaboration and constitutional counter-balancing can take place in constitutions with a strong constitutional protection of rights, those with a parliamentary protection of rights, and those which have adopted a commonwealth model of rights protections. It will confirm our suspicion that institutional interactions take place in a variety of constitutional systems, and that there is a range of interactions which can occur in a legal system with a commonwealth model of rights protections. Nevertheless, it will argue that there is a marginal advantage to adopting a commonwealth model of rights protection. These models establish formal or legal mechanisms of constitutional counter-balancing. This, in turn, may make it easier for the legislature and the courts to interact in a manner which facilitates constitutional collaboration, helping to provide a better protection of rights.

Chapter 5 examines why inter-institutional interactions are valuable. It investigates the extent to which democratic dialogue can provide a better protection of rights, focusing in particular on Gardbaum's claim that the commonwealth model of rights protections provides a better protection of human rights by maximizing the benefits and minimizing the disadvantages of a predominantly legal or political protection of human rights. We will discover that democratic dialogue can combine the advantages of political and legal protections of rights. To do so, it is important that both institutions take account not just of reasons for and against a particular resolution of rights-issues, but also of reasons which would require each institution to give weight to the resolution of the other. How this occurs depends upon the distribution of constitutional powers between these institutions. The extent to which this should occur depends upon the institutional features of the legislature and the courts. These factors are used to refine our account of both constitutional counter-balancing and constitutional collaboration.

Chapter 5 also explores further justifications for democratic dialogue. In particular, we will explore the extent to which democratic dialogue engages citizens and can facilitate deliberation. In addition, we will argue that democratic dialogue can provide effective checks and balances, as well as aiming to balance constitutional stability and constitutional evolution. These features will be used to further refine our account of constitutional counter-balancing and constitutional collaboration mechanisms. We will then draw together the arguments to provide a normative framework of democratic dialogue.

Before we can apply our normative framework to a particular constitution, we need to examine further precisely what democratic dialogue is. As discussed in this introduction, 'democratic dialogue' has been used to refer to: a particular form of constitutional design; a distinct method of protecting human rights; a theory which advocates a particular way in which institutions should exercise their powers when determining rights-issues; and as a means of providing an accurate description of constitutional reality. Chapter 6 will argue that democratic dialogue is best described as a constitutional model. It provides an account of a constitution which incorporates normative ideals, but which recognizes the need for certain factual assumptions to be met in order to assess the extent to which these normative ideas can be achieved in a particular constitution.

Having defined democratic dialogue, Chapter 6 then assesses the extent to which democratic dialogue is a suitable model for the UK constitution. It recognizes that the main challenge of the application of democratic dialogue to the UK comes from the doctrine of parliamentary sovereignty. If this is understood as requiring that Parliament is supreme, and so can always override the judiciary, then this means that the constitutional counter-balancing component of democratic dialogue is not satisfied and democratic dialogue is not suited for application to the UK constitution. Chapter 6 will propose a specific understanding of bipolar sovereignty, explaining how this can be applied to the UK constitution. This form of bipolar sovereignty satisfies the specific assumptions on which democratic dialogue is based, meaning that it can be applied to the UK constitution.

Chapter 7 provides an account of the plethora of human rights protections in the United Kingdom, explaining how human rights are protected through the common law and from European Union law in addition to the Human Rights Act 1998. This array of human rights protections provides a range of inter-institutional interactions between both the legislature and the courts and between domestic and European courts. We will focus first on providing a framework of inter-institutional interactions between the legislature and the courts, using this in Chapter 7 to provide examples of where inter-institutional interactions between the legislature and the courts facilitate the normative values of democratic dialogue. Chapter 8 analyses inter-institutional interactions between the UK and European courts. We will first explain how the normative model of inter-institutional interactions needs to be modified when applied to exchanges between courts as opposed to between courts and legislatures. We will then provide a framework for dialogue between the UK courts and the European Court of Human Rights, providing examples of where interactions between these two courts may facilitate democratic dialogue, followed by a separate analysis of interactions between domestic courts and the Court of Justice of the European Union.

Constitutional law in the twenty-first century rarely stands still. In the process of writing this book, what started as initial calls from certain factions in the Conservative Party for modification of the Human Rights Act 1998 progressed into a proposal from the Party setting out reforms and, following the general election in May 2015, a renewed pledge on the part of the government to 'scrap' the Human Rights Act 1998 and replace it with a British Bill of Rights. This pledge has been repeated in the Queen's Speech of both 2015 and 2016, with a statement that the government will bring forth proposals for a British Bill of Rights. To date, no such proposals have appeared. In addition, the European Union's Charter of Fundamental Rights has been applied in UK law so as to disapply legislative provisions, requiring this book to take account of the influence of European Union law. Both of these changes pale in comparison to the monumental decision of the UK public on 23 June 2016 to vote in favour of leaving the European Union. The conclusion will reflect on the referendum outcome and the criticisms of the Human Rights Act 1998 which led to a desire to see it replaced by a British Bill of Rights. It will argue that an understanding of democratic dialogue casts doubt on the assumptions on which criticisms of the Human Rights Act are based, in addition to the claims of some wishing to leave the European Union that to do so would mean that the United Kingdom regained its lost sovereignty and would take back control from the European Union. Moreover, it will argue that both developments may undermine the ability of the UK constitution to facilitate democratic dialogue.

1

The Problem with Control

Democratic dialogue theories aim to provide a novel form of human rights protections. Instead of advocating that either courts or the legislature should definitively determine the content of human rights, they argue that both should play a role. Dialogue between the two institutions is regarded as a better means of protecting human rights. It is designed to maximize the benefits of both legal and political determinations of human rights, whilst minimizing their disadvantages. The Introduction examined these arguments through the lens of prisoner voting rights. It cast doubt on the claims of democratic dialogue, recognizing in particular that democratic dialogue appeared to be either ubiquitous or non-existent. This suspicion was based on the difficulty of providing a distinct account of democratic dialogue. Rather than identifying a clear distinction between a purely legal and a purely political protection of rights, with democratic dialogue theories occupying the middle ground, the line between these three accounts appeared to be vague, with each account blurring into the other. The aim of this chapter is to pursue this issue further. In doing so, it will expand on our earlier discussion in three ways. First, the discussion will not just examine prisoner voting rights but will discuss the protection of human rights more generally. Second, it will look at arguments justifying different ways of protecting human rights, focusing in particular on the debate between legal and political constitutionalism. Third, it will investigate arguments concerning legislative and judicial control of executive actions in addition to controls over human rights.

The chapter will focus predominantly on the tension between political and legal constitutionalism. This will help to frame our discussion of human rights protections more generally as well as the issue of control over the executive. The tension between these two theories of constitutionalism pervades recent UK scholarship on constitutional theory and underpins arguments for stronger legal or political protections of rights. Legal constitutionalism in UK scholarship is connected to accounts of common law constitutionalism. In his work tracking the secondary literature developing theoretical accounts of common law constitutionalism, Thomas Poole refers to the recent scholarship of Trevor Allan, Sir John Laws, Dawn Oliver, and Paul Craig, each of whom he identifies as a supporter of common law constitutionalism.[1] Although each provides a different account, Poole argues that they are all common law constitutionalists as they each advocate 'the reconfiguration of public law as a species of constitutionalised politics centred on the common law court'.[2] For Poole, common law constitutionalism is predominantly concerned with the identification of the common

[1] T Poole, 'Back to the Future? Unearthing the Theory of Common law Constitutionalism' (2003) 23 OJLS 435. NB Paul Craig disagrees with this classification of common law constitutionalism, recognizing in particular that it fails to provide an accurate account of the long-standing history of common law constitutionalism and fails to refer to the primary materials from the seventeenth to nineteenth centuries. In particular, this means that the theory provides an unrepresentative narrative of the foundations of common law constitutionalism. See P Craig, *The Hamlyn Lectures: UK, EU and Global Administrative Law. Foundations and Challenges* (Cambridge University Press 2015).

[2] Poole (n 1) 43.

Democratic Dialogue and the Constitution. First Edition. Alison L Young. © Alison L Young 2017. Published 2017 by Oxford University Press.

law courts as the main source of, and actors in, public law. Each theorist focuses on the development of constitutional law as a series of controls over the constitution, and over executive powers, from the common law courts. This contrasts with the model of political constitutionalism, advocated most prominently by JAG Griffith, and later built on, most notably, by the work of Adam Tomkins and Richard Bellamy. Political constitutionalism places politics and political institutions at the centre of the constitution.[3] This account of the constitution advocates more political as opposed to legal controls over the constitution and over executive powers.

This overview is, of necessity, brief and runs the risk alerted to in the Introduction of providing an inaccurate caricature of legal and political constitutionalism. However, it serves to recognize that issues of regulation and control play a central role in the distinction between legal and political constitutionalism. We can see, also, how this relates to the debate as to whether human rights should be protected by legal or political institutions. Political constitutionalism prefers parliamentary protections of human rights and legal constitutionalism advocates legal protections of human rights. However, before we investigate whether we can provide a distinct account of democratic dialogue theory which occupies the middle ground between legal and political constitutionalism, we need to ensure that this focus is neither too parochial, nor too concerned with what may turn out to be a contemporary and potentially short-lived approach to constitutional theory.

Although appearing to be a recent phenomenon, the division between legal constitutionalism and political constitutionalism is nothing new. It reflects tensions running through the history of the UK constitution. Moreover, some current theorists draw on events that took place in the seventeenth century in the United Kingdom in order to support their assertions that the United Kingdom is best described as demonstrating common law constitutionalism, or favouring the political controls of republicanism. Attention is paid in particular to the development of controls over the royal prerogative: *Prohibitions del Roy*[4] and *The Case of Proclamations*.[5]

Common law theorists, such as Paul Craig, argue that these cases demonstrate the extent to which the common law restricted the prerogative powers of the King. *Prohibitions del Roy* shows how the common law courts restricted the powers of the King over the judiciary. It was for the courts, and not the King, to interpret statutory provisions, upholding the independence of the judiciary.[6] *The Case of Proclamations* achieved a similar outcome for the distinction between the legislature and the executive, determining that prerogative powers were limited and that these limits were set by the common law, administered by the courts.[7] The common law courts determined the conditions under which the King could exercise his prerogative powers and they concluded that legislation, enacted by Parliament and interpreted by the courts, overrode prerogative powers. Interpreted in this manner, the cases lend support for legal constitutionalism. They demonstrate a move in the United Kingdom towards legal controls over the executive. Adam Tomkins, however, takes a different view of these seminal cases, using them to support his claim that the United Kingdom is best described in republican terms, demonstrating political as opposed to legal constitutionalism. For

[3] ibid. [4] (1607) 12 Co Rep 63; 77 ER 1342.

[5] (1611) 12 Co Rep 74; 77 ER 1352.

[6] PP Craig, 'Prerogative, Precedent and Power' in C Forsyth and I Hare (eds), *The Golden Metwand and the Crooked Cord: Essays in Honour of Sir William Wade QC* (Oxford University Press 1998), 65, 67.

[7] ibid, 67–69.

Tomkins, *Prohibitions del Roy* is best understood as part of a controversial move of the courts to subsume ecclesiastical law as part of the common law and not as an illustration of the courts using the common law to control actions of the executive.[8] In a similar manner, Tomkins argues that *The Case of Proclamations* does not represent a victory for Parliament over the Crown; but rather a victory for the common law and free enterprise.[9]

The argument as to the interpretation of key events of the seventeenth century is not restricted to these cases. Tomkins argues further that other cases in this era clearly demonstrate the inability of the courts to control the executive. The King continued to make Proclamations which were enforced by the court of Star Chamber.[10] Tomkins cites *Bates' Case*,[11] *The Five Knight's Case*,[12] and the *Ship Money Case*[13] as exemplifying reluctance on the part of the courts to limit the King's discretionary power. Tomkins claims that these cases demonstrate a tendency in the courts to read statutory powers as subject to, rather than limiting, the discretionary power of the King.[14] He argues that Parliament had to enact legislation to overturn these cases and limit the King's prerogative powers—showing that the United Kingdom is historically better understood as advocating political constitutionalism, with Parliament as opposed to the courts providing the main control over the executive.[15]

Craig, however, interprets these cases differently. Whilst agreeing that *Bates' Case* and The *Ship Money Case* concluded that the King's exercise of his prerogative powers was legal, he argues that this was because the common law at that time was unclear as to whether the King possessed the prerogative power to act in these cases. The King was using prerogative power to make impositions to raise money, which was not within his prerogative powers, but these cases could have been based on other prerogative powers. *Bates' Case* can be interpreted as an exercise of the prerogative power of the King to regulate foreign affairs.[16] The *Ship Money Case* can be read as an exercise of the prerogative power of the defence of the realm. In these cases, the raising of money could be seen as secondary to other purposes.[17] Therefore, the cases can still support an interpretation of legal constitutionalism. The courts are drawing on emerging principles of the common law to determine contentious issues of the scope of the prerogative powers of the executive.

Given the way in which current constitutional theorists draw on the history of the United Kingdom to support both legal and political constitutionalism, it is hard to argue that the tension between these two theories is limited to short-lived contemporary debate. The tension between legal and political constitutionalism, expressed in our discussion of the differences between Paul Craig and Adam Tomkins appears to run through history. Craig and Tomkins draw on historical cases to support their accounts of common law constitutionalism or of republicanism. It is equally hard to dismiss the issue as restricted to the United Kingdom, although this may not be expressed in terms of a divide between legal and political constitutionalism. In the United States, for example, similar issues surround the discussion of judicial review—i.e. the review by the courts of the constitutionality of legislative and executive acts. The concern is the potential harm to democracy that occurs in legal systems with a strong form of constitutional review, where courts can strike down legislation that contravenes the constitution, including constitutionally protected human rights. Advocates of legal

[8] A Tomkins, *Our Republican Constitution* (Oxford, Hart 2005), 70–71.
[9] ibid, 72–73. [10] ibid, 72. [11] (1608) 2 St Tr 371. [12] (1627) 3 St Tr 1.
[13] *R v Hampden* (1637) 3 St Tr 825. [14] Tomkins (n 8) 84.
[15] ibid, 74–76 and 86. [16] Craig (n 6) 69. [17] ibid, 70–71.

constitutionalism are more likely to support judicial review. Advocates of political constitutionalism, on the other hand, would favour less judicial review, for fear of its impact on democracy, favouring granting wider, unlimited law-making powers to the legislature. This debate is so common place that, according to one commentator, it is 'trite … to say that the legal academy is obsessed with trying to explain the seeming tension between judicial review and democracy'.[18]

Moreover, in a similar manner to contemporary UK scholarship, American scholars also turn to history, showing that the debate is not just a contemporary fad. In the United States, attention is paid to the tension inherent in *The Federalist Papers*, setting out the foundations of the practice of constitutionalism in the United States. Those advocating greater political controls focus on Madison's contributions to *The Federalist Papers*, which focus on how the separation of powers[19] and the fractioning of interest groups in a federal democracy can best control 'factions' who are 'united and actuated by some common impulse of passion, or of interest, adverse to the rights of other citizens or to the permanent and aggregate interests of the community'.[20] Madison's analysis casts doubt on the perceived dangers of democratic controls which often form the basis of an argument for greater legal controls over both the executive and the legislature. He argues in favour of a stricter separation of powers, with the legislature being able to control the executive. Also, by dividing power between the states and federal institutions, it is harder for any one group to hold sway and then use their power to harm the interests of other minority groups. Those advocating greater legal controls, however, would place more emphasis on Hamilton's contributions. He argued strongly that the judiciary as 'the least dangerous'[21] branch of the Constitution was most suited to protecting the Constitution from the danger of any one group in society forming a majority and using its powers to restrict the interests of other minority groups. By taking on this role, the court preserves the sovereignty of the people, ensuring that their will, as expressed in the Constitution, remains supreme.[22]

The tension between legal and political constitutionalism may be a theme of current academic commentaries on the UK constitution. However, the issues it raises are not unique to the United Kingdom. The issue as to the relative balance of legal and political controls over the executive, and concerns as to the impact on democracy where courts can strike down legislation, runs through legal scholarship as a whole. Friedman argues that this debate is ever-continuing as those taking part in the debate can often see the merit in both sides of the argument. It is understandable both why we would want democratic decision-making, and why we would want a strong protection of rights. Moreover, Friedman believes that constitutional scholars are wary of making normative arguments and so draw on the arguments of past scholars and on historical constitutional divisions, perpetuating this debate.[23] If democratic dialogue can provide a means of reconciling these tensions, it would prove to be an extremely attractive theory of constitutionalism.

There is definitely merit, therefore, in explaining how political and legal constitutionalism advocate political and legal controls and examining in more depth whether democratic dialogue can provide a middle ground between these two theories,

[18] B Friedman, 'The Counter-Majoritarian Problem and the Pathology of Constitutional Scholarship' (2001) 95 Northwestern University Law Review 933, 935.
[19] Madison, *No 51* in C Rossiter (ed), *The Federalist Papers* (Mentor 1961).
[20] Madison, *No 10* in C Rossiter (ed), *The Federalist Papers* (Mentor 1961), 78.
[21] Hamilton, *No 78* in C Rossiter (ed), *The Federalist Papers* (Mentor 1961), 465.
[22] Hamilton, *No 78* in C Rossiter (ed), *The Federalist Papers* (Mentor 1961), 468.
[23] Friedman (n 18) 935–42.

reconciling these tensions. However, this chapter may disappoint those readers who are hoping that democratic dialogue can resolve this long-standing debate. Further investigation of the distinction between political and legal constitutionalism reveals that the fears set out in the Introduction are realized. It is difficult to clearly delineate between legal and political constitutionalism in terms of their account of whether the executive should be controlled by, and human rights predominantly protected by, legal or political institutions. It is also difficult, in practice, to distinguish between the type of controls advocated by legal and political constitutionalism and those advocated by democratic dialogue theorists.

I. Parliament or the Courts?

The answer to the question as to which constitutional institution should control the executive and protect human rights appears to provide a clear means of distinguishing between legal theories. Political constitutionalism argues that legislatures do and should predominantly control the executive and protect human rights. Legal constitutionalism prefers to give this role to the courts. Democratic dialogue advocates both legal and political controls. It is also an easy task to find evidence in support of these assertions in the academic literature. The determination of which institution should protect human rights, or control the actions of the executive appears to dominate the distinction between legal and political constitutionalism. It is easy to see why this is the case. This determination makes the most difference in practice, leading to different conclusions as to constitutional design, and fuels disagreements as to whether judicial decisions overturning decisions of the legislature are legitimate.

We have already referred to Poole's account of common law constitutionalism in English law. Poole argues that a key feature of common law constitutionalism is that the court is the 'primary guardian' of rights and values in a particular community.[24] The role of the court is to 'apply fundamental standards of political morality, as enshrined in the principles of the common law, to protect individuals from interference by the state'.[25] Evidence of a preference for control of the courts over the executive, and in some cases also the legislature, is also easy to find in classic expositions of legal constitutionalism based on the common law. Sir John Laws argues that it is the function of the court to protect fundamental normative principles and values.[26] Its constitutional role is to act as the guardian of basic principles, derived from Kantian ethics and autonomy, expressed as negative rights.[27] Dawn Oliver recognizes the way in which judicial review has expanded, such that the courts focus more on controlling public functions as opposed to focusing on the source of power to trigger the imposition of public law controls.[28] She uses this development to recognize how courts have formulated fundamental values of good administration in the common law that apply to regulate the conduct of both public and private bodies, recommending that the courts continue this development to control powers of the executive.[29] Jeffrey Jowell regards the development of the principle of

[24] ibid. [25] ibid, 452.

[26] J Laws, 'Law and Democracy' [1995] Public Law 72, 92–93.

[27] J Laws, 'The Constitution: Morals and Rights' [1996] Public Law 622, 629.

[28] D Oliver, 'Is the Ultra Vires Rule the Basis of Judicial Review?' [1987] Public Law 543.

[29] D Oliver, 'Law, Politics and Public Accountability: The Search for a New Equilibrium' [1994] Public Law 238, 249.

legality as demonstrating the existence of constitutional principles of the common law. The principle of legality is a principle of statutory interpretation, developed by the courts, which assumes that the legislature would not grant the power to the executive to act contrary to fundamental principles of the common law through general provisions. Only specific words can empower the executive to act contrary to fundamental principles.[30] Although disagreeing about whether the logic of the common law argument requires that courts should be able to strike down legislation as well as executive actions that undermine fundamental principles of the common law, both Trevor Allan and Paul Craig argue that courts should control the executive, advocating broad principles of judicial review.[31]

A common theme running through the work of political constitutionalists is the identification of the institution tasked with controlling the executive. Both Adam Tomkins and Richard Bellamy conclude that legal constitutionalism advocates court control. Their theories of political constitutionalism are developed, at least in part, as a response to the claims of legal constitutionalism, preferring political to legal controls over the executive. Tomkins regards arguments for legal control over the executive as defining features of legal constitutionalism. He states that legal constitutionalism advocates that the extent and justification of the actions of the executive are to be determined by laws administered by the courts.[32] In addition, a further defining feature of legal constitutionalism is that law controls the government through the enforcement of specific rules and the application of the principle of legality.[33] Richard Bellamy focuses on the way in which legal constitutionalists argue that human rights form the basic fundamental principles in a democratic society. He argues that legal constitutionalists believe that the courts are the best institution to determine the content of these fundamental principles and, therefore, it is the job of the court to protect these fundamental rights from legislative intrusion.[34]

Political constitutionalists criticize the claims of legal constitutionalism, advocating in response the need for political as opposed to legal controls over executive actions generally and specifically to protect human rights. These arguments are made most forcefully with regard to the protection of human rights. Bellamy, for example, concludes that human rights are best protected by legislatures as opposed to the courts.[35] The preference for political controls over human rights is recognised as a defining feature of political constitutionalism.[36] This preference for political controls extends to controls over the executive and to the determination of constitutional principles. It is for politics and the democratic process to determine the principles according to which the executive should govern and for political institutions to hold the executive to account.[37]

[30] J Jowell, 'Beyond the Rule of Law, Towards Constitutional Judicial Review' [2000] Public Law 671.

[31] TRS Allan, 'Constitutional Dialogue and the Justification of Judicial Review' (2003) 23 OJLS 563; PP Craig, 'The Common Law, Shared Power and Judicial Review' (2004) 24 OJLS 237.

[32] Tomkins (n 8) 11. [33] ibid.

[34] R Bellamy, *Political Constitutionalism: A Republican Defence of the Constitutionality of Democracy* (Cambridge University Press 2007), 3.

[35] ibid, 4–5; R Bellamy, 'Political Constitutionalism and the Human Rights Act' (2011) 9 International Journal of Constitutional Law 86.

[36] G Gee and G Webber, 'What is a Political Constitution?' (2010) 20 Oxford Journal of Legal Studies 473.

[37] See Tomkins (n 8); K Ewing, 'The Resilience of the Political Constitution' (2013) 14 German Law Journal 2111; M Goldoni and C McCorkindale 'Why We (Still) Need a Revolution' (2013) 14 German Law Journal 2197.

In a similar manner, the requirement of collaboration between the legislature and the judiciary to control the executive and, in particular, to protect human rights is easily identified as a defining feature of democratic dialogue. Stephen Gardbaum, in his seminal work, presents the distinct nature of the commonwealth model of constitutionalism in a similar manner. If legal constitutionalism advocates court control of human rights and executive actions, and political constitutionalism advocates a political control over these matters, then the role of the commonwealth model is to provide a mid-way point, advocating both political and legal controls. Gardbaum describes political constitutionalism as a theory advocating that 'the limits on governmental power inherent in the concept of constitutionalism ... are ... or should be predominantly political in nature, enforced through the ordinary mechanisms of Madisonian-style structural constraints and especially through electoral accountability'.[38] Advocates of legal constitutionalism, in contrast, 'believe that these limits in general and rights in particular are or should be predominantly legal in nature and enforced through the power of the courts to disapply acts that exceed them'.[39]

The commonwealth model is a deliberate blend of legal and political constitutionalism. Two key features of the commonwealth model facilitate the sharing of human rights controls between the legislature and the judiciary. First, commonwealth models require pre-enactment legislative scrutiny of legislative provisions. This legislative scrutiny needs to focus on the human rights implications of legislative provisions. Second, commonwealth models require a weak as opposed to a strong judicial protection of human rights. A weak protection of human rights means that the courts should not have the power to strike down legislation in a way that precludes a legislative response.[40] Courts may instead have, for example, the power to declare legislation incompatible with human rights,[41] or an ability to strike down legislative provisions coupled with the ability of the legislature to respond by enacting legislation that takes effect and has full legal force notwithstanding the decision of the court.[42] However, the court must also possess more powers than the power of interpretation found in traditional models of rights protections, based on parliamentary sovereignty, where the court only has the power to interpret legislation according to the will of Parliament.

Gardbaum proposes four distinct features in the commonwealth model of rights protections that create a distinct institutional structure capable of providing a combined legal and political control over human rights. First, there is a need for a legalized and codified charter of rights. The charter of rights is not found in a constitutional document, distinguishing this model from constitutional protections of rights. Second, there is a requirement of mandatory rights review by the political branches of the Constitution of proposed legislative measures before they become fully enacted acts of the legislation. Third, there needs to be some form of constitutional review by the courts—i.e. some power of the judicial branch to review legislation for its compatibility with human rights—that goes beyond their ability to interpret legislative provisions so as to comply with the will of the legislature. Fourth, the formal power to definitively determine the content of legislation, including the content of human rights, must vest in the legislature by the ordinary voting procedures used by that legislative body.

[38] S Gardbaum, *The New Commonwealth Model of Constitutionalism* (Cambridge University Press 2013), 22.

[39] ibid. [40] ibid, 25.

[41] See, for example, the power of the high court or above to declare legislation incompatible with Convention rights, found in s 4 of the Human Rights Act 1998.

[42] See, for example, s 33 of the Canadian Charter of Rights and Freedoms, found in the Canada Act 1982.

These features are distinct institutional features of constitutional design, providing for a structured combination of legal and political controls over human rights.[43]

It is easy to get the impression from these statements that the distinction between legal and political constitutionalism is extremely clear-cut, and that democratic dialogue clearly and distinctly carves a middle path between these two extremes. However, the more closely we examine these theories, the harder it becomes to differentiate between them and the more they seem to merge into each other. The blurring between legal and political constitutionalism makes it hard to delineate a middle ground that can be occupied by democratic dialogue. Moreover, when we examine each of these theories more closely, their conclusions as to the scope of judicial review and the extent to which different institutions should protect human rights begin to overlap.

II. No Middle Ground?

The previous section argued that we could potentially distinguish between legal constitutionalism, political constitutionalism, and democratic dialogue when we examine constitutional design. Whilst legal constitutionalism prefers strong judicial review, political constitutionalism has no constitutional review and a judiciary which acts in order to control the executive according to the intentions of Parliament and democratic dialogue, with stronger judicial review than is found in political constitutionalism, but which stops short of strong judicial review without providing the legislature with the ability to respond to legal judgments. However, difficulties arise when we examine how these differently structured protections of human rights operate in practice. Although it may be possible to dismiss these concerns as merely demonstrating the difficulty involved in shifting institutional behaviour to new constitutional structures, this section will argue that they are indicative of a deeper problem. It is not only that it is difficult to distinguish between these theories in practice. Rather, it is hard to find a distinct normative justification for democratic dialogue models. Discussions as to how institutions should exercise their powers in a democratic dialogue model of human rights protections draw on the normative justifications for political and legal controls of human rights.

A. Practical impossibility

Mark Tushnet's work is highly critical of democratic dialogue models of rights protections, such as the commonwealth model of human rights defended by Stephen Gardbaum. Tushnet argues that these forms of human rights protections will inevitably collapse, in practice, into either strong legal or weak parliamentary protections of human rights.[44] It is easy to find evidence of this instability and potential collapse. This is particularly true when we look at how the Canadian Charter of Fundamental Rights and Freedoms operates in practice. Critics of the *Charter* argue that the original use of the 'notwithstanding clause', found in section 33 of the *Charter*, led to the clause falling into disrepute and therefore its lack of use. The clause has only been used by the Provincial or territorial legislatures, mostly by Quebec, and was last used in 2000. Moreover, of the seventeen times in which the clause has been used, it was only used once as a response to a judicial determination

[43] Gardbaum (n 38) 29–33.

[44] M Tushnet, 'New Forms of Judicial Review and the Persistence of Rights- and Democracy-based Worries' (2003) 38 Wake Forest Law Review 813.

of human rights.[45] The other times were all pre-emptive uses of the clause to remove legislation from judicial scrutiny. Moreover, earlier uses of section 33 were severely criticized, particularly the pre-emptive use of the clause by Quebec after an invalidation of laws requiring French-only road signs and the use of the clause by Alberta to protect its statutory opposition to same-sex marriages.[46] This has led some to argue that the clause has essentially lapsed into desuetude, leading to comments that Canada effectively has a strong legal protection of human rights as opposed to a democratic dialogue model.[47]

Similar arguments have been made in the academic commentary on the UK's Human Rights Act 1998. The Human Rights Act 1998 does not empower the courts to strike down legislation. Instead, section 3 of the Act requires courts to read legislation, so far as it is possible to do so, in a manner that ensures the legislation complies with Convention rights. Section 4 of the Act empowers the courts to make a declaration of incompatibility when a Convention-compatible reading of legislation is not possible. This enables the legislature to respond to the decisions of the court, as the legislature has a choice whether to remove or modify incompatible legislation. However, to date, the legislature has responded to all but one of the twenty final declarations of incompatibility, the remaining issue being that of prisoner voting where there have been no further moves to implement the recommendations of the Joint Committee on the Draft Prisoner Voting Bill.[48] A recent report of the Joint Committee on Human Rights also reported a 'significant downward trend' in the use of section 4.[49] Only three declarations of incompatibility were issued under the 2010–2015 Coalition Government, of which one is under appeal.[50] Under the current Conservative Government, there has, to date, been only one declaration of incompatibility, which is also currently under appeal.[51] In addition, the Human Rights Act 1998 incorporates Convention rights and preserves the right of individuals to petition the European Court of Human Rights. This connection between UK legislation and international human rights protections makes it difficult for the UK legislature to fail to respond to declarations of incompatibility. Again, this is seen as providing evidence that the Human Rights Act, in practice, is closer to a strong constitutional protection of human rights than a midway model.[52] Arguments are also made that commonwealth models of human rights protections, in practice, are closer to a parliamentary protection of rights. This is particularly true of the academic commentary in Australia and New Zealand, which argue that the courts have been too cautious to protect rights and that the pre-legislative scrutiny has not been insufficiently effective to ensure legislation protections human rights.[53]

[45] *Ford v Quebec (Attorney General)* [1998] 2 SCR 712.

[46] See Gardbaum (n 38) 109–10.

[47] G Huscroft, 'Constitutionalism from the Top Down' (2007) 45 Osgoode Hall Law Journal 91.

[48] Joint Committee on Human Rights, 'Human Rights Judgments' Seventh Report of Session 2014-2015 HL Paper 130 HC 1088, 11 March 2015. http://www.publications.parliament.uk/pa/jt201415/jtselect/jtrights/130/130.pdf.

[49] ibid, paragraph 4.2.

[50] *Reilly (2) v Secretary of State for Work and Pensions* [2014] UKHC (Admin) 2182; [2015] QB 573; [2016] EWCA Civ 413; [2016] All ER (D) 21 (May). It is believed that the government will appeal this decision.

[51] *R (Miranda) v Secretary of State for the Home Department* [2016] EWCA Civ 6.

[52] I Leigh and R Masterman, *Making Rights Real: The Human Rights Act in its First Decade* (Oxford, Hart 2008); A Kavanagh, *Constitutional Review under the UK Human Rights Act* (Cambridge University Press 2009); and Gardbaum, (n 38), 186–93.

[53] C Evans and S Evans, *Australian Bills of Rights: The Law of the Victorian Charter and ACT Human Rights Act* (Chatswood, Lexis Nexis 2008); R Masterman, 'Interpretations, Declarations and Dialogue: Rights Protection Under the Human Rights Act and Victorian Charter of Human Rights

Not only does the academic commentary support Tushnet's concerns of the potential collapse of democratic dialogue models of human rights protections into either strong legal or purely parliamentary protections of rights, but also it is hard to find academic commentary that rejects this perspective. The strongest argument supporting the stability of democratic dialogue models of rights protections is found in Gardbaum's defence of the commonwealth model. Gardbaum argues that this potential instability can be explained by the range of democratic dialogue models of rights protections. Democratic dialogue is a broad church, allowing for a range of mechanisms designed to combine legal and political protections of rights. Along the spectrum of democratic dialogue models on offer, Canada provides the strongest protection of human rights, empowering its courts to strike down legislation. It is unsurprising, therefore, that those wanting to demonstrate how democratic dialogue models of rights protections can collapse into strong protections of rights find the strongest support for their claims when they turn to the Canadian *Charter*. Australia and New Zealand, in contrast, have devised a system of human rights protections that focuses more on improving parliamentary protections of human rights, granting less power to the courts to read legislation to ensure its compatibility with human rights. It is equally unsurprising, therefore, when critics of the democratic dialogue model point to Australia and New Zealand as furnishing examples of the potential for democratic dialogue models to collapse into purely parliamentary protections of human rights in practice. The criticisms of the Canadian, Australian, and New Zealand models, therefore, may just reflect the range of democratic dialogue models, recognizing that each particular example of the commonwealth model may be closer to strong legal or to purely parliamentary protections of rights. There may still be the possibility of a stable model of democratic dialogue that combines legal and political protections of rights in a more equal manner, making collapse into political or legal constitutionalism less likely.

Moreover, Gardbaum recognizes that it takes time for the judiciary and the legislature to adapt to new models of rights protections. Democratic dialogue models of rights protections are relatively new. However, they are designed to resolve a longstanding problem. Traditional models of strong legal and purely parliamentary protections of rights have evolved over time to deal with the problems that arise when, for example, Parliaments undermine minority rights or courts are called upon to protect human rights in complex and controversial fact situations which may call for greater democratic involvement. Courts who possess the power to strike down legislation may not exercise that power fully when faced with these complex issues. Instead, they will defer to the legislature or executive, defining a right in a manner that provides the legislature or executive with a greater choice of rights-compatible policies, or by scrutinizing restrictions on rights less stringently. Courts which do not have the power to strike down legislation may nevertheless be more creative as to how they interpret legislative provisions, straying from a mere account of the intentions of Parliament to read legislation in a manner that protects fundamental rights. Similarly, legislatures who were used to a situation where courts could strike down legislation may regard courts as better placed to determine legal rights. As such, those legislatures may be reluctant to use provisions in a democratic dialogue model of rights protections that enable them

and Responsibilities' (2009) Public Law 112; Gardbaum, (n 38), Chapters 6 and 8; and A Geddis, 'The Comparative Irrelevance of the NZBORA to legislative practice' (2009) 23 New Zealand Universities Law Review 465; and A Geddis and B Fenton, '"Which is to be Master?"—Rights-Friendly Statutory Interpretation in New Zealand and the United Kingdom' (2008) 25 Arizona Journal of International and Comparative Law 733.

to respond to these court decisions. A newly created democratic dialogue model of rights protections provides a different tool to deal with the determination of rights and requires a new distribution of power between institutions of the constitution. It may take time, therefore, for courts and legislatures to use these new tools without being tempted to use the old tools, or to exercise the new tools in the manner in which they are used to interacting with other institutions.

My earlier work examining the responses to declarations of incompatibility under the Human Rights Act 1998 lends weight to Gardbaum's argument that democratic dialogue models of rights protections are not inherently unstable.[54] Dialogue between the courts and the legislature worked more effectively when both institutions were performing a similar function under the Human Rights Act as the one they were performing before the Act came into force. The clearest examples of democratic dialogue working in practice occurred when the court issued a declaration of incompatibility because complicated measures that could only be implemented by the legislature or the administration were needed to ensure Convention compatibility. This could be seen, for example, in *Bellinger v Bellinger* where the declaration of incompatibility reflected the difficulties faced by the court in choosing from a range of different Convention-compatible interpretations of the legislation, all of which could have had far-reaching social ramifications.[55] The legislature was more able to fully discuss the problems arising from different determinations of gender, and was able to provide for a range of administrative measures to facilitate the treatment of transgender individuals in a way that protected their rights in different situations, whilst minimizing the social-repercussions.

Dialogue was less effective when courts reverted to 'old tools' whilst applying the Human Rights Act 1998. For example, dialogue did not work as effectively when courts deferred to the legislature when determining the content of a Convention right, reaching the conclusion that legislation did not contravene Convention rights, without providing a justification for exercising deference, or where courts failed to provide an account of a Convention right, merely accepting that any conclusion reached by the legislature must be correct. By deferring in this manner, the court did not add its voice to the discussion as to the determination of the content of a right. In a similar manner, dialogue failed to work effectively when the legislature viewed the conclusion of the court, as expressed in the declaration of incompatibility, as a definitive and authoritative definition of a right.

When read in this light, the collapse of the democratic dialogue model does not appear to be inevitable, lending credence to the idea that democratic dialogue can provide a stable, midway protection of rights combining the advantages and minimizing the disadvantages of strong legal and purely parliamentary protections of rights. Although we can point to examples of where the current forms of democratic dialogue model appear to operate in practice as if they are strong legal or purely parliamentary protections of rights, this need not lead us to the conclusion that democratic dialogue models are inherently unstable. Rather, we reach the conclusion that they are novel and that greater experimentation is needed to determine how to combine legal and political protections of rights in a stable and advantageous manner. In addition, more time is needed to allow courts and legislatures to adapt to their new powers and to exercise them in a manner that facilitates effective dialogue. Democratic dialogue models are not unstable. They just need time to develop.

[54] AL Young, 'Is Dialogue Working under the Human Rights Act 1998?' [2011] Public Law 773.
[55] [2003] UKHL 21; [2003] 2 AC 267.

However, it is not possible to rescue democratic dialogue in this way. It is true that it takes time for institutions to change their behaviours and for experience to demonstrate the best way in which the legislature and the courts can work together. However, it is difficult to know how the legislature and the courts should interact unless we have a normative framework from which to assess the nature of their interactions. It is here that further difficulties arise. The current normative justifications for democratic dialogue models focus on the arguments used by political constitutionalists and legal constitutionalists to justify why legislatures or courts should protect human rights. We can see this when we analyse the academic commentary discussing how institutions should use their relative powers in democratic dialogue models of rights protections. If there is no new normative framework for democratic dialogue, how can it become a stable, novel model of the constitution?

B. Normative impossibility

Gardbaum's work on the Commonwealth model of rights protections examined how the law in Canada, the United Kingdom, Australia, and New Zealand was being applied in practice. His work criticizes the lack of academic commentary providing a normative account of how institutions should exercise their powers.[56] The academic commentary on the model of human rights protections in the United Kingdom, New Zealand, Australia, and Canada tends to focus more on criticisms of the model of rights protections for failing to protect rights as strongly as would be found in strong, constitutional protections of human rights, or for protecting them too far and therefore damaging the necessary political input into the protection of rights.[57] Not only is it difficult to find normative justifications of mid-way protections, but, moreover, there are often criticisms of those that are designed to justify mid-way protections of rights. It is claimed that these theoretical justifications collapse into advocating that institutions should use their powers in a way that brings mid-way theories of human rights protections closer to either the strong protection of human rights found in legal constitutionalism, or the purely parliamentary protection of human rights found in political constitutionalism.

This criticism is particularly true of the academic commentary surrounding the interplay between sections 3 and 4 of the Human Rights Act 1998. Early academic writing on the Act polarized around two points of view: the desire to use the Human Rights Act 1998 to incorporate human rights as far as possible and those who criticized the Act for giving too much power to the judiciary.[58] Those in favour of human rights protections, influenced by ideologies of legal constitutionalism, advocated that courts should mostly use section 3 to protect Convention rights. The more willing the courts are to use section 3, the more they are able to protect rights. Courts could use section 3 to provide a protection as close as possible to a strong protection of human rights, making it rare for the court to find it impossible to read and give effect to legislation

56 Gardbaum (n 38), 77–79.

57 ibid, 111–14, 144–51, 179–93, and 217–21. See also T Hickman *Public Law after the Human Rights Act* (Oxford, Hart 2010) 57–68 as regards the academic commentary on the Human Rights Act 1998.

58 See, for example, K Ewing, 'The Futility of the Human Rights Act' (2004) Public Law 829; K Ewing, *The Bonfire of the Liberties* (Oxford University Press 2011); K Ewing and J Tham, 'The Continuing Futility of the Human Rights Act' (2008) Public Law 668; T Hickman, *Public Law after the Human Rights Act* (Oxford, Hart 2010); G Phillipson, 'Deference, Discretion and Democracy in the Human Rights Era' (2006) 60 Current Legal Problems 40.

in a manner that protects Convention rights. Section 4 declarations of incompatibility would be restricted to extreme circumstances, focusing in particular on the legislature's better ability to remedy human rights breaches.[59] Those critical of the Act for giving too much power to the judiciary, influenced by arguments from political constitutionalism, advocate that the courts should mostly use section 4, empowering Parliament to have a greater final say on the content of Convention rights.

This tension is also replicated in the work of commentators who refer to their theories as ones of democratic dialogue. One clear example of this can be found in the diverse views on dialogue found in the work of Danny Nicol and Tom Hickman. Nicol's theory is one of democratic dialogue, and provides a mid-way protection of human rights in that it requires both the legislature and the courts to play a role in the protection of rights, as well as requiring both to provide a strong account of rights when expressing their opinions. He advocates a strong preference for the use of section 4 over section 3. He argues that this is required to ensure that both the legislature and the courts play a role in determining the content of rights.[60] As such, Nicol argues that both the courts and Parliament should interpret rights robustly, expressing their true positions as to the definition of contestable rights. There is no need for the courts to exercise deference. In addition, Parliament should not regard the courts as providing the right definition of a Convention right, but should regard any court decision as to the interpretation of a right as one possible definition, requiring consideration and rational response from Parliament, which maintains the final word on the definition of a Convention right.[61]

Nicol's theory can best be understood as one which advocates that courts should not defer to the opinion of the legislature when determining rights, in a manner similar to the argument of Francesca Klug.[62] For the legislature to be equally bold requires no more than that the legislature recognizes that it has a role to play in the determination of human rights. The determination of rights is not merely to be determined by the courts and the legislature should also not defer to the opinion of the courts when defining rights. However, when interpreted in this manner, it is hard to distinguish Nicol's theory of dialogue from those who interpret the Human Rights Act in order to further political constitutionalism as opposed to a dialogue model of rights protections.[63] For example, it is hard to distinguish Nicol's theory from that of Tom Campbell.[64] Campbell argues that a broad reading of section 3 will lead to the judiciary making moral decisions as to the content of rights, and that such decisions are best left to political actors. Therefore, courts should interpret legislation according to its plain meaning, minimizing the use of section 3 and ensuring that declarations of incompatibility under section 4 are routine and unproblematic.[65] Like Nicol, Campbell relies on the contestability of interpretations of human rights. A reading of section 3 requiring courts to pay attention to the clear meaning of statutory language does not prohibit the courts from giving a clear account of what they believe a contestable human right

[59] See, for example, the work of Gavin Phillipson in G Phillipson, 'Mis-reading Section 3 of the Human Rights Act' (2003) 119 LQR 183 and 'Deference, Discretion, and Democracy in the Human Rights Act Era' n 58.

[60] D Nicol, 'Law and Politics after the Human Rights Act' [2006] Public Law 722, 744–45.

[61] ibid, 744–46.

[62] F Klug, 'Judicial Deference Under the Human Rights Act 1998' [2003] European Human Rights Law Review 125.

[63] Hickman (n 58) 58–61.

[64] T Campbell, 'Incorporation through Interpretation' in T Campbell, KD Ewing, and A Tomkins (eds), *Sceptical Essays on Human Rights* (Oxford University Press 2001) 79.

[65] ibid, 99.

to mean, enabling Parliament to continue to hold the final authority to determine the content of rights, as preferred by Campbell, as Parliament can respond as robustly as the courts when determining the content of human rights.[66] Nicol too, advocates that Parliament has the final say, responding robustly to court determinations of human rights.

Hickman rejects Nicol's weak form of democratic dialogue and proposes his own theory of strong form dialogue. Hickman draws on the work of Bickel and Dicey, which he interprets as exemplifying theories of dialogue, using these accounts of dialogue to propose a different role for the courts and the legislature under the Human Rights Act 1998. Hickman argues that section 4 should be used sparingly, reserved for those occasions where the declaration of incompatibility can be used 'as a device that allows courts to vent their scorn on a piece of rights-defying legislation, thus excluding it from the integrity of the law'.[67] It can also be understood as a mechanism of dealing with those situations where the court is not best-placed to remedy a situation when legislation fails to comply with Convention rights, enabling Parliament to use its law-making function to provide a better remedy.[68] Section 3 should 'not be read minimally in order to favour the use of section 4 declarations, but equally should not be read maximally so as *always* to find Convention compliance' according to the 'proper limits of judicial law-making and the dictates of prudence' as they arise in the context of each particular case.[69]

Hickman's interpretation can be seen as a midway reading, aimed at preserving dialogue, as it rules out extremes. It rules out using the provisions of sections 3 and 4 as a means of adhering to political or legal constitutionalism indirectly. To read section 3 so minimally as to ensure that section 4 is rarely used, as advocated by Campbell and Nicol, runs the danger that the Human Rights Act collapses into a purely parliamentary protection of rights as advocated by political constitutionalists. To read section 3 as meaning that it is always possible to interpret legislation so as to comply with Convention rights runs the opposite risk that the Act becomes a strong legal protection of Convention rights in all but name. However, there is a wide range of possible ways of reading sections 3 and 4, making it hard to define the specific middle view proposed by Hickman.

It is also hard to gain further clarity by drawing on the theories of Bickel and Dicey relied upon by Hickman. Both Bickel and Dicey refer to the specific role of the court to protect long-standing values found in a particular society. But they do so against different constitutional settings. Bickel advocates the use of judicial minimalism in a legal system where courts have the power to strike down legislation. He advocates that these passive devices of the judiciary are utilized to enable the judiciary to manage political issues. Courts grant a wider area of discretionary judgment to the executive or the legislature when determining whether measures which restrict human rights are justified.[70] Dicey's theory requires courts to interpret legislation in a manner that draws attention to the extent to which legislation harms the rule of law as reflected in long-standing principles of the common law. Although courts cannot contradict the clear and specific words of Parliament when they harm these principles, the courts can ensure that Parliament uses clear words, showing that it is fully aware of the consequences of its actions and fully intends to restrict the rule of law in this manner.[71] Neither Bickel nor Dicey give an account of how courts should use their powers under sections 3 and 4 of the Human Rights Act 1998. Neither refers to dialogue. Bickel and Dicey

[66] ibid, 100. [67] Hickman (n 58) 83. [68] ibid, 83. [69] ibid.
[70] ibid, 72–76. [71] ibid, 76–81.

provide accounts of how courts should use their powers under different constitutional structures. Bickel is advocating judicial minimalism in a constitutional structure that provides for a strong legal protection of human rights. Dicey is providing an account of how the judiciary should exercise its powers of interpretation in a legal system with a purely parliamentary protection of rights.

Nevertheless, Dicey's account of the extent to which courts should interpret legislation to preserve long-standing common law principles of the rule of law is similar to the role of the court under section 3. It could, therefore, help explain what Hickman means when he advocates that courts should use section 3 predominantly, but not always, and not when this would contradict the clear wording of legislation. However, to read Hickman's theory in this manner makes it difficult to differentiate his theory from that of Gavin Phillipson, whom Hickman regards as falling into what he calls the 'incorporationist' camp—i.e. those who advocate a strong protection of rights in line with legal constitutionalism.[72] Phillipson shares Hickman's preference for section 3 as the main way through which courts should use their powers to protect rights under the Human Rights Act 1998.[73] One difference between Hickman and Phillipson is that Phillipson argues in favour of a robust reading of Convention rights, arguing that courts should only exercise deference to the legislature or executive on the facts and not as concerns the definition of human rights.[74] Hickman later advocates the use of deference to determinations of rights and this may provide a means of distinguishing between Hickman and Phillipson.[75]

However, without further clarity as to what is meant by a robust interpretation of Convention rights, and how this differs from a strong, but not robust interpretation, or the difference between deference as to the definition of a right and deference as to the facts, it becomes extremely difficult to delineate between Hickman's dialogue reading of the Human Rights Act and Phillipson's reading guided by the strong protection of human rights advocated by legal constitutionalism. The more we try and discern what is meant by a reading of the Human Rights Act based on dialogue, the more impossible it becomes to determine. This leads to the further suspicion that democratic dialogue models of human rights protections are inherently unstable. If we see the distinction between these theories as resting on arguments as to whether the legislature, judiciary, or both should control the executive and protect human rights, then there would appear to be no middle ground between legal and political constitutionalism for these theories to occupy.

III. Overlap

The prospect of new democratic dialogue models being able to provide a stable theory of human rights protections, or a sound account of constitutionalism, appears bleak. We have argued that it can be difficult to define what is meant by a commonwealth model of rights protections and that, in practice, examples of commonwealth models of rights protections appear to collapse either into strong legal protections of rights or purely parliamentary protections of rights. This would not appear to be a temporary problem. Rather, the difficulty appears to be more fundamental. There would appear to be no distinct theory of democratic dialogue because theories of legal and political

[72] ibid, 58–63.
[73] Phillipson, 'Deference, Discretion and Democracy in the Human Rights Act Era' (n 58) 68.
[74] ibid, 71–72. [75] Hickman (n 58) 128–72.

constitutionalism merge into one another. There is no middle ground for democratic dialogue to occupy. Rather, we find a range of constitutional theories regarding the protection of rights. Some provide more control to the legislature. Others provide more control to the courts. All of the theories overlap and merge with one another. The difference between them is merely one of degree.

However, the above discussion does not provide a conclusive argument against democratic dialogue theories. It may be possible to provide an account of democratic dialogue that is distinct from legal and political constitutionalism. If we have not been able to find such an account in the literature to date, that might not be because it does not exist. It could be because such a theory is difficult to formulate and earlier attempts need to be worked on. Moreover, the accounts we have examined so far have focused on human rights protections and on democratic dialogue theories. If we are to demonstrate conclusively that, when understood in terms of control, there is no middle ground for a distinct democratic dialogue account to occupy, we need to expand our analysis, looking at accounts of human rights protections more generally and also at theories of judicial review.

It would be impossible to cover all of the theories of constitutional review in a section of one chapter, so this section will necessarily have to be selective. It will examine, first, the work of Jeremy Waldron and Richard Fallon. This work was selected as Waldron's account is widely regarded as providing the strongest account against a strong legal protection of rights. His account rests on a range of assumptions. Fallon's reply to Waldron, which favours a strong legal protection of rights, rests on Waldron's assumptions. This enables a fair comparison between the theories to see if they provide distinct accounts, or whether they begin to merge into one another. When looking at judicial review more generally, we will focus on the work of Adam Tomkins and Paul Craig. Tomkins is one of the strongest advocates of political constitutionalism in the United Kingdom and one of the few to have provided an account of judicial review from the perspective of political constitutionalism. Craig is a legal constitutionalist who has focused on Tomkins' argument, providing a clear rebuttal of its arguments. This therefore provides a clear basis on which to discern whether legal and political constitutionalism, when analysed in terms of advocating either legal or political control, are distinct and can therefore be distinguished from a separate theory of democratic dialogue which takes a distinct middle path between the two.

A. Core cases for and against strong judicial protections of human rights

Waldron provides what is generally regarded as the strongest argument against a strong legal protection of human rights.[76] His argument examines both process and outcome justifications for providing courts with the power to strike down legislation. He argues that, in societies where the four assumptions on which his argument is based apply, the arguments from process strongly favour the legislature over the courts and the arguments as to outcome, although they may favour courts, nevertheless fail to provide a justification for courts to strike down legislative determinations of rights. In order to explain and evaluate Waldron's argument, we need first to establish the assumptions on which it is based. Waldron's first assumption is that the societies contemplating whether to adopt a strong or weak protection of human rights have democratic institutions that

[76] J Waldron, 'The Core of the Case Against Judicial Review' (2006) 115 Yale Law Journal 1346.

operate in reasonably good order. Such societies should have representative democracy, with universal adult suffrage and they should value political equality and responsible deliberation.[77] Second, these societies should have judicial institutions that are also operating in a reasonably good manner. This requires judicial institutions that are independent of political influence, which settle individual disputes and uphold the rule of law.[78] Waldron's third assumption is that most officials and individuals in society need to have a commitment to the idea of the protection of individual and minority rights.[79] His fourth assumption is that there will exist persistent, substantial, and good faith disagreement about rights.[80] This disagreement will be at both the philosophical level and when determining the application of abstract rights to specific situations.[81] So, for example, when analysing whether prisoners should be entitled to vote, there may be disagreement both as to why we protect the right to vote and the conceptions of democracy on which this right to vote is based, as well as disagreement about which prisoners, if any, should be allowed to vote.

In societies fulfilling these four criteria, Waldron concludes that there are good arguments for not granting courts the power to strike down legislation that does not comply with human rights. Arguments in favour of granting this power to the court focus on outcomes and procedures. In terms of outcomes, it is argued that courts are better at the type of reasoning required to determine rights-issues. Courts are more likely to determine the right answer to whether, and if so which, prisoners should be given the right to vote. Proponents of a strong legal protection of rights argue that courts are better able to reach the right answer to a specific rights issue as courts focus on specific individuals and can refer to clear texts to help shape the debate as to the content of a right. As such, courts use legal reasoning, which is akin to moral reasoning, applying general principles to the individual situation before the court to determine that specific rights-issue. Moreover, courts have to state reasons for their conclusions. This shapes their discussion and debate, further ensuring that they use rational principles enabling them to reach better conclusions on rights-issues.

Waldron argues against these propositions by challenging the facts on which they are based. Although individuals do appear before courts, he argues that the focus of the court in constitutional human rights decisions is not on the specific individual's situation. Rather, courts are more likely to reason in an abstract manner, applying general principles. It is hard to conclude, therefore, that the court reasons in a more specific and less abstract manner than the legislature.[82] Moreover, Waldron argues that the focus on legal texts and precedent that characterizes legal reasoning does not necessarily ensure that courts engage in more logical or rational discussions than are found in legislative deliberations. Instead, Waldron asserts that court arguments focus too greatly on determining how they should interpret legal texts, or on the extent to which they should rely on precedent as opposed to thinking carefully about the nature of rights and how they should be applied to a particular case.[83] Although courts do provide reasons for their outcomes, legislatures also often provide reasons which need not focus specifically on the interpretation of a text or a precedent. Therefore, Waldron concludes that it is not the case that courts will always provide better reasons for a conclusion as to the definition of a right than the legislature.[84] Consequently, it is hard to conclude that courts will always reach a better outcome as to a rights-issue than the legislature.

[77] ibid, 1360 and 1361.
[78] ibid, 1360 and 1363–64.
[79] ibid, 1360.
[80] ibid.
[81] ibid, 1367.
[82] ibid, 1360, 1379–80.
[83] ibid, 1360, 1380–82.
[84] ibid, 1360, 1382–86.

When analysed in terms of process, Waldron argues that it is clear that the legislature provides a better means through which to protect human rights. The issue here is as to the legitimacy of the means through which each institution reaches conclusions as to rights determinations. In particular, given his assumption that we are dealing with a society in which there are deep-seated, reasonable disagreements as to the nature of rights and as to their application to a particular situation, Waldron argues that rights-issues need to be determined in a manner that provides individuals with a good reason to accept the outcome, even if this is one with which they find it reasonable to disagree. Waldron argues that all of the arguments relating to process favour the legislature over the courts. When legislatures determine rights issues, they use a process which takes account of a wider range of viewpoints, valuing them equally. Moreover, legislatures will determine rights in a manner that is in line with the majority of viewpoints.[85] This is not true of courts, who can only take account of the views of those before the court. The arguments in favour of a strong judicial protection of rights are no longer persuasive when applied to a society in which there is reasonable disagreement about rights because of the relative weaker legitimacy of the way in which courts take decisions about rights.[86]

Richard Fallon's argument in favour of a strong legal protection of rights accepts all of Waldron's assumptions.[87] He also accepts Waldron's factual assessments of the way in which courts and the legislature reason about rights, recognizing that courts often reason in abstract terms and focus more on determining theories of precedent and interpretation than they do on arguments relating to the nature of rights. Furthermore, he accepts the legislature's greater claim to legitimacy when it comes to determining contestable rights-issues. Nevertheless, he concludes that there are good reasons for a strong, legal protection of rights, empowering courts to overturn decisions of the legislature where the court believes that the legislation has contravened human rights. His argument rests on the presumption that it is better for rights to be over- as opposed to under-protected. Allowing the court to overturn legislation that it believes breaches human rights will provide for a stronger protection of rights. This is because this empowers both the legislature and the courts to veto legislation that they believe to be contrary to human rights. The legislature's veto arises as the legislature, in a society based on Waldron's assumptions, will not enact legislation that it believes is contrary to human rights. The court's veto arises from its ability to strike down legislation the court believes to be contrary to human rights. Although this may frustrate the legislature's policies, and may lead to an over-protection of rights, Fallon argues that this is a price worth paying as it is better for rights to be over-protected in this way, than under-protected in a situation where courts cannot strike down legislation which contravenes human rights.

Fallon's argument also rests on a series of assumptions. First, although it accepts Waldron's argument that courts are not necessarily better than legislatures at determining rights-outcomes, it nevertheless argues that courts have a distinctive process of determining rights-outcomes that is different from that used by legislatures. As such, courts may be able to determine errors in the legislature's definition of a particular right that would have been missed by the legislature. It does not matter what the precise differences are between how courts and legislatures reason about rights. What matters is that their processes are different from one another. Second, Fallon assumes

[85] ibid, 1360, 1386–93. [86] ibid, 1360, 1393–1401.

[87] R Fallon, 'The Core of an Uneasy Case for Judicial Review' (2008) 121 Harvard Law Review 1693.

that legislative inaction is more likely to harm rights than legislative action. As such, there is a need for constitutional structures to err in favour of checking legislation that may violate rights. He likens this assumption to that underpinning the strong procedural protections in criminal trials. We err on the side of caution, even if this means that sometimes the guilty may go free, because we think it is better for the guilty to go free than for the innocent to be convicted. In a similar manner, we should err on the side of providing a stronger as opposed to a weaker protection of rights. It is better for rights to be over-protected, and some policy objectives of the legislature not to be achieved, than it is for the legislature to be able to achieve its objectives at the cost of harming human rights. Third, Fallon assumes that there is a hierarchy of rights, such that some rights are more important and more deserving of protection than others. Fourth, Fallon assumes that it is possible to design a system of judicial review such that the moral costs of over-enforcement of rights are lower than the possible costs of under-enforcement of rights.[88]

Fallon recognizes that there are circumstances in which his argument would not provide a justification for strong judicial review. This would be the case, for example, if a particular society assumed that the right to vote was more important than any other right. More fundamentally, Fallon's argument only applies where legislatures 'seek to promote the rights of one class of citizens without threatening the fundamental rights of another'[89] and does not apply to 'zero-sum controversies in which fundamental rights are pitted against one another and the over-enforcement of one entails the under-enforcement of the other'.[90] Where there are zero-sum controversies, the potential over-protection of rights for one group in society may come at the cost of the under-protection of rights for another group in society. This makes it difficult to assume that an extra veto of rights for the court will lead to rights being over-protected. It may cause other rights to be under-protected.

This overview of Waldron's and Fallon's accounts of human rights protections does appear to provide a clear line between legal and political constitutionalists. Whilst agreeing on the same background assumptions and factual assertions as to the relative ability of legislatures and the courts to reach the right conclusion on rights-issues, or to reason in a more or less legitimate manner, Waldron concludes in favour of political constitutionalism and Fallon in favour of legal constitutionalism. Their disagreement is as to the relative importance of a potential over- or under-protection of rights. Fallon prefers constitutional protections of rights which err on the side of an over-protection of rights. Waldron argues against this conclusion, concerned that the over-protection of rights undermines democratically enacted legislation.

However, when we examine these two theories more closely, the clear line between legal constitutionalism, with its strong legal protection of rights, and political constitutionalism with its parliamentary protection of rights, appears to blur. Although the distinction appears to rest on a difference as to whether it is better to over- or under-protect rights, it may be that in reality the distinction really turns on the application of the same theoretical arguments to a different set of assumptions. This argument is made by Tushnet.[91] Tushnet reaches this conclusion when he analyses the assumptions underpinning Fallon's argument for a strong, legal protection of rights, particularly the assumption that the protection of rights for one group in society does not lead to the reduction of rights in another society—leading to zero sum controversies. Fallon

[88] ibid, 1700. [89] ibid, 1712. [90] ibid, 1712–13.

[91] M Tushnet, 'How different are Waldron's and Fallon's Core Cases For and Against Judicial Review?' (2010) 30 Oxford Journal of Legal Studies 49.

appears to assume that zero-sum controversies occur rarely. However, if these were to occur more often, as Tushnet argues it is reasonable to believe that they might, then the distinction between Fallon and Waldron disappears in practice. Were these zero-sum controversies to occur frequently, both Tushnet and Waldron would argue against a strong legal protection of human rights.

Tushnet's analysis leads him to conclude that the difference between Waldron and Fallon may merely be one of perspective. Theorists from a background of a legal system with a strong constitutional protection of rights start with a presumption that such a protection is justified, modifying its application in situations where a strong constitutional protection of rights appears to cause more harm than good. Those from a background with a parliamentary protection of rights assume that rights protections are not needed, whilst recognizing the need to provide a stronger protection of rights when faced with potential weaknesses in a purely political protection of rights. Fallon justifies a strong protection of rights which does not apply when faced with rights conflicts. Waldron focuses on the need to prevent a strong protection of rights when faced with rights conflicts. Disagreement arises between their theories as to their assessment of the frequency with which rights conflict with one another in societies which adhere to Waldron's assumptions: where there is a reasonably well functioning legislature and court structure; where reasonable disagreements about the content of rights exist; and where there is a general commitment to the protection of rights from both the citizens and officials in a particular society.

The more we examine the distinction between legal and political constitutionalism in terms of whether it advocates that different institutions should control human rights, the more this distinction appears to collapse. Similar arguments are used to explain the relative skills of courts or legislatures to protect human rights. Where disagreements arise, the focus is on whether the facts on which these arguments are based are correct or not. Or they become ones of perspective. Those in societies with purely political protections of human rights can see the problems that arise with parliamentary controls and seek to argue towards stronger legal controls. Those in societies with a strong legal protection of human rights can see the problems with legal controls and so seek to move towards more parliamentary controls over rights. Given this account, there is no wonder at the popularity of democratic dialogue accounts of rights protections with their promise of blending the advantages and minimizing the disadvantages of political and legal controls. However, it is hard to see these theories as offering something new and distinct. It is much easier to see these arguments as yet another way of blending legal and political controls in a similar way to the solutions we already find in arguments based on legal and political constitutionalism arguing for a strong legal or a weak parliamentary protection of rights. Whilst this may appear to paint an even bleaker picture, it does not provide a conclusive argument, as we have only focused on human rights protections. The next section will examine arguments from legal and political constitutionalism in relation to the control of the executive more generally.

B. Legal constitutionalism, political constitutionalism, and control of the executive

When assessed in terms of control, the distinction between legal and political constitutionalism would appear to be straightforward. Legal constitutionalists advocate legal controls over the executive. Political constitutionalists prefer political controls over the executive. Therefore, whilst we would expect to find a range of theories of judicial review from the perspective of legal constitutionalism, we would not expect to find theories of judicial review from political constitutionalists. Whilst it is true that there is a plethora of accounts of judicial review from legal constitutionalists—indeed too many to cover in a sub-section of one chapter—theories of judicial review from the perspective of political constitutionalism are rarer, but they do exist. The most prominent of these is that proposed by Adam Tomkins, who has given the most complete account of judicial review from the perspective of political constitutionalism. However, when we examine his account, the same problem arises of the potential collapse between legal and political constitutionalism. Tomkins' first account of his theory provides insufficient clarity to distinguish his account of judicial review from theories of judicial review based on legal constitutionalism. Tomkins later refines his account of judicial review in order to provide this clarity. However, in doing so, it becomes difficult to distinguish his account from that of Matthias Kumm, whom most would classify as a legal constitutionalist, and from that of David Dyzenhaus, whose account of the culture of justification could be viewed as occupying a midway position between legal and political constitutionalism. This adds more evidence to the argument that there is no middle ground between legal and political constitutionalism for theories of democratic dialogue to occupy.

Tomkins' first account of judicial review from the perspective of political constitutionalism argues that, in addition to enhanced political controls over the executive, political constitutionalism would allocate three specific roles to the courts.[92] These roles are designed to enhance the control of the executive by the legislature. First, Tomkins argues that the courts should play a role when enforcing procedural rights. Courts have particular expertise in determining the procedures that should be followed in order to ensure legitimate decision-making. As such, even under a political constitution, courts should ensure that executive bodies adhere to legitimate procedures, both in terms of adhering to the procedures set by legislatures and those required by natural justice as developed by the courts.[93] Second, courts have a role to play when adjudicating upon tightly defined issues of absolute rights. This occurs when there is clear legislative authority prohibiting the executive from acting in a manner that contradicts a specific absolute right. Tomkins defines an absolute right as a specific civil liberty that is so important that it can be expressed in the form of an absolute right. He gives the example of an absolute prohibition on torture.[94] Third, courts should ensure that the executive has legal authority for any decision that it makes, particularly when the executive restricts civil liberties. Specifically, courts should not interpret broad legislative provisions as empowering the executive to act in a manner that restricts civil liberties. The power to act in a manner that harms liberty can only be granted by specific words of the legislature.[95]

The mere existence of an account of a legitimate form of court control over the executive from the perspective of political constitutionalism is not enough to blur the distinction between legal and political constitutionalism. The distinction between the two may be more nuanced, with legal constitutionalism advocating more judicial controls over the executive whilst political constitutionalism argues for more

[92] A Tomkins, 'The Role of the Courts in the Political Constitution' (2010) 60 University of Toronto Law Journal 1 and 'What's Left of the Political Constitution?' (2013) 14 German Law Journal 2275.

[93] Tomkins 'Role of the Courts' (n 92) 6 and 'What's Left?' (n 92) 2280.

[94] Tomkins 'Role of the Courts' (n 92) 6–7 and 'What's Left?' (n 92) 2281.

[95] Tomkins 'Role of the Courts' (n 92) 7–10 and 'What's Left?' (n 92) 2280.

political controls, but this does not blur the distinction between the two in and of itself. Political constitutionalists advocate a more limited role for the courts. The legislature provides the main control over the executive and the courts merely supplement its role. Legal constitutionalists advocate a larger role for the courts. Courts go beyond merely supplementing the legislature's control over the executive. Courts have their own, independently justified controls that go beyond a merely supplementary role. For example, legal constitutionalists are more likely to advocate a general test of rationality or proportionality performed by the courts to limit actions of the executive. Tomkins expressly rejects these controls in his first account of the scope of judicial review.[96] There is still, therefore, a distinction between legal and political constitutionalism assessed in terms of the relative role of the courts and the legislature in the control of executive powers.

However, the lack of precision in Tomkins' first account of the extent to which the court should control the executive means that his account is remarkably similar to theories of judicial review proffered by legal constitutionalists. Paul Craig's assessment of Tomkins' account of judicial review clearly illustrates the way in which Tomkins' theory of court control over the executive may be hard to differentiate from theories of legal constitutionalists.[97] Craig argues that, in common with Griffith, Tomkins believes that the determination of rights is a political issue more suited to political as opposed to legal institutions. It is this assessment of the nature of rights, underpinning an assessment of the relative role of the legislature and the courts as to the protection of rights, which identifies Tomkins as a political constitutionalist. Tomkins classifies assessments of rationality or proportionality as political issues. These involve the balancing of rights or the balancing of different interests when assessing executive policies. As such, they are best left to politically accountable institutions as opposed to the judiciary. However, Craig argues, inter alia, that the lack of clarity in Tomkins' account of court control over executive decisions means that his theory fails to ensure that courts do not engage with similar issues of balancing that arise when applying rationality and proportionality. As such, Tomkins' account does not provide a distinct account of judicial control over the executive and is hard to distinguish his account of judicial control under political constitutionalism from the accounts of judicial control found in theories of legal constitutionalism.

Craig interprets Tomkins' theory as containing both negative and positive aspects on the role of the courts. The negative aspects proscribe what courts should not do. For Tomkins, courts should not apply tests of rationality or proportionality given that these require balancing that is best performed by a political institution. Instead, courts can ensure that the executive does not transgress absolute rights. The determination of absolute rights does not require the same balancing as the tests of rationality and proportionality and so is suited to control by the courts. Craig argues that Tomkins posits two positive criteria of judicial review—i.e. standards of judicial review which courts should be positively encouraged to carry out. First, courts should ensure that the executive has proper legal authority for all of its actions, striking down actions of the executive that are beyond the scope of its legal authority. Second, courts should ensure that they err on the side of caution when faced with a restriction on civil liberties, ensuring that general provisions do not empower the executive to restrict civil

[96] Tomkins 'Role of the Courts' (n 92) 1–5.

[97] P Craig, 'Political Constitutionalism and the Judicial Role: A Response' (2011) 9 International Journal of Constitutional Law 112.

liberties and ensuring that any restriction of civil liberties by the executive has clear legal authority found in the express and precise wording of legislation.

Craig argues that both the negative and the positive components are so hard to specify in practice that it becomes impossible to distinguish Tomkins' account of political constitutionalism from legal constitutionalism. With regard to the negative component, Craig argues that it is difficult to delineate precisely between absolute and non-absolute rights.[98] Tomkins provides the example of the right against torture as an absolute right.[99] Craig explains that, to apply this absolute right, courts need to define torture. Yet to delineate the scope of torture may involve an assessment of proportionality and rationality. It may be easy to give clear examples of torture. Waterboarding, for example, is clearly torture. However, other examples are not so clear-cut. Is it torture, for example, to force prisoners to listen to heavy metal music?[100] To assess whether this amounts to torture may require assessments of rationality and proportionality. Playing loud heavy metal music is more likely to amount to torture when this has the purpose of disorientation, or where individuals are forced to listen to music whose style or lyrics are intended to annoy, than if the reason for forcing the listening to loud music is to broaden music appreciation or educate individuals on an aspect of a particular culture. Proportionality assessments would also play a part. Forcing individuals to listen to heavy metal music is more likely to amount to torture if this is played for more rather than fewer hours, at a higher as opposed to a lower volume, or when it is devised to interrupt sleep as opposed to amuse during waking hours. Such assessments may require the same inquiries as rationality inquiries when applying non-absolute rights.

Craig reaches similar conclusions with regard to Tomkins' positive component of judicial review over the executive. Tomkins argues that courts should control procedural issues, ensuring the executive acts according to the correct procedures. However, Craig argues that determining whether procedural rights have been breached may involve considerations of rationality and balancing, particularly when assessing recent cases that aim to balance procedural rights and the interests of national security.[101] As such, allowing the courts to control procedural issues may require courts to control the executive in a manner that Tomkins believes should be performed by the legislature and not the judiciary. Similarly, Tomkins argues that courts should ensure that only express words in legislation can empower the executive to restrict civil liberties. However, to ensure this is applied properly, courts need to determine the precise scope of civil liberties. Craig argues that this too requires courts to make proportionality and rationality assessments. Yet Tomkins argues that courts should not make proportionality and rationality assessments as these are best left to the legislature.[102]

In addition, Tomkins argues that courts should ensure that executives have the proper legal authority to act. Craig argues that legal authority can be interpreted in a range of ways. It could mean, for example, courts should only ensure that the executive has the proper authority to act, because there is a statute or a prerogative empowering the executive to perform that specific task. Second, it may require courts to assess whether a court is acting within its proper sphere of jurisdiction. This form of control by the court may extend to ensuring that the executive makes no legal errors when it acts, or that its actions are not based on factual errors. Third, determining whether an executive is acting within its lawful authority may extend to include the legality component of the *Wednesbury* unreasonableness test. Interpreted in this manner, courts

[98] ibid, 121. [99] Tomkins 'Role of the Courts' (n 92) 4–7.
[100] http://www.theguardian.com/world/2008/jun/19/usa.guantanamo.
[101] Craig (n 97) 121. [102] ibid, 127–29.

would be able to control decisions of the executive which are based on irrelevant considerations, or which fail to consider relevant considerations, or where the actions of the executive are exercised for an improper purpose, or in bad faith.

The lack of clarity as to the meaning of control for lawful authority means that the account of control over the executive by the courts proffered by political constitutionalism could easily merge into the same forms of judicial control advocated by legal constitutionalism. This is particularly true if legal authority extends to include the legality, but not the rationality component of the *Wednesbury* unreasonableness test. The distinction between these two components is a matter of degree. It depends upon the specificity with which one defines relevant and irrelevant considerations. For example, the classic description of an irrational decision, applying the *Wednesbury* unreasonableness test, is the dismissal of a teacher because she has red hair. However, we could argue that having red hair is an irrelevant consideration. Hair colour is not relevant to an assessment of whether an individual makes a good teacher or not. However, it becomes the classic example of irrationality if we define the criteria more widely, arguing that personal characteristics are relevant to an assessment of whether an individual makes a good teacher. To dismiss a teacher for having red hair on this assessment is not to apply an irrelevant consideration, but to act irrationally.[103]

Craig concludes that Tomkins' account of a theory of judicial review over the executive based on political constitutionalism undermines the basis on which his theory is based. Tomkins wishes to provide a theory of judicial review based on political constitutionalism, which regards rights-issues as political and therefore unsuited for court assessment. However, Tomkins' own account of judicial review appears to require the courts to apply proportionality and rationality controls, thereby undermining its own foundations.[104] It would appear, therefore, that accounts of court controls over the executive from political constitutionalism, in practice, are little different from arguments of court control based on legal constitutionalism. Political and legal constitutionalism overlap. There is no space left to be occupied by democratic dialogue accounts of combined legal and political controls over the executive.

Tomkins' most recent account of the role of the courts in a political constitution responds to these criticisms, aiming to provide a more detailed account of how political constitutionalism can provide a distinct account of the extent to which courts should control the executive that does not overlap with a similar account from the perspective of legal constitutionalism. However, the greater clarity provided by Tomkins fails to provide a distinct account. When we analyse his argument further, Tomkins' account of the role of the court as advocated by political constitutionalism looks remarkably similar to the account of judicial review provided by Matthias Kumm's defence of a strong legal protection. Tomkins' account also resembles the culture of justification developed by David Dyzenhaus. The more we examine different accounts of judicial control of the executive, the more they appear to merge.

Tomkins provides two further clarifications of his account of judicial control over the executive. First, he explains what is meant by legality when used by courts to determine whether the executive is acting within its lawful authority. Courts should look to the express wording of legislation to determine whether the executive has lawful authority to act. Adopting Craig's first interpretation, he argues that courts need to ensure that the executive has lawful authority to act granted to it by clearly worded legislation.[105] Second, Tomkins accepts that his account of judicial review over the executive will

[103] ibid, 122–27. [104] ibid, 129–31. [105] Tomkins 'What's Left?' (n 92) 2283.

require courts to use tests of proportionality and rationality. However, he argues that the way in which these tests are used according to an account of political constitutionalism is different from that advocated by legal constitutionalism. Tomkins advocates both that these tests are applied in a different manner, and that they may have a different remedy from that found in judicial review as advocated by legal constitutionalism.

This difference in approach and remedy also explains how courts should apply their check on whether the executive has lawful authority for its actions, as well as the application of the principle of legality. Tomkins does not advocate that courts should determine the scope of civil liberties, or assess whether an action of the executive is rational or proportionate. Rather, he argues that courts should ensure that they scrutinize the evidence of the executive. The executive needs to provide a justification for why it believes it has lawful authority to act. The court scrutinizes these reasons to determine whether they provide a reason for the executive to act.[106] In addition, in those situations where the court is unable to scrutinize reasons without assessing the political merits, the courts can use a different remedy. Instead of striking down the decision as unlawful, courts can refer the matter back to the executive to re-decide, taking into account the criticism of its reasons provided by the judiciary.[107]

These differences in approach and remedy play a key role in Tomkins' explanation of how political constitutionalism provides a different account of the extent to which the court can control the executive than that provided by legal constitutionalism. To understand it clearly, it helps to use an example. In *Quila* the Supreme Court ruled on the legality of a change in immigration rules, designed to protect those in forced marriages.[108] Before the change in rules, a UK citizen who married a non-UK national would be able to obtain a marriage visa, granting the right to the non-UK national to reside in the UK with his or her spouse, provided that both parties to the marriage were 18 or over. In order to protect girls, in particular, who were forced into marriage, the Home Secretary changed the immigration rules, increasing the ages of the parties to the marriage from 18 to 21. The parties before the court argued that this placed a disproportionate restriction on the right to marry protected under article 8 ECHR. In a majority decision, the Supreme Court concluded that the change in immigration rules disproportionately restricted article 8.

The judgment of Lord Wilson illustrates the approach advocated by Tomkins. Lord Wilson applied the four-stage proportionality test to determine whether article 8 ECHR had been breached.[109] He concluded that the Home Secretary had failed to provide sufficient evidence to support the change in immigration rules. First, the Home Secretary had sought to demonstrate that a change in age from 18 to 21 was justified as most forced marriages involved individuals between the ages of 18 and 21. However, this was insufficient, logically, to justify increasing the age of consent to tackle the problem of forced marriages. In order to ensure that the increase in the age of consent was a proportionate restriction on the right to marry, there was a need to compare the number of forced and consensual marriages between those of the ages of 18 and 21. The mere fact that most forced marriages occurred between these ages did not provide evidence to suggest that a significant proportion of the marriages of those between the ages of 18 and 21 were forced marriages. Insufficient further evidence had been provided to give an account of the number of forced or consensual marriages taking place between the age of 18 and 21. In addition, the advice from interest

[106] ibid, 2280, particularly 2287–89.
[107] Tomkins 'Role of the Courts' (n 92) 20.
[108] *R (Quila) v Secretary of State for the Home Department* [2011] UKSC 45; [2012] 1 AC 621.
[109] ibid, [45].

groups had both advocated that the change in the rules may help girls forced into marriage and that it may also make the problem worse. The forced marriages might still go ahead, but with no right to reside in the United Kingdom being granted to the spouse of the UK citizen, the girl in the forced marriage may be forced to live overseas until she reached the age of 21. In those three years the girl may have less protection from potential abuse in the forced marriage than she would receive in the United Kingdom.[110]

Although Lord Wilson struck down the decision of the Home Secretary, at no stage did he himself balance the competing article 8 ECHR rights not to be forced into a marriage with the rights of those who freely wished to marry. In this manner, the court, exemplified through Lord Wilson, was able to apply proportionality in a manner that checked on whether the executive had the proper lawful authority to act, without himself performing what Tomkins would see as the task of the executive or legislature—balancing the competing rights to determine if they had been correctly balanced in substance. Although the decision was struck down, the Home Secretary still has the freedom to tackle forced marriages and may even do so by re-enacting the rule to raise the age for marriage visas from 18 to 21, provided that she can provide sufficient evidence to demonstrate that this rule would be suited to tackling this issue and was not too great a restriction on consenting marriages. It also provides a stronger protection of civil liberties. This can be seen by the contrast of the approach of Lord Wilson with that of Lord Brown in the minority, who would not have struck down the rule, arguing that an assessment of whether increasing the age for marriage visas was a suitable means of tackling forced marriages was an assessment of competing policy issues, best left to the executive. As such, he deferred to the opinion of the executive, deciding that the changed immigration rule was lawful.

Understood in this manner, however, Tomkins' account of the legitimate role of the court is similar to that advocated by David Dyzenhaus. Dyzenhaus advocates the adoption of a 'culture of justification'. One of the key aspects of his theory is that courts should not determine whether decisions of the executive are justified, but whether they are justifiable.[111] If a court is determining whether a decision is justified it is usually asking whether the decision coincides with the decision the court would have taken, were it to have been given the power of taking the decision. If a court is determining whether a decision is justifiable, it is 'asking whether the decision maker has shown it to be defensible, taking all of the important considerations into account'.[112]

Dyzenhaus' theory can be regarded as steering a middle path between legal and political constitutionalism. Rather than referring to legal and political constitutionalism, Dyzenhaus describes different legal cultures. In particular, he distinguishes between the culture of reflection and the culture of neutrality. The culture of reflection resembles political constitutionalism. Legislation is regarded as reflecting the wishes of the people. As such, legislation is the superior form of law-making and it is for legislation to empower the executive and to set limits on the actions of the executive. The role of the courts is to check that the legislature acts within the proper sphere of its powers, as designated by the legislature. The culture of neutrality, in contrast, advocates a series of liberal principles that are superior to legislation. These principles determine the legitimacy of actions of the executive and the role of the court is to enforce these

[110] ibid, [47]–[59].

[111] D Dyzenhaus, 'Law as Justification: Etienne Mureinik's Conception of Legal Culture' (1998) 14 South African Journal of Human Rights 11, 27–28 and 31–37.

[112] ibid, 28.

liberal principles. Dyzenhaus is critical of both of these cultures, advocating instead a culture of justification. The culture of justification regards legislation as the primary source of law, in common with the culture of reflection. In addition, it draws from the culture of neutrality that there is a need for principles against which to evaluate the law. However, it does not advocate adherence to liberal principles. It argues instead that principles emerge from discussion, advocating a need to facilitate participation and accountability.[113]

Although it might appear odd that Tomkins, a strong advocate of political constitutionalism, should devise a theory of adjudication that is remarkably similar to that proposed by an advocate of a constitutional theory which appears to take a middle path between legal and political constitutionalism, this is unsurprising given that Tomkins concludes that '[t]he British constitution is indeed now a "mixed constitution"'.[114] Tomkins presents this as a descriptive observation. He sets out evidence, in the British constitution, of a combination of parliamentary and judicial controls over the executive, both generally and in terms of the protection of civil liberties.[115] However, he also argues for a normative defence of his theory, arguing that it provides a good way of balancing the four constitutional goods of: promoting rational decision-making; allowing the government of the day to govern; accountability and the recognition that the government of the day is chosen by force of democracy.[116] This is similar to Dyzenhaus' normative justification of his theory.[117]

This similarity suggests that it is difficult to provide a clear distinctive theory of democratic dialogue determining the extent to which courts should control the executive. It also suggests that it may be hard to provide an account of judicial review over the executive from the perspective of political constitutionalism without this overlapping with other accounts. The picture of overlapping accounts is reinforced when we recognize the similarities between Tomkins' account of judicial review and Matthias Kumm's argument in favour of strong judicial review, as advocated by legal constitutionalists. Kumm's starting point is that the US model, in which most arguments for strong protections of rights are based, is quite unique. It provides for a series of broad constitutional rights, prohibiting the making of laws that restrict these rights. This places a large responsibility on the courts to interpret the meaning of these broad constitutional rights. This approach can be contrasted with that found in Germany, or in the European Court of Human Rights. Here one finds a protection of both absolute and qualified rights. The absolute rights, like those protected in the US constitution, prohibit the making of laws that breach these rights. However, these absolute rights tend to be more narrowly defined than those found in the US Constitution. The non-absolute rights proscribe a human right that is to be protected, but where restrictions on the right are permitted provided that these restrictions are by law, pursue a legitimate objective and are a proportionate restriction on the right. Kumm describes this approach as the 'rationalist human rights paradigm'.[118]

Kumm's justification for judicial review rests on the way in which the application of the proportionality test creates a form of Socratic contestation. When applying the

[113] Dyzenhaus (n 111) and D Dyzenhaus, 'The Legitimacy of Legality' (1996) 46 University of Toronto Law Journal 49.

[114] Tomkins, 'What's Left?' (n 92) 2276.

[115] ibid, 2275–80.

[116] ibid, 2284–89.

[117] Dyzenhaus (n 111) 31.

[118] M Kumm, 'Institutionalising Socratic Contestation: The Rationalists Human Rights Paradigm, Legitimate Authority and the Point of Judicial Review' (2007) 1 European Journal of Legal Studies 1; and M Kumm, 'Democracy is not Enough: Rights, Proportionality and the Point of Judicial Review' (2009) New York University Public Law and Legal Theory Working Papers, Paper 118, 1.

proportionality test, courts question the justifications provided by the executive or the legislature for restricting human rights. The role of the court is not to think that it has the right answer to whether a restriction on a right is proportionate, but to question whether sufficient reasons have been provided to demonstrate that a restriction on a right is proportionate. The rationalist human rights paradigm tends also to lead to a broader definition of rights, requiring courts to question whether legislatures or the executive have provided sufficient justifications for restricting a broadly defined right.

Kumm argues that a judicial protection of human rights exercised in this manner is better both in terms of outcome and in terms of legitimacy. In terms of outcomes, Kumm argues that the rationalist human rights paradigm corrects legislative pathologies—i.e. aspects of legislative decision-making that may detract from rational justifications for action. For example, legislatures may enact rules based on an adherence to tradition, culture, or preference. Yet these rules may further prejudice. By scrutinizing the justification provided by the legislature, the court can allow adherence to tradition, culture, or preference where justified, whilst challenging those rules which further prejudice. In a similar manner, the Socratic contestation found in the application of the proportionality test can challenge legislative measures that do not reflect public reasoning or where general or ideological legislation fails to take account of reality such that its specific application may undermine its aims or inadvertently limit individual rights; or where the technical nature of the legislation means that it inadvertently favours particular interest groups, where favourable treatment is hidden in the technical details of the legislation. In all of these situations, courts inquire into the justifications of the restriction of a right, determining that the proper justification has been provided, correcting those situations in which legislatures were not able to perform at their best.

Kumm also argues that that rationalist human rights paradigm provides greater legitimacy. Although agreeing with Waldron that democracy provides the most legitimate form of decision-making, modern societies can only have a form of representative democracy. This means that although legislation and the actions of the legislature may represent the wishes of the people, it is difficult for individuals to participate effectively in these decisions. Allowing individuals to go to court to challenge actions of the executive and legislature can enhance participation, allowing individuals to challenge those decisions they feel are not representative of their views. In addition, democracy is justified because it promotes political equality, enhances participation of individuals, but also because decisions have a logical and rational basis. As judicial review aims to facilitate rational decision-making, it thereby enhances the legitimacy of democratic decision-making.

Although Kumm's account focuses on human rights protections, the method of judicial reasoning it proposes to control human rights is similar to that advocated by Tomkins. Both assign to courts a strong role in the protection of absolute rights. Tomkins argues that courts can strike down decisions of the executive which breach absolute rights. Kumm argues that absolute rights are an example of where the legislature has provided an authoritative determination of how a particular right is to be applied in a particular circumstance. If there is any scope for judicial interpretation here, it is at the margins. Not only does Kumm's theory appear to mirror Tomkins' approach, but his theory provides an explanation for Tomkins' approach to absolute rights which could be supported by political constitutionalism. It may also, by analogy, justify why courts should have the power to strike down executive actions when the executive has clearly stepped beyond the boundaries of its powers as established by clear legislative provision, explaining why Tomkins' theory equates 'lawful authority' with the clear and express words of the legislature. The express words are a legislative determination of the powers of the executive. This legislative determination is an authoritative assessment, deriving legitimacy from the democratically representative manner in which it is made. Courts should control the executive in order to ensure that it too complies with legitimate, democratic, and authoritative determinations of the scope of its powers.

Kumm's account of how courts should apply the proportionality test is similar to Tomkins' explanation of how courts should apply proportionality and rationality when examining executive actions. Kumm argues that the court uses the proportionality test to create a more structured inquiry, focusing on whether good reasons have been provided by the legislature or the executive. He advocates a four-stage test. The first stage, assessing whether there is a legitimate aim, requires the court to establish whether the legislature or executive acted to achieve a legitimate objective. This is a question of textual interpretation, the aims being set out in the human rights document. The second stage of suitable means is an empirical question, where the court assesses whether the proposed measure is capable of achieving the outcome of the legitimate aim. When assessing the final two stages of necessity and balancing the right with the legitimate aim, the court again is assessing reasons. The role of the court is to assess whether there are good reasons for the measure. In a similar manner, Tomkins advocates that courts should scrutinize reasoning to determine whether rationality and proportionality have been satisfied.

This is not to argue that the theories are precisely the same. First, Kumm advocates that courts can strike down legislative acts whereas Tomkins only focuses on the control of the courts over executive actions. But this cannot be the distinguishing line between legal and political constitutionalists. Craig, for example, is a legal constitutionalist, but he does not argue that courts should be able to strike down legislative in addition to executive acts. A second difference between Kumm and Tomkins may stem from whether their theories permit courts only to review the reasons provided by the executive for their actions, or whether courts are able to review the possibility of whether any reason could exist to justify the actions of the executive. Tomkins' theory appears to focus on an assessment of the reasons provided by the executive. Kumm's theory appears to be more general, allowing the courts to scrutinize decisions according to principles of practical reasoning, beyond the assessment of the reasons provided. Kumm's approach appears to provide a more active role for the judiciary, allowing them to use principles of practical reasoning to determine if the action of the executive is justified. Tomkins' approach provides courts with a more restrictive power, allowing them only to evaluate the reasons provided by the executive. However, this seems a rather tenuous line to draw between a theory of judicial review drawn from principles of legal constitutionalism and one drawn from political constitutionalism. It may also be a difficult distinction to maintain in practice. Were a court to realize that the executive had not provided a good justification, but there were clear rational grounds for its conclusion, it is hard to see how a court would strike the measure down due to its lack of rationality. It would also appear odd in this situation if political constitutionalism, which generally advocates less control over the executive, would be more activist in this scenario than legal constitutionalism, striking down a decision of the executive where the reasons provided by the executive were flawed, despite the existence of clear reasons justifying the actions of the executive.

The more we examine accounts of legal and political constitutionalism, the harder it appears to provide a clear line between these two theories. No account of legal constitutionalism argues that only courts should control the executive or protect human rights. No account of political constitutionalism advocates that only legislatures should control the executive or protect human rights. Both theories aim to provide different roles to both institutions, favouring either legal or political controls. But it can be extremely difficult to delineate between their accounts both in theory and in practice. The accounts merge and overlap with one another. If this is the case, then it is hard to see how democratic dialogue can provide a new account. There would appear to be no middle ground for such a theory to occupy. Moreover, as both legal and political constitutionalism advocate a combination of legal and political controls over the executive, democratic dialogue appears to be nothing more than a labelling exercise. Political constitutionalism, legal constitutionalism, and democratic dialogue appear to advocate remarkably similar protections of human rights and principles of judicial review over the executive. They merely provide different labels for their accounts.

IV. Conclusion

It is difficult to find conclusive proof for any argument. This is particularly true when you are aiming to prove a negative. Nevertheless, our account of the extent to which democratic dialogue can provide a distinct theory of human rights protections, or a unique account of the extent to which courts should control actions of the executive, provides strong evidence that, if such a theory exists, it is not one that distinguishes itself from other theories in terms of control. It is not the case that political constitutionalism advocates only political controls and legal constitutionalism advocates only legal controls. Both theories offer both types of control. Although they may prefer political or legal controls, the line as to the precise balance between these controls is hard to define. This does not mean that there is no distinction between political and legal constitutionalism. It does make it difficult, however, to provide an account of democratic dialogue if this is merely to be expressed in terms of control. If both political constitutionalism and legal constitutionalism advocate a combination of both legal and political controls, then, if you are optimistic, democratic dialogue is ubiquitous and both political and legal constitutionalism are best understood as democratic dialogue theories. If you are pessimistic, there is no space between political and legal constitutionalism for democratic dialogue to occupy. It may sound like a nice idea to combine legal and political controls, but this is already done in theories of both legal and political constitutionalism.

Moreover, the distinction between legal and political constitutionalism appears to be more of a dispute as to the nature of the world. Both theories recognize the same relative abilities of the legislature and the courts to protect rights and to control the executive. Where they disagree is as to the facts. Political constitutionalists think rights are more contestable and more likely to require political assessments of competing interests. Legal constitutionalists think rights are less contestable and therefore require more moral reasoning from courts to ensure political balances of interests do not remove rights from minority groups. Some political constitutionalists think rights are merely expressions of interest and therefore should be determined by the political process. Other political constitutionalists think that democratic decision-making bodies are less likely to harm minority rights than courts.[119]

[119] See P Craig, *UK, EU and Global Administrative Law: Foundations and Challenges* (n 1) Chapter 1.

This conclusion is hardly surprising. Although legal constitutionalism is often paraphrased as focusing on a preference for legal controls, as Craig's work on the origins of legal constitutionalism clearly establishes, the focus of the early case law establishing common law constitutionalism in the United Kingdom was not one of establishing legal controls and restraints per se, but rather one of recognizing the need to regulate the executive, sometimes doing so to further the legislative aims of Parliament in establishing a particular regulatory body and sometimes establishing principles of the common law to further administrative efficiency in addition to the maintenance of the rule of law. To merely express legal and political constitutionalism in terms of legal and political control, with democratic dialogue occupying a middle position, is a caricature which glosses over the subtle aspects of both legal and political constitutionalism, despite the apparent commonality of this perception. If we are to find a distinction between legal and political constitutionalism, therefore, we need to start looking elsewhere than at the question of whether a theory advocates a predominantly legal or political control of human rights or a predominantly legal or political control over the executive.

2

Democratic Dialogue and the Dynamic Approach

This chapter continues our search for an understanding of the meaning of democratic dialogue. The previous chapter investigated one claim as to the distinct nature of democratic dialogue. Democratic dialogue advocates a combination of legal and political controls over human rights and administrative acts, and in some legal systems, legislation. This contrasts with theories of legal constitutionalism and political constitutionalism. Legal constitutionalism argues that law should be used to control the administration and protect human rights, whereas political constitutionalism prefers political controls. The previous chapter explained how this was inaccurate. Neither political nor legal constitutionalism claims exclusivity for legal or political controls. Rather, the difference between the two theories is better understood as one of degree—a preference for legal or political controls. As such, this leaves theories of democratic dialogue in a precarious position. They are either ubiquitous or non-existent. If both political and legal constitutionalism advocate a need for a combination of legal and political controls, then it would appear that every constitutional theory is one of democratic dialogue. If so, it is hard to see this theory as a distinct understanding of the constitution. The other alternative seems equally bleak. If both political and legal constitutionalism advocate a combination of legal and political controls then there is no middle ground for theories of democratic dialogue to occupy.

This brings us to a second account of a possible distinguishing feature of democratic dialogue: democratic dialogue is dynamic; theories of legal and political constitutionalism are not. Democratic dialogue does not rest on providing an account of a particular set of values against which constitutions should be evaluated. Rather, it advocates that values should be formed and re-formed through a process of inter-institutional interaction. It is easy to argue that democratic dialogue theories are dynamic. This dynamic element appears to have two components. First, values, or rights, are not fixed but fluid. This is best understood not as a rejection of the existence of fixed, constant, or objective abstract values, but of the recognition that the way in which values are applied to give specific solutions to distinct problems evolves over time. Second, democratic dialogue includes interaction between institutions.

The Introduction examined the issue of prisoner voting across a range of common law countries. Each of the legal systems examined recognized the value of democracy and the need for democracy to include a right to vote. They also recognized that those convicted of crimes should be punished in a manner that is proportionate to their crime, which may include their removal from the electoral franchise. However, different solutions arose as to how to reconcile these values: how serious should the nature of an offence be to deprive a prisoner of the right to vote, and for how long, if at all, should this prohibition remain in place? Not only do different countries reach different solutions to these issues, but also the answer to this issue has evolved over time. New Zealand, for example, shifted from a legal system which allowed some prisoners to vote to one which re-introduced a blanket ban on prisoner voting. The law in the

United Kingdom appears to be moving in the opposite direction with the existence of a Draft Bill and the recommendations of the Joint Committee on the Draft Bill that some prisoners should be given the right to vote. Moreover, in each of the countries we examined, solutions evolved through the interaction of the legislature, executive, and judiciary. It seems easy to argue, therefore, that our answer to rights-issues may evolve over time as society changes.

However, as with our assessment of control in the previous chapter, to regard this dynamic element as a defining feature of democratic dialogue runs the risk, yet again, that we will reach the conclusion that democratic dialogue theories are either ubiquitous or empty. Evidence of dynamic interaction between institutions of the constitution, giving rise to the evolution of values over time, can be found in theories of both legal and political constitutionalism. Moreover, there are some theories of legal and political constitutionalism that place as much importance on this element of dynamic interaction, or the evolution of values, as is found in theories of democratic dialogue. If dynamic interaction is a defining feature of democratic dialogue theories—then either many, if not all, theoretical accounts of the constitution are ones of democratic dialogue, or theories of democratic dialogue do not really exist, being merely subsumed into accounts of legal or political constitutionalism.

I. Democratic Dialogue is Dynamic

It is easy to find evidence of a dynamic element in accounts of democratic dialogue. This is hardly surprising. Dialogue, after all, involves more than one party and encourages interaction between the parties involved in the dialogue. The seminal account of descriptive democratic dialogue is found in the work of Peter Hogg and Alison Bushell,[1] who define dialogue as follows:

> Where a judicial decision is open to legislative reversal, modification or avoidance, then it is meaningful to regard that relationship between the Court and the competent legislative body as a dialogue.[2]

This definition emphasizes the need for interaction between two institutions of the constitution—the judiciary and the legislature. Dialogue occurs when the legislature has a chance to respond to the actions of the judiciary. If there is no ability for the legislature to respond, then there is no dialogue. In addition, Hogg and Bushell define dialogue as giving rise to a relationship between the two institutions. This focus on an element of interaction and the dynamic development of rights is also found in their account of democratic dialogue occurring under the Canadian *Charter*. Hogg and Bushell argue in favour of dialogue by giving an account of the way in which decisions of the court have been responded to by actions of the legislature. Any form of legislative response to a decision of the court was counted as evidence of democratic dialogue; indicating interaction between two institutions of the constitution.[3]

Hogg and Bushell are not the only academics who focus on an account of dynamic interactions as a feature of democratic dialogue. In his account of different forms of democratic dialogue theory, Kent Roach identifies the common feature of dialogue as the recognition that courts need not have the final word on the definition or

[1] PW Hogg and AA Bushell, 'The *Charter* Dialogue Between the Courts and Legislatures (Or Perhaps the *Charter of Rights* Isn't Such a Bad Thing After All)' (1997) 35 Osgoode Hall Law Journal 75.
[2] ibid, 79. [3] ibid, 97–98.

interpretation of a legally protected human right, given the ability of the legislature to respond to the decision of the court.[4] He places more emphasis on the dynamic element of dialogue than is found in the account of Hogg and Bushell, ascribing a post-modern characteristic to theories of democratic dialogue as dialogue 'can go on and on and it does not presuppose final or right answers to the difficult questions that we as a society discuss'.[5] His theory does not merely describe institutional inter-actions, but also recognizes how answers to rights-issues evolve over time.

Roach describes three different accounts of democratic dialogue, differing according to the relative roles given to the legislature and the courts. The first, 'co-ordinate construction', occurs where the legislature is free to ignore rules of the court. The second, 'dialogue based on court accountability', occurs where judicial decisions are held to account before majority decision-makers, allowing the views of a strong majority to override the decisions of the court. Roach's third account of dialogue occurs where the legislature and the courts have distinct but complementary roles. All three accounts contain a dynamic element as they involve interaction between the legislature and the courts. The legislature may either ignore, override, or modify decisions of the judiciary.[6] On Roach's third, preferred, account, interaction occurs between the two institutions both when the legislature reacts to a decision of the judiciary by modifying or overturning its conclusions and when the legislature chooses to accept the decision of the court. Interaction can also occur when the court decides to uphold legislation as well as when the court strikes down or re-reads legislation. On this account, dialogue can be seen as an endless conversation. The legislature and the judiciary interact in a series of events to refine legal definitions of rights.[7]

The recognition of inter-institutional interaction as a key feature of accounts of democratic dialogue is not restricted to Canadian accounts of dialogue. It also features in accounts of democratic dialogue in the United Kingdom. Richard Clayton, for example, who applies Hogg and Bushell's work to the Human Rights Act 1998, regards the Canadian experience as giving rise to 'a more dynamic interaction among the branches of governance', thereby enhancing the democratic process as institutions of the constitution are made accountable to one another.[8] Tom Hickman and Danny Nicol propose divergent accounts of democratic dialogue for the Human Rights Act 1998. Yet, both of their accounts refer to dynamic interaction between the legislature and the judiciary, albeit in divergent ways. Nicol prefers democratic dialogue to occur through an application of section 4 of the Human Rights Act 1998. He advocates that judicial output should be 'reconceptualised as a contestable entity', where courts provide their honest and forthright account of the meaning of a human right, providing Parliament with the opportunity to respond to this account either by accepting the opinion of the judiciary, or substituting its own interpretation of a human right.[9] Nicol recognizes that rights can modify and change over time.[10] Both the courts and the legislature should engage in full and frank debates over the meaning of rights, 'turning disagreement into a creative force' so as to reconfigure the meaning of rights through inter-institutional disagreement.[11]

[4] K Roach, 'Constitutional and Common Law Dialogues Between the Supreme Court and the Canadian Legislatures' (2001) 80 La Revue du Barreau Canadien 481, 489.

[5] ibid, 490. [6] ibid, 490–503. [7] ibid, 496–501.

[8] R Clayton, 'Judicial Deference and "Democratic Dialogue": The Legitimacy of Judicial Intervention under the Human Rights Act 1998' [2004] Public Law 33, 44.

[9] D Nicol, 'Law and Politics after the Human Rights Act' [2006] Public Law 722, 743.

[10] ibid, 743. [11] ibid, 749.

Hickman disagrees with Nicol's account, both in terms of its descriptive accuracy and its normative desirability.[12] He prefers dialogue to occur through section 3 as opposed to section 4. Courts should be prepared to read legislation to provide as strong a protection of Convention rights as possible, with section 4 being reserved for extreme circumstances where this is not possible.[13] Nevertheless, interactions between the legislature and the judiciary are central to his account. Hickman not only recognizes that the Human Right Act lends itself to democratic dialogue given the built-in ability of the legislature to respond to human rights decisions of the judiciary, but also regards dialogue as occurring through both sections 3 and 4 of the Act, as well as providing an account of dialogue that includes an assessment of the further response of the judiciary following the legislature's reaction to the court's initial judgment.[14]

The importance of dynamic interactions between institutions of the constitution is also found in Gardbaum's account of the commonwealth model of rights protections, encompassing Australia and New Zealand in addition to the UK and Canada. Gardbaum establishes four key features of the commonwealth model: (i) a legalized and codified charter of rights; (ii) mandatory rights review by the political branch before enacting legislation; (iii) a form of constitutional review by the courts that is beyond interpretation; and (iv) the ability of the legislature to have the final say on the content of the law through use of the ordinary legislative procedure.[15] These features facilitate interactions between the legislature and the court, particularly as both can respond to the determinations of the other. Moreover, dynamic interaction is present in the account of dialogue taking place in the US constitution found in the work of Friedman, Fisher, and Burt. Courts can initiate and facilitate dialogue by hearing rights cases and entering into debate about the interpretation of a right. Courts are able to do this as their power to protect rights goes above and beyond the ability to interpret legislation by ensuring that its interpretation matches the intention of the legislature. Legislatures are in a better position to continue the dialogue as legislatures have the final say, giving them the ability to respond to court decisions. There are more options open to the courts than in systems, like the USA, with a strong constitutional protection of rights, where legislatures are able to respond through legislative amendment, constitutional amendment, or through the response of the executive to administer judgments in a manner slightly different from that proscribed by the courts.[16]

Gardbaum's theory goes beyond a mere descriptive account of inter-institutional interactions. He also provides a normative justification for the commonwealth model that is based on the dynamic interaction between the legislature and the judiciary. These interactions between the legislature and the judiciary facilitate the combination of the relative advantages of both legal and political constitutionalism, whilst minimizing the disadvantages of purely legal or purely political protections of human rights. It provides a better means of facilitating interaction, making this part of the design of the constitution as opposed to a side effect, or a possible interpretation of the constitution.

[12] T Hickman, 'The Courts and the Politicians after the Human Rights Act' [2008] Public Law 84.

[13] T Hickman, 'Constitutional Dialogue, Constitutional Theories and the Human Rights Act 1998' [1995] Public Law 306 and T Hickman, *Public Law after the Human Rights Act* (Hart 2010) Chapter 3.

[14] Hickman, 'Constitutional Dialogue, Constitutional Theories and the Human Rights Act 1998', ibid, 328–9.

[15] S Gardbaum, *The New Commonwealth Model of Constitutionalism: Theory and Practice* (Cambridge University Press 2013) 29–31.

[16] See L Fisher, *Constitutional Dialogues: Interpretation as Political Process* (Princeton University Press 1988) 201–28.

In the commonwealth model of rights protections, dialogue occurs through predominantly legal as opposed to political means, the use of the ordinary law-making procedure making it easier for the legislature to respond to judicial interpretations of constitutional rights with which it does not agree.

Nor is this recognition of a dynamic element as a necessary feature of democratic dialogue restricted to those theories which focus on a democratic dialogue protection of rights in commonwealth models of rights protections. A dynamic element of dialogue is also found in theories which explain how democratic dialogue provides a more descriptively accurate account of the relationship between the legislature, executive, and judiciary in constitutional systems with a strong, constitutional protection of rights. Barry Friedman, for example, provides an account of how the interpretation of the US constitution is best-described as an 'elaborate discussion between judges and the body politic'.[17] Debates as to the meaning of a constitutional provision take place before the court. A government body starts the process by taking a decision, legislating or acting in a way that an individual believes is contrary to his or her constitutional rights—for example by restricting speech contrary to the First Amendment. The individual takes this dispute to the courts. The courts then enter into the debate as to the meaning of a constitutional provision by resolving this dispute. In doing so, the court provides its interpretation of the broadly worded constitutional text. The role of the court, however, goes beyond merely giving its interpretation and, in so doing, becoming part of the inter-institutional discussion of the meaning of a constitutional provision. For Friedman,

> [t]he Court dictates how the dialogue will proceed by choosing one interpretation. The process of reaching an interpretative consensus on the text is dynamic. The Court may offer an interpretation that is operative for a time, but the Court's opinions lead debate on a path that often ultimately changes that interpretation. Not coincidentally, the accepted interpretation shifts and changes as constituencies shift and grow in strength.[18]

Friedman argues that the debate over abortion rights in the United States is an example of this dynamic, dialogic process. Although the Supreme Court may take the final, legally binding decision as to whether state laws enabling abortion are contrary to the Constitution, its decision is the culmination of debate surrounding the legislative enactment, debate, and discussion in prior court decisions, and debate and discussion in the media and in society more generally. Nor does a decision of the Supreme Court bring this debate and discussion to an end. Media institutions and society more generally will react to the decision of the Supreme Court. This, in turn, may lead to potential future legislative amendment or constitutional amendment, re-starting the interactive process of interpreting constitutional rights.

Friedman gives an account of two distinct roles of the court in this dynamic process of inter-institutional interactions. First, the court plays a role as a speaker. The courts at various levels give their interpretation of a constitutional right by providing their interpretation of the constitutional right in their judgment. Second, the court acts as a facilitator of debate. It does so by synthesizing the views of society, focusing the debate, and acting as a catalyst for debate. Courts synthesize the views of society by the way in which courts look to views in society to help them in their interpretations of constitutional provisions. This may be through reading media accounts, or academic debates, or through the *amicus curiae* or *Brandeis* briefs submitted to the court. Their

[17] B Friedman, 'Dialogue and Judicial Review' (1993) 91 Michigan Law Review 577, 653.
[18] ibid, 654.

judgments focus debate through the process of bringing the debate to the attention of the public through hearing the issue before the court, as well as through their analysis of constitutional interpretations in their specific judgments. Courts can act as a catalyst for debate in a similar manner, drawing an issue to the attention of the public through hearing the case and through reaching a particular outcome. Courts can motivate other institutions of the constitution to act or to enter into the debate. They also moderate the debate through their judgments.[19] This dynamic element of interaction is common to other accounts of descriptive democratic dialogue in the US.[20]

Dynamic interactions between the legislature and the judiciary are clearly a necessary component of democratic dialogue. However, the fact that the requirement of dynamic interactions between the legislature and the judiciary is common to accounts of commonwealth models of rights protections, and to accounts which aim to provide a more accurate account of the way in which rights are protected in legal systems which provide for a strong, constitutional protection of human rights, may already begin to cast doubt on the extent to which dynamic interactions is a sufficient criterion of theories of democratic dialogue. Gardbaum is aware of this problem, and the similarities between descriptions of dialogue in legal systems with a strong protection of human rights and his account of the commonwealth model, which is designed to facilitate these interactions through legal as opposed to political means. Whilst this may be a means of delineating commonwealth models of rights protections, this cannot provide a means of distinguishing democratic dialogue. These problems are exacerbated when we examine accounts of legal and political constitutionalism further and realize that dynamic interactions can be as much a feature of these constitutional models as it is a feature of democratic dialogue.

II. Dynamic Legal Constitutionalism

The clearest example of a dynamic theory of legal constitutionalism can be found in the work of Trevor Allan. Allan is one of the, if not the, leading advocates of common law constitutionalism in the UK. In his three seminal books on constitutional theory, Allan advocates a theory of the constitution founded on the rule of law.[21] His account of the rule of law goes beyond purely formal accounts, as found for example in the account of Joseph Raz, but does not go as far as complete substantive liberal accounts of the rule of law, as found for example in the theories of Hayek. Allan's account argues that the rule of law requires adherence to formal principle of due process and equality, and also with substantive principles reflecting the common good in that particular society, consistent with the principle of equal citizenship.[22]

Allan asserts that it is the primary job of the court to determine the content of the rule of law. There are both institutional and constitutional reasons for granting this role to the court. Law stands as the bulwark between the governors and the governed.[23]

[19] ibid, 669–72.

[20] See, for example, Fisher (n 16) and R Burt, *The Constitution in Conflict* (Harvard: Belknap Press 1995).

[21] TRS Allan, *Law, Liberty and Justice* (Oxford University Press 1994); TRS Allan, *Constitutional Justice: A Liberal Theory of the Rule of law* (Oxford University Press 2003); and TRS Allan, *The Sovereignty of Law: Freedom, Constitution and Common Law* (Oxford University Press 2013).

[22] Allan, *Law Liberty and Justice* (n 21) chapter 3; Allan, *Constitutional Justice* (n 21) chapter 3; and Allan, *Sovereignty of Law* (n 21) chapter 3.

[23] See Allan, *Constitutional Justice* (n 21) chapter 1; Allan, *Sovereignty of Law* (n 21), chapter 1; and Allan, *Law Liberty and Justice* (n 21) chapter 1.

Institutionally, courts are best-suited to determining the content of the rule of law as the reasoning process used by the common law applies principles of practical reasoning in order to determine the specific content of the rule of law in a particular situation. The rule of law is an ideal best expressed as an aspect of practical reasoning.[24] The exemplar of practical reasoning is the reasoning process found in the ordinary courts applying ordinary principles of the common law.[25] Constitutionally, the courts are the best institution to determine the content of the rule of law as courts are independent arbiters in disputes between the state and individuals. The judiciary determine these issues not according to their own principles and values, but according to the general principles of practical reasoning,[26] ensuring there is a justification for any executive act or legislative provision that does not match the principles of equal citizenship.[27]

Allan does not regard the UK constitution as currently giving the power to the courts to strike down legislation that is incompatible with the rule of law. Nor does he unequivocally argue that his theory necessarily requires a general principle that courts should be able, in every situation, to strike down legislation which contravenes the rule of law. Nevertheless, he argues that courts should ensure that legislative provisions are interpreted so as to be compatible with the provisions of the rule of law—the line between re-interpreting legislation so as to comply with the rule of law and of striking down legislation when this is not possible being particularly fine. The law enacted by the legislature should be such that it is capable of being obeyed by its citizens. The legislature should also adhere to principles of practical reason, adhering to the ideals of formal and substantive equality and respect for the principle of equal citizenship, determining how these principles are to apply when balancing different values.[28] Otherwise the legislation enacted is not law in its true sense; it is not capable of giving rise to obedience.

The sovereignty of the Westminster Parliament rests on a prior, unwritten constitution requiring that the legislature enact its powers for the good of the people. Despite this lack of a clear argument that courts do or should have the power to strike down legislation that is incompatible with the rule of law, Allan's account is a theory of legal constitutionalism. His theory advocates a preference for control over the executive and the legislature by the courts. Moreover, the principle at the heart of Allan's theory is the rule of law, understood as a process of practical reasoning through which the general principles of due process and equal citizenship are determined, harnessing ideals of procedural and substantive equality. The values that emerge from this process of practical reasoning determine the legitimacy of executive and legislative enactments. Courts determine these values through the common law reasoning process, their process of adjudication determining the law on a case-by-case basis.

Allan's theory is clearly dynamic in terms of the content of the rule of law. We can see this in the way in which Allan's account sees the rule of law as synonymous with the results of the reasoning process of the common law.[29]

As the basic principle of the British constitution, underpinning its character as a liberal democratic polity, the rule of law means the sovereignty of the principle of liberty: it upholds the

[24] See Allan, *Constitutional Justice* (n 21) chapter 1.

[25] See Allan, *Sovereignty of Law* (n 21) chapter 3; and Allan, *Constitutional Justice* (n 21) 290–2.

[26] See Allan, *Sovereignty of Law* (n 21) 293.

[27] See ibid, chapters 1 and 8; and Allan, *Constitutional Justice* (n 21) chapter 1.

[28] See Allan, *Law, Liberty and Justice* (n 21) chapter 1; Allan, *Constitutional Justice* (n 21) chapters 1 and 9; and Allan, *Sovereignty of Law* (n 21) chapters 3 and 8.

[29] When analysing Allan's theory in more depth, reference will be made predominantly to the most recent iteration of his theory in *The Sovereignty of Law* (n 21).

freedom and dignity of those independent citizens who comprise the political community. While, however, the rule of law prohibits the violation of citizens' basic rights—allowing only (modest) limitations and restrictions when really necessary for the public good—it does not prescribe the detailed content of the laws.[30]

Although the rule of law 'means the sovereignty of the principle of liberty', for Allan, the principle of liberty is insufficiently precise to determine the detailed content of laws. Instead:

The ideal of the rule of law is most fully realized in the common law, which is the ultimate foundation for the authority of court decisions, even those that apply statutory provisions. For the scope and limits of parliamentary authority, and the content of the principles of statutory interpretation, are themselves elements of the legal order, whose nature and implications are worked out, case by case, in the evolution and development of the common law.[31]

The dynamic element inherent in Allan's account of the rule of law is illustrated by the way in which Allan's account does not provide a detailed list of the precise content of the rule of law, or the liberal principles and the content of the principle of equal citizenship on which it is based. Rather, the detailed content of the rule of law evolves on a case-by-case basis. Each case before the court requires the judge to apply principles of practical reasoning to the specific facts, a process that requires evaluation of what the rule of law requires in those particular circumstances. Just as the common law evolves over time through a process of analogical reasoning, so does the content of the rule of law which is derived from this series of common law decisions.

This dynamic element is present not only in the way in which courts rely purely on principles of the common law to develop the rule of law on a case-by-case basis over time, but also when courts interpret legislative provisions. Allan's account of statutory interpretation illustrates this inter-institutional element of his account of legal constitutionalism. His theory sees the content of the rule of law evolving through the actions of the legislature, the executive, and the judiciary. Allan argues that courts should interpret statutory provisions according to his account of the rule of law, in the same manner that courts should use the rule of law when developing the common law. But this does not mean that the courts should ignore statutory provisions. Parliament, in addition to the courts, plays a role in determining specific applications of the rule of law. Allan recognizes that Parliament has authority to determine the way in which general principles deriving from formal equality and the principles of equal citizenship are to be applied and balanced in particular circumstances. He recognizes the democratic credentials of Parliament to enact legislation, seeing its legislation as commanding authority when enacted in line with the principles of the rule of law.[32] However, Parliament enacts measures through legislation, which are examples of general rules. These general rules will naturally be over and under inclusive. As such, although Parliament's legislation is designed to provide a democratically legitimate balance between different aspects of the rule of law, it may nevertheless be the case that the general rule, when applied to a specific situation, fails to uphold the rule of law. When interpreting legislation, courts should pay attention to the general rule as enacted by Parliament, whilst ensuring that it interprets the provisions of the rule according to the requirements of the common law. Courts also need to pay attention to the reason for employing a general rule as opposed to adopting a series of individual decisions to determine the precise content of the rule of law as applied to a particular set of circumstances.[33] In other words, the

[30] Allan, *Sovereignty of Law* (n 21) 91–92. [31] ibid, 121. [32] ibid, chapter 3.
[33] ibid, 177–79.

legislature and the judiciary work together to determine the requirements of the rule of law in particular circumstances.

Allan also requires courts to pay attention to the role of the executive, recognizing that the way in which the executive implements general rules can determine how well the values of the rule of law are maintained when general rules are applied to specific situations. Allan explains how this may occur in practice through his analysis of the *Pretty* case.[34] *Pretty* concerned a blanket ban on assisted suicide. Section 2(1) of the Suicide Act 1962 criminalizes assisting another individual to take his or her own life. Pretty was too disabled to take her own life and wished to enlist the help of her husband. However, she also did not wish for her husband to be prosecuted and sought assurances that he would not be prosecuted should he assist her to take her own life. When assessing whether the Suicide Act 1962 restricted Pretty's rights too greatly, Allan argues that the court can pay regard to the fact that the best way of balancing the different interests may be through a blanket ban. This may be due to the fact that it is too complicated to devise a more precise rule that can delineate clearly deserving cases of assisted suicide without running the risk that more mercenary individuals will be able to use the newly formed rule to assist individuals to commit suicide where there was insufficient clarity that this was according to the wishes of the individual.

The argument in favour of a general rule is bolstered by the ability of the executive to exercise discretion when implementing the general rule. In this instance, discretion arises from the ability of the Director of Public Prosecutions to decide whether to prosecute an individual who has aided another to commit suicide. This executive discretion could help to alleviate cases of over and under classification that may arise under a general rule. In this case, it could help to ensure that the general rule did not result in the prosecution of individuals who had helped someone to commit suicide where it was clear that this assistance was used to help further the right of the individual concerned to decide when to terminate his or her own life when suffering from a debilitating terminal illness. For this executive discretion to comply with the requirements of the rule of law, it would require the publication of guidelines, in order to promote certainty and personal autonomy.[35] This solution was reached in English law, following a series of decisions on assisted suicide in the House of Lords,[36] the European Court of Human Rights,[37] and the Supreme Court.[38] Allan argues that this line of cases provides a role for the legislature, executive, and courts, with the courts requiring the publication of criteria which can then inform public debate and further scrutiny over this issue. For Allan:

> [s]uch a dialogue between court and executive officials can generate a wider public discussion, in which questions of fair enforcement may broaden into consideration of the proper scope of the criminal law.[39]

Allan's account of dialogue is evidence of a dynamic interaction between the legislature, the judiciary, and the executive. The legislature enacts a general rule. In doing so the legislature should take account of the values found in the rule of law and aim to balance different interests in society in line with the principle of equal citizenship. Courts interpret this legislation. They do so substantively, ensuring that the general

[34] *R (Pretty) v Director of Public Prosecutions* [2001] UKHL 61, [2002] 1 AC 800.
[35] Allan, *Sovereignty of Law* (n 21) 179–84.
[36] *R (Pretty) v Director of Public Prosecutions* (n 34).
[37] *Pretty v United Kingdom* (Application 2346/02) [2002] ECHR 2346/02, 35 EHRR 1.
[38] *R (Purdy) v Director of Public Prosecutions* [2009] UKHL 45, [201] 1 AC 345.
[39] Allan, *Sovereignty of Law* (n 21) 184.

rule enacted by the legislature does not contradict the rule of law. Second, courts assess whether despite the harm to the rule of law caused by the over and under-inclusiveness of general rules, there may nevertheless be good reasons for enacting a general rule such that the legislation should be maintained and not read by the courts in such a way as to ensure its provisions do not contravene the rule of law.

The executive should also implement general rules to provide for further discretion to uphold the rule of law when the general rule is applied to individual cases. Courts control the substantive outcomes of these exercises of administrative discretion to ensure that they uphold the rule of law. In addition, courts will enforce due process requirements and further requirements of more formal aspects of the rule of law. Courts may sometimes require the publication of clear criteria on which the exercise of this discretion is made, in order to reduce arbitrariness and to further personal autonomy through the publication of clear rules—as has occurred with regard to assisted suicide. These inter-institutional interactions develop the rule of law in a dynamic way. In addition, they may prompt public discussion in a manner similar to that described by Burt, Fisher, and Friedmann in their accounts of a democratic dialogue interpretation of the US constitution. It is hard to see, therefore, how a dynamic element is unique to theories of democratic dialogue. Inter-institutional interactions are advocated by Trevor Allan, yet his theory is clearly an example of legal constitutionalism and not of democratic dialogue.

It may be possible to argue against our conclusion that democratic dialogue can be just as significant a feature of accounts of legal constitutionalism as it is in theories of democratic dialogue, given that different accounts may place more or less weight on the importance of dynamic interactions. Allan may provide an account of inter-institutional interactions, but his theory focuses more on the rule of law than it does on dialogue between the legislature, the judiciary, and the executive. However, on closer examination, it becomes clear that this dynamic element is a fundamental component of Allan's common law theory of the constitution. In the most recent account of his theory, Allan draws a distinction between the internal and the external perspective. Lawyers and legal theorists can only adopt the internal viewpoint, not the external viewpoint. Any account of law, from the internal viewpoint, is an interpretative process, requiring an evaluation of general principles and their specific application to the facts of the case. This is true of both statutory interpretation and of the common law. Although legislation enacts general rules, we do not know how the general rule applies to a particular situation until we have evaluated different opinions of the general rule and determined its application to that particular situation according to this evaluation. In a similar manner, we cannot know what the law is when applying and developing the common law. We do not know how the common law regulates a particular situation until common law precedents have been evaluated in light of the rule of law and applied to the particular situation before the court.

Any conclusion as to what the law is before this evaluative process has occurred is, for Allan, an external account of academic opinion about the law. For Allan:

> An account of common law rules and principles, in any field of law, is necessarily a theory about how best to understand why courts have reached certain decisions—not in the sense of explaining social or psychological phenomena, but rather of presenting reasons of justice or political morality for reading them in one way rather than another.[40]

[40] ibid, 6.

As law is always an interpretation of precedent and statutory provision, this interpretation requiring an evaluation of the requirements of the principle of equal citizenship and due process, Allan argues that

> We cannot, then, distinguish (as is often supposed) between an account of the present law, as it simply is for the time being, and our opinions about what, ideally, it ought to be, if the statutes and precedents were better understood.[41]

This is not to argue that lawyers and academics provide their own account of law according to their own personal system of values, however derived. Rather, it is to recognize that a determination of the law requires an evaluation of precedent and general rules according to the rule of law. The rule of law itself requires an evaluation of how the broad principles of formal and substantive equality, understood in line with the principle of equal citizenship, apply to the particular scenario before the court.

This account of the law is key to Allan's defence of his theory of the constitution. If law is as Allan describes, then lawyers and legal theorists have no choice but to interpret the constitution according to Allan's account. Any other interpretation of the constitution is criticized by Allan as external and therefore invalid. It cannot, by definition, be an account of a legal theorist. It can only be an account of external facts about the UK constitution as opposed to an account of the UK constitution itself. It is also clear that this account of law is dynamic. Law evolves over time. As Allan explains:

> There is no simple fact-of-the-matter about any questions of public law, however comparatively local or trivial: any statement of law is always the conclusion of an interpretative argument over how best to read the relevant legal materials. The United Kingdom has a common law constitution not merely in the sense that it is the product of history and tradition, but also in the sense that its content is a complex mixture of shared understandings and theoretical argument. Every doctrine, no matter how well established or exalted, is embraced as a rough approximation to the applicable balance of reasons—adequate for most purposes, perhaps, but subject to reappraisal and refinement when tested in novel circumstances or in the light of changing moral attitudes.[42]

Any statement of the law is open to constant re-evaluation and re-interpretation. It evolves as it is applied to new situations and as moral attitudes change. It is hard to see this as anything other than an assessment of law as itself inherently dynamic. As such, it is hard to conclude that dynamic interactions have smaller importance to Allan's account of legal constitutionalism than they would do in an account of democratic dialogue. In both theories, dynamic interactions appear to be necessary and central.

Allan's account of legal constitutionalism, therefore, provides a strong challenge to the argument that democratic dialogue is distinct because of its dynamic nature. Allan's account of common law constitutionalism includes an account on inter-institutional interactions between the legislature, the judiciary, and the executive. These interactions occur both when the courts develop the common law and when they interpret legislation. In addition, his account of law, where law is interpretive, evolving over time as general principles are applied to specific facts arising in legal cases, is best understood as a dynamic account of the law. Democratic dialogue theories regard the resolution of rights-issues as evolving over time. In a similar manner, Allan argues that the answer to any legal question can only be determined by applying general principles to specific situations. The general principles may appear the same, but the resolution of rights-issues may evolve over time as these general principles are applied to a series of distinct factual situations.

[41] ibid, 7. [42] ibid, 7–8.

This example of a dynamic theory of legal constitutionalism, therefore, undermines the idea that democratic dialogue is distinct because it is dynamic. This dynamic component can only be a sufficient criterion of democratic dialogue if Allan's theory is really an example of democratic dialogue. However, this conclusion hints at the same difficulties we faced in the previous chapter. If democratic dialogue is distinct because it is dynamic, but we can find examples of legal constitutionalism that are also dynamic, then we may once again be faced with the conclusion that democratic dialogue is either non-existent or ubiquitous.

III. Dynamic Political Constitutionalism

The starting point for most evaluations of political constitutionalism is the seminal article of JAG Griffith, *The Political Constitution*.[43] Having coined the phrase 'the political constitution', Griffith's work has become synonymous with political constitutionalism. However, when we analyse his classic account of political constitutionalism and his later articles written in response to emerging theories of common law constitutionalism and calls for reform of the UK constitution, we can find clear evidence of a dynamic component. In his work, Griffith makes frequent reference to conflict in society. He states that there are continuing disagreements about controversial issues.[44] Debate and disagreement stem from his assessment that all societies are naturally authoritarian. This, in turn, derives from Griffith's account of the human condition. All humans are at one and the same time both individuals and social animals. For Griffith, this position 'sets up conflicts from which we can never be free'.[45] Conflict appears to be inevitable as, for humans to be able to live together in any society, they have to work together to achieve common desires. But as each individual desires different things, this gives rise to inevitable conflict and debate. The purpose of politics, and of law, is to perpetuate or to resolve, albeit temporarily, these debates.

There is nothing novel in recognizing that conflict is an essential element of Griffith's account of the political constitution. Carol Harlow,[46] Thomas Poole,[47] Graham Gee, and Grégoire Webber[48] and Christopher McCorkindale and Marco Goldoni[49] all recognize this. When we analyse Griffith's account of conflict we can see how his theory also includes a dynamic aspect of the generation of values and constitutional principles, although Griffith would not describe the outcomes of conflicts as either values or constitutional principles but as political claims that are legally recognized, or as the content of the constitution. Conflicts may give rise to temporary resolutions, but they are regarded by Griffith as what is and not what ought to be.

The dynamic role of conflict can be seen in Griffith's account of rights. One of Griffith's key arguments against legal constitutionalism is his claim that rights are best understood as political claims—'so-called human rights are no more and no less than

[43] JAG Griffith, 'The Political Constitution' (1979) 42 Modern Law Review 1.

[44] ibid, 12. [45] ibid, 3.

[46] C Harlow, 'The Political Constitution Reworked' in R Bigwood (ed), *Public Interest Litigation: New Zealand Experience in International Perspective* (New Zealand, Lexis Nexis 2006) 189.

[47] T Poole, 'Tilting at Windmills? Truth and Illusion in "The Political Constitution"' (2007) 70 Modern Law Review 250.

[48] G Gee and G Webb, 'What is a Political Constitution?' (2010) Oxford Journal of Legal Studies 273 and G Gee, 'The Political Constitutionalism of JAG Griffith' (2007) 28 Legal Studies 20.

[49] M Goldoni and C McCorkindale, 'Why We (Still) Need a Revolution' (2013) 14 German Law Journal 2197.

political claims made by individuals on those in authority'.[50] Each individual is able to make a political claim in favour of a right. If the individual has enough power, or joins with a sufficiently large group of other like-minded individuals, she may be able to persuade the legislature to enact legislation transforming her political claim into a legal right. The content of these legal rights changes over time as different groups gain different levels of power and as culture and morality change over time.[51]

Griffiths argues in addition that it is not only rights, but also that constitutions—in the sense of the rules that constitute the institutions of government and the relationship between the governors and the governed in a particular society—are dynamic in nature. They evolve over time. Moreover, their derivation illustrates the second aspect of a dynamic theory that we argued was a necessary criterion of a theory of democratic dialogue—the interaction between different institutions of the constitution.[52] Griffith regards constitutions as taking their shape from political upheavals and rival solutions to contentious disputes.[53] They also take their shape from the relationship between the different institutions of the constitution, in turn influenced by the personalities of those in office and the prevailing cultural and political attitudes.[54] For example, when reflecting on what was then the recent history of the UK constitution, Griffith argued that the government was most dominant in the immediate post-war period and through the Thatcher government of the 1980s, with Parliament being more dominant in the early 1960s and late 1970s and the judiciary growing in strength in the 1960s and declining in the 1980s and regaining its strength in the 1990s.[55] The inter-institutional dynamic reflects prevailing culture and the characteristics of the members of the institutions. Legally recognized rights, and the content of the rules regulating relations between institutions and between the governed and the governors, change over time as a result of the change in the nature of the relationships between governmental institutions.

It is also arguable that this aspect of conflict, and its dynamic generation of legal rights and the content of the constitution, is central to Griffith's account of political constitutionalism and to political constitutionalism more generally. Graham Gee argues that conflict is central to Griffith's version of the political constitution, stating that the recognition of the agonistic element of Griffith's account is key to understanding his theory.[56] Gee argues that Griffith regards conflict as inevitable, undeniable, and permanent. It is inevitable as it stems from the human condition itself. It is undeniable as it is clearly present in all political societies. It is permanent as any potential resolution of a conflict is only temporary, itself open to future change following further conflict and disagreement.[57] An understanding of the centrality of conflict to Griffith's account of the constitution is key to understanding how Griffith's theory appears to proscribe political over legal resolutions of conflicts, a prescriptive account of the constitution, whilst also stating that everything that happens in the UK constitution is, by definition, constitutional, a descriptive account. Gee argues that this potential contradiction is countered by Griffith's account of politics. Griffith advocates political resolution of conflicts because this is the accepted means of resolving conflicts. As such,

[50] Griffith (n 43) 19. [51] ibid, 12, 17, and 19.

[52] JAG Griffith, 'The Brave New World of Sir John Laws' [2000] 63 MLR 159, 165; and JAG Griffith, 'The Common Law and the Political Constitution' [2001] LQR 42, 42.

[53] Griffith, 'The Brave New World of Sir John Laws' (n 52) 176.

[54] Griffith, 'The Common Law and the Political Constitution' (n 52) 64. [55] ibid, 42.

[56] G Gee, 'The Political Constitutionalism of JAG Griffith' (2007) 28 Legal Studies 20.

[57] ibid, 23–27.

political mechanisms should still be used, provided that they remain an effective means of resolving conflicts and are themselves open to questioning and modification.[58]

Goldoni and McCorkindale go further, arguing that the centrality of conflict is key not only to understanding Griffith's account of political constitutionalism, but it is also a key component of political constitutionalism itself.[59] They argue that recent accounts of political constitutionalism, particularly the work of Tomkins and Bellamy, have focused too greatly on Parliament, examining constituted as opposed to constitutive power. Political constitutionalism needs to recognize the ability of the citizens, who hold constitutive power, to challenge current political arrangements. Conflict needs to be central to political constitutionalism, including the recognition of the power of the governed to challenge the institutional arrangements enjoyed by the governors.

Our examination of political constitutionalism, therefore, appears to lead to the same conclusion. Not only are there examples of dynamic accounts of political constitutionalism, but also there are arguments that dynamic interactions between institutions of the constitution are central to political constitutionalism. We cannot distinguish democratic dialogue from political or legal constitutionalism either by arguing that a dynamic component is unique to democratic dialogue, or by arguing that this dynamic component plays a more important role in democratic dialogue than it does in either legal or political constitutionalism.

IV. Conclusion

Our analysis of the dynamic component of democratic dialogue appears to have moved us no further in our search to define democratic dialogue as a distinct constitutional theory with its own unique account of the way in which the legislature and the judiciary should work together, dynamically, to protect human rights and to control the actions of the executive. Whilst inter-institutional interactions between the legislature and the judiciary, and the dynamic evolution of the resolution of rights-issues are clearly components of democratic dialogue, these are also found in accounts of both legal and political constitutionalism. Trevor Allan's account of legal constitutionalism contains similar dynamic elements, as does Griffith's theory of political constitutionalism. However, if this is the case, then, as with our assessment of the extent to which democratic dialogue differs from legal and political constitutionalism in terms of control, we appear to be reaching the conclusion that democratic dialogue is either non-existent, or ubiquitous. We either have to conclude that both Trevor Allan and JAG Griffith provide accounts of democratic dialogue, or that the accounts of democratic dialogue found in the academic literature do not provide a sufficiently clear and distinct constitutional theory.

[58] ibid, 44.

[59] Goldoni and McCorkindale (n 49).

3

Re-defining Democratic Dialogue

The previous two chapters criticized the general understanding that democratic dialogue provides a midway point between legal and political constitutionalism, advocating a combination of legal and political means of protecting human rights and controlling executive power through dynamic interactions between the legislature and the judiciary. The first chapter argued that, when analysed more closely, theories of political and legal constitutionalism appeared to merge, leaving the suspicion that either the label of democratic dialogue was ubiquitous, capable of applying to any account of constitutions, drawn from theories of both legal and political constitutionalism, or that the theory of democratic dialogue was non-existent, there being no middle ground between legal and political constitutionalism for it to occupy. Moreover, we discovered that there were theories of both legal and political constitutionalism which advocated inter-institutional interactions. Whilst a dynamic component may be necessary for any theory of democratic dialogue, its existence in any account of the constitution is not sufficient to classify that theory as an example of democratic dialogue. This seems a rather depressing start for a book which aims to examine, and defend, a distinct account of democratic dialogue.

Despite the problems which arise when we try and discover an account of democratic dialogue in terms of control, this chapter will argue that democratic dialogue is capable of providing a unique account of constitutionalism. However, we need to take care as to the extent of this claim. Any account of democratic dialogue has to come to terms with the fact that the distinction between legal and political constitutionalism is vague. Any account of a 'middle ground' to be occupied by democratic dialogue, therefore, will always appear to merge with either political or legal constitutionalism. When we assess legal constitutionalism or political constitutionalism, we come across an array of accounts of the constitution. It is hard to see these accounts as anything other than broad schools of thought—sometimes it is hard to see these broad schools of thought as anything other than a form of myth or ideology, or an account of fictional groups that do not really exist.[1] Similar problems arise when we try to define democratic dialogue. We are faced with an array of accounts which draw on ideas from both legal and political constitutionalism and, as we discussed in the Introduction when analysing the accounts of Nicol and Hickman regarding the Human Rights Act 1998, there are divergent accounts of democratic dialogue.

This chapter will argue that an account of democratic dialogue has value and can help to resolve some of the questions surrounding the relative role of the judiciary and the legislature when protecting human rights. However, again, it is important at this stage to take care over the modest nature of these claims. This chapter will not argue that an account of democratic dialogue is a form of holy grail. It does not provide a miraculous means of squaring the circle, automatically resolving all of the issues surrounding which institution is best suited to protecting human rights. It is also important to

[1] See, for example, P Craig, *UK, EU and Global Administrative Law* (Cambridge University Press 2015) 96–103.

recognize that, just as with legal and political constitutionalism, democratic dialogue is a broad church and there can be different theories of democratic dialogue in the same way that there can be different theories of legal and political constitutionalism. This chapter, therefore, will lay the ground for developing a distinct account of democratic dialogue, whilst recognizing its modest claims, with later chapters providing a specific account of democratic dialogue and applying this to the UK constitution.

In order to explain how democratic dialogue can be sufficiently distinct to operate as an account of constitutionalism which is different from both legal and political constitutionalism, we need to revisit another possible means of distinguishing between legal and political constitutionalism which also recognizes the inherent vagueness between the theories, but which can nevertheless provide the seeds of explaining how democratic dialogue can add to the current literature and help to resolve current constitutional issues. A possible understanding of the difference between political and legal constitutionalism depends not upon a preference for political or legal controls, but arises at a more abstract level, stemming from different assumptions. I will argue that this analysis runs the risk of pushing definitions of legal and political constitutionalism to extreme poles, thus artificially providing a middle ground to be occupied by democratic dialogue. Nevertheless, it provides an insight as to how the difference between these theories is based on a different starting point, meaning that theorists classified as advocating either legal or political constitutionalism focus on different questions, albeit often reaching similar solutions.

It is the case that democratic dialogue starts from different assumptions from legal and political constitutionalism and that it asks distinct questions. Political constitutionalists start with an assessment of political controls, focusing on the value of democracy. This does not mean that they reject the value of legal controls, or of liberal principles. However, it means that they focus predominantly on strengthening democratic controls, linking in an assessment of legal controls which supplement political controls. Legal constitutionalists start with an assessment of legal controls, examining how courts control the executive or the legislature. They do not dismiss the value of democracy or of democratic controls by the legislature over the judiciary. Indeed, they advocate the modification of legal controls to take account of those situations in which there are good reasons for preferring political controls. Democratic dialogue, however, has a different focus. It shifts away from merely asking whether we should use legal or political controls and asks a further question—how should these legal and political controls interact with one another? Democratic dialogue builds on existing accounts of institutional advantages of legal and political controls and asks whether there is value in encouraging interactions between these two forms of control, and if so, which types of interaction are more or less capable of achieving these values?

This different starting point also requires an examination of different forms of inter-institutional interactions, distinguished according to their purpose. The chapter will argue that there are two forms of inter-institutional interactions that are necessary components of an account of democratic dialogue: constitutional counter-balancing and constitutional collaboration. Constitutional counter-balancing mechanisms are required in accounts of democratic dialogue in order to ensure that effective dialogue can take place between institutions. For dialogue to occur, it must not be the case that either the legislature or the court can always have the final word. Constitutional counter-balancing mechanisms are designed to ensure that this does not occur. Constitutional collaboration mechanisms are required to facilitate one of the normative advantages of democratic dialogue—the achievement of a better resolution of rights-issues through combining the reasoning processes of both the legislature and the judiciary. These mechanisms aim to provide a means through which the legislature and the judiciary may work together to achieve a better and more legitimate resolution of a rights-issue.

I. Constitutional Foundational Assumptions

Constitutional theories do not emerge from the ether. Nor are they found in a vacuum. They are normally based upon an assessment of current practice, case law, or a reflection on normative values. Moreover, these theories often contain latent, or sometimes explained, assumptions upon which these theories are based. We have already looked at assumptions when discussing the differences between legal and political constitutionalism. Waldron, for example, provides a justification for rejecting a strong, constitutional protection of rights which is based on four key assumptions:

(i) That democratic institutions in a State are in reasonably good working order
(ii) That the judicial institutions of the State are in reasonably good working order
(iii) That there is a general commitment both amongst officials and the citizens of a particular State to protect human rights
(iv) That there exists reasonable disagreement as to the content of rights.[2]

All of these assumptions are made at a very general and abstract level. This, in turn, means that it can be reasonable to disagree about whether these assumptions are met. How many instances of either the democratic or the judicial institutions of the state failing to act in an acceptable manner, for example, are required before a conclusion is reached that either the first or the second of Waldron's assumptions has not been met?

It is also easy to understand how different assumptions, and different conclusions about whether assumptions have been met, can explain the differences between legal and political constitutionalism that were explored in the first chapter. In the first chapter, for example, we examined the differences between Jeremy Waldron's rejection of a legal protection of human rights and the accounts of Richard Fallon and Matthias Kumm, who argued in favour of a legal protection of human rights. Fallon accepts Waldron's four main assumptions. However, he adds to these a further assumption; that courts may sometimes be better at recognizing certain types of errors which may be made by the legislature when enacting legislation which may harm human rights. This is because courts and legislatures reason about rights in different ways. Fallon combines this observation with two further assumptions: that it is better for rights to be over- as opposed to under-protected and that rights are harmed more greatly by legislation than by a lack of legislation. These differences lead Fallon to conclude in favour of a constitutional protection of rights.[3] Kumm shares Fallon's concerns. His account of legislative pathologies—where he argues for example that legislatures may err on the side of protecting cultural traditions without examining the reasons behind these traditions whereas courts are more likely to look for rational justifications for restrictions on rights—questions Waldron's first assumption.[4]

[2] J Waldron, 'The Core of the Case Against Judicial Review' (2006) 115 Yale Law Journal 1346.

[3] R Fallon, 'The Core of an Uneasy Case for Judicial Review' (2008) 121 Harvard Law Review 1693.

[4] M Kumm, 'Institutionalising Socratic Contestation: the Rationalists Human Rights Paradigm, Legitimate Authority and the Point of Judicial Review' (2007) 1 European Journal of Legal Studies 1 and 'Democracy is not Enough: Rights, Proportionality and the Point of Judicial Review' (2009) New York University Public Law and Legal Theory Working Papers, Paper 118, 1.

The different assumptions underpinning the accounts of Fallon and Waldron lead them to reach radically different conclusions as to the normative value of a strong, constitutional protection of human rights where courts can strike down legislation which breaches human rights. We could also interpret the difference between Waldron and Kumm as illustrating a reliance on different assumptions. Kumm is arguably questioning whether a general reasonably good working order is sufficient to justify the power of the legislature to legislate in a manner which is unchecked by the judiciary. Even when the legislature is operating to a reasonably good working order, legislative pathologies may occur that question the ability of the legislature to protect human rights. Kumm's rationalist human rights perspective does not argue that courts are necessarily better than the legislature at protecting human rights more generally. Instead Kumm explains how, adopting his different assumption, courts are required to counteract legislative pathologies through the application of the proportionality test which focuses on analysing the justifications provided for any legislation which potentially restricts human rights.

The difference between these theories may also be accounted for as differences in the facts required to establish the accuracy of the assumptions on which these theories are based. Waldron's theory is a more general, abstract account than Kumm's theory. When faced with precise examples that challenge his assumptions, Waldron might change his analysis, or reach a contrary conclusion with regard to a particular state. This can be illustrated by the debate surrounding the re-introduction of a blanket ban for prisoners in New Zealand. Andrew Geddis, for example, concludes that the debate on the Bill to reintroduce the blanket ban on prisoner voting in New Zealand did not satisfy Waldron's criteria of a minimal deliberative threshold.[5] In particular, Geddis points out that the Bill was sent to the wrong committee,[6] that the committee recommended the Bill, despite receiving fifty-one submissions from the public against the Bill and only two submissions in favour,[7] and that there was a lack of engagement in the debate at the committee stage.[8] In addition the Bill became law by a very narrow majority (sixty-three votes to fifty-nine at the first reading; sixty-three to fifty-five at the second reading; sixty-four to fifty-seven at the committee stage; and sixty-three to fifty-eighty at the third reading), with the ACT party supporting the National Party, despite no member of ACT specifically speaking in favour of adopting the legislation.[9] It is also hard to find evidence of statements of clear reasoning in favour of the Bill. Paul Quinn for example, who introduced the Private Members' Bill, based its provisions on a feeling that he was acting in favour of the wishes of his constituents and of the need to be seen to be tough on crime. Little if any response was given by the supporters of the Bill to rational arguments pointing out weaknesses in the legislation; for example its potential differential impact on aboriginal populations and the disparities that would arise with regard to individuals who committed the same crime, but where one received home detention, and so would be able to vote, and the other a prison sentence, losing the right to vote. The differential treatment here would be due to the different nature of their family circumstances and not due to the serious, or otherwise, nature of their crime.

Waldron has also been critical of the New Zealand legislative process in general.[10] Could these facts about how the New Zealand legislature introduced its blanket ban on

[5] A Geddis, 'Prisoner Voting and Rights Deliberation: How New Zealand's Parliament Failed' [2011] New Zealand Law Review 443.

[6] ibid, 463. [7] ibid, 464. [8] ibid, 466. [9] ibid, 467.

[10] J Waldron, 'Compared to What? Judicial Activism and New Zealand's Parliament' [2005] New Zealand Law Journal 441.

prisoner voting cause Waldron to argue that New Zealand no longer met his assumptions, challenging the lack of a strong protection of human rights in New Zealand, or would Waldron require more evidence showing that this example was fairly typical of the way in which New Zealand enacts legislation to conclude that it did not have legislative processes which operate at a reasonable standard? Maybe the only difference between Kumm and Waldron, if they were to focus on this example from New Zealand, would be that Kumm would conclude that the New Zealand experience illustrated a specific legislative pathology which the court could correct, justifying judicial review. Waldron, however, might conclude that one example of a particular legislative pathology is not enough to challenge his general argument against a constitutional protection of judicial review. Legislatures may make mistakes, but they still do generally work well and provide a better protection of rights than the courts, even when courts are working reasonably well.

Differences in facts and their evaluation may also explain Tomkins' account of judicial review over executive powers. The first chapter recognized that, although Tomkins is a political constitutionalist and presents his argument as to the extent of judicial control over the executive as stemming from political constitutionalism, Tomkins also accepts that the United Kingdom is best described as a mixed constitution. This potential shift in his theory is probably best explained as a change in the facts about the UK constitution leading to a different, more general conclusion as to the state of the UK constitution. The adoption of the Human Rights Act 1998, for example, with its greater political scrutiny through the work of the Joint Committee on Human Rights, in addition to the greater legal controls over the executive in section 6 and the legislature through sections 3 and 4 of the Act, illustrate a move towards what Tomkins would refer to as a 'mixed' constitution. This, in turn, influences Tomkins' account of judicial review. Although originally critical of the way in which courts intruded on executive decisions, Tomkins is more willing to accept recent, more restrained examples of judicial review.[11] However, he is still wary of 'the twin constitutional dangers of parliamentary under-performance and judicial power-grabbing'.[12] It is not that his theory has changed. Rather, a change in the facts about the UK constitution means the account of judicial review from the perspective of political constitutionalism has changed.

This discussion of assumptions helps us to understand one possible, but ultimately flawed way, in which we might distinguish between legal and political constitutionalism, whose exploration can help to pave a better understanding of the relationship between legal and political constitutionalism and the contribution that could be made by an account of democratic dialogue. A possible way of arguing that there can be a clear distinction between legal and political constitutionalism, with a distinct middle ground which can be occupied by democratic dialogue, is based upon the argument that assumptions are playing a bigger role than merely providing an account of factual premises upon which a normative conclusion rests. Rather, the assumption plays a foundational or organizing role. I will refer to this as a constitutional foundational assumption, in order to distinguish this as a specific form of assumption. It could be argued that legal and political constitutionalism are based on different constitutional foundational assumptions. A constitutional foundational assumption is a specific type of assumption. It is an assumption which aims to provide a normative foundation for a

[11] A Tomkins, 'What's Left of the Political Constitution?' (2013) 14 German Law Journal 2275, 2275–80.

[12] ibid, 2280.

constitutional theory, the assumption being used to justify other aspects of a particular constitutional theory.

Waldron refers to assumptions in order to clarify the extent of the application of his argument. He argues that, if and only if the four assumptions he mentions are satisfied, then there are good reasons against establishing a strong constitutional protection of human rights. His theory rests on the ability to provide sufficient evidence to demonstrate the plausibility of applying these assumptions to a particular legal system. To the extent that this evidence is not provided, Waldron's conclusion against strong, constitutional protections of human rights by the judiciary loses its justification when applied to a particular legal system. The assumptions on which Waldron's account rests need to be rationally sound in order to support the justification of his conclusion. A constitutional foundational assumption goes further. If Waldron's assumptions were to form a constitutional foundational assumption, then evidence would need to be provided to demonstrate the plausibility of the reasonably good working order of the legislature and the judiciary, the general commitment to the protection of human rights and that it was reasonable to disagree about the content of rights. However, these premises would not need to be proved to be true. Rather, sufficient evidence would need to be provided that these four premises were plausible; that the assumptions were rationally sound.

A constitutional foundational assumption is 'foundational' as it grounds a particular model of the constitution. What I mean by this is that other aspects of a constitutional model are derived from, or are justified through, their connection to the constitutional foundational assumption. For example, when examining Fallon's argument in favour of constitutional review in the first chapter, we discussed Fallon's libertarian presumption. This presumption argues that more harm occurs to the protection of human rights in a particular society when there is too much legislation, than when there is too little legislation. Fallon derives his argument in favour of judicial review from this principle.[13] Both the courts and the legislature can play a role in the protection of human rights and both may make mistakes when protecting rights. However, once we accept the libertarian presumption, an argument can be made in favour of allowing courts to have the power to strike down legislation. The consequence of allowing courts to strike down legislation is that legislation may be struck down when the court mistakenly believes that the legislation breaches a right. However, given the libertarian presumption, the cost of striking this legislation down is smaller than the cost of not striking legislation down, which may mean that the court fails to strike down legislation that harms human rights. Fallon's conclusion of the case for a strong, constitutional protection of rights is justified by the libertarian presumption. In this sense, the presumption is acting as a foundation for his argument in favour of a strong constitutional protection of human rights. It is also important to recognize that this presumption is an assumption. It is assumed that the harm from striking down legislation is greater than the harm which comes from legislation which may harm human rights. However, this is not self-evidently true and may not reflect reality in every legal system. It is at least arguable, for example, that striking down legislation sanctioning reverse discrimination designed to ensure that there were more female Chief Executive Officers of the companies listed on the FTSE 100, because this was seen to breach equality by giving women an unfair advantage, may be more likely to harm the protection of human rights than allowing the legislation to stand.

[13] R Fallon, 'The Core of an Uneasy Case for Judicial Review' (2008) 121 Harvard Law Review 1693.

Another way of understanding what it means for a constitutional foundational assumption to be 'foundational' is to draw on its similarity with, and differences from, Kelsen's Grudnorm. Kelsen's theory of jurisprudence argues that each norm in a legal system can be derived from a higher norm in the legal system. The highest norm in that legal system derives its validity from the Grundnorm. For Kelsen, the Grundnorm was a fiction. If it has a particular content, it is an assumption as to the legitimacy of the makers of the constitution or of the law in a particular legal system.[14] Like a Grundnorm, a constitutional foundational assumption can be referred back to in order to establish the validity of a more specific principle. Also, in common with some interpretations of the Grundnorm, a constitutional foundational assumption is a presumption. However, unlike a Kelsenian Grundnorm it is not a fiction. The presumption underpinning a constitutional foundational assumption needs to be plausible. In this sense it is related to facts about the world. In addition, a constitutional foundational assumption is not a presumption as to the legitimacy of the authors of a law or of a constitution.

In playing this foundational or organizing rule, the assumption is acting as a normative principle. Understood in this sense, a constitutional foundational assumption is not merely providing a plausible generalization of the facts. Rather, the constitutional foundational assumption has an evaluative or normative component. It is not a description of what is, but is an assertion of what ought to be. Again, this may be best explained through an example. The first chapter investigated the distinction between legal and political constitutionalism and, in doing so, drew on accounts of common law constitutionalism. However, although common law constitutionalism is used to classify a particular approach to the role of the courts in the control of the executive and of the protection of human rights, it is a broad term that includes a wide range of theories. Paul Craig, for example, is seen as a leading advocate of common law constitutionalism. However, there is a big difference between Craig's approach and that found in the early work of Sir John Laws, another key advocate of common law constitutionalism. The difference between these theories turns, at least in part, on the extent to which each theorist is providing a normative or a descriptive account of the UK constitution.

Craig's account of common law constitutionalism is based on arguments as to the nature of the UK constitution. If courts have the power to develop principles of judicial review under the common law, it is because this is an accurate description of the powers of English courts in the UK constitution. English courts, save for the Supreme Court, are courts of inherent jurisdiction. As such, they can determine the scope of their own powers through developing the common law. This extends to the power to use the common law to develop principles of judicial review. There can be no normative difference between courts developing the common law to provide for principles of judicial review and courts developing the common law to provide for the principles which regulate private law—for example, through developing the laws of real property or the principles of tort law.

Sir John Laws' earlier work argued that courts should have the ability to protect human rights because of his commitment to Platonic principles.[15] Laws is making a normative assertion as to the value of liberal principles that underpin democracy and should override simple majoritarian decision-making. This constitutional foundational

[14] H Kelsen, *Pure Theory of Law*, M Knight (trans) (2nd edn, University of California Press 1967) Chapter 1.

[15] J Laws, 'Law and Democracy' [1995] Public Law 72.

assumption grounds his argument for judicial review. Craig, on the other hand, is not deriving his account of common law constitutionalism from an evaluation of how the courts should exercise their powers, but on an account of the powers the English courts have in the UK constitution. This is not to argue that Craig does not believe that it is right for the courts to have the power to review actions of the executive so as to comply with common law principles. It is rather to recognize the different nature of the argument Craig is making in support of judicial review in his academic writings on English administrative law. Courts should have the power to develop principles of judicial review, because as a matter of English constitutional law, courts have inherent authority and historical evidence supports their long-standing power to develop the law in terms of the development of both public and private law. Craig then provides other arguments for why he believes that there is normative value in allowing courts to check the power of the executive. However, Craig's argument is not designed to provide a strong normative justification of judicial review as a whole, but rather an account of why courts have the power to develop these principles as a matter of English constitutional law.

This account may explain how a constitutional foundational assumption is foundational. It is also important to note that constitutional foundational assumptions have normative value and that these normative values are used to justify specific conclusions. A constitutional foundational assumption is constitutional purely in a descriptive sense. A constitutional foundational assumption grounds a theory about constitutions. By this I mean a theory about how we should distribute and exercise governmental powers and who should control the exercise of these governmental powers. In particular, this book has been investigating which institution should play a primary role in controlling actions of the executive and in protecting human rights. However, a constitutional foundational assumption need not be limited to these aspects of constitutional law.

The next section will investigate whether it is plausible to delineate between legal and political constitutionalism because they use different constitutional foundational assumptions, with constitutional foundational assumptions being understood as different normative assumptions which organize political and legal constitutionalism and which are then used to provide different justifications for the conclusions reached by these different theories as to whether the courts or the legislature should play the predominant role when controlling executive power or protecting human rights. If this is true, does this provide a means of providing a distinct account of democratic dialogue, which is based on a different constitutional foundational assumption? The section will argue that this too breaks down, again leading to the danger that democratic dialogue is non-existent or ubiquitous. Nevertheless, it provides our most fruitful means of explaining how democratic dialogue can add to current accounts of political and legal constitutionalism.

II. Does Democratic Dialogue Rest on a Different Constitutional Foundational Assumption?

In order to assess whether democratic dialogue rests on a different constitutional foundational assumption than legal and political constitutionalism, we need to revisit our analysis of the distinction between legal and political constitutionalism based on control, which we examined in Chapter 1. A good starting place is Sir John Laws' most recent account of common law constitutionalism and his assessment of good principles of constitutionalism.[16] Laws argues that a good constitution aims to find a balance between two moralities: the morality of law and the morality of government. The morality of law refers to the good of personal autonomy and the protection of the rights of the individual. The morality of government looks to the good of the people as a whole, often using principles of utilitarianism to maximize the good of all.[17] Laws argues that this more abstract account of the different moralities of law and government is reflected in more concrete disputes. With regard to disputes in the UK constitution, it is reflected in assessments as to whether the UK constitution has shifted away from a political towards a legal constitution as well as being reflective of the even more concrete issue as to whether there is a need for a strong, constitutional or a purely political protection of human rights. Different theorists reach different conclusions as to whether human rights should be protected predominantly through legal or political means as they rely to varying extents on the morality of law or the morality of government.

A similar argument is found in Dyzenhaus' account of the culture of justification. The first chapter explained Dyzenhaus' aim to provide an account of constitutionalism that was able to resolve the tension between the culture of reflection and the culture of neutrality.[18] Both the culture of reflection and the culture of neutrality are understood at an abstract level. The culture of reflection is based on the assumption that legislation reflects the wishes of the people. As such, it advocates an account of political constitutionalism given the greater claim to legitimacy of legislation. Legislation reflects the wishes of the electorate as a whole. Judicial decisions do not. The culture of neutrality is based on the need to protect a series of liberal values. The culture of neutrality accepts that these liberal values underpin democracy and override simple majoritarian calculations as to the wishes of the people. As such, the judiciary, who are better able to identify and protect these liberal principles, should be responsible for protecting human rights, which reflect these liberal principles, from intrusion by the legislature. The culture of neutrality, therefore, underpins accounts of legal constitutionalism.

Other discussions which operate at a similar abstract level focus on ideas of sovereignty. We recognized in Chapter 1 that one area of dispute between legal and political constitutionalism turned on the interpretation of seminal cases from the seventeenth century.[19] Jeffrey Goldsworthy provides a different account of the same case law. He distinguishes between royalist, parliamentarian, and common law theories. These theories are differentiated from each other in terms of their account of sovereignty. For royalists, sovereignty was vested in the monarch. For parliamentarians, sovereignty was with the people, represented through Parliament. For common lawyers, sovereignty was vested in the common law, which in turn created and restricted the powers of the King. Arguably, political constitutionalists base their constitutional theory upon preserving the sovereignty of the people, represented by Parliament, whereas legal constitutionalists vest sovereignty in the law, either expressed through principles of the common law or through a constitutional document.

These more abstract analyses hint at a further distinction between political and legal constitutionalism. Political constitutionalism could be connected to Laws' account of the morality of government, and Goldsworthy's analysis of the sovereignty

[16] J Laws, 'The Good Constitution' (2012) 71 Cambridge Law Journal 567.

[17] Ibid, 572–73.

[18] D Dyzenhaus, 'Law as Justification: Etienne Mureinik's Conception of Legal Culture' (1998) 14 South African Journal of Human Rights 11.

[19] PP Craig, 'Prerogative, Precedent and Power' in C Forsyth and I Hare (eds), *The Golden Metwand and the Crooked Cord: Essays in Honour of Sir William Wade QC* (Oxford University Press 1998) 65; and A Tomkins, *Our Republican Constitution* (Oxford, Hart 2005).

of Parliament, or of the sovereignty of the people who had vested their sovereignty in Parliament as a body representing the will of the people. Legal constitutionalism, on the other hand, could be connected to Laws' account of the morality of law and Goldworthy's account of the sovereignty in the common law. These connections reflect different constitutional foundational assumptions.

A. Re-evaluating the difference between legal and political constitutionalism

Keith Ewing's most recent account of political constitutionalism helps to demonstrate how examining the difference between legal and political constitutionalism in terms of competing constitutional foundational assumptions could provide a more accurate account of these competing theories.[20] Ewing's account of political constitutionalism clarifies the constitutional foundational assumption on which political constitutionalism is based. His version of political constitutionalism is based on the constitutional foundational assumption of the sovereignty of Parliament. Ewing states that '[t]he legal principle of the sovereignty of Parliament provides both the source of legal authority and the source of legal restraint of the power of government in a political constitution'.[21] When referring to the sovereignty of Parliament, Ewing is not referring to Dicey's account of a legal rule, or determining whether, as a matter of English law, Parliament can or cannot bind its successors. Instead, Ewing is drawing on the normative force of the sovereignty of Parliament. Parliament, for all its faults, is the institution best designed to represent the will of the people. The sovereignty of Parliament reflects the ideology of popular sovereignty. In Ewing's words:

> the legal principle of parliamentary sovereignty—as the core legal principle of the political constitution—evolved in such a way as to become no more and no less than the legal principle underpinning the political principle that in a democracy there should be no legal limit to the wishes of the people.[22]

The political principle of democracy, expressed as a lack of legal limits on the wishes of the people, is foundational. The legal principle of parliamentary sovereignty is necessary to ensure courts adhere to the political principle. The political and legal principles are expressions of the constitutional foundational assumption that Parliament, as the institution designed to express the wishes of the people, should have the ultimate authority in a particular constitution. The role of the courts is to ensure that legislation is enacted according to the rules Parliament itself establishes for the enactment of valid legislation. In this way courts enforce the constitutional foundational assumption of parliamentary sovereignty by ensuring that only Parliament, as Parliament itself has decided to establish itself, is able to enact legally valid legislation.[23] Where there are legal controls of the courts over the executive, these should also have the aim of facilitating popular sovereignty. Legal controls should focus more clearly on ensuring that there is effective participation in the democratic process, as well as facilitating accountability and representation.[24]

[20] K Ewing, 'The Resilience of the Political Constitution' (2013) 14 German Law Journal 2111.
[21] ibid, 2118. [22] ibid.
[23] For a similar defence of the manner and form account of parliamentary sovereignty, see M Gordon, *Parliamentary Sovereignty in the UK Constitution: Process, Politics and Democracy* (Oxford, Hart 2015).
[24] Ewing (n 20) 2135.

In contrast, Ewing argues that legal constitutionalism rests on an assumption of the normative value or sovereignty of fundamental principles. Some legal constitutionalists regard these principles as capable of underpinning democracy. As such, these principles should not be removed by simple majoritarian decision-making.[25] Others recognize the value of fundamental principles, but do not advocate that these principles should override legislation. This may be because their accounts are descriptive of common law constitutionalism as it is understood in the United Kingdom.[26] Other theories are based on a description of law as an interpretative concept which requires judges and academics to engage in assessments of how fundamental principles apply to specific facts arising in each different case before the courts, recognizing that, currently, the law of the United Kingdom does not conclusively empower the judiciary to strike down legislation contrary to fundamental principles of the common law.[27] The need to balance fundamental principles and democracy, and how this balance should occur, may depend upon the particular constitution to which this is applied.[28] Legal constitutionalism entails a commitment to normative fundamental principles, however defined, which underpin the law. These principles justify the ability of courts to provide a control over the executive, independent of their controls to ensure the executive only acts within the proper confines of its power as defined by the legislature. These principles may also, for some legal constitutionalists, justify empowering the judiciary to strike down legislation, either through the means of an entrenched constitution or through the enforcement of fundamental principles of the common law.

The recognition of these divergent constitutional foundational assumptions appears to provide a better delineation between legal and political constitutionalism than a focus on whether a theory advocates a preference for legal or political protections of human rights and legal or political controls over executive powers. For example, linking political constitutionalism to its constitutional foundational assumption of popular sovereignty, giving rise to a legal principle of the sovereignty of Parliament, can help to explain Tomkins' account of the role of the courts in a political constitution and the way in which this is distinct from accounts based on legal constitutionalism. Courts ensure that the executive has proper legal authority by examining whether its actions are within the scope of its authority as established by legislation. When protecting absolute rights, courts are again enforcing popular sovereignty. The legislature enacts valid legislation reflecting the wishes of the people, concretizing a particular right. Courts protect the right as expressed in the legislative provision, thereby protecting the wishes of the people. This may seem to give the courts too great a power, given ambiguities and vagueness that arise in legal language. However, political constitutionalists would argue that courts should exercise their powers in line with the constitutional foundational assumption of democracy, parliamentary sovereignty, or popular sovereignty. As such, courts should aim to determine the will of Parliament when interpreting legislation. Where this is not possible, perhaps different remedies can be used, as is the case with

[25] Laws n 15; J Laws, 'The Constitution: Morals and Rights' [1996] Public Law 622; and J Jowell, 'Beyond the Rule of Law: Towards Constitutional Review' [2000] Public Law 671.

[26] PP Craig, 'Competing Models of Judicial Review' [1999] Public Law 428; PP Craig and N Bamforth, 'Constitutional Analysis, Constitutional Principle and Judicial Review' [2001] PL 763; PP Craig 'The Common Law, Shared Power and Judicial Review' (2004) 24 Oxford Journal of Legal Studies 237; and Craig (n 1) 125–55.

[27] TRS Allan, *Law, Liberty and Justice* (Oxford University Press 1994); TRS Allan, *Constitutional Justice: A Liberal Theory of the Rule of Law* (Oxford University Press 2003); and TRS Allan, *The Sovereignty of Law: Freedom, Constitution and Common Law* (Oxford University Press 2013).

[28] Laws (n 16); and J Laws, *The Common Law Constitution* (Cambridge University Press 2014).

section 4, allowing courts to give their interpretation as to whether legislation breaches Convention rights, whilst leaving the final authoritative voice to Parliament. That way, the sovereignty of the people can prevail, as Parliament has the opportunity to more clearly express those wishes in its response to a decision of the court.

The same is true of the control of the court over executive actions. The legislature remains free to respond to court decisions, overturning the decision of the courts should this be required to ensure that the executive only acts within the sphere of its powers as determined by the legislature and not by the courts.[29] Although these controls may appear to collapse, or to closely resemble principles of judicial review advocated by legal constitutionalism, the legal principle of the sovereignty of Parliament, understood as an expression of the political principle of popular sovereignty, provides a different justification for these legal controls. Moreover, this legal principle restricts the way in which the powers of the court are exercised.

In a similar manner, reference to the constitutional foundational assumption of popular sovereignty underpinning political constitutionalism can be used to distinguish Tomkins' account of the application of proportionality from that of Kumm. In Chapter 1, it was suggested that the only distinction between the two theories may be as to the breadth of the inquiry when applying proportionality, suggesting that the difference between the theories may merely be one of degree. Kumm's theory is broader, allowing the courts to examine, through the series of questions established by the four-stage proportionality test, whether the actions of the legislature or executive are justifiable in the abstract. Tomkins' focus appeared to be more specific, requiring the courts to assess whether the reasons provided by the executive to justify its actions were justifiable. Tomkins' focus is narrower given the need to ensure that courts exercise controls over the executive in accordance with popular sovereignty. By focusing on an assessment of whether the reasons provided by the executive are justifiable, rather than a broader assessment of the issues, there is less of a risk that courts will use their own assessment of the merits of a decision as the context from which to assess whether the decision of the executive is justifiable. Courts are restricting their analysis in proportionality decisions in order to preserve the sovereignty of Parliament. No such concern limits the approach to proportionality provided by Kumm.

A focus on constitutional foundational assumptions, therefore, may provide a means of explaining why political and legal constitutionalism are distinct, even though both may advocate a combination of political and legal controls over the executive and a combination of legal and political means of protecting human rights. Although a clear delineation between these two theories may not be clear from their analysis of the legal and political controls which they advocate, their reasoning for these conclusions is distinct because it is based on differing constitutional foundational assumptions. If this is the case, does this mean that we can provide a distinct constitutional foundational assumption of democratic dialogue which occupies the middle ground between legal and political constitutionalism?

B. Democratic dialogue: occupying the middle ground?

The above discussion appears to provide a better means of distinguishing between legal and political constitutionalism, thus providing us with a means of providing a distinct account of democratic dialogue which does not run the risk of making democratic

[29] See, for example, *Burmah Oil Company Ltd v Lord Advocate* [1965] AC 75 and the War Damages Act 1965. See also the discussion in Chapter 4.

dialogue ubiquitous or non-existent. However, it is important to recognize the dangers of this approach. To delineate between legal constitutionalism, political constitutionalism, and democratic dialogue in this manner runs a similar risk of imagining legal and political constitutionalism as distinct poles, a middle ground only being occupied by democratic dialogue as this middle ground has been artificially created by providing overly narrow and artificial accounts of legal and political constitutionalism. Nevertheless, an understanding of constitutional foundational assumptions helps to provide a means of understanding why theories of political constitutionalism, legal constitutionalism, and democratic dialogue appear to blend into one another. If we are to provide a normative account of democratic dialogue, then we need to recognize its connection to legal and political constitutionalism. Its distinct nature stems from its different starting point. It aims to examine inter-institutional interactions, drawing on the different constitutional foundational assumptions of legal and political constitutionalism in order to provide a more detailed normative framework of inter-institutional interactions.

In order to make this argument, we must first explain why it would be wrong to argue that we can distinguish between legal constitutionalism, political constitutionalism, and democratic dialogue because they are based on different constitutional foundational assumptions. Whilst legal constitutionalism regards liberal normative principles as more important than democracy, political constitutionalism regards democracy as more important than liberal normative principles. Democratic dialogue arguably embraces both, claiming that neither is more important than the other. It can thus appear to occupy a clear middle ground between legal and political constitutionalism.

It is easy to explain why this account is incorrect. At the beginning of this section, we referred to the arguments of Sir John Laws and David Dyzenhaus in order to explain the possible different constitutional foundational assumptions of legal and political constitutionalism. Laws refers to a tension between two political moralities.[30] One morality rests on the autonomy of the individual. The other rests on the good of society as a whole. These two moralities are presented in an abstract manner. The morality of the autonomy of the individual is reflected in Kantian philosophy and the recognition of fundamental rights. The morality of the good of society as a whole is reflected in principles of utilitarianism, as found in Bentham's account of the law. If we were to use this as a means of delineating between the constitutional foundational assumptions of legal and political constitutionalism, then we would expect to find that John Laws, a prime example of a common law constitutionalist, would argue for the supremacy of the morality of the autonomy of the individual. However, when we examine his later work, we realize this is not the case. Laws argues that these two moralities are in tension with one another. Neither one morality nor the other should form the basis of a constitution, but both.

These tensions are replicated when we analyse the constitution in a less abstract manner, concentrating on specific tensions between human rights and calculations of social welfare, or between the institutions designed to protect rights and the public good. For example, tensions between the protection of individual rights and the protection of democracy are reflections of the tension between individual autonomy and the need to promote the good of society as a whole. Fundamental and human rights are frequently based on principles of personal autonomy. These individual rights can clash with policies designed to protect the greater good, as expressed through democratic

[30] Laws (n 160) and *The Common Law Constitution* (n 28).

settlements of competing interests. In turn, courts are the institution charged predominantly with the protection of fundamental rights. The legislature is the institution charged with protecting the good of society as a whole.

Laws LJ argues that a good constitution 'requires that the two political moralities are in harmony; each of them served to the least prejudice of the other'.[31] Each needs to be given substantial weight in the good constitution, with neither having the ability to expunge the powers of the other.[32] This is not only to balance out the competing tensions between the courts and the legislature, but also to protect against the inherent weaknesses of each. Laws provides no specific prescription of how the tension between these two is to be resolved, regarding each state as balancing these different tensions in different ways, dependent upon its own particular circumstances.[33] This account is compatible with a constitutional foundational assumption resting on the tension between fundamental principles—the political morality of personal autonomy and the political morality of the good of society as a whole. Laws LJ is recognizing the tension between these two principles, as well as recognizing the need for balance and interaction between the legislature and the courts.

We reach a similar conclusion when we analyse David Dyzenhaus' account of the culture of justification. It too can be explained as resting on a constitutional foundational assumption which recognizes the value of both popular sovereignty and the protection of fundamental rights, with neither one nor the other having the ability to usurp the other. Dyzenhaus provides a more detailed account of how the legislature and the courts interact to protect human rights and to control the executive than found in Laws' more abstract analysis. Dyzenhaus describes the culture of justification as providing a middle ground between the extremes of the culture of reflection and the culture of neutrality.[34] The culture of reflection can be illustrated by the theories of Bentham, who advocated legislation as the ideal form of law-making, reflecting the majority choices of the citizens governed by this legislation. The role of the judge is merely to interpret legislation, ensuring that their interpretations correspond to the wishes of the legislature, in turn reflecting majority preferences. Law is legitimate because it reflects majority preferences. By contrast, the culture of neutrality regards legitimacy as stemming from liberal principles, which in turn underpin democracy. The role of the judiciary is to uphold these liberal principles, ensuring that they are not overridden by democratic decision-makers. The culture of reflection is related to political constitutionalism. The culture of neutrality, in turn, is connected to legal constitutionalism.

Dyzenhaus' two contrasting cultures are reflected in two competing models of judicial review.[35] The culture of reflection is related to the *ultra vires* theory of judicial review. According to this theory, judicial review is justified as a means by which the judiciary can ensure that the administration does not transgress the scope of powers granted to it by the legislature. If the administration were to act beyond the scope of its powers, it would be transgressing its indirectly democratically justified mandate. Parliament, as the representative of the people, has determined the scope of powers of the administration and it is only legitimate for the administration to act within its powers as determined in this manner. In addition, were the courts to strike down actions of the administration for any reason other than it having transgressed the scope

[31] Laws (n 16) 573. [32] ibid, 575–76. [33] ibid, 577–78.

[34] D Dyzenhaus, 'The Legitimacy of Legality' (1996) 46 University of Toronto Law Journal 129.

[35] The term model is used here to recognize that the justifications presented here are 'broad brush' and are meant to provide an account of general themes running through schools of thought that underpin more specific and precise theories of justification of judicial review.

of its powers, then courts would be acting beyond the sphere of their powers; declaring unlawful an action that was within the scope of the powers of the administration as determined by Parliament. As such, courts would be contravening democratic will and, therefore, acting illegitimately.

The culture of neutrality is reflected in certain interpretations of the common law theory of judicial review, which regard judicial review as legitimate when it upholds constitutional principles found in the common law. Common law theories of judicial review, broadly defined, regard common law principles as providing an alternative justification for judicial review. Actions of the administration are legitimate not because they are within the sphere of power granted to them by the legislature, but because they comply with legitimate principles of the common law. These principles derive their legitimacy, for the majority of common law theorists, from the value of the substantive principles reflected in the common law.

An understanding of how the culture of justification can hold this middle ground between these two competing models can be gleaned from examining Etienne Mureinik's approach to administrative law. Mureinik developed his theory of the culture of justification in the context of justifying actions of the judiciary in the face of the apartheid regime. Mureinik classified the prevailing culture under apartheid in South Africa as a culture of authority—one where the legislature took actions that were upheld by the judiciary, often due to the existence of ouster clauses removing judicial review, but where legislation did not reflect the view of the majority of the electorate. As such, an application of an *ultra vires* theory of administrative law failed to provide a justification for judicial review. Courts would uphold the views of the legislature; however these views were not necessarily legitimate as there was no verifiable connection between the views of the legislature and the views of the people. Apartheid also posed problems for the culture of neutrality, particularly where this was based upon Dworkin's justification of law as integrity. Apartheid laws are hard to fit with the liberal principles of morality needed to overturn it, yet without this element of fit and integrity it was in turn hard to justify the role of the judiciary to uphold these liberal principles over the will of the legislature unless these principles could be justified as universal or objective. However, Mureinik doubted the ability of the judiciary to provide a clear set of objective, non-contestable principles that could be used to justify overriding legislation.

Mureinik's theory was aimed at responding to these pressures. The culture of justification aims to promote democracy and accountability which can provide a more justifiable means of promoting substantive values when these values may not be reflected in the law. It stops short of advocating that the judiciary should strike down actions of the legislature that undermine liberal principles, whilst also advocating that the judiciary must do more than merely seek to uphold the will of the legislature. Rather, the judiciary are required to promote accountability and transparency, seeking justifications for the actions of the executive and legislature, requiring reasons to be provided for their actions. By requiring such justification and transparency, courts do not merely enforce the will of the legislature; promoting transparency may require courts to develop stronger procedural protections perhaps in the face of apparently contradictory legislation.[36] However, such protection stops short of empowering courts to

[36] A possible example of this in English law could be *R v Home Secretary, ex parte Al Fayed* [1998] 1 WLR 763, where the court required sufficient notice of a decision to be provided to the applicants to enable them to exercise their appeal rights, despite an express statement in statutory provisions that reasons need not be provided for the decision.

protect substantive liberal principles to strike down actions of the administration or the legislature.[37]

The culture of justification has been used by David Dyzenhaus and Murray Hunt to justify a theory of human rights adjudication based upon the principle of proportionality combined with a doctrine of deference as respect. Deference as respect occurs when 'the court gives some weight to a decision of a primary decision-maker for an articulated reason, as part of its overall review of the justifications for the decision'.[38] It is contrasted with deference as submission, which occurs 'when the court treats a decision or an aspect of it as non-justiciable, and refuses to enter on a review of it because it considers it beyond its competence'.[39] A culture of justification requires that courts examine the reasons provided by the executive or legislature to justify their actions, ensuring that any purported restriction of a right is justifiable. When scrutinizing the decision, courts give varying weight to the reasons provided by the legislature or executive. The weight to be provided to these justifications depends upon an analysis of the relative constitutional and institutional features of the legislature, executive, and the courts. Constitutional features are those relating to the relative constitutional positions of these institutions, referring to the democratic mandate of the legislature as well as the constitutional function of the court to uphold the rule of law. Institutional features refer to the relative expertise of the legislature, executive, and courts. Both depend upon the specific context of the decision or action falling to be examined by the courts.

However, despite Laws, Dyzenhaus, Mureinik, and Hunt all appearing to base their theories on the constitutional foundational assumptions underpinning both legal and political constitutionalism, all of these theorists are regarded as advocates of legal as opposed to political constitutionalism. If we are to define democratic dialogue as resting on a constitutional foundational assumption which accepts the need to respect both democracy and liberal principles, then we have devised a distinct theory which appears to include nearly every account of political and legal constitutionalism. We are again forcing 'legal' and 'political' constitutionalism to occupy extreme poles, with legal constitutionalism referring to any theory which argues that liberal principles always override democracy and political constitutionalism referring to any theory which requires democracy to always override legal principles. In essence, we are merely replicating the arguments made in Chapter 1 but at a more abstract level.

Nevertheless, our analysis of constitutional foundational assumptions helps to explain how democratic dialogue is sufficiently different from political and legal constitutionalism to provide a distinct means of determining whether rights are better protected if relatively more power is given to the legislature or to the judiciary. First, rather than trying to forge a separate middle ground for democratic dialogue, we need to recognize and embrace the vague nature of the distinction between legal and political constitutionalism. Both theories recognize the value of both democracy and of liberal principles and human rights. If there are differences between these theories, they can best be understood as a matter of degree. Unsurprisingly, legal constitutionalists tend to place more value on liberal principles and human rights. They tend to advocate greater judicial control over the executive and the legislature and a greater role for the

[37] E Mureinik, 'A Bridge to Where? Introducing the Interim Bill of Rights' (1994) 10 South African Journal of Human Rights 31; and D Dyzenhaus, 'Law as Justification: Etienne Mureinik's Conception of Legal Culture' (1998) 14 South African Journal on Human Rights 11.

[38] M Hunt, 'Sovereignty's Blight: Why Contemporary Public Law Needs the Concept of "Due Deference"' in N Bamforth and P Leyland (eds), *Public Law in a Multi-Layered Constitution* (Oxford, Hart 2003) 337, 347.

[39] ibid, 346–47.

court in the protection of human rights. Where these theories have a dynamic component, they tend to focus on providing mechanisms of interaction which focus on the role of the courts, suggesting means through which courts may modify the stringency with which they exercise their legal controls in order to give greater decision-making opportunities for the legislature. Equally predictably, political constitutionalists tend to place more value on democracy than on liberal principles and human rights, advocating a greater role for the legislature and, where there is any dynamic element, giving the legislature the predominant role in any interactions taking place between the legislature and the judiciary.

It is important to recognize that just because the distinction between legal and political constitutionalism is vague, this does not mean that the distinction between the two does not exist. The distinction between 'night' and 'day', for example, is vague, when we apply this distinction to the United Kingdom where we experience dawn and dusk, as well as days and nights of varying length. It may be difficult to determine the precise level of light needed to determine when it is sufficiently light to classify a particular period of time as day or night. Nevertheless, we can give clear examples of night and day which do not rely on day referring merely to noon and night referring to midnight. We also recognize the existence of dawn and dusk. We do so by recognizing not that dawn and dusk occupy a middle ground through a specific blend of light and dark which represents a tenable middle ground between night and day. Rather, we recognize that dawn and dusk are distinct as they mark a specific period of transition between night and day as the sun rises and sets. These terms, therefore, add value to our assessment of night and day. In a similar manner, recognizing democratic dialogue can add value to our analysis of legal and political constitutionalism, despite the fact that it draws on a blending of similar constitutional foundational assumptions as those which underpin legal and political constitutionalism.

First, we can recognize that democratic dialogue is distinct in that it asks different questions, these questions arising because democratic dialogue has a different focus, or starting point, from legal and political constitutionalism. We have argued that it is not the case that political and legal constitutionalism are based on distinct constitutional foundational assumptions given that both legal and political constitutionalism recognize the constitutional foundational assumptions of democracy and the protection of liberal rights. However, the arguments found in legal and political constitutionalism have a different focus or starting point. Theories of political constitutionalism tend to focus on the role of Parliament, analysing the role of courts in terms of how they may supplement parliamentary controls. Legal constitutionalists tend to start their arguments with an analysis of legal controls, modifying the stringency of legal controls in order to recognize those circumstances where weight needs to be given to political controls or political reasoning about rights. Democratic dialogue asks a different question. It adds a further dimension to the discussion of the relative merits of legal and political controls by examining interactions between institutions, asking how these interactions can best be used to achieve normative values. In the field of human rights, for example, the focus or starting point of theories of democratic dialogue examines how legislatures and the judiciary can best work together to provide for better outcomes and more legitimate means of resolving rights-issues.

In examining interactions, theories of democratic dialogue will draw on the same competing constitutional foundational assumptions used by theories of legal and political constitutionalism. In common with legal and political constitutionalism, democratic dialogue examines the relative merits of legal and political controls of human rights. In the same manner that different conceptions of legal and political constitutionalism will differ from each other in terms of degree, so different conceptions of democratic dialogue may differ in terms of the relative power given to the legislature and the judiciary as regards the interactions between the two institutions when determining rights-issues.

The difference between legal constitutionalism, political constitutionalism, and democratic dialogue may be less pronounced than at first perceived by the overly simplistic claim that democratic dialogue can occupy a middle ground between legal and political constitutionalism. Nevertheless, this does not mean that democratic dialogue is incapable of adding value. Democratic dialogue can further the arguments of legal and political constitutionalism in two ways. First, by focusing on interactions it can provide a framework through which to determine which interactions between the legislature and the judiciary are better able to draw on the relative strengths of these two institutions in order to provide a better resolution of rights-issues. Second, an analysis of interactions between the legislature and the judiciary illustrates how interactions can add to the legitimacy of the resolution of rights-issues. This can occur through a form of self-correcting mechanism, where each institution is aware of the anticipated reactions of the other, in addition to the anticipated reaction of the individuals governed by the legislature and the judiciary. The next section will re-visit the dynamic element of democratic dialogue in order to lay the groundwork for explaining how democratic dialogue can add to current theoretical analyses, with later chapters building on this foundation by drawing on the constitutional foundational assumptions of legal and political constitutionalism.

III. Re-visiting Inter-institutional Interactions

In the previous chapter we argued that theories of democratic dialogue need a dynamic component, recognizing the need for interactions between the legislature and the judiciary. However, we also recognized that inter-institutional interactions were also present in accounts of legal and political constitutionalism, meaning that this dynamic component, whilst necessary, was not sufficient to differentiate democratic dialogue from legal and political constitutionalism. Just as with our assessment of constitutional foundational assumptions, it could be argued that an easy way in which to delineate accounts of democratic dialogue from legal or political constitutionalism would be to demonstrate that, although institutional interactions take place in all three theories, the institutional interactions taking place in legal constitutionalism, political constitutionalism, and democratic dialogue are different. We would expect political constitutionalism to focus on inter-institutional interactions which grant more power to the legislature to authoritatively determine disputes; legal constitutionalism to grant more power to the judiciary to resolve these disputes; and democratic dialogue to focus on equalizing the relative power of the legislature and the judiciary.

It is the case that we can find examples of theories which grant different roles to the legislature and the judiciary when they interact and that these distinctions can give rise to different legal doctrines. However, these distinctions are best understood as deriving from differences in the relative weight given to democracy and liberal rights, or differences in conceptions of human rights and different understandings about how different institutions reason about rights. A closer examination of these differences helps to explain three points. First, it reinforces the argument that the line between political and legal constitutionalism is vague and that this causes problems for the clear delineation of legal and political constitutionalism as well as problems for democratic dialogue. Second, it helps to illustrate how different inter-institutional interactions can facilitate the achievement of different values. This suggests that it is valuable to examine how institutions interact, focusing in particular on which interactions can promote or hinder the achievement of different normative principles. It is true that accounts of democratic dialogue may draw on different values when determining interactions more precisely. However, the same is true of accounts of legal and political constitutionalism. There are different conceptions of these theories which draw on different normative values. If this diversity undermines the distinct nature of democratic dialogue, then it also undermines the distinct nature of legal and political constitutionalism. Third, it provides a means of introducing two different forms of inter-institutional interaction: constitutional counter-balancing and constitutional collaboration. Constitutional counter-balancing mechanisms are designed to ensure that no one institution is consistently able to authoritatively resolve rights-issues. If it is the case that one institution always wins any form of exchange as to the determination of a rights-issue, then it is difficult to see how any form of effective dialogue can take place between these institutions. Constitutional counter-balancing mechanisms are designed to counteract this. Constitutional collaboration mechanisms focus on drawing on the different ways in which legislatures and courts reason about rights, investigating how institutional interactions can better combine the relative strengths and minimize the relative weaknesses of each institution when reasoning about rights. In addition, the combination of constitutional counter-balancing and constitutional collaboration mechanisms helps to provide a form of self-correcting mechanism which adds legitimacy as well as acting as a safety valve, helping to provide a balance between stability and flexibility.

A. Dynamic legal and political constitutionalism re-visited

Chapter 2 concluded that both JAG Griffith and Trevor Allan include a dynamic element in their theories of legal and political constitutionalism. However, there are clear distinctions between their two approaches. The clearest difference, understandably, can be seen in the relative roles Griffith and Allan give to the judiciary and the legislature. Each theory recognizes the role of both the legislature and the judiciary in the dynamic evolution of values. However, whereas Allan places more importance on the role of the judiciary in developing the law in line with his conception of the rule of law, Griffith focuses predominantly on the role of the legislature, modifying laws in line with temporary resolutions of conflicts and changing societal opinions and values. When we re-examine accounts of the dynamic component of their theories, we can see that the different roles they grant to the legislature and the judiciary stem from different normative values; in particular differences in conceptions of the rule of law and of the nature of human rights.

There exists a stark division between Griffith's and Allan's conceptions of human rights. Griffith famously rejected the ideology of fundamental rights, rejecting the idea of abstractions of justice as 'nonsense on stilts'—a phrase borrowed from Jeremy Bentham.[40] His objection to the incorporation of a legally enforceable Bill of Rights was two-fold; political and philosophical. His political objection states that legal rights are really political claims. To provide an answer to whether a specific situation breaches a human right requires an assessment of political as opposed to legal issues.[41] His

[40] JAG Griffith, 'The Political Constitution' (1979) 42 Modern Law Review 1, 18.
[41] ibid, 14–16.

philosophical argument rejects the existence of fundamental rights. Although we may refer to rights as fundamental, for Griffith this was merely to recognize that a particular group in society had managed to persuade the majority of members of that society that this right should be protected. Griffith believes in a priori principles. However, he argues that the application of a priori principles to specific issues is always the subject of conflict. If it is to be decided by politicians it is not because they are better at ensuring that the right resolution of this conflict is reached. Rather, they should resolve these conflicts as they are removable and can be replaced in line with shifting temporary resolutions of these conflicts as the composition of groups in society changes and different majorities are formed.[42]

For Allan, constitutional rights are 'implications of human freedom and dignity' that 'enjoy a fundamental status'.[43] They condition the validity of legislative and administrative acts. Any application of a general right to a specific situation requires not just the application of legal reasoning as to the meaning of the role and its application to the specific case, but also moral reasoning. What Griffith regards as a specification reflecting the opinions of stronger and weaker groups in society, Allan regards as a substantiation of general principles of human freedom and dignity to a specific situation. This specification is derived from a combination of interpretation of statutory provisions and case law in line with moral as well as legal reasoning. If this reasoning process is performed correctly, the specification is objectively true. However, care needs to be taken over the meaning of 'true' here. Allan is assessing truth from the internal perspective—that is, the lawyer, judge, or academic involved in determining the application of legal rights and principles to a specific case. If legal and moral reasoning are applied correctly, the outcome is the correct application in that particular legal system from that internal perspective. This is not to argue that the judiciary do not make mistakes. Rather, it is to recognize that, as law is an interpretative concept, a correct interpretation of the law is a correct specification of objectively correct general principles as applied in that legal system.[44]

In addition to radically different conceptions of rights, Allan and Griffith also adopt radically different conceptions of the rule of law. Griffith adopts a narrow, formal interpretation of the rule of law.[45] For Griffith, the rule of law encapsulates the ideology of ensuring that there is no punishment without law. It ensures adequate machinery for implementing the law, including dealing with breaches of the law, as well as ensuring that public bodies do not exceed their powers.[46] For Allan, the rule of law is substantive as well as formal, with Allan arguing that it is not possible to clearly distinguish between these two approaches. The rule of law should guide actions of all institutions of the constitution—the executive, legislature, and the judiciary. Allan does not provide a complete list of substantive rights or principles similar to the ones that are often found in liberal accounts of the substantive rule of law. Rather, he argues that the rule of law, as a general principle, aims to guarantee individual freedom, understood in terms of personal autonomy and equality for all. It aims to achieve the public good. Its precise content evolves as it is applied to specific situations.[47]

These differences explain their distinct accounts of inter-institutional interactions from the perspective of political and legal constitutionalism. If legal rights are mere temporary resolutions to political claims, then we would expect them to change over

[42] ibid, 18–20. [43] Allan n 27 243. [44] ibid, 284–85.
[45] PP Craig, 'Formal and Substantive Conceptions of the Rule of Law: An Analytical Framework' [1997] Public Law 467.
[46] Griffith (n 40) 15. [47] Allan (n 27) Chapter 3.

time as the composition of different groups, and their relative political strength, changes over time. If we can point to a general shift towards granting greater voting rights to prisoners, for example, this can only be because those groups who would support such a right have grown in strength. If the Westminster Parliament has been slow to adopt the decision of the European Court of Human Rights requiring a modification of the blanket ban, and if New Zealand has recently reversed this trend, this can only be because those in favour of granting voting rights to prisoners in these countries have less political power. There is no history of evolution towards the right answer reflecting general legal principles to determine whether prisoners should have the right to vote. Rather, there are different temporary resolutions.

Consequently, there is no normative claim in Griffith's theory that a dynamic element produces the 'right' outcome. There are also no underlying principles used to guide dynamic interactions between institutions. Griffith famously remarked that

> [t]he Constitution of the United Kingdom lives on, changing from day to day for the constitution is no more and no less than what happens. Everything that happens is constitutional. And if nothing happened that would be constitutional also.[48]

Regardless of whether we read this phrase as demonstrating that Griffith adopted a purely descriptive as opposed to a normative account of the constitution, it demonstrates how Griffith regarded constitutional change. Disagreement and conflict may fuel dynamic shifts in constitutional values. However, we cannot regard these shifts as progress towards an ideal, or as the shifting application of general principles to changing social situations. If prisoners get the right to vote, for example, this is because those who have power currently believe they should. If this is lost, it is because those who do not want prisoners to have the vote had gained more power. The different resolution of this issue in different countries merely reflects that there are different balances of power between different interest groups in these societies.

Trevor Allan, however, regards law as constantly evolving and changing as we apply general moral principles to specific situations. As general rights are applied to specific situations they become legal rights that form legal doctrines. However, Allan is careful to point out that legal doctrines never fully determine the answer to a specific legal issue engaging the application of general principles. This always requires an application of moral reasoning. The dynamic development of legal rights is mediated through the application of general principles of the substantive rule of law. It is not the result of a conflict of values determined by the relative strength of different political groups in society, but the result of the application of principles of practical reasoning applying legal and moral principles. Reasons are required. The dynamic development of rights occurs according to the strength of these legal reasons, not because of political or numerical strength, or shifts in favour. If there is a shift towards an acceptance of voting rights for some prisoners it is because the justifications provided for failing to provide voting rights do not provide sound moral reasons for restricting these rights. Different countries may grant different rights to vote to prisoners reflecting the application of general moral principles to the specific facts in these different countries.

It is undeniable that the dynamic component found in the work of Griffiths is different from that of Allan. It is also uncontroversial that this means that Griffith and Allan would grant different roles to the legislature and the judiciary when determining the interactions which should take place between these institutions. Allan would give a greater role to the judiciary and Griffith would give a greater role to the legislature.

[48] Griffith (n 40) 19.

These differences depend on differing accounts of the rule of law and the means of determining the content of rights. However, to see this as the main distinguishing feature between legal and political constitutionalism also collapses into a matter of degree. Neither Allan nor Griffith place the sole role of determining rights-issues in the hands of either the judiciary or the legislature respectively. Nor do their theories require that either the judiciary or the legislature should always have the authoritative final say in any interactions between the two institutions. We therefore return to our common theme of recognizing that democratic dialogue appears to be either non-existent or ubiquitous. We can find a space for theories of democratic dialogue only by creating a middle ground by modifying our definitions of legal and political constitutionalism to such an extent that it only covers extremely radical versions of either theory. This conclusion is reinforced when we examine theories that appear to occupy this middle ground, but which, in reality, illustrate how different normative values, including conceptions of the rule of law and of human rights, are being used to determine different types of inter-institutional interaction. This can be illustrated through an analysis of the 'culture of justification' developed by David Dyzenhaus and Etienne Mureinik, which is used specifically by Sandra Fredman to discuss inter-institutional interactions which go further than the account found in theories of democratic dialogue, building into her account an assessment of which inter-institutional interactions are more able to facilitate deliberative democracy.

B. Dialogue and the culture of justification: a stable middle ground?

The culture of justification is developed by David Dyzenhaus drawing on the work of Etienne Mureinik. It will be recalled that Dyzenhaus distinguishes between two cultures, the culture of reflection and the culture of neutrality. The culture of justification aimed to occupy a middle position between these two competing cultures. The culture of reflection resembles accounts of political constitutionalism. The culture of reflection is based on the ideology that the content of the law should reflect the wishes of the people. In a manner similar to political constitutionalism, the culture of reflection prioritizes democracy, preserving the sovereignty of the people. Drawing on the positivist theories of Bentham, the culture of reflection rejects the ideologies of moral or legal fundamental rights. Legislation is regarded as the best form of law-making and legislation is justified as and when it reflects the wishes of the people. It is easy to see the parallels between Dyzenhaus's account of the culture of reflection and Griffith's account of the dynamic evolution of legal rights. Griffith also rejects fundamental rights. Griffith's account of political constitutionalism also shares a preference for laws to be enacted by legislation as opposed to through the development of the common law. Moreover, his account of the dynamic changes in the content of rights over time shows how rights mirror the political and social preferences of the people.

In a similar manner we can draw a connection between the culture of neutrality and Allan's account of legal constitutionalism. Theories belonging to the culture of neutrality are based on principles of liberal government. Dyzenhaus refers to these theories as the culture of neutrality as they aim to ensure that laws uphold liberal principles whilst being neutral as to different ways of life, in order to promote personal autonomy. Although Allan does not proscribe a precise set of liberal principles, his concern with ensuring law's legitimacy through its promotion of principles of good government, based on a concern for equal citizenship, shares the ideology of the culture of neutrality. This is reflected in the dynamic component of his theory. Legal rights evolve through the application of legal and moral reasoning to determine how general principles of the rule of law apply to specific situations.

The culture of justification takes a middle path between the culture of neutrality and the culture of reflection. It shares with the culture of reflection the preference for laws to be enacted through legislation, whilst also sharing with the culture of neutrality the need for principles to determine the legitimacy of the law. This middle position also appears to lead to different conclusions as to the relative roles of the legislature and the judiciary with regard to the protection of human rights, in addition to proposing different types of interactions between these two institutions. The culture of justification does not require the judiciary to strike down laws that contravene liberal principles. Rather, the culture of justification argues that the principles that should be used to determine the legitimacy of the law derived from a specific form of reasoning about rights. It is not the job of the court to perform this task. Rather, the job of the courts is to require justification for actions by the legislature and the executive. Both should provide reasons for their actions, explaining why they believe that legislation or administrative action is justified. Courts are to scrutinize these reasons, ensuring that they provide a sound justification. Their role is to ensure that actions are justifiable as opposed to justified.

Sandra Fredman's account of a bounded deliberative approach in the field of prisoner voting rights provides an example of an account of inter-institutional interactions between the legislature and the judiciary which draws on the culture of justification.[49] Fredman proposes a theory of inter-institutional interaction based on a deliberative model, which she sees as going beyond democratic dialogue models of adjudication. She draws on Habermas' distinction between two forms of co-ordination; interest-formed and value-orientated. Interest-formed co-ordination occurs when different groups express their interests, without seeing a space for negotiation or compromise. Co-ordination occurs through the weight of numbers or political influence. Value-orientated co-ordination occurs when arguments are based on reasons; where parties are prepared to weigh up competing reasons and reach compromises in the light of reasoning and justification. The culture of justification prioritizes value-orientated as opposed to interest-formed co-ordination.

Fredman's deliberative model is designed to facilitate dynamic developments which derive from value-orientated co-ordination. Value-orientated co-ordination can be found in both political and judicial debate. However, there is more of a risk of legislative deliberation focusing on interests as opposed to values as legislative decisions are determined by the number of votes. Political pressures can be used to persuade individuals to vote according to shared interests and the views of their political party, even when this is contrary to their values, or when arguments appear to suggest that this position is mistaken. Judicial independence provides a safeguard against this pressure towards interest-orientated co-ordination. Courts can, and should, steer the legislature towards value-orientated co-ordination, requiring legislatures to provide reasons for their actions which can then be scrutinized by the courts. In addition, courts provide a forum for value-orientated co-ordination through hearing the justifications and arguments of the parties before the court in addition to providing the possibilities of further deliberative forums outside the courtroom as society comments on court decisions. It is not, however, the job of the court to dictate the outcome. It is the role of

[49] S Fredman, 'From Dialogue to Deliberation: Human Rights Adjudication and Prisoners' Right to Vote' [2013] Public Law 292.

the legislature to balance rights or to provide detailed accounts of what rights require in specific circumstances, provided that they are able to provide clear reasons for their decision.

Inter-institutional interactions take place in accounts of legal constitutionalism, political constitutionalism, and the culture of justification. The inter-institutional interactions in the three accounts of these constitutional theories are different. Griffith would give a greater role to the legislature to determine rights-issues, with the judiciary focusing predominantly on ensuring that legislative provisions adhered to the wishes of the people expressed through legislative provisions. Allan would give a greater role to the court, with the judiciary providing the predominant role in the determination of rights-issues, whilst recognizing areas where the nature of the right itself would dictate that a greater discretionary area of judgment could be granted to the legislature. Fredman's account of inter-institutional interactions focuses on the need for the court to scrutinize the reasons provided by the legislature for their policy choices, ensuring that any restriction of a right is sufficiently justified. However, despite these differences, it is hard to clearly delineate between them. All draw on different accounts of normative values or principles—for example the rule of law or a conception of rights—using these values to provide a specific account of inter-institutional interactions which give different relative roles to the legislature and the judiciary in these interactions.

We can see further evidence of the blurring between the accounts when we re-examine Dyzenhaus' account of the rule of law. This appears to take a middle ground between the accounts of the rule of law provided by Griffith and Allan. Griffith provides a formal account of the rule of law. For Griffith, the rule of law is desirable for all when it merely requires that there be a 'proper and adequate machinery' for dealing with criminal offences and ensuring that public authorities do not exceed their powers, so that punishments are only for those who have broken the law.[50] He rejects substantive accounts of the rule of law, which he regards as a means of creating a 'protective sanctity around certain legal and political institutions and principles' which those seeking to protect this substantive conception of the rule of law 'wish to preserve at any cost'.[51] Allan, on the other hand, provides an account of the rule of law that is both formal and substantive. However, he does not provide a conception of the rule of law which contains a complete account of the substantive principles the rule of law is designed to protect. Rather, the rule of law aims to preserve the liberty of citizens, only allowing incursions on individual liberties when they are a proportionate restriction to achieve the public good. Democratic institutions determine this precise balance, subject to scrutiny by the court. Both the legislature and the courts should ensure their actions are justified by the requirements of the rule of law.[52]

Dyzenhaus' account of the rule of law is designed to differ from that of both Allan and Griffith. It is best understood when placing his account of the rule of law in the context of his constitutional theory as a whole. As well as distinguishing between the culture of neutrality and the culture of reflection, Dyzenhaus also refers to the distinction between natural lawyers and positivists. He describes the positivist account of the rule of law as one which focuses on formal requirements and does not include substantive requirements. For positivists, the ideal of the rule of law is to ensure government according to the law. The role of the judiciary when enforcing the rule of law is to ensure that they enforce validly enacted law, interpreting its provisions to ensure that it enacts the will of the legislature. Dyzenhaus links the positivist account of the rule

[50] Griffith (n 40) 15. [51] ibid. [52] Allan (n 27) Chapter 3.

of law with the culture of reflection. Law, when validly enacted through legislation, reflects the wishes of the majority and it is the role of the judiciary to interpret legislation as it is enacted, to ensure that the law as enforced also reflects the wishes of the majority. Dyzenhaus contrasts positivist accounts of the rule of law with natural law accounts of the rule of law. Natural law accounts focus on substantive as opposed to formal requirements of the rule of law. This is not to deny that natural law accounts of the rule of law also include formal characteristics. Natural law accounts, however, add substantive requirements to their account of the rule of law. This in turn influences the role of the judiciary. To apply the requirements of the rule of law, the judiciary need to ensure not only that the law is validly enacted, but also that it adheres to substantive requirements of the rule of law. Dyzenhaus connects this account of the rule of law with the culture of neutrality.

Dyzenhaus arguably provides an account of the rule of law that falls between the account of natural lawyers and the account of positivists, aiming to avoid the pitfalls of both accounts of the rule of law. He is critical of positivist accounts of the rule of law as they are unable to protect society from bad laws. His criticism can be illustrated in Griffith's account of the rule of law. Griffith recognizes that political values and opinions change over time and legislation, in turn, reflects these changes. All of these changes are 'constitutional'. Legislation requiring unfavourable treatment of a distinct minority group would be just as constitutional as legislation based on egalitarian principles. To uphold the rule of law, the judge would be required to enforce both as valid law, reflecting the views of a racist or egalitarian society.

Dyzenhaus argues that natural law conceptions of the rule of law are problematic given the difficulty of justifying the content of the substantive principles incorporated into the account of the rule of law. Dyzenhaus aims to develop an account of the rule of law that responds to these difficulties. His account of the rule of law goes beyond the mere formal requirements of the rule of law found in positivist accounts, but does not incorporate a substantive component as found in natural law accounts of the rule of law. Drawing on Fuller's account of the inner morality of law,[53] Dyzenhaus focuses on formal features such as clarity and publication of the law. However, unlike Raz's account of a formal theory of the rule of law,[54] Dyzenhaus does not regard these formal requirements of the rule of law as a means of ensuring law is an effective tool, nor does he conclude that the formal requirements of the rule of law can indirectly promote personal autonomy through removing some of the ways in which the way the law is formulated may restrict personal liberty. Instead, Dyzenhaus connects the formal requirements of the rule of law to law's legitimacy. Dyzenhaus believes that legislation should be the main form of law-making. Adhering to the formal requirements of the rule of law may not guarantee that the substantive content of the law will be 'good'. However, requirements of clarity, publication and, in particular, providing reasons will enable citizens to scrutinize the content of the law. Providing justifications for legislation is more likely to ensure the quality of its content. Judges can further the requirements of the rule of law by requiring justifications for restrictions on rights, determining whether sound reasons can be provided.

However, it is difficult to delineate this account of the rule of law as occupying a clear middle ground between Griffith and Allan. Griffith and Allan would also agree that clarity, publication, and the provision of reasons were necessary components of the rule of law. Also, it is hard to see their accounts as disagreeing over the need for scrutiny

[53] L Fuller, *The Morality of Law* (2nd edn, Yale 1969).
[54] J Raz, 'The Rule of Law and its Virtue' (1977) 93 Law Quarterly Review 195.

to ensure that the content of legislation has a good content through the scrutiny of the reasons provided for this content. Where they differ is as to the reasons they would regard as acceptable. It would be hard to find an account of political constitutionalism that did not allow for the courts to scrutinize the reasoning of the legislature to ensure that it had not made a logical mistake when reaching its conclusion. A legal constitutionalist would also accept a scrutiny of the reasons of the legislature to ensure that a policy choice was justified. But this scrutiny would draw not just on rational arguments but also on substantive values incorporated in the rule of law. Moreover, the requirements of transparency, publication, and the provision of reasons also draw on substantive values. Would these requirements of a formal theory of the rule of law be present if it were not for their connection to the facilitation of personal autonomy?[55]

The similarities between the 'middle ground' and legal and political constitutionalism are even more apparent when we recognize the similarities between Dyzenhaus' account of the rule of law and that of Trevor Allan. Allan also develops an account of the rule of law that is predominantly formal and which does not contain a precise or complete list of substantive principles of the rule of law. He also argues that democratic institutions have a role to play in determining the precise content of the substantive principles of the rule of law. However, Dyzenhaus regards his account as distinct from that of Allan, given Allan's substantive content of the rule of law, recognizing the need to respect equal citizenship.[56] Allan agrees that this difference in content delineates between their two theories. But he regards this as a difference in focus. Whilst Allan focuses on the substance of the law, Dyzenhaus is more concerned with the participation of citizens in the legal order.[57] It is hard to disagree with Allan's conclusion, particularly as Allan himself also recognizes the need for Parliament to adhere to the rule of law. A better understanding of these accounts is that there is no clear-cut distinction between legal constitutionalism and political constitutionalism, with democratic dialogue accounts being free to occupy a middle ground. Rather, all three theories draw on normative principles, placing emphasis on, or more focus on, different aspects of these values, or giving more weight to different normative principles. Whilst Allan focuses on the substantive content of the rule of law and Dyzenhaus focuses on participation, Fredman focuses on democratic deliberation. If there is a space for democratic dialogue it is one of focus, examining the nature of inter-institutional interactions and using this examination as its starting point to reach conclusions as to the resolution of rights-issues, rather than focusing purely on whether normative values favour giving either the courts or the legislature the main role in the resolution of rights-issues.

Similar problems arise when we focus on conceptions of rights. Fredman's account of inter-institutional interactions draws on Habermas' distinction between interest-formed and value-orientated forms of co-ordination, expressing a preference for value-orientated co-ordination. If we were to focus on Griffith's account of political constitutionalism, with its rejection of rights as anything other than the expression of the interests of a particular group in society, it is not too great a leap to argue that his account would focus more predominantly on interest-formed co-ordination. In a similar manner, Allan's account of legal constitutionalism would focus predominantly on value-orientated co-ordination, with the precise content of these substantive rights

[55] NW Barber, 'Must Legalistic Conceptions of the Rule of Law Have a Social Dimension?' (2004) 17 Ratio Juris 474.

[56] D Dyzenhaus, 'Form and Substance in the Rule of Law: A Democratic Justification for Judicial Review' in C Forsyth (ed), *Judicial Review and the Constitution* (Oxford, Hart 2000) 141, 170–72.

[57] Allan (n 27) 26–27.

being drawn from the rule of law. However, neither political nor legal constitutionalism adopts a model of only interest-formed or value-orientated co-ordination. We can see this more clearly if we reason through an example. To return to our theme of prisoner voting; how would each of these theories respond were the United Kingdom to enact legislation granting prisoners the right to vote when serving sentences of less than twelve months, enabling prisoners to register to vote in the last six months of their sentence, as recommended by the Joint Committee on the Draft Prisoner Voting (Eligibility) Bill?[58]

We have described the dynamic component of Griffith's theory of political constitutionalism as focusing predominantly on interest-formed co-ordination. The solution suggested by the Joint Committee would be regarded by Griffith as demonstrating a shift in the balance of interest groups, away from the view in support of a blanket ban towards a support of granting limited voting rights for prisoners. This shift would have occurred through a shift in the relative power of those promoting the interests of voting rights for prisoners. Or the shift may have occurred because of the recognition of the need to change the law, even if those in power do not believe in granting voting rights to prisoners. This may be because those with more power believe that the United Kingdom should comply with decisions of the European Court of Human Rights, even if this requires protecting interests which they would not otherwise protect. The role of the court would be to interpret the legislation in line with the interests of Parliament. Here that would require courts to ensure that voting rights were granted to those serving sentences of less than twelve months and not, for example, to re-interpret the legislation so as to grant voting rights to a prisoner serving a sentence of fourteen months because the court believed that the twelve months limit was arbitrary and sentences of fourteen months were for offences which were not sufficiently more serious than those which attracted a twelve-month sentence.

The dynamic component of Allan's theory of legal constitutionalism prioritizes value-orientated co-ordination, regarding the courts as better suited to determining this issue. When faced with legislation granting the right to vote for prisoners serving less than twelve months, the court would be able to scrutinize both the substance and the justification for the legislation. If the legislation were to breach principles of equal citizenship, then courts should interpret the legislation so as to remove this breach. For example, the use of a twelve-month sentence or less to trigger voting rights may fail to delineate between those serving sentences of more than twelve months for a series of minor offences, all of which alone would attract a sentence of less than twelve months, and those serving sentences of less than twelve months for a major offence which normally attracts a sentence of more than twelve months, but where the sentence was reduced to reflect that the prisoner helped the police with their investigation. Allan's theory of legal constitutionalism would require the courts to evaluate whether a person who committed a series of minor offences should be treated in the same way as one who committed a major offence, or whether this individual should be allowed to vote given the offences they committed were less serious. Also, it would require courts to work out whether helping the police with their inquiries was enough of an indication of good citizenship to enfranchise a prisoner even though the offence they committed would normally be serious enough to remove the right to vote. The court should assess the value of equal citizenship for itself, re-interpreting legislation where required to ensure equal citizenship is maintained.

[58] Joint Committee on the Draft Voting Ability (Prisoners) Bill, 'Draft Voting Eligibility (Prisoners) Bill', HL Paper 103, HC 924, 2013–14 Session.

Fredman's account of dynamic interaction, based on the culture of justification as developed by Dyzenhaus, would analyse the situation differently. The role of the court would be to assess whether the solution of the legislature was properly justified. It would scrutinize the reasoning of the legislature. If, for example, the legislature had chosen the solution of granting the right to vote to prisoners serving less than twelve months because these prisoners were normally middle class and therefore more likely to vote responsibly, then the court would challenge the legislation, explaining why this justification was insufficient. Even if the court were empowered to strike down the legislation, the legislature would be able to respond to this decision, even to the extent of re-enacting the same content, if it is able to provide a sound reason for the legislation which takes into account the explanation of the court as to why the legislature's previous justification had failed. In common with ideals of political constitutionalism, this theory recognizes that it is predominantly for the legislature to determine which prisoners should be able to vote. In common with legal constitutionalism, the court needs to check whether the legislation undermines values. However, it may not be the job of the court to decide this issue for itself; there is a need also for input from the legislature.

However, although there may be differences in approach, it is easy to see how each theory could reach similar solutions, or draw on different facts, assumptions, and values such that it is difficult to determine whether a judicial approach reflects a conception of legal or political constitutionalism. The more we regard a rights-issue as contestable, for example, the more we will see this as being one which requires a higher degree of interest-formed as opposed to value-orientated co-ordination. Advocates of legal constitutionalism may incorporate this element into their accounts of judicial reasoning by concluding that the judiciary should respect the democratic resolution of the legislature, or by determining that the nature of the right, when fully understood, is capable of being respected in a wide variety of ways. For example, the judiciary may give weight to the democratic resolution of the legislature that twelve-month sentences are the right length by which to determine whether a prisoner should be granted the right to vote, or may determine that the right to vote can be satisfied by a range of possible solutions to when prisoners should be granted the right to vote and that the sentence requirement of less than twelve months is within this range of possible solutions. Whilst the culture of justification may require justifications, less justification would be required of those measures seen as suited for interest-formed collaboration than those deemed suited for value-orientated collaboration. The less contestable the nature of the rights-issue, the greater the likelihood that value-orientated reasoning will be required in order to ensure that the legislature's resolution of the rights-issue is justified. Or the difference in the interactions between institutions may depend upon whether we place more value on representative democracy, deliberative democracy or the protection of individual rights, with different theorists giving different relative weights to these values depending upon the nature of the rights-issue.

C. Is democratic dialogue defunct?

It is clear that democratic dialogue is difficult to define. However, it need not follow that accounts of democratic dialogue are defunct. The common understanding of democratic dialogue is that it operates in the middle ground between legal and political constitutionalism. However, we have argued that it is difficult to define democratic dialogue in this manner without pushing definitions of legal and political constitutionalism to such extremes that they begin to resemble fictional accounts that are adhered to by nobody. The distinction between legal and political constitutionalism is vague.

Therefore, any attempt to provide a clear line between legal constitutionalism, political constitutionalism, and democratic dialogue runs the risk of classifying all accounts as ones of democratic dialogue, or appears to suggest that democratic dialogue is not a separate theory of constitutionalism.

However, having recognized that the distinction between legal and political constitutionalism is vague, similar problems arise for these theories. Nevertheless, we find it useful to recognize a distinction between legal and political constitutionalism, albeit one which recognizes that there is a range of different accounts of legal and political constitutionalism and that the difference between legal and political constitutionalism may best be understood in terms of a starting assumption or question, with different facts and normative values being used to explain how theories may reach similar conclusions, but do so through a different reasoning process. In a similar manner, democratic dialogue focuses on different questions, examining not just the relative powers of the legislature and judiciary to determine rights-issues, but also focusing on which interactions between these institutions are more valuable. A more in depth discussion of the normative values of democratic dialogue, and the range of inter-institutional interactions that may facilitate the achievement of these values, can be found in the following two chapters. This section will pave the way for this more in-depth analysis.

i) Inter-institutional interactions and contestability

A re-examination of Fredman's account of bounded deliberation helps to illustrate the first way in which an account of democratic dialogue can be valuable. Despite the differences discussed above, there is nevertheless a common theme running through the accounts of inter-institutional interactions in legal constitutionalism, political constitutionalism, and the culture of justification. Each theory aims to resolve the same problem—how should a particular society make authoritative determinations of rights when faced with situations where it can be reasonable to disagree about how a right should apply in a particular situation? In previous writing, I have referred to this problem as the resolution of contestable rights-issues.[59] Contestability arises where there is reasonable disagreement. A rights-issue refers to the determination of the answer to a specific question about rights. A rights-issue is less abstract than a right in two ways. First, a rights-issue looks at whether a particular activity is or is not within the scope of the right—for example when determining whether the right to vote includes the right for prisoners to vote in general elections for legislatures. Second, a rights-issue determines the application of the right to a specific individual in a specific set of circumstances—for example determining whether a prisoner convicted of manslaughter and sentenced to ten years should have the right to vote in the general election occurring a year before his release.

Each of the theories discussed so far has a different account of the nature, extent, and potential resolution of contestable rights-issues. Griffith regards contestability as arising because of the nature of rights. Rights are interest claims. As such, contestability is resolved through a battle of interests. The dynamic element in his theory arises as the composition of different interest groups in society changes. These tensions between different groups cause dynamic changes to the resolution of rights-issues. If this resolution is justified, it is because of the value in the democratic process—it is more legitimate for rights to be determined by a body which represents the interests

[59] AL Young, 'Is Dialogue Working under the Human Rights Act 1998?' [2011] Public Law 773.

of the people it governs. Therefore, contestable rights-issues should be predominantly resolved by the legislature with courts ensuring the will of the legislature is applied to the specific issue before it. As Griffith regards all rights as expressions of interests, his account can be viewed as one which views all rights-issues as contestable. It can be reasonable to disagree about how to resolve any rights-issue as any question as to the application of a right to a specific issue requires an assessment of competing interests about which it is reasonable to disagree. Where there is no contestability—because the legislature has balanced competing interests and provided a specific and clear account of a right—courts enforce the right and apply it to the rights-issue before the court. There is, therefore, still a role left for the court in determining the meaning of legislative provisions and how they would apply to the specific rights-issue before the court.

Allan, however, resolves this problem in a different manner. He recognizes that rights-issues are contestable. However, he internalizes this issue, making contestability part of the right. Courts look to substantive principles, either in the abstract or as they are expressed in a particular social and legal context, to determine a rights-issue. When doing so, they pay attention to the nature of the right. When there is a range of solutions that would be compatible with the right in question, the courts recognize this, granting a wider area of discretionary judgment to the executive or the legislature. Rights-issues should be resolved by the courts. Courts determine the extent to which any further decision-making power is left to the legislature. However, in practice, this means that both the legislature and the courts play a role in the resolution of contestable rights-issues.

Fredman's account of bounded deliberation also relies on a combination of the legislature and the courts to determine contestable rights-issues. Fredman's account of bounded deliberation prioritizes value-orientated over interest-formed co-ordination. The legislature balances competing interests and the courts draw on values when resolving rights-issues. When dealing with contestable rights-issues, courts respect the interest-formed co-ordination of the legislature, whilst ensuring that this co-ordination, expressed in a legislative provision, has not transgressed values. Courts draw on substantive values when assessing whether the legislative resolution is justified, checking both its adherence to substantive values and principles of human rights found in constitutional or legal texts in addition to checking for logical errors. As with our account of legal and political constitutionalism, both institutions play a role in the resolution of rights-issues. The legislature balances interests, and the courts ensure that this balance of interests is justified and does not undermine values. Moreover, the more contestable the rights-issue, the more each theory allocates a greater role for interest-formed co-ordination, which is regarded as better performed by the legislature both in terms of its better ability to reach a good outcome and the more legitimate process through which this outcome is achieved.

These differences can be explained, at least in part, due to each theorist adopting a different account of how we reason about rights. Griffith regards rights as mere interest-claims. As such, rights-issues are resolved through weighing up competing interests. The legislature provides a better means of balancing competing interests than the courts and so the legislature should resolve these issues. Allan regards rights as objective. There is one right answer to a specific rights issue, albeit a right answer for that particular legal system and which may recognize that there is a range of right answers. Reasoning about rights is a form of moral reasoning. As Allan argues that judges are better at moral reasoning than the legislature, rights-issues should be resolved by the courts. Legal rights are determined by legal cases, applying general and specified principles to specific situations. This can only be carried out by the courts. Fredman accepts that rights are both determinate and indeterminate. This feature of rights makes them particularly suited for resolution by deliberative democracy, focusing on value-orientated as opposed to interest-formed co-ordination. Both the judiciary and the legislature have a role to play in facilitating value-orientated reasoning and justification.

This recognition of how different institutions reason about rights points to one of the values that can be achieved through an account of democratic dialogue. If we accept that different institutions have different strengths and weaknesses when reasoning about rights, then it is valuable both to examine how institutions reason about rights and also how interactions between these institutions can better combine the relative strengths of how institutions reason about rights. It is this focus on interactions which explains how Fredman's account adds value to accounts of legal and political constitutionalism. Fredman's argument investigates how courts can enhance value-orientated co-ordination through focusing on assessing reasons for specific resolutions of rights-issues, whilst also recognizing the better ability of the legislature to provide interest-formed co-ordination. A focus on how legislatures and courts interact when reasoning about rights may help to provide a better protection of rights by drawing on the relative strengths of how legislatures and courts reason about rights. Fredman's account does so by drawing on the value of deliberative democracy, her account of interactions being one designed to facilitate deliberative democracy. The account of democratic dialogue found in this book is broader in two respects. First, although it recognizes how inter-institutional interactions can facilitate deliberative democracy, it will argue that this is neither the only nor necessarily the main value whose realization can be facilitated through inter-institutional interactions. This argument will be developed further in the following chapters. Second, Fredman's argument draws on interest-formed and value-orientated co-ordination about rights-issues. The account of democratic dialogue advocate here also draws on other forms of reasoning about rights, adding in other dimensions to our assessment of inter-institutional interactions.

ii) Different forms of inter-institutional interaction: constitutional collaboration and constitutional counter-balancing

The previous section explained how democratic dialogue can provide accounts of inter-institutional interaction which may add to accounts of legal and political constitutionalism. These accounts may help to provide a better account of how legislatures and courts can work together to combine their relative institutional and constitutional strengths and weaknesses when reasoning about rights. This will be explored further in the following chapters. It is this type of inter-institutional interaction which has been the main focus of existing theories of democratic dialogue. I will refer to these forms of inter-institutional interaction as examples of constitutional collaboration. The aim of these inter-institutional interactions is collaboration, to facilitate interactions which allow each institution to work effectively with the other to achieve a better protection of rights. It is not the purpose of this book to argue that institutions should, or that they have a duty to collaborate with each other in this manner. Rather, this book aims to describe and evaluate different mechanisms of constitutional collaboration, assessing the extent to which these mechanisms can facilitate a better resolution of rights-issues. The extent to which institutions should use these different mechanisms of constitution collaboration depends upon the institutional and constitutional features of the legislature and the judiciary in legal systems, in addition to normative assessments of their relative roles.

This book will argue that, in addition to mechanisms of constitutional collaboration, accounts of democratic dialogue also need to examine a different form of inter-institutional interaction which I will refer to as constitutional counter-balancing. These mechanisms focus on ensuring that inter-institutional interactions are capable of facilitating dialogue. The need for constitutional counter-balancing mechanisms can be seen in criticisms of accounts of democratic dialogue theories, particularly in the work of Luc Tremblay.[60] Tremblay distinguishes between two forms of dialogue: dialogue as conversation and dialogue as deliberation. Both require interaction between two or more persons, who are recognized as equal partners, who exchange words, ideas, feelings, emotions, intentions, desires, judgments, and experiences within a shared space of inter-subjective meaning.[61] Dialogue as conversation is informal and spontaneous, with no specific purpose other than to further understanding and knowledge amongst the participants, or merely for entertainment. As such, it does not provide any means of furnishing normative legitimacy.[62] Dialogue as deliberation, however, is dialogue for a mutual practical purpose, such as determining the content of a constitutional right or resolving a rights-issue.[63]

Tremblay argues that only dialogue as deliberation is capable of providing normative justification to the outcomes reached through this form of inter-institutional interaction. Dialogue as deliberation is also more suited to achieving collaboration between the legislature and the judiciary when reasoning about rights. However, it is not necessary for inter-institutional interactions to take the form of dialogue as deliberation. It is possible for constitutional collaboration to occur inadvertently, providing a better protection of rights than would be achieved were there to be no interaction between institutions. Nevertheless, Tremblay is right to recognize that inter-institutional interactions require a form of equality if they are to facilitate constitutional collaboration. Tremblay argues in particular that

> [e]ach participant must be equally entitled to put forward theses, to make proposals, to defend particular options, and to take part in the final decision. No one should be excluded from the dialogue, no one should impose by fiat where the dialogue should lead, and no hierarchy must confer in advance on one or more of the participants the authority to settle the disagreements.[64]

He argues further that equality requires either that each participant has equal expertise to determine an issue, or that each has an equal right to participate.[65]

Constitutional counter-balancing mechanisms are means through which this necessary component of equality can be maintained. Accounts of democratic dialogue do not need complete parity or equality between the legislature and the courts, such that both institutions must be the same, or must enjoy an equal role in the determination of rights-issues. Each institution may be better able to resolve particular types or rights-issue and each reasons about rights in a different manner. As such, constitutional collaboration may require different institutions to play different roles, with each playing a more or less decisive role in determining different rights-issues. However, if constitutional collaboration is to take place, then there has to be a means of ensuring that no one institution is able to 'impose by fiat where the dialogue should lead'. Although different features of the legislature and the courts may make it appear as if their relative roles, and importance in settling rights-issues, is determined in advance, nevertheless

[60] LB Tremblay, 'The Legitimacy of Judicial Review: The Limits of Dialogue Between Courts and Legislatures' (2005) 3 International Journal of Constitutional Law 617.

[61] ibid, 630. [62] ibid, 630–31. [63] ibid, 631–34. [64] ibid, 632.

[65] ibid, 632–33.

it cannot be the case that one institution is always able to dictate the outcome of the resolution of rights-issues. Constitutional counter-balancing mechanisms help to provide a means of ensuring that each institution has the ability of responding to the other when it transgresses its proper constitutional role, aiming to authoritatively resolve a rights-issue without considering the view of the other. In this way, constitutional collaboration can be facilitated. It is for this purpose that accounts of democratic dialogue have to accept the complementary roles of the legislature and the judiciary.

Accounts of democratic dialogue need to recognize these different mechanisms of constitutional collaboration and constitutional counter-balancing, providing a framework to help explain how these different forms of inter-institutional interaction can work together to facilitate a better protection of human rights. In addition, it will be argued that this combination of constitutional collaboration and constitutional counter-balancing can achieve other values, including providing a self-correcting mechanism which may provide further legitimacy to the resolution of contestable rights-issues, in addition to providing a safety-valve function which helps to provide a balance between flexibility and stability.

IV. Conclusion

The introduction set out what appeared to be a fundamental criticism of democratic dialogue. Rather than providing a new, and better, means of protecting human rights and controlling executive actions, the accusation was made that dialogue theories were either non-existent or ubiquitous. This conclusion was reinforced in the first and second chapters of the book. This chapter reinforces the conclusion that the distinction between legal and political constitutionalism is vague. Although political constitutionalism may tend to focus more on the role of the legislature, giving more weight to the value of democracy, with legal constitutionalism focusing more on the role of the courts and the value of the protection of human rights and liberal principles, both theories recognize a role for both institutions. In a similar manner, accounts of legal and political constitutionalism may both recognize interactions between the legislature and the judiciary, with greater roles being given to the judiciary and the legislature. However, again, the distinction between these theories is vague.

The vague nature of the distinction between legal and political constitutionalism means that regarding democratic dialogue theories as accounts which occupy a middle ground between these two poles is unrealistic. If it is achievable, it comes at the cost of redefining accounts of legal and political constitutionalism in overly simplistic and radical terms, such that all accounts of political constitutionalism regard rights as only being protected validly by legislatures, with no role for courts, or requiring democratic determinations to always override judicial determinations—and vice versa. It is understandable, therefore, that critics of democratic dialogue dismiss the theory as either non-existent or ubiquitous.

However, if we are to accept that the distinction between legal and political constitutionalism is vague, than we need to recognize that this poses problems not only for accounts of democratic dialogue but also for accounts of legal and political constitutionalism, particularly those that include an assessment of dynamic interactions between the legislature and the judiciary. Legal constitutionalism, political constitutionalism, and democratic dialogue are all best understood as broad churches, which can include a variety of incarnations. If there is a way of delineating between these theories in the abstract, it stems from recognizing that these theories may ask different questions, or start from a different set of assumptions. Whilst political constitutionalists may focus more on the role of legislatures, and legal constitutionalists on the role of the judiciary, accounts of democratic dialogue focus on inter-institutional interactions. In doing so, accounts of democratic dialogue will rely on the institutional and constitutional features of the legislature and the judiciary, drawing on different conceptions of democracy, the rule of law and human rights when assessing the relative roles to be given to these institutions and the types of interactions which are more or less likely to provide a better resolution of rights-issues. Democratic dialogue adds to accounts of legal and political constitutionalism through this focus on inter-institutional interactions.

This chapter has argued that there are two forms of inter-institutional interactions—constitutional collaboration and constitutional counter-balancing. Constitutional collaboration focuses on the means through which the legislature and the judiciary can work together to better protect rights. Constitutional counter-balancing mechanisms aim to ensure that inter-institutional interactions facilitate collaboration by providing a means of ensuring that no one institution consistently authoritatively resolves rights-issues. As well as facilitating a better protection of rights, combinations of constitutional collaboration and constitutional counter-balancing mechanisms may help to provide further legitimacy to the resolution of contestable rights-issues, as well as serving the purpose of balancing the conflicting needs for constitutions to be both flexible and sufficiently rigid. The following two chapters will explain these arguments in more detail. First, we need to investigate the different means of inter-institutional interactions between the legislature and the judiciary, explaining how these interactions can take place in constitutional systems with a strong constitutional protection of rights, a weak parliamentary protection of rights and in Gardbaum's commonwealth models of rights protections which are specifically designed to facilitate democratic dialogue. This analysis, in Chapter 4, will recognize that there is a range of inter-institutional interactions which can be used to facilitate constitutional collaboration and constitutional counter-balancing. Chapter 5 will then move on to assess the claims of how inter-institutional interactions can facilitate normative values, focusing on the argument that these interactions can be used to provide a better protection of rights, in addition to facilitating deliberative and participatory democracy and acting as a pressure value to alleviate constitutional crises, before building on this analysis to provide a normative framework for inter-institutional interactions which facilitate these normative values, setting out a specific account of democratic dialogue.

4

Inter-institutional Interactions

The previous chapters have challenged the argument that democratic dialogue can provide a distinct theory of constitutionalism. Instead, we have argued that dialogue appears to be ubiquitous or non-existent. Either we have to accept that dialogue occurs in all constitutional systems, or we have to recognize that dialogue, as a distinct account of constitutionalism, is untenable. The previous chapter suggested that, rather than being a weakness, the broad nature of dialogue could be a strength. Dialogue requires us to examine constitutions in a different way, recognizing that institutional interactions can occur in a range of constitutions and using this to prompt a new focus of analysis, examining institutional interactions to delineate between those which are valuable and those which are not. The previous chapter already suggested one distinction between forms of institutional interactions. This distinction is best understood in terms of the aim of these interactions. We distinguished between constitutional collaboration, which aims to encourage institutions to interact to determine human rights, or refine our understanding of values, and constitutional counter-balancing which aims to ensure that interactions between institutions are not such that one institution's analysis always dominates that of another.

This conclusion contradicts a further traditional understanding of democratic dialogue, which appears to be inevitably connected to issues of constitutional design. Arguments advocating democratic dialogue began to gain prominence in the United Kingdom when applied to the Human Rights Act 1998.[1] This is not surprising given the Act's design. The Act does not give courts the power to strike down legislation that is contrary to Convention rights, merely requiring courts to read and give effect to legislation so as to comply with Convention rights, so far as this is possible,[2] and empowering them to make a declaration of incompatibility when this is not possible.[3] The legislature is free to determine whether, and if so how, to respond to such declarations of incompatibility. As such, the Act clearly provides a midway, or commonwealth protection of rights and it is these models of rights protections that attract arguments of democratic dialogue.

However, dialogue can take place in legal systems that do not adopt a mid-way protection of human rights. This is because inter-institutional interactions can take place in a range of constitutional systems. There is no necessary correlation between democratic dialogue and the commonwealth model of rights protections. If we are to understand democratic dialogue further, we need to explain more clearly the distinction between a democratic dialogue model of rights protections and a democratic dialogue reading of other models of rights protections. The distinction is two-fold. First, the distinction relies upon issues of constitutional design. A democratic dialogue

[1] As Tom Hickman's work clearly explains, although not referred to as 'democratic dialogue' this theory could provide an accurate account of Dicey's work, suggesting that arguments from democratic dialogue have greater longevity than originally thought. See T Hickman, *Public Law After the Human Rights Act* (Oxford, Hart 2010) Chapter 3.

[2] Human Rights Act 1998, s 3. [3] ibid, s 4.

Democratic Dialogue and the Constitution. First Edition. Alison L Young.
Published 2017 by Oxford University Press.

model of rights protections refers to a constitutional, or legal, protection of rights that is designed to facilitate dialogue. It is part of the model of rights protections that the legislature has the means to respond to the decisions of the judiciary as to the definition of human rights. A democratic dialogue reading can be provided for any form of rights-protection, including those that are not designed to provide the legislature with the means to respond to decisions of the judiciary. Although the facilitation of dialogue was not part of the design of the constitution or legal system, nevertheless a democratic dialogue reading will read legal provisions differently, in order to describe or advocate democratic dialogue, either advertently or inadvertently. Second, a democratic dialogue model of rights protections provides specific legal powers to different institutions to facilitate dialogue. A democratic dialogue reading of rights protections, however, either provides an account of how dialogue between different institutions can occur through political means, or advocates the facilitation of dialogue by recommending that institutions exercise their powers in a manner that would facilitate dialogue, this may include refraining from exercising their powers, or exercising them to a lesser degree than is legally possible.

Recognizing this distinction can help to explain why inter-institutional interactions can take place in a range of legal systems and how arguments can be made that dialogue can occur in legal systems with a constitutional protection of rights, a purely parliamentary protection of rights and with a democratic dialogue model of rights protections. In addition, it can explain why arguments can be made that some democratic dialogue models of rights protections can collapse into purely parliamentary or strong legal protections of rights. This may be because of arguments that the powers of the judiciary and the legislature should be read in a manner which places more power in the hands of the legislature or the judiciary, essentially ensuring that the inter-institutional interactions taking place in a legal system with a democratic dialogue model of rights protections resemble those which take place in a strong legal or purely parliamentary protection of rights. If we are to develop an account of democratic dialogue, we need to assess how institutions can interact, evaluating whether some interactions are better able to facilitate the achievement of the values of dialogue than others. Our analysis will take part in two stages. This chapter will set out different forms of inter-institutional interaction, with the following chapter drawing on the values that inter-institutional interactions can promote in order to provide a specific account of democratic dialogue. Although this chapter will evaluate inter-institutional interactions, it will do so in order to explain better or worse means of interaction.

I. Mechanisms of Inter-institutional Interaction

Institutions of the constitution can interact with each other in a range of constitutional systems. Nevertheless, an analysis of commonwealth models serves as a good starting point for our analysis of inter-institutional interactions. In particular, it provides a means of helping to delineate between mechanisms which are better able to achieve the aim of constitutional collaboration and those which may be more likely to achieve constitutional counter-balancing. Having classified how inter-institutional interactions may take place in commonwealth models, we can then expand our analysis to include other models of rights protections. It is not possible to provide a full account of all of the possible range of mechanisms through which institutions may interact across every legal system. This section will focus instead on analysing mechanisms of dialogue found in systems with a strong legal, a parliamentary, or a democratic dialogue protection of rights, drawing predominantly from the United States, Canada, and the United Kingdom, both prior to and post the Human Rights Act 1998.

A. Institutional interactions under the commonwealth model of rights protections

Stephen Gardbaum's account of the commonwealth model provides the classic account of a constitutional model designed to provide a democratic dialogue model of rights. Gardbaum argues that the commonwealth model requires political scrutiny of human rights at the pre-legislative stage, enabling rights scrutiny to take place before legislative enactment, and a weak form of judicial review. He provides four necessary and sufficient criteria of the commonwealth model. First, his theory requires a codified Bill of Rights. This Bill of Rights should be found in legislation and should be used both by political institutions, when performing pre-legislative scrutiny of human rights, and by courts applying their post-legislative scrutiny. Second, the pre-legislative scrutiny performed by a political body needs to be mandatory. There is a need for a legal requirement of such scrutiny, as opposed to a mere practice or a discretionary power. Third, courts need to be empowered to scrutinize legislation in a manner that is more stringent than an interpretative presumption that the legislature does not intend to enact legislation that contradicts human rights. Fourth, there must be a formal power for the legislature to have the final word, being able to respond to judicial post-legislative determinations of human rights through the ordinary law-making procedure.[4] Gardbaum concludes that the protection of human rights found in Canada,[5] the United Kingdom,[6] New Zealand,[7] the Australian Capital Territory,[8] and the Australian State of Victoria[9] satisfy these requirements. Dialogue occurring in these legal systems, therefore, can be said to operate by design.

Each of these four components is designed to facilitate inter-institutional interactions. By placing the protection of rights on a legislative basis, accompanied with pre-legislative scrutiny, interactions can occur as courts can respond to the pre-legislative scrutiny, referring to this assessment in their judgments and drawing on the reasoning provided by the legislature for why a provisions does, or does not, comply with human rights. Placing rights on a legislative basis also ensures that the court does not always have the upper hand, being able to strike down all and any legislation which contravenes human rights, thereby ensuring its determinations of human rights are always finally determinative. In a similar manner, by empowering courts to interpret legislation so as to protect human rights, specifically ensuring that this interpretation of legislation is not merely to ensure that legislation complies with the will of the legislature, courts are able to effectively interact with the legislature. It is not the case that the legislature always has the upper hand; courts are able to read legislation so as to protect rights, even when this appears to contradict non-ambiguous legislative provisions. However, as the legislature can always respond to these determinations, any

[4] S Gardbaum, *The New Commonwealth Model of Constitutionalism: Theory and Practice* (Cambridge University Press 2013) 29–31.

[5] Charter of Fundamental Rights and Freedoms, found in the Constitution Act 1982 (Canada), Canada Act 1982 (UK).

[6] Human Rights Act 1998.

[7] New Zealand Bill of Rights Act 1990 (New Zealand).

[8] Human Rights Act 2004 (Australian Capital Territory: Australia).

[9] Charter of Human Rights and Responsibilities 2006 (Victoria: Australia).

interaction prompted by the way in which courts interpret legislation ensures that the court does not always have the upper hand.

This brief discussion demonstrates how commonwealth models of rights protections can facilitate constitutional counter-balancing. The features of the model are designed to ensure that institutions can interact by responding to the decisions of the other and are also designed to ensure that one institution does not have the ability to consistently authoritatively determine rights. If these interactions facilitate constitutional collaboration, this is because of the way in which these mechanisms are used. Rather than being deployed as a means of asserting relative decision-making power, the legislature and the courts interact in order to achieve a better understanding of a constitutional right, or a better means in which to achieve a policy decision. The judiciary and the legislature can draw on the reasoning of the other, refining definitions of rights and feasible policy objectives.

If we are to understand mechanisms of constitutional collaboration and constitutional counter-balancing, therefore, we need to recognize that whilst some mechanisms may be understood as more likely to achieve collaboration and others appear to be more focused on ensuring constitutional counter-balancing, nevertheless whether the mechanisms achieve collaboration or not may depend on how they are used. Despite this blurring of the line between constitutional counter-balancing and constitutional collaboration, we can gain a better understanding of how commonwealth models of rights protections facilitate inter-institutional interactions through examining different examples of the commonwealth model to determine whether the mechanisms included in these models are more likely to facilitate constitutional collaboration, or are better understood as designed to ensure constitutional counter-balancing.

Perhaps the clearest example of a mechanism designed to facilitate constitutional counter-balancing is the notwithstanding clause found in section 33 of the Canadian *Charter*. The Canadian Supreme Court is empowered to strike down Canadian legislation that is contrary to the *Charter*. The Canadian legislature can respond by using section 33 to enact legislation notwithstanding the provisions of the *Charter*, this legislation being only valid for five years. This provision does not focus on ensuring that the legislature works with the judiciary in order to provide a better protection of *Charter* rights. Rather, it is perhaps better understood as a means of ensuring that the legislature can respond to judicial determinations of rights with which it disagrees. This stops the judiciary from always having the final say on rights. As such, constitutional counter-balancing occurs with the legislature using its power to legislate in a manner contrary to judicial determinations of human rights.

We can also find mechanisms which are more likely to facilitate constitutional counter-balancing than constitutional collaboration in the United Kingdom, the Australian Capital Territories, Victoria, and New Zealand. However, these mechanisms differ from those found in the Canadian *Charter* given that these legal systems do not provide the courts with the ability to strike down legislation that is contrary to human rights. Rather, these legal systems focus on providing more power to the court, whilst preserving legislative supremacy as regards human rights. As such, it is not the case that the legislature needs to be provided with mechanisms of constitutional counter-balancing in order to disagree with court-determinations of rights. Rather, these commonwealth models require that courts are given more power to achieve a better distribution of relative authoritative decision-making between the legislature and the courts, with these powers stopping short of striking down legislation which contravenes rights. Under the Human Rights Act 1998, for example, courts are required to read and give effect to legislation in a manner which complies with Convention rights, so far as it is possible to do so.[10] In addition, section 4 of the Act empowers the courts to issue a declaration of incompatibility. A declaration of incompatibility does not affect the legal force, validity, or effect of the legislation. However, the political pressure created by declarations of incompatibility, in addition to the judicial reasoning that can influence public debate and guide legislative responses, provides the courts with a form of constitutional counterbalancing. This may influence the way in which the legislature decides to exercise its discretion to either ignore the declaration of incompatibility, or to amend legislation.

Whether sections 3 and 4 under the Human Rights Act achieve constitutional collaboration or constitutional counter-balancing depends more upon how the judiciary and the legislature exercise their powers under these sections than the nature of the provisions themselves. These provisions can be used to facilitate constitutional collaboration when each institution uses these provisions to listen to the rights determination of the other, refining their understanding of human rights in the light of the reasoning of the other institution. However, they may also be used merely as a means of ensuring constitutional counter-balancing when used as a means of ensuring that the other institution's determination of rights does not prevail. We can see this when we analyse some of the accounts of theorists who advocate that sections 3 and 4 should be applied so as to facilitate different types of dialogue between legislatures and the courts.

When discussing the Human Rights Act 1998, Tom Hickman distinguishes between what he refers to as principle-posing, or weak form dialogue and strong form dialogue. His distinction is expressed in terms of the way in which the provisions of the Human Rights Act 1998 can be interpreted so as to give relatively greater power to the legislature or to the judiciary to determine rights issues. Weak form dialogue gives more relative authority over the determination of rights-issues to the legislature. Hickman regards Danny Nicol's account of democratic dialogue to be a classic account of principle-posing or weak form dialogue. Hickman argues that the role of the court in principle-posing dialogue is to merely provide a clear account of the principles governing how to resolve a rights-issue, whilst leaving the resolution of this rights-issue to the legislature. When the legislature responds to the decisions of the court, following a declaration of incompatibility issued under section 4, the legislature is not expected to give any special weight to the view of the judiciary. The legislature need only take account of the opinion of the judiciary to the extent merited by the content of that opinion. There is no need to give any weight to the opinion of the court because it came from a court.[11] Nicol argues that the courts should use section 4 as often as possible, providing strong interpretations of rights, enabling Parliament to determine whether to accept the reasoning of the courts. Although Nicol recognizes that, in most instances, Parliament is likely to agree with the courts, he argues that

> when parliamentarians disagree with judicial conceptions of rights they should say so—and say why—forthrightly, and should reiterate the compelling reasons of principle why Parliament, not the courts, remains sovereign.[12]

Nicol regards both the legislature and the courts as performing a political function. He does recognize that there are differences between the decision-making processes of the legislature and the judiciary. First, the decision-making process of the judiciary is more teleological. Their decision-making process requires courts to focus on legal values when determining rights-issues. This not only means that they are immersed in

[10] Human Rights Act 1998, s 3. [11] Hickman (n 1) 69–71.
[12] D Nicol, 'Law and Politics after the Human Rights Act' [2006] Public Law 722, 746.

these values, but also that these values provide a common ideological foundation to the decisions of the judiciary. This may help the judiciary to 'draw Parliament's attention to a perspective it might otherwise forget'.[13] Second, the judiciary has greater independence. Judicial independence ensures that the judiciary can focus on the content of rights without having to place this in the context of the pursuit of a particular political policy. Consequently, this enables courts to provide a 'candid conception of rights, and can help ensure that Parliament approves such measures only in the conscious knowledge of their adverse effect on rights'.[14] Parliament plays the predominant role, deciding whether to accept or reject the arguments of the courts on the basis of Parliament's analysis of the value of the arguments provided by the courts. There seems little role for the courts to play here, other than to draw the attention of the legislature to potential errors, which the legislature can decide to accept or reject.

Hickman's discussion of Nicol's approach to the Human Rights Act 1998 is designed to criticize the extent to which it gives more power to Parliament than to the courts. However, Nicol's account of how the courts and the legislature should use their powers under sections 3 and 4 provides an example of a reading of the Act which favours inter-institutional interactions which are more inclined to serve the aim of constitutional counter-balancing than to facilitate constitutional collaboration. Nicol encourages both the legislature and the judiciary to express clearly and forthrightly their own account of an interpretation of a right. However, there is no mention of either institution paying attention to, or responding to the interpretation of the other in a manner which reflects upon the determination of a right by the other institution. Rather, courts prepare their justification of why legislation has or has not breached Convention rights independently, based on the judiciary's own assessment of policy and rights, and the legislature decides whether it agrees or disagrees with the courts. If there is collaboration over rights it is inadvertent. Any apparent collaboration would arise because both institutions have separately reached the same conclusion. Moreover, Nicol encourages parliamentarians to disagree forthrightly when they disagree about rights, drawing on their constitutional position as sovereign law-maker, with the power to make authoritative determinations on human rights. The focus on this interaction, therefore, is on the legislature protecting its constitutional role, ensuring that it is able to respond to court determinations of rights when the legislature believes that this determination has transgressed the proper constitutional role of the court.

Hickman's account of strong form dialogue differs from weak form as it regards the courts as playing a vital role in protecting fundamental principles. Under strong form dialogue, courts

> do not simply have a subordinate or formal task, but must capture and insulate the enduring long-term values and principles of the community. Furthermore, it is the courts, and not Parliament or the executive, which determine the meaning of fundamental principles.[15]

Courts can and do recognize the role of the legislature, but they must do so through exercising prudence and restraint when determining rights-decisions. It is still the role of the court to authoritatively determine the content of long-standing principles of human rights, albeit through recognizing that these long-standing principles may provide a greater or smaller range of acceptable policy choices to the legislature which would not harm these long-standing principles.[16] Hickman sees the court as the dominant institution in protecting rights.[17] He therefore favours the use of section 3 as opposed to

[13] ibid. [14] ibid, 743–44. [15] Hickman (n 1) 71. [16] ibid, 69–72.
[17] T Hickman, 'Constitutional Dialogue, Constitutional Theories and the Human Rights Act 1998' [2005] Public Law 306, 322–26.

section 4 as the best means through which to facilitate democratic dialogue between the legislature and the judiciary.[18]

Hickman argues that section 3 facilitates institutional interactions as Parliament has the ability to respond to court decisions that read and give effect to legislation so as to promote Convention rights. Parliament may respond in four ways: (i) through re-enacting the legislation that was previously found to be incompatible with Convention rights; (ii) by enacting legislation that specifically repeals the judicial decision; (iii) by repealing the legislation and enacting a modified provision; and (iv) by doing nothing. If Parliament does nothing, then this can be seen as an acceptance of the interpretation provided by the judiciary. In situation (i), courts should continue to provide their Convention-compatible reading of the newly passed, but essentially the same, legislative provision, unless Parliament provides good reasons for why this provision is Convention-compatible which are acceptable to the courts. In situation (ii), courts should issue a declaration of incompatibility under section 4 if it is clear that Parliament wishes to legislate contrary to Convention rights or, where this is not clear, should continue to provide a Convention-compatible interpretation under section 3. In situation (iii), courts should determine whether the new legislation is Convention-compatible, paying regard to the need to distinguish between core and penumbral aspects of absolute Convention rights and to the need for balance when interpreting non-absolute rights, ensuring it does not merely accept the newly enacted provision of Parliament, but also ensuring that it does not merely reject it.[19] Courts should use section 4 either to vent scorn against the legislature when faced with legislation that cannot be read or given effect in a manner compatible with Convention rights, or where it would not be possible for the court to provide the specific remedy needed to provide an adequate protection of Convention rights.[20]

Hickman's account of how the legislature may respond to judicial readings of legislation so as to comply with Convention rights demonstrates how section 3 could be used to facilitate constitutional collaboration or as a means of constitutional counter-balancing. Regardless of whether the legislature responds by specifically repealing the legislation interpreted in a Convention-compatible manner, re-enacting legislation which reinforces its original intention, specifically modifying a judicial interpretation, or through doing nothing, the legislature would facilitate constitutional collaboration if its response was focused upon an evaluation of the judicial determination and a reasoned response to that determination. However, if the legislature's response was to merely respond to the judicial determination without providing reasons or justifications, or was motivated to respond because of a perception that the courts had transgressed their proper constitutional role, then this is better understood as achieving constitutional counter-balancing as opposed to constitutional collaboration. The legislature is aiming to preserve its constitutional position as regards the determination of rights rather than working with the judiciary to provide a protection of rights where both institutions have worked together to interpret the right.

The difference between constitutional collaboration and constitutional counter-balancing is further illustrated by Hickman's account of how the judiciary should respond to the legislature. Hickman focuses on how, when using section 3, courts should focus on the legislature's response and on whether the legislature has provided a justification for its modification or repeal of legislation. Where these justifications are found,

[18] ibid, 327. [19] ibid, 328. [20] ibid, 327.

Hickman advocates that courts should continue to use section 3 and should incorporate the legislature's reasons when determining rights-issues. This form of interaction between the legislature and the courts helps to facilitate constitutional collaboration. The judiciary and the legislature are working together to define Convention rights or to balance rights against legislative policy objectives. Hickman advocates that courts should use section 4 to declare legislation incompatible with Convention rights when it is clear that the legislature wishes to continue to legislate contrary to Convention rights, despite this Convention-incompatibility having been drawn to the attention of the legislature. In this sense, the judiciary is venting scorn at the response of the legislature through its use of section 4. Here, the judiciary are using section 4 as a means of achieving constitutional counter-balancing. This occurs if the judiciary are concerned that the legislature is failing to fulfil its proper constitutional role through legislating in a manner to effectively derogate from human rights. Their declaration of incompatibility, therefore, may be used to send a signal that the judiciary believes that the legislature is not fulfilling its proper constitutional role. However, this need not mean that every use of section 4 is only to achieve the purpose of facilitating constitutional counter-balancing. Hickman recognizes that section 4 can be used when the legislature is better placed to provide a remedy for a breach of Convention rights. Section 4 may also be used when it is not linguistically possible to read legislation so as to comply with Convention rights. In these circumstances, section 4 is better able to achieve constitutional collaboration and is not used predominantly to pursue constitutional counter-balancing.

B. Refining our understanding of inter-institutional interactions

Our analysis of commonwealth models illustrates how inter-institutional interactions can facilitate both constitutional collaboration and constitutional counter-balancing. Although some legal mechanisms may be designed to favour collaboration over counter-balancing, or counter-balancing over collaboration, the way in which provisions are used by institutions plays just as important a role as the nature of the provision itself when determining whether the inter-institutional interaction which occurs is more likely to facilitate constitutional collaboration or constitutional counter-balancing. From our brief overview, the more confrontational the mechanism, the more this is likely to focus on constitutional counter-balancing as opposed to constitutional collaboration. The more the interaction is based on reasoning, justifications, and respect for the other institution, the more the interaction will be likely to facilitate constitutional collaboration.

Similar conclusions arise when we analyse inter-institutional interactions which take place in legal systems that do not use a commonwealth model of rights protections. Barry Friedman, for example, analyses dialogue which can occur in the US constitution, arguing that inter-institutional interactions may facilitate three forms of dialogue: co-operative; educative; or push/shove dialogue. The first two provide a means through which courts and legislatures may work together to determine constitutional rights. Co-operative dialogue occurs when one branch seeks assistance from the other. Educative dialogue occurs when the institution sets out to educate the other as to the limits of rights.[21] Push/shove dialogue, however, focuses predominantly on facilitating constitutional counter-balancing.

[21] B Friedman, 'A Different Dialogue: The Supreme Court, Congress and Federal Jurisdiction' (1990) 85 North Western Law Review 1.

Co-operative and educative dialogue can facilitate constitutional collaboration both when courts act as a speaker and as a facilitator. Courts facilitate inter-institutional interactions as a speaker when they provide clear and reasoned accounts for their conclusion as to why legislation complies with or breaches constitutional rights. Courts encourage constitutional collaboration as a facilitator of institutional interactions by exercising restraint, prodding the legislature into responding. Moreover, courts can facilitate dialogue through responding to the views of the public. Courts may incorporate public opinion into their deliberations on human rights, as well as drawing attention to issues through deciding matters of constitutional importance to the public. In all of these instances, the focus of the court is not in challenging the authority of the legislature, pushing back against its authority, but in facilitating inter-institutional collaboration.[22]

An examination of Friedman's three-fold classification of dialogue helps to further refine our understanding of constitutional collaboration and constitutional counter-balancing. If dialogue can be co-operative, educative, and 'push/shove' then this would appear to suggest that co-operative dialogue is better able to achieve the objectives of constitutional collaboration required to provide a better protection of rights. However, if this is the case, then this may cause problems for our refinement of constitutional collaboration in terms of its ability to provide a better protection of rights. It is hard to find examples of co-operative dialogue, particularly outside commonwealth models of rights protections, as it is rare to find evidence of courts or legislatures expressly seeking the advice of the other. In order to illustrate co-operative dialogue in the United States, Friedman provides the example of the habeas corpus cases. When interpreting the Habeas Corpus Act 1867, the courts first read the legislation in a restricted manner, before adopting a broader interpretation in the 1950s. Friedman states that the courts adopted a broader interpretation without paying regard to Congressional intent as expressed in the more narrowly worded legislation. The broadening of the availability of habeas corpus led to the development of more precise rules as to its application. Friedman argues that these rules were developed through a process of co-operative dialogue with the judiciary developing principles that were later re-enacted in legislative amendments by Congress reflecting these judicial developments; where judicial interpretations were indirectly sanctioned by Congress, or where Congress enacted legislation overturning these judicial developments, with the courts later acquiescing to this change.[23]

If we follow Friedman's example of co-operative dialogue, constitutional collaboration occurs whenever there is evidence of either institution acquiescing to the opinion of the other. There is no need for express evidence of either institution actively seeking advice from the other. Rather, dialogue is co-operative whenever there are amicable exchanges between institutions, regardless of whether this is evidenced through the legislature accepting the view of the judiciary or vice-versa. Co-operation, therefore, can occur actively or passively. Active co-operation arises when one institution actively seeks or gives advice to the other. Passive co-operation occurs when inter-institutional interaction reaches an amicable solution. This may occur in a variety of ways. First, the institutions may just happen to agree. Second, given the different complementary constitutional roles of the legislature and the courts, it may be that a co-operative solution arises as both institutions perform their proper constitutional role. Third, passive co-operation may occur through each institution taking account of the anticipated

[22] B Friedman, 'Dialogue and Judicial Review' (1993) 91 Michigan Law Review 577, 666–71.
[23] Friedman (n 21) 11–13.

reactions of the other, using these anticipated reactions as a means of modifying the way in which each institution performs their own specific function. This may be, for example, in order to avoid anticipated adverse reactions from the other institution, or where institutions take account of the anticipated reaction of the general public to a rights-determination of the legislature or the court.

However, if we understand co-operation in this manner, then it becomes difficult to differentiate Friedman's example of co-operation from his account of push/shove dialogue. Push/shove dialogue takes place when each institution aims to resist, or push against, the actions of the other. Nicol's theory of democratic dialogue in the United Kingdom, for example, could be regarded as providing an example of push/shove democratic dialogue. As discussed above, Nicol encourages courts to use section 4 of the Human Rights Act 1998 in preference to using section 3. When doing so, courts should decide the rights-issue for themselves. The same is true of the legislature. The tension between these assertions leads to a resolution of the rights-issue through an agonistic process. Courts push one way and the legislature pushes back in the opposite direction.[24] In these situations, it may be that the courts and the legislature agree, or that they act politely, responding in an amicable manner to the reactions of the other, or they may modify their account of rights in anticipation of, or in reaction to, the account of the other. If the difference between co-operation and push/shove is whether exchanges between institutions are amicable or not, then it becomes even more difficult to differentiate between mechanisms which may facilitate constitutional collaboration and those which facilitate constitutional counter-balancing. The only additional aspect appears to be that, under Friedman's account of push/shove dialogue, institutions are influenced more by their potential power vis-à-vis the other institution, and thus their ability to win in an eventual conflict. However, passive co-operation is also based on anticipated reactions of the other institution, which may also turn on the relative power of each institution.

Our analysis suggests, therefore, that it is hard to draw a clear line between forms of inter-institutional interaction which are more likely to facilitate constitutional counter-balancing and those which are more likely to achieve constitutional collaboration. The following sections will focus first on how mechanisms of inter-institutional interaction can be used to achieve constitutional counter-balancing as these mechanisms become more important in legal systems which provide for a strong legal or a weak political means of protecting rights. In legal systems which provide courts with the power to strike down legislation, the balance of power to determine rights is placed with the judiciary. By contrast, those with a parliamentary protection of rights are designed to facilitate parliamentary or legislative supremacy. It is the role of the legislature to have the final determinative say. Constitutional counter-balancing, therefore, takes on a more important role. Without these mechanisms, it may be impossible for constitutional collaboration to operate effectively, given that without constitutional counter-balancing, it may well be that one institution can always have the final say, effectively cancelling out the role of the other institution when collaborating over the definition of rights, or the refinement of public policy. Having established aspects of inter-institutional interactions which may facilitate constitutional counter-balancing, we will evaluate how these mechanisms may also achieve constitutional collaboration to assess whether there are some mechanisms of inter-institutional interaction which are better able to facilitate constitutional collaboration than others.

[24] Nicol (n 12).

II. Inter-institutional Interactions outside the Commonwealth Model

Constitutional counter-balancing takes on a more important role in those constitutions that have not adopted a commonwealth model of rights protections. In systems which have adopted a constitutional protection of rights, these mechanisms can either be found through the adoption of measures which reduce the powers of the court, advocating, for example, that the court should not always exercise its powers to strike down legislation in order to provide a greater possible range of decision-making power to the legislature, or through mechanisms that the legislature may use to respond to judicial determinations. In legal systems where courts do not have the power to strike down legislation, constitutional counter-balancing may occur through mechanisms which allow the judiciary to provide a stronger protection of rights, applying non-legal or legal pressure on the legislature to comply with human rights. This may also occur through the legislature refraining from exercising their powers. These mechanisms may also provide a means of facilitating constitutional collaboration. Whether constitutional collaboration occurs or not depends, at least in part, on the way in which these mechanisms are used and whether there is the motivation on the part of the legislature or the executive to collaborate regarding the definition of a human right or a general principle. Nevertheless, it is still the case that some mechanisms are more likely to achieve constitutional collaboration than others.

A. Courts

(i) Judicial restraint

The main mechanism through which courts can interact with legislatures in legal systems with a constitutional protection of rights is through exercising a form of judicial restraint. When analysing the ways in which courts can facilitate dialogue in the US Constitution, Heise distinguishes between active and passive judicial participation. Active judicial participation occurs when courts give advice to the legislature or the executive, either through dicta or through giving advisory opinions. Passive judicial participation occurs when the court refrains from exercising its powers. The court may exercise passive judicial participation either by refusing to hear a case, or by hearing a case, but doing so in a manner that is more restrained than striking down legislation.[25] When analysing these mechanisms, passive judicial participation may be more likely to facilitate constitutional counter-balancing, with constitutional collaboration occurring more inadvertently. Active judicial participation, however, may be more likely to facilitate constitutional collaboration. As such, this section will focus first on mechanisms of passive judicial participation, before assessing the extent to which active judicial participation may facilitate constitutional collaboration. Having distinguished between active and passive judicial participation, Michael Heise distinguishes further between two forms of passive judicial participation, when the court declines to hear a case and where the court hears a case, but declines to issue a remedy. Both may be used as a means of facilitating constitutional counter-balancing in order to help achieve

[25] M Heise, 'Preliminary Thoughts on the Virtues of Passive Dialogue' (2000) 34 Akron Law Review 73, 76–77.

successful constitutional collaboration in legal systems with a strong, constitutional protection of rights.

The classic example of a way in which constitutional counter-balancing can be maintained through the court refusing to hear cases is Alexander Bickel's account of the passive virtues in the US Constitution.[26] Since the seminal case of *Marbury v Madison*, the US Supreme Court has been empowered to hear individual petitions that legislation is unconstitutional and to grant remedies in these cases, including striking down unconstitutional legislation.[27] However, just because the court is empowered to hear such cases, does not mean that the court should hear every individual petition that is put before it. The US Supreme Court has a discretionary power to determine which cases it will hear. Bickel refers to how the Supreme Court determines issues of ripeness, standing, whether there is a case or controversy, and whether the issue is a political question when determining whether the court has the power to hear a case.

Ripeness is determined by the Ashwander rules. In *Ashwander v Tennessee Valley Authority*, Brandeis J, delivering a concurring opinion, set out a series of rules that the Supreme Court had developed through its case law, governing when the Supreme Court would avoid passing judgment upon constitutional issues that were nevertheless within its jurisdiction.[28] The court should: (i) refuse to hear a case in a 'friendly, non-adversary proceeding';[29] (ii) not hear a case which would 'anticipate a question of Constitutional law' deciding an issue when it is not necessary to do so;[30] (iii) ensure it only determined the narrow issue before it on the facts, not broadening this beyond what is required to decide the case;[31] (iv) not decide a case on Constitutional grounds if there are other grounds for determining the outcome of the case;[32] (v) not hear the case if the applicant has not suffered any damage or injury caused by the alleged unconstitutionality;[33] (vi) refuse to hear a case brought at the instigation of an individual who has benefitted from the measure that is claimed to be unconstitutional;[34] and (vii) not declare a statute unconstitutional if it is possible to resolve this unconstitutionality through interpreting the statute so as to render it compatible with the Constitution.[35] The Supreme Court may also decline to exercise jurisdiction through refusing to grant a writ of certiorari, or refusing to hear a case 'for want of a substantial federal issue'.[36]

Bickel argues that the Supreme Court does not determine these issues through a mechanical application of legal rules in a constructionist manner. Instead he argues that these provisions grant the Supreme Court a discretionary power as to whether to hear the case before it. In Bickel's words:

> The Court is able to play its full role … maintaining itself in the tension on which our society thrives, because at least in modern times it nearly always has three courses of action open to it: it may strike down legislation as inconsistent with principle; it may legitimate it; or it may do neither. When it does neither, it need not forsake its educational function, nor abandon principle. Indeed, very often it engages in a Socratic dialogue with the other institutions and with society as a whole concerning the necessity for this or that measure, for this or that compromise.[37]

Louis Fisher's account of dialogue in the United States provides clear examples of how the exercise of these passive virtues, through refusing to decide a case, may have been

[26] A Bickel, 'Foreward: The Passive Virtues' [1961] Harvard Law Review 40; and A Bickel, *The Least Dangerous Branch: The Supreme Court at the Bar of Politics* (New York, Bobs-Merrill Company 1962).
[27] *Marbury v Madison* (1803) 5 US 137 (US Supreme Court).
[28] *Ashwander v Tennessee Valley Authority* (1936) 297 US 288 (US Supreme Court).
[29] ibid, 346. [30] ibid, 346–47. [31] ibid, 347. [32] ibid.
[33] ibid, 347–48. [34] ibid, 348. [35] ibid.
[36] Bickel, 'Foreward: The Passive Virtues' (n 26) 46. [37] ibid, 50.

used as means of facilitating constitutional counter-balancing between the legislature, the judiciary, and also the executive.[38] The 'political question' issue is the clearest example of a mechanism that could be used to maintain constitutional counter-balancing. When determining that an issue raises a 'political question', the court is effectively deciding that it is an issue that should be authoritatively decided by a different institution. The test essentially evaluates whether the issue is one that is suited for judicial resolution. By determining that the issue is 'political', the court is essentially determining that the legislature or executive have the authority to resolve that particular issue. Constitutional counter-balancing is maintained through the delineation of what is legal and what is political, enabling political institutions to take some decisions free from the legal checks performed by the courts.[39]

Other passive virtues may also be used to maintain constitutional counter-balancing. Fisher suggests that ripeness may be used as a means of avoiding a socially sensitive issue. For example, in *Naim v Naim*[40] the Supreme Court refused to hear a case challenging the constitutionality of a Virginia statute preventing interracial marriages on the grounds of the inadequacy of the record and the lack of a federal question. Fisher, drawing on Bickel's analysis of the case, suggests that the Supreme Court refused to exercise jurisdiction in this case to buy time, waiting for the issue to become less controversial, allowing it to strike down legislation in the future when the principle of desegregation had been more clearly established.[41] Understood in terms of constitutional counter-balancing, *Naim v Naim* provides a potential example of where the Supreme Court did not exercise its power to strike down constitutional legislation for fear of an anticipated reaction from the legislature and from the people. By exercising this restraint, the Court maintained constitutional counter-balancing through enabling the legislature to enact what was potentially unconstitutional, albeit popular, legislation.

In addition to refusing to hear a case, courts may exercise their powers in a more restrictive manner. James Thayer's account of judicial minimalism may be best regarded as an example of judicial restraint that facilitates constitutional counter-balancing.[42] Thayer argued that courts did, and should, exercise powers of constitutional review in a restrained manner. It was not the job of the court to authoritatively determine the meaning of a constitutional provision, correcting any legislation that did not correspond to the courts' determination. The court should not strike down legislation as unconstitutional 'merely because it is concluded that upon a just and true construction the law is unconstitutional'.[43] Rather, Thayer argued that a rule of administration had developed in tandem with the petition for constitutional review established in *Marbury v Madison*. The rule of administration proscribes that the court 'can only disregard the Act when those who have the right to make laws have not merely made a mistake, but have made a very clear one—so clear that it is not open to rational question'.[44] Thayer developed this rule out of respect and comity for the constitutional authority of the law-maker. It can be interpreted as a means of maintaining constitutional counter-balancing. The court does not exercise its power to correct the legislature. Rather, it gives greater decision-making power to the legislature, only striking down legislation that

[38] L Fisher, *Constitutional Dialogues: Interpretation as a Political Process* (Princeton University Press 1988).

[39] ibid, 110–16. [40] (1955) 350 US 891.

[41] Fisher (n 38) 108–09; and Bickel, *The Least Dangerous Branch* (n 26) 174.

[42] JB Thayer, 'The Origin and Scope of the American Doctrine of Constitutional Law' (1893) 7 Harvard Law Review 129.

[43] ibid, 144. [44] ibid.

manifestly disregards constitutional principles. The court operates more as a back-stop to correct mistakes, as opposed to an institution with sole and full authority to determine the meaning of constitutional provisions.

Michael Perry's account of judicial minimalism draws on the work of Thayer. He argues for a position of originalism when determining the meaning of constitutional terms, coupled with judicial minimalism when it comes to the specification of individual rights and liberties contained in the broad constitutional provisions. Courts should interpret the meaning of constitutional terms by determining the intentions of the original authors of the Constitution. However, this needs to be coupled with the specification of constitutional terms. Specification occurs not when we ask what speech means when determining whether a particular provision is contrary to the First Amendment, preventing laws restricting free speech, but when, for example, the court determines whether a law empowering Internet Service Providers to disclose the identity of internet trolls is a law restricting free speech. Judicial minimalism at the stage of the specification of the right occurs when the court assesses whether the legislation is rational, within a reasonable range of possible specifications of the First Amendment, as opposed to specifying the right for itself and correcting the legislation where this is contrary to the conclusion reached by the court.[45]

Although Perry does not expressly regard his account of judicial minimalism as a means of obtaining constitutional counter-balancing, this can be implied both from his justification of minimalism and also his avocation of the adoption of the Canadian model of rights protections in the United States. Perry's preference for minimalism stems from a recognition of the lack of either the legislature or the courts to claim conclusive authority to determine the specification of human rights against a backdrop of moral pluralism. It can be reasonable to disagree with rights specifications of both institutions. To allow the legislature to also be able to make reasonable specifications of rights respects their constitutional authority to make these determinations, especially when recognizing that this helps to foster democracy, facilitating individuals and their representatives to take rights seriously, focusing on developing their own specifications of rights as opposed to merely accepting the specifications provided by the courts.[46] Second, Perry argues in favour of the Canadian system of rights protections, focusing on the notwithstanding clause found in section 33 of the *Charter*. He argues that this is a better means of protecting rights than using principles of judicial minimalism, given that this system still permits the courts to play a full and active role in the determination of rights, whilst ensuring that the judicial voice is not privileged.[47]

Another way in which the judiciary could exercise its powers so as to help maintain constitutional counter-balancing is to employ what Ronald Krotozynski calls constitutional flares.[48] Krotozynski argues that Federal Courts in the United States deploy constitutional flares when they fire warning shots at the legislature. They do so by refraining from striking down legislation as unconstitutional, whilst making it clear to the legislature that there are problems of constitutionality and warning the legislature

[45] M Perry, 'The Constitution, the Courts and the Question of Minimalism' (1993) 88 Northwestern University Law Review 93; and M Perry, 'Protecting Human Rights in a Democracy—What Role for the Courts?' (2003) 38 Wake Forest Law Review 635.

[46] Perry, 'The Constitution, the Courts and the Question of Minimalism' (n 45) 115–53; and Perry, 'Protecting Human Rights in a Democracy—What Role for the Courts?' (n 45) 679–88.

[47] Perry 'The Constitution, the Courts and the Question of Minimalism' (n 45) 153–160 and Perry 'Protecting Human Rights in a Democracy—What Role for the Courts?' (n 45) 689–96.

[48] R Krotozynski, 'Constitutional Flares: On Judges, Legislatures and Dialogue' (1998) 83 Minnesota Law Review 1.

that, should no changes be made, the legislation could be struck down in future as unconstitutional. Krotozynski provides Calabresi's concurring opinion in *US v Then* as an example of a constitutional flare.[49] The case concerned legislation which established sentencing for crack cocaine offences relative to those for cocaine. The sentencing ratio was 100:1 for crack cocaine compared to cocaine offences. Then argued against his sentence for a crack cocaine offence. He claimed that the sentencing guidelines were unconstitutional, breaching the equal protection clause, given that members of the Afro-Caribbean community were more likely to be convicted for offences relating to crack cocaine than to cocaine. Calabresi, in agreement with the majority, concluded that the sentencing guidelines were not unconstitutional as the applicant had not established any intention to discriminate on the part of the sentencing commission who established the 100:1 ratio. However, he also remarked that the sentencing ratio was 'deeply troubling'.[50] Although the information concerning the discriminatory impact that was available at the time the sentencing decision was made would not be sufficient to establish a discriminatory intention, he could foresee that 'constitutional arguments that were unavailing in the past may not be foreclosed in the future'.[51] His judgment, therefore, warned the legislature that, should facts be available in the future to demonstrate the discriminatory impact of the sentencing ratios, the court would strike down the legislation.

Krotozynski argues that constitutional flares may encourage interactions between the judiciary and Congress. In particular, he argues that the use of constitutional flares helps to facilitate inter-branch comity. It can prevent direct conflict in the future through providing the legislature with a warning that continued action may give rise to unconstitutionality. This warning provides the legislature with the opportunity to respond, should it wish to do so, to avoid future problems.[52] Krotozynski's focus on comity, inter alia, demonstrates how his constitutional flare can be used to facilitate constitutional counter-balancing. It provides the legislature with an opportunity to reflect upon legislation that may be deemed unconstitutional, in a manner similar to the use of the declaration of incompatibility under the Human Rights Act 1998. In doing so, the legislature can determine whether it believes that the court has transgressed its proper constitutional role, which may then influence the legislature's response.

Krotozynski's argument also shows how these interactions may facilitate constitutional collaboration as well as constitutional counter-balancing. A constitutional flare provides the legislature with the opportunity to take a second look at legislation, being aware that, although currently constitutionally valid, there are serious concerns as to its potential impact on human rights which may lead to the conclusion in the future that the legislation is constitutionally invalid. Krotozynski's account of constitutional flares draws on the work of Guido Calabresi, who argues for a greater use of forms of judicial review that enable the legislature to take a second look at legislation, using the power to strike down legislation as a last resort.[53]

Whilst Krotozynski focused on how Calabresi's second look doctrine could encourage constitutional counter-balancing, focusing predominantly on issues of comity, Dan Coenen draws on the same work as a means of facilitating constitutional collaboration between the legislature and the court. Coenen advocates that courts should focus not on the substance of decisions, but on how the decision is made, focusing in particular

[49] *US v Then* (1995) 56 F 3d 464. [50] ibid, 467. [51] ibid.

[52] Krotozynski (n 48) 57–60.

[53] G Calabresi, 'Foreword: Anti-Discrimination and Constitutional Accountability (What the Bork/Brennan Debate Ignores)' (1991) 105 Harvard Law Review 80.

on procedural flaws. Coenen draws on the *Ashwander* principles, for example where the court requires clear legislative statements to demonstrate an intention on the part of the legislature to enact provisions that are contrary to constitutional rights. Coenen also relies on examples of where courts focus clearly on examining whether evidence cited by the legislature really does support its aims and Ely's focus on the protection of discrete and insular minorities. Coenen argues that this focus facilitates collaboration as the court is able to provide a detailed account of why a provision is or is not contrary to Constitutional rights, whilst striking down the decision on process as opposed to substantive grounds. This enables the legislature to further its policy through re-enacting the legislation through the proper procedure, taking account of the court's justifications for potential substantive incompatibility. In this manner, the second look at the hands of the legislature may be used as a means of working together with the courts to balance constitutional rights and legislative policies.[54]

When exercised in this manner, constitutional flares are more akin to a form of active as opposed to passive judicial participation. The court is not merely refraining from exercising its powers, thereby giving greater relative decision-making power to the legislature. Rather, the judiciary is providing detailed advice and guidance as to why a provision may undermine human rights. In a similar manner, the way in which the judiciary exercises judicial minimalism may determine the extent to which inter-institutional interactions may facilitate constitutional collaboration. When discussing judicial minimalism, we focused on how judicial restraint could facilitate constitutional counter-balancing through providing the legislature with decision-making power despite the ability of the courts to strike down legislation which contravenes constitutionally protected human rights. Cass Sunstein also advocates judicial minimalism in the face of reasonable debate as to the resolution of the particular rights-issue before the court, advocating an approach focusing on narrow and shallow as opposed to deep and wide judicial decisions. Narrow and shallow decisions focus on giving a specific response to the question. They do not provide broader principles or consequences, or give deeply theorized justifications in the same way as broad and wide judicial decisions. Sunstein argues that judicial minimalism can facilitate democracy, as judicial minimalism may prompt discussion and deliberation in the legislature.[55] Discussions and deliberations, in turn, facilitate constitutional collaboration.

Sunstein's work investigates how judicial determinations can be democracy-permitting, democracy-forcing, and democracy-restricting, favouring judgments which permit or force democracy. Shallow and narrow decisions may permit democracy by leaving more space for deliberation by legislatures. They can be particularly useful when faced with contestable rights issues. Broader and more deeply theorized judgments can force democratic decision-makers to deliberate further. For example, the court may strike down overly vague provisions in order to facilitate democracy. A vaguely worded provision in legislation will leave greater leeway to the executive to

[54] DT Coenen, 'A Constitution of Collaboration: Protecting Fundamental Values with Second Look Rules of Interbranch Dialogue' (2001) 42 William and Mary Law Review 1575; DT Coenen, 'Structural Review' (2001) 42 William and Mary Law Review 1881; and DT Coenen, 'The Rhenquist Court, Structural Due Process and Semi-Substantive Constitutional Review' (2002) 75 Southern California Law Review 1281.

[55] See C Sunstein, *One Case at a Time: Judicial Minimalism and the Supreme Court* (Harvard University Press 1999); C Sunstein, 'Leaving Things Undecided' (1996) 110 Harvard Law Review 6; C Sunstein, 'Incompletely Theorised Agreements' (1995) 108 Harvard Law Review 1733; C Sunstein, 'Beyond Judicial Minimalism' (2007) 43 Tulsa Law Review 825; and C Sunstein, *The Partial Constitution* (Harvard University Press 1993).

enact detailed measures to clarify vague provisions. If the court strikes down the legislation, it can encourage legislatures to deliberate to provide these details, substituting executive discretion with deliberatively reasoned conclusions.

Sunstein also recognizes a role for the court to take account of anticipated public reactions to their decisions, particularly when there would be outrage in response to a judicial determination. He focuses predominantly on consequentialist grounds. If, despite the judicial determination to protect a particular right, it would not be achieved in practice because of public outrage, then there may be good consequentialist grounds for the court to take this potential outrage into account. There may also be epistemic grounds for taking public reactions into account, based on considerations of humility. It may be that the public are better placed to decide some issues and intense public disagreement may suggest that a judicial determination is wrong. However, it is important for the judiciary to be wary of systemic bias in public reactions, weakening the epistemic justification for courts to pay attention to public reaction.[56]

(ii) Judicial maximization

In a legal system where courts do not have the power to strike down legislation which contravenes human rights, constitutional counter-balancing requires courts to exercise their powers in a manner which may provide them with a greater ability to protect rights than they would appear to be given by the constitution. I have referred to this as 'judicial maximization' to recognize that this need not carry the connotation the inter-institutional interactions entail going beyond the understood constitutional limits of the power of the judiciary which may be entailed by the use of the term 'judicial activism'. Inter-institutional interactions can arise through the way in which courts exercise their powers to interpret legislation or to provide remedies for abuses of rights. Constitutional counter-balancing occurs in common law legal systems when courts use the common law to strengthen their ability to protect human rights. The more these developments are seen as a means of specifically pushing back against the legislature, or pushing at the boundaries of the constitutional limits of the judiciary, the more interactions will be perceived as a means of achieving constitutional counter-balancing. The more the judiciary provide reasons for their conclusions, or provide space for legislative response, the more these interactions will help to facilitate constitutional collaboration, particularly when these interactions are accompanied by a clear statement of reasons as to why legislative provisions contravene human rights.

The clearest example of inter-institutional interactions which predominantly achieve constitutional counter-balancing as opposed to collaboration is found in a series of decisions of the UK courts where the judiciary have made clear assertions of judicial sovereignty. The UK constitution is widely regarded as being based upon parliamentary sovereignty. This is reflected in the lack of the ability of the UK courts to strike down legislation. Nevertheless, there are examples in UK case law of judicial statements to the effect that parliamentary sovereignty, including the legal understanding that courts cannot strike down legislation, is itself a principle of the common law. As such, this can be modified by the courts, including to the extent of recognizing that

[56] C Sunstein, 'If People Would be Out-raged by Their Rulings Should Judges Care?' (2007) 60 Stanford Law Review 155. See also C Bateup, 'The Dialogic Promise: Assessing the Normative Potential of Theories of Constitutional Dialogue' (2006) 71 Brooklyn Law Review 1109; and C Bateup, 'Expanding the Conversation: American and Canadian Experiences of Constitutional Dialogue in Comparative Perspective' (2006) 21 Temple International and Comparative Law Journal 1.

specific legislation is constitutionally invalid. The clearest example of this assertion originates in the statements of Laws LJ in *Thoburn*.[57] In this case, concerning the validity of directly effective EU law, Laws LJ distinguished between constitutional and ordinary statutes. The main aspect of this distinction was that constitutional statutes were immune from implied repeal, requiring instead clear and precise words to illustrate an intention to override the provisions of a constitutional statute, this perhaps only being achieved through express repeal. According to Laws LJ:

> The common law has in recent years allowed, or rather created, exceptions to the doctrine of implied repeal: a doctrine which was always the common law's own creature. There are now classes or types of legislative provision which cannot be repealed by mere implication. These instances are given, and can only be given, by our own courts, to which the scope and nature of Parliamentary sovereignty are ultimately confided.[58]

The assertion that it is the courts who determine the scope of parliamentary sovereignty can be best understood as giving rise to an interaction with the legislature which is designed to maintain constitutional counter-balancing. Rather than focusing on interactions with the legislature which may facilitate constitutional collaboration over the doctrine of implied repeal and its application to directly effective EU law, the statements of Laws LJ seem more to be intended to push-back against the legislature. Following *Thoburn*, legislatures wishing to overturn constitutional statutes must either do so through express repeal, or through specifically worded legislation which makes clear the legislature's intention to enact provisions which contradict a constitutional statute. This empowers the courts to push back against a move by the legislature to remove human rights, or other constitutionally important principles, in two ways. First, it is the courts that determine which statutory provisions are constitutional. As such, courts can determine whether the legislature needs to provide specific or express words to overturn a particular legislative provision. Second, it is the courts who determine whether legislation purporting to overturn a constitutional statute has expressed this will of the legislature clearly enough in order to achieve its objective.

More fundamentally, by asserting the ability of the common law to determine the content of parliamentary sovereignty, the judiciary are asserting their ability to play a role in the determination of the distribution of constitutional powers between the legislature and the courts, as well as the potential distribution of powers between the United Kingdom and the European Union. This can be illustrated in dicta of the UK courts concerning the potential of the judiciary, in extreme circumstances, to not recognize an Act of Parliament as valid legislation, particularly as regards legislation that would undermine constitutional principles, specifically that which would remove the power of the courts to carry out judicial review.[59] In addition, judicial statements by Justices of the Supreme Court in *HS2* set out that the courts can use constitutional statutes, constitutional instruments and constitutional principles as a means of limiting the extent to which the UK courts will regard the United Kingdom as having transferred law-making power to the European Union.[60] All of these measures provide an example of constitutional counter-balancing, with the courts asserting their right to play a major role in the determination of the UK constitution.

[57] *Thoburn v Sunderland City Council* [2002] EWHC 195 (Admin), [2003] QB 151.

[58] ibid, [60] (Laws LJ).

[59] *R (Jackson) v Attorney General* [2005] UKHL 56, [2006] 1 AC 262, [102] (Lord Steyn) and [107] (Lord Hope); *AXA General Insurance v Lord Advocate* [2011] UKSC 46; [2012] 1 AC 868, [51] (Lord Hope).

[60] *R (HS2) v Secretary of State for Transport* [2014] UKSC 3, [2014] 1 WLR 324.

Inter-institutional interactions that are more likely to achieve constitutional counter-balancing than constitutional collaboration can also be found in legal systems with a written constitution. One example of this is provided by the implied rights cases in Australia. Although Australia has a written Constitution, with constitutional review for the provisions protecting Australia's federal structure, the Australian Constitution does not include a Federal Bill of Rights. Nevertheless, the Australian High Court concluded that the Constitution, founded on principles of representative democracy, included implied rights, specifically the implied right of political communication.[61] The implied right, once read in to the Constitution, had constitutional status. Therefore, it could be used to strike down legislation contrary to the implied right of political communication. By reading implied rights into the Constitution, the courts, arguably, gained a measure which could facilitate constitutional counter-balancing, providing courts with the power to strike down legislation, despite the courts not having this power with regard to the right of political communication specifically, or freedom of expression or human rights more generally.

Constitutional counter-balancing can also occur when courts devise new remedies or procedures. *Marbury v Madison* provides an example of a means through which the US Supreme Court facilitated constitutional counter-balancing in this way.[62] The US Supreme Court implied a power to grant a remedy into the US Constitution, empowering the courts in a system of constitutionally protected rights to push-back against the legislature by effectively enforcing constitutional provisions. By allowing individual petitions against unconstitutional legislation, in addition to the ability to strike down unconstitutional legislation, the US Supreme Court redressed a perceived imbalance in their constitutional powers. Similarly, the recent New Zealand High Court decision in *Taylor*, where the court decided that it had the power to issue a declaration of inconsistency against legislation which could not be read so as to be compatible with the New Zealand Bill of Rights Act 1990 can also be interpreted as a means through which the court can achieve constitutional counter-balancing.[63] This is because the court read this power into the legislation, despite the 1990 Act not including a provision empowering the courts to issue a declaration of inconsistency.

Constitutional collaboration is more likely to occur when courts use their existing powers to provide stronger protections of rights, with collaboration being more likely when courts provide justifications for their conclusions. One example of a means through which courts may facilitate constitutional collaboration is provided by the principle of legality, developed in English law. The principle of legality is a principle of statutory interpretation. It recognizes that Parliament does not legislate in a vacuum. Rather, it legislates against a backdrop of principles of the common law. As such, broad legislative terms are to be interpreted in a manner which complies with this backdrop of common law principles. Parliament would have understood, when legislating, the context of these principles and so is not to have been taken to have intended to legislate in a manner that contradicts these principles unless it clearly and specifically expresses its intention to do so. Although originally used to ensure that broad legislative principles were not interpreted so as to remove the rights of natural justice and procedural fairness,[64] the principle was later interpreted to extend to include a presumption that Parliament would not intend to legislate contrary to substantive principles of the

[61] *Australian Capital Television v Commonwealth* (1992) 177 C LR 106 (High Court Australia).
[62] 5 US 137 (1803).
[63] *Taylor v Attorney-General of New Zealand* [2015] NZHC 1706.
[64] See, for example, *R v Home Secretary, ex parte Doody* [1994] AC 531.

common law. For example, in *Leech* the principle was used to conclude that a statutory provision that empowered the creation of general prison rules would not empower the restriction of communications between prisoners and their solicitors due to this being in conflict with common law principles.[65] In *Witham* a general provision empowering the Lord Chancellor to set legal fees did not empower the Lord Chancellor to set fees that would preclude individuals from pursuing legal cases, thus restricting the common law principle of access to justice.[66]

Courts may go further to facilitate constitutional collaboration by providing an outline of the way in which the legislature may respond in order to ensure that future legislation can be made compatible with human rights. The clearest example of this is Neal Katyal's account of constitutional road maps, in his assessment of the US Constitution.[67] This occurs when the courts couple restraint with advice to the legislature as to how it could achieve its objectives without breaching constitutional rights. Courts may facilitate constitutional collaboration through a process of clarification, pointing out potential ambiguities in legislative provisions and providing a means of resolving these difficulties, or advising of future potential problems and suggesting possible resolutions of these difficulties. In addition, courts may strike down a provision as unconstitutional, but then provide dicta as to how the legislature may achieve the same policy goal without breaching the constitution. Alternatively, it may uphold a statute as constitutional, whilst making it clear that legislation going beyond these provisions would be struck down as unconstitutional. All of these mechanisms may facilitate constitutional collaboration, through providing general, reasoned advice to the legislature. Although provided as an account of the powers of the court under a constitutional structure where courts can strike down legislation which contravenes constitutionally protected human rights, the ability to outline possible human-rights compatible solutions could also be used in legal systems where courts can issue declarations of incompatibility or of inconsistency.

B. Law-makers

The previous section recognized how constitutional counter-balancing can occur through inter-institutional interactions in a system with a constitutional protection of rights through forms of judicial restraint. In contrast the judiciary needed to either be activist, or maximize their exercise of constitutional powers if they were to produce achieve constitutional counterbalancing in a system with a parliamentary protection of rights. The arguments are, understandably, reversed when we analyse the mechanisms of inter-institutional interaction which may be triggered by law-makers. Legislative restraint is needed to facilitate constitutional counter-balancing in legal systems where legislatures have the final say over rights, with more active legislative action being needed in legal systems where courts can strike down legislation which contravenes constitutionally protected human rights.

It is difficult to find direct evidence of legislature's refraining from exercising powers in order to maintain constitutional counter-balancing in a system with parliamentary sovereignty. Where this occurs, it can be seen through legislatures adhering to legal advice. There is more evidence of constitutional counter-balancing mechanisms exercised by the law-maker in legal systems with a constitutional protection of rights. In a

[65] *R v Secretary of State for the Home Department, ex parte Leech* [1994] QB 198.
[66] *R v Lord Chancellor, ex parte Witham* [1998] QB 575.
[67] N Katyal, 'Judges as Advice Givers' (1998) 50 Stanford Law Review 1709.

system of constitutional supremacy, there are nevertheless mechanisms that the legislature and executive can use to achieve an element of constitutional counter-balancing, enabling them to respond to judicial determinations of rights. As well as these more radical means through which constitutional counter-balancing can be achieved, there are addition mechanisms that could be used to maintain constitutional counter-balancing. Some of these may be more or less likely to also facilitate constitutional collaboration. In their analysis of UK law, Carol Harlow and Rick Rawlings distinguish between clamping down and striking back mechanisms, both of which focus on maintaining constitutional counter-balancing.[68] Constitutional amendment and legislative reversal are both examples of striking back, where the law-maker reacts to modify a specific court decision. Clamping down occurs when the law-maker prospectively enacts measures that can restrict the power of the courts. These clamping down measures may be direct, specifically removing powers of the court, or indirect, measures that may make it more difficult for courts to exercise their powers or for individuals to commence legal actions.

We can find examples of striking-back mechanisms by constitutional amendment and through legislative reversal of judicial determinations of rights. The legislature can respond to a judicial determination striking down legislation as unconstitutional by amending the Constitution, such that legislation can be re-enacted following this constitutional amendment. This may be difficult to achieve, depending on the mechanisms used in a particular legal system to entrench constitutional protections. Nevertheless, examples of constitutional amendments that were introduced to respond to court decisions can be found even in the US constitution, which is one of the most difficult Constitutions to amend. Fisher, for example, cites the example of the Thirteenth, Fourteenth and Fifteenth Amendments of the US Constitution enacted to reverse the infamous *Dred Scott*[69] decision of the US Supreme Court, which held that blacks were not citizens and therefore were not protected by the Constitution.[70]

Similarly, in a legal system where courts have the power to strike down unlawful actions of the executive, legislation can be enacted to overturn the decisions of the court. This is particularly pertinent in the UK constitution, where the executive can initiate legislation and rely upon its majority in the House of Commons to ensure the legislation is enacted. Harlow and Rawlings draw attention to examples where legislation has been enacted to achieve this purpose, describing how the UK Government has even been prepared to enact retrospective legislation.[71] For example, the UK enacted the War Damages Act 1965 to retrospectively overturn the impact of the House of Lords decision in *Burmah Oil v Lord Advocate*.[72] *Burmah Oil* examined whether the UK government had the power, under the prerogative, to destroy property in order to prevent this falling into enemy hands in a time a conflict. The House of Lords concluded that this prerogative power did exist, but that the prerogative required the payment of compensation from the Government to those whose property had been destroyed. The War Damages Act 1965 retrospectively abolished the prerogative power, including the requirement to pay compensation. A more recent example in the United Kingdom can be found in the Terrorist-Asset Freezing (Temporary Provisions)

[68] C Harlow and R Rawlings, '"Striking-Back" and "Clamping-Down". An Alternative Perspective on Judicial Review' presented to the Cambridge Public Law Conference, September 2015. Cited with kind permission of the authors.

[69] *Dred Scott v Sandford* (1857) 60 US 393.

[70] Fisher (n 38) 201–06.

[71] Harlow and Rawlings (n 68).

[72] *Burmah Oil Company Ltd v Lord Advocate* [1965] AC 75.

Act 2010, which retrospectively validated measures taken to implement the United Nation's requirements concerning the freezing of assets connected to terrorism, which had been struck down under an application of the principle of legality in *Ahmed v Her Majesty's Treasury*.[73] The Terrorist Asset-Freezing etc Act 2010 then placed similar measures on a legislative footing. In a legal system where the court has no power to strike down legislation, this essentially made these measures immune from future legal challenge.

Examples of legislation enacted to reverse judicial decisions are not confined to what may be broadly defined as emergency situations—for example, responding to war and conflict or to the global threat of terrorism. The Jobseekers (Back to Work Scheme) Act 2013 was not only retrospective, overturning a judicial decision to strike down the Jobseeker's Allowance (Employment, Skills and Enterprise Scheme) Regulations 2011, but also interfered with legal proceedings currently before the court.[74] Nor are legislative reversals restricted to the UK with its lack of strong constitutional review. Fisher provides examples of legislative reversal in the US, where the US Congress can enact new legislation in response to a particular interpretation of federal legislation by the US Supreme Court.[75]

It is also possible to find examples of clamping-down measures. In his analysis of the US constitution, Fisher provides examples of legislative delay, outright non-compliance, or where the court is able to enact the same measure using a different procedure. Fisher provides the example of Congress's reaction to the Supreme Court decision in *INS v Chadha*, which required any alteration of the powers, rights or duties of the executive to be enacted through the full legislative process.[76] This effectively prevented Congress from relying on a 'legislative veto' as a short-cut through which to control executive agencies. However, despite these implications of the *Chadha* decision, legislative vetoes were still placed in bills and these bills were in turn still signed into law by the President.[77]

Examples of direct clamping down can also be found in the UK, for example in ouster clauses. The US equivalent is found in legislation withdrawing jurisdiction from the Supreme Court. Article 3 of the Constitution grants appellate jurisdiction to the Supreme Court 'with such exceptions and under such regulations as Congress shall make'.[78] This appears to grant the power to the US Congress to limit the jurisdiction of the Supreme Court.[79] Although experience in both the US and the UK constitution would suggest that these extreme measures are not taken lightly by the court, resulting in push back mechanisms.[80] A similar adverse reaction is given to direct clamping down through the use of the impeachment process to remove members of the judiciary, or to examples of court-packing.[81] Indirect clamping down measures may include undercutting judicial review through measures that remove or cut funding for judicial review actions,[82] or

[73] [2010] UKSC 2, [2010] 2 AC 534.

[74] *Reilly (2) v Secretary of State for Work and Pensions* [2014] UKHC (Admin) 2182; [2015] QB 573, [2016] EWCA Civ 413, [2016] All ER (D) 21 (May). It is believed that the government will appeal this decision. See also C Harlow, 'Judging Parliament: The Jobseekers Case' UK Const. L. Blog (3 October 2014) (available at http://ukconstitutionallaw.org).

[75] Fisher (n 38) 206–09. [76] 462 US 919, (1983). [77] Fisher (n 38) 224–29.

[78] US Constitution, Art 3.

[79] HM Hart, 'The Power of Congress to Limit the Jurisdiction of Federal Courts' (1953) 66 Harvard Law Review 1362; L Sager, 'Foreward: Constitutional Limitations on Congress' Authority to Regulate the Jurisdiction of the Federal Courts' (1981) 95 Harvard Law Review 17.

[80] Fisher (n 38) 215–21; R Rawling 'Review, Revenge and Retreat' (2005) 68 MLR 378.

[81] Fisher (n 38) 143–49. [82] Harlow and Rawlings (n 68).

which restrict standing,[83] or by altering the remuneration of members of the judiciary.[84] The experience of both UK law and US law demonstrate that, when the law-maker uses these mechanisms to remove or limit jurisdiction, the courts do not merely acquiesce in the removal of this power, with such actions often resulting in a series of exchanges between the law-maker and the courts.

Constitutional collaboration may arise through the manner in which the law-maker utilizes striking-back mechanisms. In particular, constitutional collaboration is facilitated when legislatures have the opportunity to respond to court decisions, or when court decisions prompt modifications to the constitution. When motivated to collaborate, legislatures can use the detailed accounts of courts to help facilitate further legislative debate, taking on their advice to help inform legislative responses. A similar process may occur when there is discussion of constitutional modification. The latter may also prompt wider public debate. However, constitutional collaboration is not facilitated when legislatures are unaware of judicial changes, or where legislative responses are unreflective acts of defiance. The more transparency and reason-giving occurs, the greater the opportunities for constitutional collaboration.

III. Evaluation of Inter-institutional Interactions

As the above discussion has demonstrated, inter-institutional interactions may take place in a range of systems of rights protections, occurring in legal systems with no constitutional protection of rights and those where the courts have the power to strike down legislation which contravenes constitutionally protected human rights. Consequently, there is no need to adopt a commonwealth model of rights protections in order to achieve the values of democratic dialogue. This should come as no surprise to those who have studied US constitutional law. After all, it is at least arguable that the theories of Madison and Jefferson, which Christine Bateup refers to as an account of co-ordinate construction,[85] advocate a shared enterprise of constitutional interpretation, with the legislature and the courts working together to promote democracy whilst tempering its potential dangers when democracy is taken over by factions.[86] Moreover, as discussed above, particularly given that the distinction between constitutional collaboration and constitutional counter-balancing may depend more upon how a mechanism of inter-institutional interaction is used, as opposed to the nature of the mechanism through which the interaction is produced, adopting a commonwealth model of rights protections is not sufficient to achieve the benefits of democratic dialogue.

There are, however, differences between the way in which constitutional counter-balancing and constitutional collaboration are achieved under commonwealth models and other models of rights protection. Margit Cohn, for example, distinguishes between formal and implied dialogue, where formal dialogue occurs when there is a legal mechanism governing the interaction between different institutions. Commonwealth models produce formal dialogue as they include legal mechanisms

[83] ibid. See also Criminal Justice and Court Act 2015, ss 84–90, which restrict standing, remedies, and also court costs.

[84] Fisher (n 38) 149–52.

[85] Bateup, 'The Dialogic Promise: Assessing the Normative Potential of Theories of Constitutional Dialogue' (n 56) 1137–43.

[86] Madison, *The Federalist Papers* No 10 and No 51, in C Rossiter (ed), *The Federalist Papers* (Mentor 1961).

to facilitate inter-institutional interactions. Implied dialogue occurs where there are no specific legal provisions facilitating dialogue, but where dialogue occurs due to the general constitutional structure itself and the power of the judiciary to interpret and re-shape the law. Christine Bateup provides a different account of inter-institutional interactions which take place in legal systems which have not adopted a commonwealth model of rights protections. She distinguishes between political and legal dialogue. Legal dialogue occurs through legal mechanisms, focusing on inter-institutional interchange. It is therefore coterminous with formal dialogue. Political dialogue focuses on political constraints placed on the way in which courts and legislatures can exercise their powers.

These differences help to demonstrate one possible advantage of commonwealth models of rights protections, in addition to possible disadvantages. Commonwealth models provide for legal mechanisms of constitutional counter-balancing. We argued in the previous chapter that constitutional collaboration requires sufficient constitutional counter-balancing. There is no dialogue between institutions if one institution is always able to enforce its will over the other. This would suggest that commonwealth models, with their legal provisions designed to achieve constitutional counter-balancing are a better means of facilitating dialogue. This may indirectly facilitate constitutional collaboration, by ensuring some element of constitutional counter-balancing. Moreover, we argued above that the distinction between constitutional collaboration and constitutional counter-balancing may depend upon how mechanisms of inter-institutional interaction are used. The more inter-institutional interactions focus on providing reasons and justifications, and reflecting upon the reasons and justifications provided by other institutions, the more inter-institutional interactions may achieve constitutional collaboration. However, the more interactions draw on mechanisms which focus on striking-back, clamping-down or pushing back against the other institution in a bid to ensure that constitutional powers of institutions are not transgressed, the harder it is for inter-institutional interactions to facilitate constitutional collaboration. If, as the next chapter will argue, democratic dialogue is best achieved through constitutional collaboration as opposed to constitutional counter-balancing, then this may appear to argue in favour of commonwealth models of rights protections as opposed to inter-institutional interactions in other legal systems.

It may also provide a means of preferring some forms of commonwealth models over others. For example, it may suggest that commonwealth models of rights protections need to ensure that the legal mechanisms which facilitate inter-institutional interactions provide an effective balance between the legislature or the judiciary, otherwise each institution may use other means through which to protect their constitutional position which may, in turn, undermine the ability of that commonwealth model to achieve constitutional collaboration. This is illustrated, for example, in New Zealand where the lack of an ability of the court to provide a remedy for legislation which was not able to be interpreted in line with the human rights protected in the New Zealand Bill of Rights Act 1990 led to the judiciary implying this remedy into the Act.[87] This has been met by a negative reaction by the New Zealand Government, motivated both by the outcome of using this mechanism to declare legislation imposing a prisoner voting ban to be inconsistent with the New Zealand Act in addition to the way in which the judiciary implied a power to issue such declarations of inconsistency.

[87] *Taylor v Attorney-General of New Zealand* (n 63).

It may also suggest a preference for commonwealth models whose legal mechanisms focus on the provision of reasons and justifications, as these legal mechanisms are more likely to facilitate constitutional collaboration. Section 19 of the Human Rights Act 1998, for example, requires the Minister promoting a Bill to make a statement to the House as to the compatibility of the proposed Bill with Convention rights. Drawing attention to the Convention-compatibility of legislation in this manner is designed to further debate, providing the legislature with the opportunity to discuss human rights implications. When discussed in a manner that provides justifications for conclusions and reflects discussion of the views of society as to a particular human right, this pre-legislative scrutiny can help to facilitate constitutional collaboration. In addition, the UK's joint committee on human rights can help to further facilitate constitutional collaboration through producing clear and reasoned reports, setting out detailed assessments of whether legislative provisions contravene Convention rights. These reports can help provide information for legislatures and courts. Legislatures can also respond specifically to these reports, setting out their own account of why they are drawing a particular balance between a right and a legislative policy objective. Courts may also draw on these reports, using information in the reports to help them to assess whether legislation contravenes Convention rights.[88]

The Australian commonwealth models may also provide a good facilitation of constitutional collaboration through their requirement of reasons in Ministerial statements. The Australian Capital Territory's Human Rights Act requires the Minister to provide reasons when making a statement of incompatibility.[89] The Victorian Charter provisions require Ministers to provide justifications for both statements of compatibility and of incompatibility.[90] This account of reasons can facilitate constitutional collaboration through shaping debate in the legislature and in the courts. In addition, reasons help to facilitate collaboration as courts can engage with these justifications. It helps each institution to work together to determine the content of rights.[91] The Victorian Charter may also be better at facilitating constitutional collaboration through their use of declarations of inconsistent interpretation as opposed to the declaration of incompatibility found under the UK's Human Rights Act.[92] The formulation of this declaration may be better able to facilitate collaboration as the declaration makes it clear that the court is providing its interpretation of human rights, declaring that it is not possible to interpret legislation according to its interpretation of human rights. A declaration of incompatibility is more likely to leave the legislature with the impression that the court makes a final authoritative declaration of human rights. This may lead to the expectation that the legislature should only respond to a section 4 declaration of incompatibility by amending legislation so as to ensure its compatibility with Convention rights. A declaration of inconsistent interpretation may better convey to the legislature that its role is to collaborate with the court over the definition

[88] H Hooper, 'The Use of Parliamentary Materials in Proportionality Judgments' in M Hunt, H Hooper, and P Yowell (eds), *Parliament and Human Rights: Redressing the Democratic Deficit* (Oxford, Hart 2015) Chapter 19; A Kavanagh, 'The Joint Committee on Human Rights: A Hybrid Breed of Watchdog' in M Hunt, H Hooper, and P Yowell (eds), *Parliament and Human Rights: Redressing the Democratic Deficit* (Oxford, Hart 2015) Chapter 6; and A Kavanagh, 'Proportionality and Parliamentary Debates: Exploring Some Forbidden Territory' (2014) 34 Oxford Journal of Legal Studies 443.

[89] Human Rights Act 2004 (Australian Capital Territory: Australia), s 40B(1)(b).

[90] Charter of Human Rights and Responsibilities 2006 (Victoria: Australia), s 28(3)(a).

[91] R Masterman, 'Interpretations, Declarations and Dialogue: Rights Protections under the Human Rights Act and Victorian Charter of Human Rights and Responsibilities' (2009) Public Law 112.

[92] Charter of Human Rights and Responsibilities 2006 (Victoria: Australia), s 36(2).

of rights, as opposed to accepting the court's conclusions as a definitive authoritative determination.[93]

Cohn's account of the distinction between formal and informal dialogue also recognizes how institutional interactions can take place informally in legal systems which have adopted a Commonwealth model of rights protections. She argues, for example, that the general limitations clause found in the Canadian *Charter* is best understood as an example of informal dialogue. Dialogue occurs here not because there is a legal provision establishing inter-institutional exchanges, but because of the power of the judiciary to interpret and re-shape the law, coupled with the general structure of the constitution, including the ability of the legislature to respond to judicial interpretations by enacting new legislation.[94] In addition to reinforcing our conclusion that commonwealth models of rights protection need not facilitate inter-institutional interactions, or that the interactions they facilitate may depend on how these provisions are used in addition to the nature of these legal mechanisms, Cohn's analysis points to a further potential problem which may arise in commonwealth models—the danger of double counting.

Difficulties can arise when institutions act in a manner to facilitate constitutional collaboration, by modifying the way in which they use their power, when the powers they possess have been designed to facilitate inter-institutional interactions. As discussed above with regard to the interpretation of the Human Rights Act 1998, issues arise as to how the courts should apply section 3 of the Act. This provision helps to facilitate democratic dialogue as there is the ability of the legislature to respond to judicial determinations. The legislature can respond through re-enacting legislation, taking account of the reasoning of the court. As such, section 3 provides a legal mechanism for facilitating dialogue between the legislature and the court as to the determination of a human rights issue. The issue arises, therefore, as to whether, when exercising powers of interpretation under section 3, the UK courts should use similar mechanisms of dialogue as employed by the Canadian courts, for example using deference, when interpreting *Charter* rights. To do so would give rise to different issues. The Canadian courts do have the power to strike down legislation. Therefore, dialogue is facilitated through the Canadian courts exercising judicial deference, for example, through giving greater discretionary areas of judgment to the legislature by applying the proportionality test less stringently. This mechanism may not be needed in the UK constitution, where the legislature may respond by re-enacting legislation. However, if we regard a response of the legislature to a section 3 interpretation as a mechanism designed to achieve constitutional counter-balancing, then democratic dialogue under that section may be better facilitated through deference as opposed to a reliance on the ability of the legislature to re-enact legislation. Deference may be a better means of facilitating constitutional collaboration through the application of section 3.

The above discussion is not provided, at this stage, in order to advocate a particular approach to section 3 of the Human Rights Act 1998. Rather, it is provided to illustrate that care needs to be taken in systems with legal mechanisms designed to facilitate inter-institutional interactions. The benefits of democratic dialogue will not be achieved when courts fail to provide a strong interpretation of rights in situations where the legislature is willing and able to respond to judicial rights-determinations.

[93] Masterman (n 91).

[94] M Cohn, 'Sovereignty, Constitutional Dialogues, and Political Networks: A Comparative and Conceptual Study' in R Rawlings, P Leyland, and AL Young (eds), *Sovereignty and the Law: Domestic, European and International Perspectives* (OUP 2013) 236, 241–44.

In a similar manner, democratic dialogue may not be facilitated if one institution relies on the other to exercise a legal power to facilitate dialogue when the institution is reluctant to do so.

As well as understanding the problems that may arise with double counting, we also need to recognize issues which arise from recognizing the distinction between political and legal means of facilitating inter-institutional interactions. Bateup's account of interactions which take place outside the commonwealth model focuses on how these interactions may take place through political as well as legal means. This may arise because of the political as well as the legal constraints which influence how the legislature and the courts exercise their powers. Both courts and legislatures may be sensitive to public opinion, as well as to the way in which the other institutions of the constitution may react. This may govern behaviour of institutions of the constitution as they take account of anticipated reactions. The anticipation of a negative reaction from the public or from another institution of the constitution may constrain the way in which either the legislature or the judiciary exercise their legal powers.

Failing to take account of the political means through which institutional interactions may occur may also give rise to elements of double counting, where legal and political means are used to facilitate constitutional counter-balancing. A failure to take account of political as well as legal constraints may mean that the balance of relative decision-making authority between the legislature and the judiciary is tipped too far in favour of one institution. This can be illustrated by section 4 of the Human Rights Act 1998. A declaration of incompatibility does not affect the legal force, validity or effect of the legislation declared incompatible with Convention rights. As such, it stops short of providing the courts with the ability to strike down legislation that is incompatible with Convention rights, leaving Parliament with the last word. However, the political pressure created by declarations of incompatibility, in addition to the judicial reasoning that can influence public debate and guide legislative responses, strengthens the position of the court. It may be very difficult for the legislature to resist the political pressure to change legislation so as to ensure that this is compatible with Convention rights. If this is the case, then it may be that the court is better using informal mechanisms of inter-institutional interactions, through a use of judicial minimalism or deference, as a means of facilitating constitutional collaboration. Otherwise the delicate balance of constitutional counter-balancing may not be achieved.

Bateup's account of political dialogue has a wide scope, moving away from inter-institutional interactions to incorporate discussions of rights by society at large. The actions of the legislature or the judiciary may prompt discussion of an issue by the public at large. This discussion may also cause the legislature or the judiciary to act differently, in anticipation of the public's reaction, or in direct response to the reaction of the public to legislation or a judicial decision.[95] This recognition illustrates how inter-institutional interactions may act as a pressure value in society, in addition to furthering deliberative and participatory democracy—both of which will be explained in more detail in the following chapter. To focus predominantly on legal mechanisms of inter-institutional interaction, without accompanying this with an account of political means of interaction, may undermine constitutional counter-balancing, and may also mean that inter-institutional interactions fail to achieve these further values. This is particularly pertinent in commonwealth models of rights protection, where there is a focus on facilitating legal mechanisms of inter-institutional interaction which may, in

[95] Bateup, 'Expanding the Conversation: American and Canadian Experiences of Constitutional Dialogue in Comparative Perspective' (n 56).

turn, be accompanied by a lack of recognition of political means of inter-institutional interaction.

IV. Conclusion

Hogg and Bushell's account of democratic dialogue in the Canadian *Charter* acted as a catalyst for the adoption of commonwealth model of rights protections. Understanding how institutions of the constitution interact with each other is able to provide a more accurate account of the relative powers of the legislature and the judiciary, as well as helping us to understand whether the commonwealth model is a necessary or sufficient component of democratic dialogue, or whether its adoption will facilitate a better form of inter-institutional interactions than those found in legal systems with a strong constitutional protection of rights, or those where courts are not empowered to strike down legislation with contravenes human rights. Our refinement of accounts of inter-institutional interactions, focusing on those which maintain constitutional counter-balancing and those which facilitate constitutional collaboration, provides a further means of accurately understanding how constitutions operate in practice.

This understanding can help us to evaluate commonwealth models and provide a more accurate account of the reality of the distribution of power between the legislature and the judiciary in legal systems which have not adopted the commonwealth model. For example, it can help to evaluate arguments which are made to reject the classification of Canada's *Charter* as an example of the commonwealth model of rights protections. First, the argument is made that section 33 of the *Charter*, the 'notwithstanding' clause, has not only fallen into disuse but has become unusable. However, unlike the New Zealand, UK and Australian versions of a democratic dialogue model of rights protections, the Canadian Supreme Court has the power to strike down legislation. If the notwithstanding clause is unable to be exercised, then the Canadian *Charter* would appear to provide for a strong as opposed to a midway protection of rights, making it indistinguishable from the US's model of rights protections.[96] Second, although dialogue may occur more frequently in Canada through the general restrictions clause found in section 1 of the *Charter*, the argument is made that this is insufficient to provide a distinct form of protection of rights given that dialogue may occur in a similar fashion in Constitutions like the US which has no distinct general limitation clause. This may arise as courts internalize the limitation on the right within their account of the definition of the right. For example, whilst a constitution with a general limitations clause might assess whether the removal of prisoner voting rights was a valid restriction on the right to vote, a constitution without a general limitations clause may achieve the same result by analysing the justifications for restricting prisoner voting rights when determining the content of the right to vote. The former could conclude that prisoners had a right to vote, but that the restriction of this right to exclude prisoners who were serving sentences for serious crimes was a valid restriction on the right to vote. The latter could conclude that the right to vote did not include the right of prisoners who had committed serious crimes to vote.[97]

[96] G Huscroft, 'Constitutionalism from the Top Down' (2007) 45 Osgoode Hall Law Journal 91, 96–97; and A Petter, 'Taking Dialogue Theory Much too Seriously (or perhaps Charter Dialogue isn't Such a Good Thing After All)' (2007) 45 Osgoode Hall Law Journal 147, 160–62.

[97] Huscroft (n 96) 96; and Petter (n 96) 157–60.

An accurate account of different mechanisms of inter-institutional interactions helps to clarify this debate. First, it is clear that the notwithstanding clause and the general limitations clause facilitate different types of inter-institutional interaction. The notwithstanding clause maintains constitutional counter-balancing as it provides a means through which the legislature can respond to judicial determinations of rights. To empower the courts to strike down legislation with no ability of response from the legislature would give the courts the power to enforce its determination of rights over the legislature. Without some mechanism for the attainment of constitutional counter-balancing, the commonwealth model is difficult to distinguish from other forms rights protections. The general restrictions clause is more suited to facilitating constitutional collaboration, providing a means through which the courts and the legislature can work together to determine the content of rights and principles. Arguments as to whether the lack of use of the notwithstanding clause damages the democratic dialogue model of rights protections, therefore, may depend upon one's preference for different forms of inter-institutional interaction. The more one values the facilitation of constitutional collaboration over the maintenance of constitutional counter-balancing, the more one will recognize that the Canadian constitution still provides for sufficient inter-institutional interactions between the legislature and the courts, even if the notwithstanding clause has lapsed into desuetude.

In addition, the existence of the clause still distinguishes Canada's commonwealth model from a strong constitutional protection of rights given that it is an example of a legal as opposed to a political means of ensuring constitutional counter-balancing. The same is true of the general limitations clause. Even if, in practice, the US and the Canadian constitution give rise to the same amount of constitutional collaboration, this collaboration will still remain distinct. In Canada, the general limitations clause provides a legal mechanism for facilitating collaboration. Although the courts may apply the general limitations clause differently, providing for stronger or weaker protections of rights, nevertheless the court still has to apply the clause, requiring it to assess the nature of the restriction and whether this is a disproportionate restriction of a right. Even when the court strikes down legislation as providing a disproportionate restriction on a right, the reasoning of the court when applying the general limitations clause helps to inform the legislature as to how to achieve the policy aim of its earlier legislation, without giving rise to a disproportionate restriction on rights. The structure of the legal test helps to facilitate constitutional collaboration because the legal test structures the analysis of the court, providing better guidance to the legislature. Although the American constitution can be read in a manner which facilitates inter-institutional interactions, this occurs when the court refrains from fully exercising its powers to correct constitutional interpretations. This restraint may not structure the reasoning of the court in the same manner, which in turn may weaken constitutional collaboration. Constitutional collaboration may also arise inadvertently, where the court is motivated to exercise restraint when exercising its powers for other reasons, for example because of potential adverse public reaction to a judgment. These differences between the Canadian and US legal arrangements means that the Canadian situation is distinct, even if inter-institutional interactions occur in both legal systems.

Nevertheless, commonwealth models do have on advantage over other models of rights protections. Commonwealth models can maintain constitutional counter-balancing through legal as opposed to non-legal means. This can make it easier to achieve constitutional counter-balancing under the commonwealth model. Moreover, this may also make it easier to achieve constitutional collaboration under the commonwealth model. Given the legal mechanisms that can help to maintain constitutional counter-balancing, collaborations between the legislation and the judiciary may be better able to reach outcomes which draw on the relative abilities of both institutions to reason about rights, or to determine the better content of policies. Whilst this analysis of inter-institutional interactions is useful in terms of helping to provide descriptive accuracy, as well as helping to understand the connection between commonwealth models of rights protections and democratic dialogue, it is only a step along the way to developing an account of democratic dialogue. To progress further, we need to assess the way in which inter-institutional interactions are valuable, using this normative framework to provide a specific account of democratic dialogue.

5

From Inter-institutional Interactions to Democratic Dialogue

In the search to provide an account of democratic dialogue, it is hard not to turn to the seminal work of Hogg and Bushell,[1] even though, as discussed in the previous chapter, inter-institutional interactions take place in a wide range of constitutional systems and despite the fact that the commonwealth model found in the *Charter* is not the first form of rights protections in Canada to focus on providing a role for both the legislature and the judiciary in the protection of rights, the first being found in the Canadian Bill of Rights 1960.[2] However, it is important to recognize that Hogg and Bushell did not provide a detailed normative justification of democratic dialogue. Rather, their theory provided a description of whether, when, and how the legislature had responded to determinations of rights provided by the Canadian Supreme Court. Their seminal account of dialogue in the Canadian constitution was designed to be descriptive as opposed to normative. Hogg and Bushell's claims were limited to explaining that, to the extent that legislatures were able to respond in this manner, doubt could be cast on the counter-majoritarian criticism of judicial protections of human rights.[3]

The idea that an account of inter-institutional interactions provides a more accurate account of the relationship between the legislature and the judiciary is not restricted to descriptions of the Canadian constitution. There is a wealth of literature from political scientists in the United States which focuses on the extent to which an analysis of inter-institutional interactions between the legislature and the judiciary provides a more accurate account, for example the accounts of Robert Burt,[4] and of Louis Fisher and Neal Devins.[5] Their accounts criticize the accuracy of the principle of judicial supremacy in the United States. Although the judiciary assert the constitution power to make final, authoritative determinations as to the meaning and application of the US Constitution, Burt, and Fisher and Devins argue that the claim that the US Supreme Court has the power to make final, authoritative determinations of rights does not provide an accurate reflection of reality. Rather, the US Constitution is best understood as exemplifying a series of interactions between the courts, the legislature, and the executive. Devins and Fisher provide a series of examples to support their assertions; including instances where Presidents have refused to accept judicial authority, ranging

[1] P Hogg and A Bushell, 'The Charter Dialogue between Courts and Legislatures: (Or Perhaps the Charter of Rights isn't such a Bad Thing After All)' (1997) 35 Osgoode Hall Law Journal 75; P Hogg, A Thornton, and W Wright, 'Charter Dialogue Revisited: Or Much Ado About Metaphors' (2007) 45 Osgoode Hall Law Journal 1.

[2] WS Tarnopolsky, 'The Historical and Constitutional Context of the Proposed Canadian Charter of Rights and Freedoms' (1981) 44 Law and Contemporary Problems 168; B Hovius, 'The Legacy of the Supreme Court of Canada's Approach to the Canadian Bill of Rights: Prospects for Canada' (1982–83) 28 McGill Law Journal 31.

[3] Hogg, Thornton, and Wright (n 1) 26–27 and 29.

[4] R Burt, *The Constitution in Conflict* (Harvard, Belknap Press 1992).

[5] L Fisher, *Constitutional Dialogues: Interpretation as Political Process* (Princeton University Press 1988); L Fisher and N Devins, *The Democratic Constitution* (Oxford University Press 2004).

from Abraham Lincoln's repudiation of the *Dred Scott* decision to Bill Clinton's signing of the Religious Freedom Restoration Act,[6] in addition to examples of where Congress has enacted legislation that challenges decisions of the Supreme Court and where the Supreme Court appears to refrain from exercising its powers, essentially enabling the legislature to have the final say in practice.

If we are to provide a normative justification of democratic dialogue, we need to move on from merely asserting that an account of inter-institutional interactions can provide an accurate account of the relationship between the legislature and the judiciary, or provide a tool through which to analyse these interactions. We need to ask whether these interactions are valuable, beyond their descriptive accuracy. This chapter will argue that inter-institutional interactions are valuable. In particular, they can provide a means through which to combine the way in which both the legislature and the judiciary reason about rights, they can provide a form of checks and balance to help achieve constitutional stability and act as a potential pressure value, and can also help to facilitate deliberative and participatory democracy. Having provided an account of these values, the chapter will assess the extent to which different forms of inter-institutional interaction can facilitate the achievement of these values, as well as assessing factors which may undermine inter-institutional interactions.

I. The Value of Inter-institutional Interactions

A. A better protection of human rights

The most common argument in favour of democratic dialogue is that democratic dialogue is able to provide a better protection of rights. The most comprehensive account of how democratic dialogue may provide a better means of protecting human rights is found in Gardbaum's seminal work on the commonwealth constitution.[7] Gardbaum argues that the commonwealth model, with its focus on inter-institutional interactions, is able to combine the relative strengths of a purely legal or political protection of rights, whilst minimizing their respective weaknesses.

Gardbaum argues that purely political or legal protections of rights are defended according to the relative ability of either the legislature or the courts to reach better and more legitimate outcomes when reasoning about rights. In terms of outcome, legislatures have more freedom to balance rights without having to do so within the confines of legal doctrine. In addition, they are able to take account of a broader range of interests than the courts, which focus on the arguments of the two parties to a particular dispute. In terms of legitimacy, legislatures are democratically representative and democratically accountable. However, Gardbaum also recognizes the relative weaknesses of a purely political protection of rights. There are legislative pathologies—i.e. circumstances in which specific aspects of the reasoning process of democratic decision-makers may lead to a weaker protection of rights. For example, legislatures tend to represent majority as opposed to minority interests, meaning that they may fail to provide a sufficiently strong protection of minority rights. In addition, legislatures focus on enacting general, forward-looking measures to resolve broad problems or issues facing society as a whole. This may mean that legislatures inadvertently legislate

[6] Fisher and Devins (n 5) 221.

[7] S Gardbaum, *The Commonwealth Model of Constitutionalism: Theory and Practice* (Cambridge University Press 2013).

contrary to long-standing principles, or legislate in a manner which may generally protect rights, but which fails to protect rights when applied to a particular individual in a specific set of circumstances. Moreover, although purely political protections of rights can be normatively justified through their promotion of democracy, they may fail to provide a sufficiently strong protection of rights or social justice.[8]

When assessing the relative strengths and weaknesses of purely legal protections of rights, Gardbaum recognizes that these are almost the opposite side of the coin to the arguments for and against a political protection of rights. A strong legal protection of rights is regarded as advantageous as the courts are able to remedy the specific problems that may arise with a purely political protection of rights. Courts are more likely to recognize when general legislation overrides long-standing principles given the way in which courts reason on a case-by-case basis. Moreover, courts look specifically at the circumstances before them, being in a better position to ensure that general provisions do not harm individual rights in their specific application. A legal protection of rights also counters the problems of a lack of legitimacy, providing a means of protecting rights and social justice in addition to democracy. In addition, it is argued that courts may provide a means of reasoning about rights that counters the potential under-protection of minority rights that may occur in purely political protections of rights. By focusing on legal principles and rights, courts may be more likely to reach morally correct decisions and will be less likely to be swayed by majority opinion and, perhaps, prejudice. In addition, a legally protected Bill of Rights may facilitate education about rights. This knowledge about the rights that individuals possess may empower them to be better able to protect their rights.

The relative strengths of human rights protections are accompanied by the relative weaknesses. An awareness of the court's lack of legitimacy may lead courts to under-protect rights, exercising deference when determining the content of rights or when assessing the appropriate remedy for a breach of rights. This is particularly true when courts are called upon to balance rights and legitimate restrictions placed on rights to achieve policy objectives or to protect other rights and interests. Or, the opposite may occur, with courts failing to recognize the bounds of their power leading to an over-protection of rights. Problems also arise from the *ex post* as opposed to *ex ante* nature of judicial protections. As such, rights have to be breached before they can be protected by the courts. A better protection of rights would include *ex ante* provisions, helping to ensure that measures which breached human rights were prevented from being enacted rather than being corrected once enacted. In addition, although courts rule on specific applications of rights regarding individuals before the court, their decisions often serve as precedents in the legal system, essentially establishing a broad principle or rule that will be applied to others. However, courts are in a less justifiable position to enact broad, general measures of rights, given their lack of democratic legitimacy and their relative inability to take account of the broader situation or the wider range of interests affected by these measures than those represented through the arguments of the parties before the court. Finally, a strong protection of rights arguably harms democracy, as courts can strike down measures enacted by a democratically elected and democratically accountable institution.[9]

The commonwealth model of rights protections proposed by Gardbaum accepts some and rejects other arguments as to the relative strengths and weaknesses of legal and political protections of rights. Gardbaum does not accept that either the legislature

[8] ibid, 51–61. [9] ibid.

or the courts are better, in the round, at reasoning about rights such that a protection of rights by purely legal or purely political means would always lead to better outcomes in terms of rights protections. Courts may be too timid to protect some rights, through fears as to their legitimacy to resolve some rights issues. Legislatures can fail to protect rights because of their particular pathologies, leading to a protection of rights which undermines the protection of rights in specific circumstances or where rights are protected generally, but undermined when applied to specific individuals in particular situations. Gardbaum agrees that courts can correct the pathologies which arise in a purely political protection of rights. However, he argues that considerations of legitimacy advocate that legislatures should still maintain the final say over rights, ensuring an adequate protection of democracy.

The commonwealth model of rights protections aims to maximize these relative strengths and weaknesses. First, the model requires an *ex ante* parliamentary discussion of rights. This aims to encourage political as well as legal reasoning about rights, as well as correcting the problems that can arise from a purely legal, *ex post facto* protection of rights. The advantages of political reasoning about rights can also be preserved through the ability of legislatures to respond to court determinations of rights-issues. The stronger legal protection of rights aims to protect against the pathologies of legislative reasoning about rights, particularly given its focus on assessing detailed reasons provided for rights decisions by legislatures. As legislatures have the final say, this remedies the problem of legitimacy that may arise due to the challenge to democracy that occurs with a purely legal protection of human rights. By allowing both institutions to reason about rights, Gardbaum argues that there is a better ability of reaching the right outcomes as legislative and court pathologies are corrected, in addition to a greater legitimacy to these decisions as both legislatures and courts combine to protect both democracy and rights and social justice.[10]

The argument that democratic dialogue can provide a better means of protecting rights is not confined to Gardbaum's justification of the commonwealth model of rights protections. Tom Hickman, for example, argues that dialogic approaches to constitutionalism, illustrated in the work of Bickel and of Dicey, also aim to balance the competing advantages and disadvantages of political and legal protections of rights.[11] Bickel's theory of judicial minimalism, advocating that the court exercise the passive virtues and refrain from deciding complex issues, is influenced by his concern for the justification of strong judicial review in the face of the counter-majoritarian difficulty—a phrase coined by Bickel.[12] By refraining from exercising the full extent of their powers, the judiciary were able to reduce the counter-majoritarian problem which arises every time a court—an unelected institution—strikes down legislation enacted by a democratically composed and democratically accountable institution. Dicey's account of the UK constitution refers to the tension between the rule of law, whose principles are protected through the courts applying the common law, and parliamentary sovereignty, designed to give priority to the authoritative determinations of the legislature. Hickman argues that Dicey's theory is best understood as one that resolves this tension. Although Parliament can ultimately overrule a judicial decision, the long-standing principles of the common law endure in their application by the courts. This allows 'for political compromises to be made and given effect to, whilst at the same

[10] ibid, 61–76.

[11] T Hickman, *Public Law After the Human Rights Act* (Hart 2010) 71–81.

[12] A Bickel, 'Foreword: The Passive Virtues' (1961) 75 Harvard Law Review 40; A Bickel, *The Least Dangerous Branch* (2nd edn, Yale University Press 1986).

time limiting the effect of such compromises and ensuring that the courts' protection of those fundamental principles to which society is committed is not undermined'.[13]

The idea that interactions between the legislature and the courts can provide for a better protection of rights is also present in other accounts of constitutionalism. In Chapter 3, we discussed how both accounts of legal and political constitutionalism do not advocate that rights should only be protected by the courts or by Parliament. Rather, they advocate a different combination of legal and political controls, placing relative power in the hands of the legislature and the judiciary. We also argued that, as well as best being regarded as a matter of degree, the differences between legal and political constitutionalism were often based on assumptions as to the nature of rights and the relative ability of the legislature and the courts to reason about rights. These differences were best illustrated in Sandra Fredman's account of bounded deliberation, which draws on Habermas' account of the distinction between interest-formed and value-orientated co-ordination. The differences between interest-formed and value-orientated co-ordination are, in turn, reflected in Gardbaum's account of the relative abilities of the legislature and the judiciary to reason about rights. If we are to build on this analysis, we need to recognize that value-orientated and interest-formed co-ordination are only two of the four accounts provided by Habermas' account of deliberation in his theory of deliberative democracy.

Habermas' account of deliberative democracy explains how a legal norm can be justified for moral reasons, for political–ethical reasons, or for pragmatic reasons. Moral reasons derive from objective moral principles and are deontological. Political–ethical reasons are different as they are teleological. They link to a specific aim or purpose. Political–ethical justifications derive from values that are geared to achieving these particular purposes. Pragmatic reasons determine how best a particular objective or end can be achieved.[14] All of these types of reasons can be relevant to value-orientated co-ordination. As such, a more refined account of democratic dialogue needs to distinguish not just between the different roles that should be played by the legislature and the court in value-orientated and interest-formed co-ordination, but should also take account of the different roles and different forms of interaction that can occur between the legislature and the judiciary as regards political–ethical and pragmatic reasoning.

To understand these differences further, we can return to our earlier example of prisoner voting. Moral arguments for prisoner voting would determine whether there are objective moral reasons for allowing prisoners to vote. This may draw on moral arguments relating to the status of prisoners as people who are as worthy of equal concern and respect as other members of society, or derive from moral arguments relating to whether a removal of the right to vote is a proportionate punishment for those who have committed crimes punishable by imprisonment. Political–ethical arguments relate to how granting or removing voting rights from prisoners achieves a particular aim for that society. It may be that a society wishes to make a stand as to their identity, recognizing themselves as a group that is more liberal, therefore granting prisoner voting rights, or which wishes to show that it takes a strict attitude to those who commit crimes, suggesting a removal of prisoner voting rights. Pragmatic reasons for and against prisoner voting rights would focus on the practical difficulties, perhaps referring to the logistical problems of transporting prisoners to polling stations in the constituency in which they would reside on release. There may also be issues regarding

[13] Hickman (n 11) 80.

[14] J Habermas, *Between Facts and Norms*, W Rehgs (trs) (Polity Press 2007) Ch 4.

the organization of postal or electronic voting for prisoners. All of these types of reason play a role in determining prisoner voting rights.

Not only do these different types of reasoning all play a role in determining rights-issues, but our understanding of these different types of reasoning may help to facilitate co-ordination. Their recognition may help individuals to reach a consensus. For example, if the pragmatic arguments relating to cost and security were overwhelmingly against granting prisoners the right to vote, this may persuade some who would otherwise have accepted the moral and political–ethical arguments in favour of prisoner voting to reject granting prisoners the right to vote. This may facilitate a consensus that rejects prisoner voting. These arguments may operate in the opposite direction. Individuals who are not persuaded by moral arguments in favour of prisoner voting, for example, may nevertheless agree that there are good political–ethical reasons to support prisoner voting in order to ensure their country retains its reputation as a liberal and progressive state.

More importantly for the establishment of a theory of democratic dialogue, the recognition of the different ways in which legal norms can be justified can be used to provide a more precise account of the nature of the inter-institutional interactions between the legislature and the courts which can facilitate a better protection of rights. Habermas argues that it is only when all of the reasons from moral, political–ethical, and pragmatic considerations fail to provide a consensus that negotiations should be used, achieving an interest-formed as opposed to a value-orientated consensus.[15] Whilst an account of democratic dialogue need not accept Habermas' conclusion as to the relative role of interest-formed and value-orientated co-ordination, nevertheless any complete account of inter-institutional interactions has to recognize different forms of reasoning about rights in order to ensure that interactions between institutions are able to facilitate the achievement of better, more legitimate resolutions of contestable rights-issues.

B. Deliberation and engaging citizens

Inter-institutional interactions may facilitate deliberation both by institutions of the constitution and by citizens. This was already suggested by our discussion in the previous chapter of informal and political means of inter-institutional interaction and how the legislature and the judiciary may take account of anticipated reactions from the public when determining the scope of rights, constitutional principles, or policies. Barry Friedman's theory of dialogue provides a more detailed account of how this may take place, focusing on the abortion debate in the United States, prompted by the Supreme Court decision in *Roe v Wade*.[16] Writing in 1993, Friedman argues that *Roe v Wade* is best understood as an example of a dynamic interaction between institutions of the constitution, as opposed to an example of judicial supremacy, or to provide grist to the mill for those who advocate the counter-majoritarian criticism of judicial supremacy.

First, Friedman argues that it is not clear that *Roe v Wade* is a clear example of 'judicial fiat' overturning democratic will. He states that polling evidence demonstrates that a majority of the US population supports the decision in *Roe v Wade*. Second, he argues that the case has to be understood in its context. There had been a number of public interest groups advocating social change on abortion prior to the decision. These groups both campaigned for change to the law and brought legal challenges to what

[15] Habermas (n 14). [16] *Roe v Wade* (1973) 410 US 113 (US Supreme Court).

they perceived to be restrictive laws. As *Roe v Wade* permitted abortion under certain conditions, the case served as a catalyst for state legislation and for national legislation in Congress, as well as prompting calls for constitutional amendment. In turn, these legislative responses were challenged in the courts. Friedman also argues that the decision pushed the issue of abortion into the public domain, leading to more general public engagement, as well as prompting the involvement of anti-abortion groups both in terms of lobbying and appearing before the courts as amicus curiae. He also argues that the decision led to appointments to the Supreme Court of those critical of the outcome in *Roe v Wade*, leading to future Supreme Court decisions.[17] Devins and Fisher agree. They conclude that, following initial more combative interactions between institutions and political groups—for example through defiant state legislation and court-packing in the Supreme Court—the abortion issue in the United States is now best understood as one where the courts and the legislature regard themselves as taking part in a dialogue.[18] These inter-institutional interactions take account of wider discussion in the public arena, indirectly engaging citizens in the determination of human rights.

The discussion of the American abortion case law demonstrates two forms of citizen engagement running in parallel with each other. First, courts can act, either directly or indirectly, as an agent of the public. By bringing actions of judicial review, the public, mostly through pressure groups, were using the courts as a means through which they could express their objection to legislation. It can be easier for public interest groups to challenge legislation or executive regulations in this manner as opposed to engaging in political lobbying. Lobbying can be expensive and it can be difficult for new groups to find channels through which to lobby effectively. It may be cheaper and easier to bring an action for judicial review. Although actions for judicial review are restricted to an analysis of legality, when groups bring a human rights challenge there is more scope for groups to provide clear arguments explaining how legislation harms human rights. This provides a further means through which the judiciary may be able to correct perceived weaknesses in which the legislature reasons about rights.

Although there is a general assumption that the legislature is able to balance values in a more legitimate manner, focusing on being able to collate views from a wide range of society, Friedman's analysis of *Roe v Wade* suggests that this may not always be the case. Legislatures may only hear the views of those who have been able to lobby effectively, meaning that some interests have not been taken into account. Judicial review may correct for this possibility through allowing such groups to bring challenges to legislation and executive actions on human rights grounds, particularly where it is felt that the legislation harms the human rights of the particular interest group in question. In addition, allowing judicial review actions may enable challenges to be brought to legislation which is felt to no longer reflect the views of society. It may be easier to bring this to the attention of the legislature through bringing an action for judicial review than it would be to lobby for legislative amendment or new legislation.

Courts may act indirectly as an agent of the public when they exercise their powers in order to reflect the views of society, or in anticipation of the possible adverse reaction of the public. When determining whether the US Constitution contained a right of abortion, for example, the judiciary may be more willing to recognize the right if it believes that this is widely recognized in society. In a similar manner, courts may refrain from developing a right to abortion if they fear strong adverse public reaction from developing this right. In this manner, courts play a role in political–ethical reasoning

[17] B Friedman, 'Dialogue and Judicial Review' (1993) 91 Michigan Law Review 577, 658–68.
[18] See also Fisher and Devins (n 5) 49, 129, and 131–39.

about rights. This role is more acceptable when courts are developing rights in the light of shifting perceptions of morality. This is more suited to the role of the court. This is particularly true of the courts in a common law system, where developments of the common law often reflect or draw upon commonly perceived views of morality.

Second, citizens are engaged in dialogue about rights because the way in which the courts and the legislature interact with each other may prompt public debate about rights. In the abortion debate, Friedman refers to how inter-institutional interactions took place between the legislature and the court as the court concluded that abortion could be permitted under certain conditions. This provided the legislature with discretion as to the conditions under which it would permit abortion. This facilitates indirect engagement with citizens. Citizens and pressure groups may lobby the legislature as to the conditions under which abortion should be lawful. Moreover, the existence of court decisions and legislative responses may give rise to further public debate.

As well as providing a link between citizens and constitutional counter-balancing, Devins and Fisher's account also explains how institutional interactions between the legislature and the court can facilitate public engagement in the protection of human rights. Cass Sunstein's work on judicial minimalism also focuses on how the courts can refrain from exercising their powers so as to stimulate public debate.[19] Sunstein's account adds on to our earlier discussion of Friedman by explaining how institutional interactions can facilitate deliberative democracy. Sunstein proposes a normative justification for judicial minimalism, which may facilitate dialogue, because of its ability to further deliberative democracy. Sunstein regards deliberative democracy as a justifiable form of government. His account of deliberative democracy requires that, for legislation to be legitimate, it needs to respect fundamental equality and provide detailed reasons for legislation. Judicial minimalism can be used to help facilitate deliberative democracy by aiming to ensure that it produces democracy-permitting or democracy-forcing judgments, as opposed to giving rise to democracy-foreclosing judgments. Sunstein's theory of judicial minimalism advocates that courts should adopt reasoning that is narrow as opposed to wide, and shallow as opposed to deep. Narrow judicial reasoning concentrates on deciding the precise matter before the courts, without broadening this to cover other related issues that are not specifically before the court. Shallow judicial reasoning focuses on reaching an agreement without the use of arguments from deep theory. It aims to reach incompletely theorized agreements, where there is an agreement as to the outcome of the case, if not as to the deep theoretical justifications for that outcome.

Judicial minimalism is regarded as valuable as it may provide an effective means of ensuring that democracy is not foreclosed. If courts make decisions that are broad and which rely on deep theory, they are more likely to foreclose democracy through cutting off discussion not only in that case, but also in the area more generally as legislatures consider issues to be decided by the broad reasoning of the court. Judicial minimalism, however, can facilitate democracy by leaving open broader issues for discussion by future legislatures. In addition, judicial minimalist judgments may act as prods and spurs for democratic deliberation. Where there has been no democratic deliberation, the court should be more willing to intervene. In doing so, its judgments can prod democratic reactions. Democratic deliberation is also more likely to follow where the court judgment is narrow, leaving more space to the legislature to respond.[20]

[19] C Sunstein, 'Leaving Things Undecided' (1996) 110 Harvard Law Review 4.
[20] ibid, 36–42.

Sandra Fredman's theory of bounded deliberation also focuses on the extent to which democratic dialogue facilitates deliberative democracy, illustrating again how this may facilitate deliberation by institutions of the constitution and by the public more generally. She provides a more detailed account of how this may work in practice when analysing prisoner voting decisions in the South African constitution. She argues that courts may facilitate dialogue in two ways. First, courts provide a deliberative forum. Courts hear the arguments of the parties before the court, allowing them to present their arguments as to the content of a particular human right and the resolution of a particular rights-issue. In addition, where intervention is permitted by third parties, for example public interest groups, courts are in a position to hear a wider spectrum of opinions. The deliberation of the courts feeds into a wider deliberation process. Decisions of the Constitutional Court may be widely reported, prompting commentary from the wider public as well as from members of the government or the legislature. Second, courts are in a position to steer legislative decision-making, ensuring that their decision-making moves away from a model that balances interests towards a model that focuses on deliberation. This occurs when courts require legislatures or executives to provide justifications, explaining why their legislation or administrative action is a legitimate restriction of human rights, or how this achieves a legitimate policy objective. This incentivizes law-makers and decision-makers to think carefully about rights-restrictions, focusing on justifications for any potential restriction of a right as opposed to merely assessing how to balance competing interests.[21] Fredman's first account of dialogue is best understood as dialogue occurring in the public forum, involving society as a whole as opposed to dialogue taking place between different institutions of the constitution. Her second account of dialogue is a form of constitutional collaboration, where the courts and the legislature can work together to determine constitutional rights.

For example, in the *August* decision, the South African Constitutional Court was asked to rule on a challenge to the Electoral Commission which had not put in place measures for prisoners to exercise their vote.[22] The court decided that, as there was no provision expressly restricting or limiting prisoner voting, it could be assumed that prisoners did have a right to vote under the South African Constitution. However, rather than providing a detailed account of the precise nature of this right to vote—for example whether it extended to all or only some prisoners and, if so, which type of prisoner would be entitled to vote—the decision of the court left space to the Electoral Commission to determine these issues. This space enabled the South African legislature to respond to the decision of the South African Constitutional Court, enacting legislation determining which prisoners had the right to vote.[23]

Inter-institutional interactions were further facilitated through the manner in which the court scrutinized the legislative response to the *August* decision. The South African legislature enacted legislation that forbade all prisoners from voting, with the exception of those imprisoned for the non-payment of a fine, which was challenged in *NICRO*.[24] The South African Constitutional Court concluded that this legislation was an unconstitutional restriction on the right to vote. In reaching this decision, the court

[21] S Fredman, 'From Dialogue to Deliberation: Human Rights Adjudication and Prisoners' Right to Vote' [2013] Public Law 292, 296–97.

[22] *August v Electoral Commission* (CCT8/99) [1999] ZACC 3 (South African Constitutional Court).

[23] Fredman (n 21) 300–01.

[24] *Minister of Home Affairs v National Institute for Crime Prevention and the Re-Integration of Offenders (NICRO)* Case CCT 03/04 [2004] ZACC 10 (South African Constitutional Court).

focused on whether the legislature had supplied sufficient justification for its approach to prisoner voting rights, both in terms of the provision of sufficient information to justify the conclusion reached and the cogency of the reasons. The court focused on whether the legislature's justifications for this restriction were convincing—concluding that they were not, given the lack of information provided in support of this legislative choice—rather than determining for itself whether the restriction on prisoner voting rights was right or wrong. In doing so, the court facilitated deliberation through providing the legislature with an incentive to focus on values when enacting legislation, as opposed to merely weighing up competing interests.[25]

In addition, the court established a framework for the debate on prisoner voting rights. It analysed the legislation in terms of the background constitutional framework, focusing in particular on the importance of universal adult suffrage in the newly formed Constitutional of South Africa following the earlier Apartheid regime.[26] This framework could be used by the legislature and also by the broader public, focusing debate on prisoner voting in the context of constitutional values and constitutional history. Although Fredman focuses predominantly on how dialogue may be facilitated through the way in which courts exercise their powers, enabling possible legislative responses, her recognition of the way in which courts may establish a framework for discussion shows how deliberation may occur outside the institutions of the constitution, with dialogue occurring in society in response to decisions of the Constitutional Court and the legislature.

C. Checks and balances and the safety valve function

Our discussion of constitutional counter-balancing has focused on the need to ensure that, in order to facilitate constitutional collaboration, no one institution is able to always definitively resolve issues surrounding rights. However, this discussion of the need to maintain constitutional counter-balancing is suggestive of possible tension between the legislature and the judiciary. This tension may give rise to potential power struggles, where one institution defends its powers from intrusion by another institution, serving as a means of preserving constitutional balance by ensuring that dialogue is not damaged as one institution is always able to authoritatively resolve any discussion on rights issues. This tension may also give rise to a form of co-operation, with agreement and consensus being reached through actions of restraint on the part of each institution due to the anticipated reaction of the other institution. Nick Barber, for example, refers to this as a relationship of friction between the institutions of the constitution. This occurs where institutions have different aims, or where there may be tension as to the relationship between their respective powers. Barber recognizes that this may often occur through threats rather than through actual conflict.[27]

Philip Joseph recognizes a similar tension, with both the legislature and the courts asserting authority, where this tension may give rise to collaboration over constitutional values.[28] These tensions may serve as checks and balances upon the legislature and the judiciary and may, even indirectly, serve to provide a form of consensus between the institutions. Fisher argues, in a similar manner, that dialogue helps to ensure the

[25] Fredman (n 21) 301–03. [26] ibid, 300–01.

[27] N Barber, 'Self-Defence for Institutions' (2013) 72 Cambridge Law Journal 558, 559–64.

[28] P Joseph, 'The Demise of Ultra Vires—Judicial Review in the New Zealand Courts' [2001] Public Law 354 and 'Parliament, the Courts, and the Collaborative Enterprise' (2004) King's College Law Journal 321.

fragmentation of power and to facilitate checks and balances. As each institution interacts with the other, it is able to check on the powers of the other. It ensures a healthy balance between the legislature and the judiciary.[29] He argues that judicial review is itself justified by ideologies of the fragmentation of powers and the need for checks and balances. We want courts to check the actions of the executive and legislature to ensure that they do not transgress the proper scope of their powers and to correct potential errors that may arise.

Devins and Fisher provide an account of this tension in the US Constitution which helps to explain how constitutional counter-balancing mechanisms may occur through inter-institutional interactions, as well as recognizing how these mechanisms can involve citizens more generally. One of the conclusions reached in their analysis of constitutional dialogue in the United States refers to how assertions of judicial supremacy by the US Supreme Court need to be understood in their political context, citing the assertion of judicial supremacy in *Cooper v Aaron* as an example.[30] The decision in *Cooper v Aaron* is one of a series of cases on school desegregation. In *Brown v Board of Education*, the Supreme Court concluded that the equal protection clause in the US Constitution could not be interpreted to mean 'separate but equal'—in other words it was not possible to achieve 'equality' through segregating schools.[31] Despite this conclusion, the Supreme Court in *Brown v Board of Education* failed to specify a remedy. Moreover, many state executives failed to implement the decision of *Brown v Board of Education*. In particular, the State Governor of Arkansas commissioned the state's National Guard to block the entrance of black students to Little Rock High School. The court's assertion of its authority was in the face of an extreme reaction by state executives refusing to accept the authority of the Supreme Court, in addition to the recognition that its earlier decisions, which had not asserted authority in a similar manner, had failed to induce compliance from some Southern states. Devins and Fisher argue that the US Supreme Court feels more empowered to issue declarations of its supremacy in these situations not merely because they are reacting to challenges from other branches of the Constitution, but also because they are linked with 'popular sentiment'.[32] President Eisenhower had reacted to the deployment of the state's National Guard by the Governor of Arkansas by sending in Federal troops. This deployment was supported by the majority of the United States, albeit not the majority of the State of Arkansas. Devins and Fisher argue that the Supreme Court realizes that its role as interpreter depends on 'public support and understanding of its decisions'.[33]

Mechanisms of constitutional counter-balancing can help to maintain a balance between flexibility and stability, as well as providing for a legitimate means of balancing flexibility and stability in particular instances. Constitutional arrangements need to be sufficiently flexible to allow constitutions to modify with changes in society, whilst being sufficiently stable to protect important rights and preserve democracy. Fisher and Devins argue that their account of democratic dialogue in the United States illustrates how these two goals may be effectively balanced against each other, through the way in which dialogue facilitates checks and balances and democratic debate, enabling society to add legitimacy to the development of constitutional principles. In their words:

> It is this process of give and take and the mutual respect the branches have for one another that permits the unelected Court to function in a democratic society. By agreeing to an open exchange among the branches, all three institutions are able to expose weaknesses, hold excesses

[29] Burt provides a similar justification, *The Constitution in Conflict* (n 4) Ch 3.
[30] (1958) 358 US 1. [31] (1954) 347 US 483. [32] Fisher and Devins (n 6) 223.
[33] Fisher and Devins (n 6) 224.

in check, and gradually forge a consensus on constitutional values. By participating in this process, the public has an opportunity to add legitimacy, vitality, and meaning to what might otherwise be an alien and short-lived document. Therein lies true stability. Therein lies respect for and understanding of the Constitution.[34]

II. A Normative Framework for Democratic Dialogue

The previous section set out the possible values of inter-institutional interactions. These interactions may facilitate a better protection of rights through drawing on the relative strengths and weaknesses of the manner in which the legislature and the judiciary reason about rights. In addition, they may provide a more stable manner in which to facilitate checks and balances in the system, helping to balance the needs of flexibility and stability. Moreover, the way in which these institutional interactions occur may help to facilitate deliberation, engaging not only institutions of the constitution, but also citizens. This engagement may occur either directly, as the public debate issues outside of the courts or the legislative process, or indirectly as anticipated public reactions influence the way in which institutions exercise their powers. If we are to provide a normative theory of democratic dialogue, we need to provide a framework through which to determine whether there are reasons for favouring a particular purpose of inter-institutional interaction, particular mechanisms of interaction, or particular means of exercising these interactions. In addition, we then need to evaluate the potential problems which may arise from facilitating institutional interactions.

A. Constitutional collaboration or constitutional counter-balancing?

Our analysis of mechanisms of inter-institutional interaction in the previous chapter explained how the line between mechanisms which facilitate constitutional counter-balancing and those which facilitate constitutional collaboration can be difficult to draw. We recognized that there are some mechanisms which appear to be predominantly focused on constitutional counter-balancing—for example the notwithstanding clause found in section 33 of the Canadian *Charter*. However, we also recognized that often, whether a mechanism maintains constitutional counter-balancing, or facilitates constitutional collaboration may well depend upon the purpose for which a particular provision is used. For example, we recognized that Tom Hickman advocated that the courts should, on occasion, use section 4 to vent scorn at the legislature. When deployed in this manner, the courts are using section 4 more as a means of redressing what they see to be a constitutional imbalance, where they regard the reaction of the legislature in response to a judicial determination of Convention rights as transgressing the respective separation of powers between the legislature and the courts. However, Hickman also argues that the courts should use section 4 when they realize that the legislature is better able to provide a remedy for a breach of Convention rights. To use section 4 in this manner is a means through which to facilitate constitutional collaboration. Here, the court is collaborating with the legislature through recognizing that practical reasons explain how the legislature can provide a better solution to a potential breach of Convention rights. By issuing a section 4 declaration, therefore, the legislature

[34] Fisher and Devins (n 6) 239.

and the courts can better work together to protect human rights. This discussion provides the beginnings of an argument in favour of constitutional collaboration over constitutional counter-balancing. There is a closer connection between constitutional collaboration and deliberation, be that deliberation which engages citizens or otherwise, and the protection of rights. Constitutional counter-balancing is more connected with the maintenance of checks and balances between the legislature and the courts. Constitutional collaboration, therefore, would appear to achieve more of the potential values of inter-institutional interaction than constitutional counter-balancing.

The connection between constitutional collaboration and the protection of rights is one that is easy to make. We argued above that inter-institutional interactions may promote the protection of human rights through recognizing that legislatures and the courts reason about rights in different ways. Whilst legislatures may be better at achieving interest-formed co-ordination in a legitimate manner, courts are regarded as better at achieving value-orientated co-ordination. Legislatures may also be better than courts at producing pragmatic solutions to rights-issues, or providing political–ethical co-ordination, where decisions are made as to the ethical or political values of a particular community and their expression through the determination of rights-issues. If we regard each institution as possessing different strengths and weaknesses, then inter-institutional interactions which allow both to play a role in protecting human rights, applying their relative strengths and weaknesses in a complementary manner is more likely to provide for a better protection of rights. This is more likely to be achieved through constitutional collaboration, where this occurs directly, than through constitutional counter-balancing, where this occurs indirectly.

It is also easy to draw the connection between constitutional collaboration and deliberation. Deliberation is facilitated when legislatures and courts provide clear reasons for their decisions. Not only does this help to ensure that there is value-orientated as well as interest-formed collaboration, but, as discussed above, it also helps to frame debate between the institutions and that taking place in society at large. In the previous chapter, we noted that the greater the element of reasoning and transparency in inter-institutional interactions, the more likely that the inter-institutional interaction will facilitate constitutional collaboration as opposed to constitutional counter-balancing.

However, this does not mean that constitutional counter-balancing has no connection to the promotion of a better protection of rights. Nor is it the case that a better protection of rights can only be facilitated through constitutional collaboration. As we concluded in Chapter 3, dialogue, if it is to be effective, requires an element of parity. It cannot be the case that one institution always wins the debate. Constitutional counter-balancing, therefore, provides a means of support for constitutional collaboration, helping to facilitate democratic dialogue through ensuring that it is not the case that one institution is always able to authoritatively determine issues concerning human rights. This explains why, in discussions assessing constitutional counter-balancing and constitutional collaboration, this book has referred to maintaining constitutional counter-balancing and to facilitating constitutional collaboration.

Constitutional counter-balancing mechanisms may also provide a means through which to facilitate a better protection of rights, given that they aim to provide an element of equality in the decision-making power of the legislature and the courts. An example of an account of democratic dialogue which aims to facilitate rights protection in this manner is found in Janet Hiebert's account of how dialogue should occur in the Canadian Constitution. Hiebert advocates that both the legislature and the judiciary should aspire to ensure that their actions comply with the values of the Canadian *Charter*, whether this be through ensuring that judgments protect *Charter* rights, or through ensuring that legislation respects *Charter* rights. She also advocates comity. Comity occurs when both the legislature and the courts respect the views of the other institution. This respect stems not from arguments as to the better ability of one or the other institution to determine rights-issues. Although Hiebert recognizes that courts focus on issues of principle and that legislatures focus on values, she makes no claim that courts or legislatures are better at resolving issues of principles or of values. Rather, her argument is that these are the respective roles that the Canadian constitution has ascribed to the legislature and the courts. Each institution should respect the resolution of the other, not because of any argument that the other institution is better able to resolve the issue, but because of the respect due to the other as an institution of the Canadian constitution.[35]

The account of democratic dialogue provided in this book, however, is based on the premise that there is sufficient evidence to demonstrate that legislatures and courts reason about rights in a different manner and that rights are better protected when each institution works together to facilitate deliberation. Institutions should aim to act in a manner which facilitates constitutional collaboration, providing reasons for their conclusions and engaging respectfully with the reasons provided for the decisions of the other institution. Constitutional counter-balancing should be used in those circumstances where one institution believes that the other has transgressed the proper bounds of their constitutional powers. As such, constitutional counter-balancing acts as more of a backstop. It aims to facilitate stability by acting as a means of resolving constitutional conflicts. Constitutional collaboration aims to smooth over the potential for conflict by facilitating institutions to work together.

B. Mechanisms

As the previous chapter discussed, there is an array of mechanisms that may be used to facilitate inter-institutional interactions. The previous chapter concluded that there was neither a necessary nor a sufficient correlation between the commonwealth model and inter-institutional interactions. Interactions can occur in legal systems that have not adopted a commonwealth model of rights protections, be they legal systems with a strong legal, a constitutional, or a parliamentary protection of rights. In addition, whether inter-institutional interactions occur within a legal system with a commonwealth model depends on how the legislature and the judiciary use the powers given to them under the commonwealth model. Nevertheless, we concluded that the commonwealth model had the advantage of adopting formal as opposed to informal mechanisms of dialogue, which may provide a wider choice of mechanisms.

In addition, commonwealth models of rights protection may be better able to facilitate democratic dialogue. First, as discussed in the previous chapter, formal mechanisms provide a legal means through which to maintain constitutional counter-balancing. This means that neither the legislature nor the judiciary need to use other mechanisms which may provoke more tension between these institutions—for example using striking back or clamping down mechanisms, or pushing back against striking back and clamping down measures. These measures may create as opposed to alleviate tension between the institutions, undermining the ability of constitutional counter-balancing to act as a pressure valve, providing a balance between stability and flexibility in the constitution. Moreover, non-legal constitutional counter-balancing mechanisms may

[35] J Hiebert, *Charter Conflicts: What is Parliament's Role?* (McGill-Queen's University Press 2002) Ch 3.

be less able to indirectly facilitate deliberation. First, non-legal or informal counter-balancing mechanisms occur mostly when either the legislature or the judiciary refrain from exercising their constitutional powers, for example through an exercise of judicial minimalism. If an institution refrains from exercising a power without providing an explanation, or without providing reasons, this may be less likely to provide a framework for deliberation either in the legislature or in the wider public sphere.

If we are to ensure democratic dialogue engages citizens in deliberations about rights, then we need to ensure that dialogue occurs through political as well as legal mechanisms of inter-institutional interaction. This may occur regardless of the mechanism used to facilitate inter-institutional interactions. Political mechanisms rely on the public reacting to either judicial or legislative determinations. The more the legislature and the courts are able to structure their reasoning in a manner that can be understood by the general public, the more political mechanisms may facilitate deliberation by the public. This aim is furthered by ensuring that the legislature and the judiciary pay attention to the public, particularly the legislature. This is also important to ensure that constitutional counter-balancing works effectively as a pressure valve.

C. Exercise

From the above discussion, it is clear that one factor that should influence the way in which inter-institutional interactions are exercised if they are to satisfy the requirements of democratic dialogue, is that both the legislature and the judiciary should focus on providing reasons and provide an account of their conclusions as clearly and transparently as possible. However, in addition, if we are to ensure that constitutional collaboration provides a better protection of rights, we also need to ensure that each institution takes account of the reasons of the other in a manner which corresponds to the relative ability of each institution to reason about rights. Most classifications of dialogue theories focus on the extent to which the theory allocates relative power to the legislature and the court to determine rights issues. Whilst some theories prefer that courts play a dominant role in the protection of rights, with a smaller role given to the legislature, others would reverse that relative balance of power, or distribute equal power to the legislature and judiciary to determine rights. This account of democratic dialogue argues, however, that the extent to which relative decision-making power should be given to the legislature or the courts depends upon the nature of the rights-issue to be resolved and how this relates to the different complementary roles of the legislature and the courts when reasoning about rights. To understand how democratic dialogue works, we need to think through accounts of the relative strength and weaknesses of the legislature and judiciary when reasoning about rights, in addition to thinking further about how each institution can respect the reasoning abilities of the other.

A common theme running through the literature on democratic dialogue is the distribution of tasks between the legislature and the judiciary according to whether the issue before the court is one of policy or one of principle, drawing on the distinction of Ronald Dworkin.[36] Hickman, for example, uses this distinction in his account of democratic dialogue. He argues that courts are better able to reach conclusions as to matters of principle. Legislatures, however, are better able to reach decisions on complex matters of policy. This is because legislatures receive information on a wide range of issues, may have more expertise in evaluating policy judgments and are better able to

[36] R Dworkin, *Taking Rights Seriously* (Harvard University Press 1977).

balance policy considerations in a legitimate manner.[37] Hickman is not alone in drawing on a distinction between principle and policy when explaining the different roles of the legislature and judiciary. Roach concludes that democratic dialogue works best when the legislature and the courts play distinct but complementary roles, again drawing on the better ability of the courts to resolve issues of principle and of the courts to resolve issues of policy. The role of the court is to question the policy decisions of the legislature, ensuring that their policy decisions do not come at the cost of overriding principles.[38] Hiebert also draws on the relative roles of the legislature and the court when providing her account of dialogue in the Canadian context.[39]

These accounts of democratic dialogue draw on generalizations as to the institutional differences between legislatures and the courts. Courts are regarding as being better at protecting fundamental principles as they reason from precedent and are immersed in a form of legal reasoning that recognizes and builds on long-standing fundamental principles. Legislatures, however, are more forward-looking, resolving problems as and when they arise, often looking to find long-term solutions. This means that courts may be better able to spot and correct errors made by legislatures who overlook long-standing fundamental principles. Courts also apply legislation or general principles to specific individuals before the courts. Legislatures enact general provisions. The possibility arises, therefore, that legislatures will not realize that legislation which is generally protective of fundamental rights fails to protect these rights when applied to a specific situation. Given the different reasoning abilities of the courts, they are in a better position to correct these potential errors as they focus on the application of general legislative provisions to specific situations.[40] These assessments, if based on valid facts about a particular legal system, can provide good reasons for arguing that courts are in a good position to recognize a potential error made by a legislature and to know that an error has been made. This, in turn, provides a justification for courts not to follow otherwise authoritative legislative resolutions of human rights issues.

However, it is important to recognize that these accounts of democratic dialogue are based on generalizations. To refine democratic dialogue further requires a specific application of general arguments about the relative ability of legislatures and courts to reason about rights to the features of these institutions in different constitutional settings. It is only when this application is made that we can assess whether dialogue is based on the relative institutional features of the legislature and the court to reason about rights, thus having the potential to provide a better protection of rights. Where we can make further progress, however, is as regards to the way in which courts and legislatures interact with one another. To explain this, however, requires a detour into an explanation of practical reasoning, focusing in particular on the distinction between first-order and second-order reasoning found in the work of Joseph Raz and others. This will not only help to explain how legislatures and courts can interact in order to facilitate democratic dialogue, but will also be helpful for the following section which analyses the potential problems of democratic dialogue, particularly arising from its potential conflict with the separation of powers and path-dependent behaviours of institutions in particular legal systems.

One of Raz's major contributions to the theory of practical reasoning was to recognize the distinction between first-order and second-order reasons.[41] First-order reasons

[37] Hickman (n 11) 85–87.

[38] K Roach, *The Supreme Court on Trial* (Toronto, Irwin Law Press 2001) 246–50.

[39] Hiebert (n 35) Ch 3.

[40] Gardbaum (n 7) 51–71; Hickman (n 11) 71–81.

[41] J Raz, *Practical Reason and Norms* (2nd edn, Oxford University Press 1999) 35–40.

are the reasons that we have for acting, or for not acting. For example, when deciding whether to accept a dinner invitation, first-order reasons would provide me with reasons for and against accepting the invitation. I may have a reason to accept the dinner invitation because I will enjoy the company, am otherwise free, and am able to find a child-minder. However, if the host is a terrible cook, or tends to invite people I do not like or find it hard to talk to, or there are no child-minders available that night, then there are good first-order reasons not to accept the dinner invitation. A second-order reason is defined by Raz as 'any reason to act for a reason or to refrain from acting for a reason'.[42] To return to my example of reasoning about the dinner invitation, it may be the case that I have promised my daughter not to accept dinner invitations on a Saturday so that we can watch episodes of *Dr Who* and *Sherlock* together. Even if the dinner I have been invited to is hosted by a marvellous cook, with the best of company, and quality child-minders are plentiful, my promise to my daughter provides a second-order reason to refrain from attending the dinner. Although my first-order reasons provide a reason to attend, my promise to my daughter excludes those considerations and I should refuse the invitation because of my promise. Similarly, if my boss has told me that I have to attend the dinner, then this command will give me a reason to attend the dinner, even if the first-order reasons would conclude that I should refuse to accept the invitation given that the host is a terrible cook, the others invited are my sworn enemies, and my daughter has to be looked after by an extremely expensive child-minder to whom she has taken an instant dislike.

Both of the examples of second-order reasons explained above are described by Raz as exclusionary reasons. The promise and the command provide a reason for me to exclude the conclusions I had reached by looking at the first-order reasons for accepting the dinner invitation. Although they are not the only form of second-order reasons, they are the type of second-order reasons that play the most important role in Raz's work. Raz develops his distinction between first-order and second-order reasoning to explain law's authority. In doing so, he gives an account of the normal justification thesis for authority. The normal justification thesis claims that A is justified in accepting the authority of B when adhering to B's conclusions is more likely to ensure that A achieves the right outcome on a balancing of first-order reasons than if A were to rely on A's own balancing of first-order reasons.[43]

Stephen Perry adds to Raz's classification by pointing out a distinction between how second-order reasons may operate in practice.[44] In the previous paragraph, we discussed reasons for and against attending a dinner. When describing the first-order and second-order reasons, we gave a series of facts about cooking, hosting skills, and the availability of child-minders. If I obey the command of my boss and attend the dinner, and the normal justification thesis applies, then by obeying my boss I may be more likely to do the right thing, on the balance of first-order reasons, than if I decide this for myself. This may be best explained through another example. My daughter wants to watch *Dr Who*, play Minecraft, and make a felt cat. However, she also has to practise piano and complete her homework. She has thought through the advantages and disadvantages of these activities and decides to only play her piano pieces, ignoring her piano scales, and to complete her homework on the school bus. I tell my daughter she cannot watch *Dr Who* or play Minecraft until her homework is complete and she has practised her contrary motion piano scales. By doing as she is asked, as opposed to

[42] ibid, 39. [43] J Raz, *The Morality of Freedom* (Oxford University Press 1986) 53.
[44] S Perry, 'Second-Order Reasons, Uncertainty and Legal Theory' (1989) 62 Southern California Law Review 913.

doing what she wants to do, my daughter is more likely to do the right thing on the balance of first-order reasons than if she were to decide this for herself. Perry refers to this as an objective second-order reason. There is a clear connection between following the exclusionary reason of the parental command and ensuring that, on the balance of first-order reasons, the right choice is made.[45]

However, Perry argues that second-order reasoning can also occur in situations of uncertainty. Imagine that I have to decide whether to take my waterproofs with me when I cycle in to work. If it is raining, then I have good first-order reasons to wear waterproofs, therefore taking the waterproofs with me, so they can be worn if it is raining when I cycle home, is the right thing for me to do. If it is not raining, then there are good reasons for me not to take my waterproofs. They take up a lot of room in my bag and cycling home in waterproofs when it is not raining is an uncomfortable experience. When deciding whether to take my waterproofs or not, I could look out of the window and try and guess whether I think it will rain or not, or I could look up weather forecasts for my local area. As the weather forecast is written by someone with more expertise in predicting the weather than myself, I may have good reasons to adhere to their advice. However, these good reasons are not necessarily connected to first-order reasons as to whether I should take my waterproofs. It may well be the case that the weather forecaster is more likely to predict whether it will rain on my cycle ride home. However, her forecast is a prediction. It is a not a fact about whether it is raining; but a prediction, or a belief that it may rain in the future. It is uncertain. This uncertainty affects the connection between the first-order reasons and the second-order reasons in a different manner. Perry calls these subjective second-order reasons.[46]

Having distinguished between objective and subjective second-order reasons, Perry delineates further between two types of subjective second-order reason—re-weighting reasons and epistemically-bounded reasons. Both occur in situations of uncertainty—that is when there is uncertainty surrounding the best outcome on the balance of first-order reasons. However, they differ in terms of the way in which an individual will reason in these conditions of uncertainty. Re-weighting reasons are reasons for giving particular weight to a first-order reason when balancing these reasons in order to determine an outcome. If I follow the advice of the weather forecaster and pack my waterproofs, even though my brief glance at the weather would suggest that they were not needed, it is because I've given greater weight to the first-order reasons of the weather forecaster. I still decide for myself whether to take waterproofs, but the weight of the advice of the weather forecaster means that the balance of first-order reasons tips in favour of taking my waterproofs even though it is not currently raining, as I have good reasons to believe that it will be raining when I cycle home.

Epistemically bounded reasons operate differently. First, they operate not when an individual is determining the balance of first-order reasons for him or herself, but when an individual is determining whether to adhere to the conclusion of another as to the balance of first-order reasons. To return to our dinner invitation, imagine this time that I have asked my boss whether I should accept an invitation to a faculty dinner. If I were applying epistemically bounded reasons, I would not be determining whether to go to the dinner, but rather whether I should adhere to the authoritative determination of my boss that I should attend the dinner. Normally I would follow the decision of my boss as he is in a position of authority over me. However, epistemically bounded

[45] Any conclusion of the reader that my daughter would reason in this manner is strenuously denied by the author's daughter!

[46] Perry (n 44) 927–31.

reasoning focuses on whether, although my boss has authority over me and normally I should adhere to his commands as he is more likely to reach the right answer, nevertheless I may be in a better position to spot and correct an error in my boss's balancing of the reasons for and against attending the faculty dinner.

For example, my boss may recommend that I attend the faculty dinner as he knows that this is the best decision, in terms of career progression. My boss is normally more likely to reach the right answer in this situation as I'm an introvert and pay too little attention to career progression. My boss is aware of these tendencies and has more experience than I in assessing what will and will not advance my career. However, when I ask my boss for an explanation of why I should attend the dinner, he informs me that the Dean normally attends this dinner, that the Dean is considering whether to recommend me for promotion, and that the Dean is concerned that I am anti-social and so wanted to test this by inviting me to a dinner that the Dean would be attending in order to assess my social skills first hand. However, I am a confidante of the Dean's partner. Because of this, I know that, although the Dean normally does attend, she will not be attending this dinner as she is going to a romantic dinner with her partner to celebrate their anniversary. Even though I would normally follow the advice of my boss, nevertheless in this instance I have very good reasons not to. There will be no negative impact on my career as the Dean will not be there to test my social skills.[47] I have information which provides me with good reasons not to follow the advice of my boss.[48]

Understanding these aspects of practical reasoning helps to clarify the nature of the relationship between the legislature and the judiciary which is more likely to provide a stable theory of democratic dialogue which, in turn, may provide a better protection of rights. First, an assessment of the relative authority of the legislature and the court needs to be based on second-order as well as first-order reasons. When determining how to respond to a judicial or legislative assessment, each institution should focus on second-order and not just first-order reasoning, based on the relative institutional abilities of the other institution to resolve rights-issues. This is for two reasons. First, without applying second-order reasons, there is a danger that accounts of democratic dialogue merely reiterate the arguments found in dynamic interpretations of legal and political constitutionalism, making it hard in practice to distinguish democratic dialogue from other accounts. Second, this focus on second-order reasoning provides a better means of ensuring that it is not the case that one institution overturns the rights-determination of the other when the other institution would have had more knowledge or expertise to determine this issue. Therefore, an application of second-order reasoning is more likely to provide for a better protection of rights.

We can illustrate the danger of a potential collapse, and the failure to deliver on the promise of a better protection of rights, if we return to the account given in the previous two chapters of Trevor Allan's account of the dynamic component of legal constitutionalism and Griffith's account of the dynamic component of political constitutionalism. Allan and Griffith both provide an account of inter-institutional interactions between the legislature and the court, but their accounts provide different relative authority to the legislature and the court to resolve rights-issues. Allan regards the court as the best institution to reason about rights. However, he is not insensitive to the

[47] Professor Anne Davies has asked me to make it clear that, despite being the current Dean of the Law Faculty at the University of Oxford, she has no powers to promote anyone and that, even if she did, social graces at a dinner would not be a relevant consideration!

[48] Perry (n 44) 932–45.

argument that there may be some rights-issues that are more difficult to resolve than others and recognizes that, in these circumstances, courts should be sensitive to these issues, defining the right in a manner which focuses on recognizing the range of ways in which the legislature can act which does not erode the right. Griffith believes that the legislature is the best institution to resolve rights-issues. The dynamic component of his theory relies on the courts ensuring rights are interpreted in line with the resolutions of the legislature, with rights evolving over time as the balance of power between different interest groups changes.

It is difficult to delineate between the account of Allan and Hickman's account of democratic dialogue for two reasons. Both give the balance of power to the courts, whilst recognizing a role for the legislature. The means through which this role for the legislature is to be accommodated also appears to be the same. Hickman refers to the courts refraining from using their powers. Allan refers to the courts focusing on the definition of the right, recognizing when the nature of the right allows for more rights-compatible balances with interests and other rights. It is hard to see the difference between these two approaches. If, for example, the court was determining whether a rule allowing prisoners to vote if they were serving sentences of less than one year breached the right to vote, it would be hard to differentiate between the courts refraining from providing a strong definition of a right and courts deciding that there were a number of ways in which the right to vote could be balanced with the interest of ensuring those who committed crimes were punished effectively. In a similar manner, it can be difficult to differentiate Nicol's account of democratic dialogue from Griffith's account of the political constitution. Both require Parliaments to play the main role when determining issues of rights.

Where a difference does arise is when we assess whether Hickman and Allan are advocating that courts apply first-order or second-order reasons. If we return to Allan's account, when courts determine the content of a right, Allan advocates that courts should only take account of features internal to the law—that is the nature of the right and its application to the specific facts before the court. Courts are to use first-order reasons, or, if second-order reasons are relevant, these are implicit as opposed to explicit and appear to be subsumed into first-order reasoning.[49] When faced with uncertainty, Allan argues that courts recognize this uncertainty by building this in to their interpretation of the right. If we were to reason in this manner in regard to the example discussed above—whether I should take waterproofs when cycling—the court would apply first-order reasoning, recognizing that I should take waterproofs if it is raining. However, faced with uncertainty as to whether it will rain later or not, the first-order reasons do not provide a definitive answer as to whether I should take my waterproofs in the morning. In a sense, I am faced with a discretionary area of judgment. I have neither a reason for, nor a reason against taking my waterproofs. In such situations, I may err on the side of caution (take my waterproofs even if it is not raining), or recklessness (never take my waterproofs unless it is raining), or decide to take my waterproofs if I think there is a reasonable chance of rain based on the predictions of a range of weather forecasts. In a similar manner, when the court is faced with the issue of whether to strike down a decision granting prisoners the right to vote if they are serving sentences of one year or less, the courts may recognize that the right to vote would be breached if no prisoners were allowed to vote, and that the interest of

[49] It can be hard to determine which of these two interpretations is the most accurate account. This chapter will adopt the first as being the most consistent with Allan's later work. I am grateful to Paul Craig for pointing out these two possible interpretations.

ensuring effective punishment would not be achieved if all prisoners were allowed to vote. The court may then decide that, as the restriction is between these two extremes it has not breached the right.

Although Hickman's theory appears similar to that of Allan, a possible distinction between the two arises when we examine Hickman's assessment of how the courts should apply deference under the Human Rights Act 1998. Deference is a means by which the court can exercise restraint, as advocated by Hickman. Hickman concludes that deference should be based only on external features, as the role of deference is not to determine the content of a right, but to determine how much weight to give to the opinions of other institutions that a particular action does not harm a Convention right.[50] When discussing these factors, Hickman is focusing on second-order reasoning. When interpreting legislation under section 3, courts should adjust the weight they give to the legislature's determination of a right when faced with a situation where the legislature may have better expertise.[51] For example, if the judiciary were convinced that the legislature had greater knowledge of, or expertise in, assessments of national security, then the court should give greater weight to the opinion of the legislature that the legislation it is scrutinizing is a legitimate restriction on a human right in order to protect national security. This is not to say that the court should adopt the conclusion of the legislature. Instead, the court may require greater evidence that the legislation has failed to find the right balance. The greater weight almost acts like a presumption in favour of legality, which can be rebutted by strong evidence. The court is determining whether there are good reasons to give weight to the opinion of the legislature, given, for example, its greater knowledge or greater expertise.[52]

The same difference, however, is not apparent when we re-examine Nicol's account of democratic dialogue. Nicol requires both the legislature and the courts to be forthright when determining rights-issues. He also advocates that both the courts and the legislature should accept or reject the conclusions of the other based solely on their assessment of the reasons each institution provides for reaching its conclusion. Neither institution should give any weight to the opinions of the other because the other institution may be better at deciding this issue.[53] In other words, each institution only uses first-order and not second-order reasons. No weight is to be given to the fact that the opinion comes from the legislature or the court, and therefore either institution may be relatively better at reasoning about rights.

The difference between the two theories is not concerned with whether, in practice, the legislature is given more discretionary power to determine the content of the right. Rather, the focus is on the way in which courts and legislatures reason. Recognizing this distinction is important if democratic dialogue is to achieve its normative claim of providing a better protection of rights. Democratic dialogue aims to minimize the disadvantages and maximize the advantages of legal and political protections of rights. As discussed in the previous chapter, this is achieved through recognizing the different ways in which both legislatures and the courts reason about rights. Their relative strengths are maximized and weaknesses minimized if both institutions are sensitive to these issues and use them to formulate second-order reasons, providing reasons to

[50] Hickman (n 11) 141–45.

[51] ibid, Ch 3; T Hickman, 'Constitutional Dialogue, Constitutional Theories and the Human Rights Act 1998' [2005] Public Law 306; and T Hickman, 'Judges and Politicians after the Human Rights Act 1998: A Comment' [2008] Public Law 84.

[52] Hickman (n 11) 145–61.

[53] D Nicol, 'Law and Politics after the Human Rights Act' [2006] Public Law 722.

follow or criticize the right determinations made by the other. To only focus on first-order reasons may be less likely to combine the role of the legislature and the court in a manner which achieves this normative aim of democratic dialogue.

This recognition also points to a potential weakness in Hiebert's account of democratic dialogue. We can see this when we use Andrew Legg's analysis of second-order reasons and their application to theories of deference and the margin of appreciation in the European Court of Human Rights.[54] Legg distinguishes between two types of justification for applying subjective second-order reasons. First, individuals may apply subjective second-order reasons based on the nature of the relationship with the individual whose reasons are operating as subjective second-order reasons. Second, individuals may apply subjective second-order reasoning because of the relative expertise of the individual whose reasons are operative as subjective second-order reasons. For example, courts may use the determinations of legislatures as subjective second-order reasons for reasons of comity—where the court respects the relative authority of the legislature to determine rights-issues based on constitutional grounds. Such justifications rely on the nature of the relationship between the legislature and the court. When, however, legislatures use the determinations of courts to provide subjective second-order reasoning based on the court's relative ability to determine rights-issues, then the legislature is justified in doing so to the extent of the relevant expertise of the legislature and the courts in determining that particular rights-issue.

Hiebert's theory is not based on the relative institutional abilities of either the legislature or the courts to reason about rights. Rather, it is based on granting comity—that is respecting the view of the other institution as providing an alternative point of view which deserves respect given the constitutional authority of the other institution. The amount of respect owed to the other institution is not necessarily based on their better institutional ability to resolve rights-issues. It appears to operate in a different manner—merely requiring that each institution does not reject the argument of the other out of hand, but considers it seriously, presumably by assessing the first-order reasons provided by each institution, although this is not clear from Hiebert's account. As such, it may be less likely that applying Hiebert's account of democratic dialogue will maximize the benefits and minimize the disadvantages of predominantly legal or political protections of rights. However, Hiebert's use of comity may help to minimise one of the potential criticisms of democratic dialogue which may also undermine its ability to deliver its normative aim of a better protection of rights; it helps to ensure that applying democratic dialogue does not undermine judicial independence and the separation of powers. We will turn to these criticisms in the next section, when evaluating the potential weaknesses of democratic dialogue.

D. Weaknesses

It is not the case that accounts of democratic dialogue automatically undermine the separation of powers and the independence of the judiciary. However, it is not hard to see how this might be the case. Kent Roach's assessment of dialogue explains clearly how different accounts of dialogue may undermine the separation of powers. Roach distinguishes between three types of democratic dialogue theory: (i) where the courts and legislature play distinct and complementary roles; (ii) where the courts and legislatures interpret the constitution for themselves; and (iii) where legislatures hold the

[54] A Legg, *The Margin of Appreciation in International Law* (Oxford University Press 2012) 24–26.

courts accountable. Roach argues that the separation of powers is particularly undermined when both the courts and the legislature interpret the constitution for themselves, or where legislatures hold courts accountable.[55]

Dialogue which takes place when courts and legislatures interpret the constitution for themselves occurs when both the legislature and the courts regard themselves as able to provide equally authoritative accounts of constitutional rights. As such, this means that the legislature is free to ignore court determinations of rights. This undermines the separation of powers because each institution of the constitution is given the same function—that of deciding rights-issues—without an account of the extent to which deciding rights-issues is a judicial or a legislative function. It is hard to know, therefore, whether one institution has begun to perform the functions of the other institution, thus breaching the separation of powers. In addition, Roach argues that accounts of dialogue where the courts and the legislature each play a role in interpreting the constitution and determining rights may undermine judicial independence given that judicial interpretations of rights have no authority other than their power to persuade the legislature based on the content of the judicial determination and the strength of the reasoning provided to reach that determination. Legislatures are free to follow or ignore these outcomes. There is the temptation, therefore, for the judiciary to determine outcomes in order to please the legislature, rather than through providing an independent account of their determination of a rights-issue.[56]

Dialogue based on legislatures holding courts accountable occurs when dialogue is designed to ensure that courts enact judicial decisions that are in line with the wishes of the majority. Again, Roach is critical of this account of dialogue as it undermines the independence of the judiciary, who may take decisions in order to avoid future criticism from the legislature, and the separation of powers, by undermining the ability of the courts to hold the legislature and the executive to account as to their record of protecting human rights, as opposed to their ability to enact decisions which reflect the views of the majority.[57]

The account of democratic dialogue advocated in this chapter, therefore, may appear to escape this criticism. Yet, if this is the case, it seems hard to understand why Hiebert's account is also seen as a means of minimizing the impact of dialogue on the maintenance of the separation of powers and the potential undermining of the independence of the judiciary, given that Hiebert's account does rest on the idea that both the judiciary and the legislature have a role to play in determining constitutional rights and her theory does not provide a specific account of the precise roles each institution should play. Rather, her account rests on arguments of comity, where each institution respects the complementary role of the other. If we are to combine the distinct roles of the legislature and the judiciary in a manner which respects their different abilities to reason about rights, without undermining the separation of powers and the independence of the judiciary, we need to think further about how these two institutions can interact, not in terms of the mechanisms of interaction, but how each institution exercises the powers given to it in any particular constitution.

We also need to be aware of a further problem that arises when applying theories of democratic dialogue. Dialogue may require courts and legislatures to act in a manner different from their traditionally perceived roles. As such, a reluctance to act in this manner may undermine the ability of democratic dialogue to achieve its objectives, particularly when institutional interactions are normally achieved through institutions

[55] Roach (n 38). [56] ibid, 241–43. [57] ibid, 243–46.

refraining from exercising legal or constitutional powers. It may also mean that interactions are more likely to achieve constitutional counter-balancing, but may be less likely to facilitate constitutional collaboration. The recent study by Janet Hiebert and James Kelly of the operation of what they refer to as parliamentary Bills of Rights in the United Kingdom and New Zealand illustrates these problems.[58] For example, Hiebert and Kelly's work concludes that there is little political engagement with human rights at the pre-legislative stage in both the United Kingdom and New Zealand, despite both having legal provisions in their commonwealth model of rights protections designed to facilitate pre-legislative scrutiny. They argue that governments are more concerned with obtaining advice as to how to minimize the risk of a human rights-based political challenge to their proposed legislation than they are to ensure that the legislation which they propose provides a good protection of human rights. Moreover, they criticize the extent to which executive dominance in both the United Kingdom and New Zealand counteracts an effective political scrutiny of rights. They conclude that parliamentary protections of rights are not going to achieve their objective of a better protection of human rights that requires the legislature and the judiciary to act in a manner different from their traditional role, but where there is little or no incentive to induce this change in behaviour.

Stephen Perry's account of subjective second-order reasons, as discussed above, can help to provide a means of ensuring that institutional interactions facilitate dialogue, whilst minimizing the impact on the separation of powers and the independence of the judiciary. Perry distinguishes between weight-adjusting and epistemically bounded subjective second-order reasons. These operate in different situations. When an individual uses weight-adjusting second-order reasoning, the individual decides for him or herself, whilst giving weight to the opinion of the other. For example, in relation to my decision as to whether to take my waterproofs when cycling in to work, I give weight to the opinion of the weather forecaster, who has greater knowledge and expertise than I have regarding the weather. I decide that her opinion that it will rain provides me with a reason to take my waterproofs. When applying epistemically bounded reasoning, however, the situation is different. Here, the individual normally adheres to the orders or commands of another, unless the individual is in a good position to know that this command is wrong and has the ability to correct this. In the example above, I would normally follow the decisions of my boss, who has authority over me. However, if I am in a position to know that information on which his decision is based is incorrect, then I have good reason not to follow his advice on this occasion.

Understanding this difference can provide a means of minimizing the extent to which democratic dialogue may undermine the separation of powers. Dialogue can work with, as opposed to working against, the separation of powers as understood in a particular legal system. As discussed above, democratic dialogue is more likely to achieve a better protection of rights when courts and legislatures use second-order as well as first-order reasoning. However, whether courts and legislatures should use weight-adjusting or epistemically bounded reasoning depends upon the relative distribution of authority between these institutions. For example, if a constitution gives courts the power to authoritatively determine rights-issues, then this alters the second-order reasoning that can be used by the legislature. The legislature should normally adhere to the reasoning of the court unless the legislature has information which calls

[58] JL Hiebert and JB Kelly, *Parliamentary Bills of Rights: The Experiences of New Zealand and the United Kingdom* (Cambridge University Press 2015).

into question the reasoning of the court and is in a good position to correct the error of the court. This helps to ensure that the legislature does not act in a manner that undermines the separation of powers and the independence of the judiciary as understood in that particular legal system.

Working with, as opposed to against, traditional understandings, or legal definitions of the relative powers of the legislature and the courts minimizes the extent to which democratic dialogue may undermine the separation of powers. It may also minimize the extent to which path-dependencies can undermine the ability of democratic dialogue to achieve its normative aims. However, this in turn recognizes that the extent to which democratic dialogue can be achieved will depend upon the constitutional and institutional features of the legislature and the judiciary. It will also depend upon the extent to which dialogue is achieved through requiring institutions to refrain from exercising their powers, through informal as opposed to formal means. This may support the conclusion of the previous chapter that dialogue may be more likely to be achieved in commonwealth models. However, it also reinforces our conclusion that dialogue may not be achieved in commonwealth models, particularly when this requires institutions to act differently from their previous patterns of behaviour.

III. Conclusion

This chapter has assessed whether inter-institutional interactions have value, using these values to develop an account of democratic dialogue. It has argued that institutional interactions can help to provide a better protection of rights, facilitate deliberation, engage citizens in the determination of rights, and act as a means of providing for checks and balances between institutions that may help to alleviate the tension between constitutional flexibility and constitutional stability.

It has also confirmed the initial findings of the previous chapter that, although there is no necessary connection between democratic dialogue and a commonwealth model of rights protections, it may nevertheless be easier to facilitate democratic dialogue in a commonwealth model given that the commonwealth model provides for formal, legal means through which to facilitate institutional interactions in addition to informal and political means. This is because we argued that democratic dialogue is more likely to be facilitated through constitutional collaboration as opposed to constitutional counter-balancing. Constitutional collaboration is better able to provide for a protection of rights which blends the relative advantages of courts and legislatures to reason about rights, taking account of pragmatic reasoning and political–ethical reasoning in addition to concerns raised by interest-orientated and value-based co-ordination. Constitutional counter-balancing needs to be maintained to facilitate constitutional collaboration. Constitutional counter-balancing should be motivated by a response to a perceived imbalance in the distribution of power between the legislature and the judiciary. Each institution should use constitutional counter-balancing mechanisms in response to a perceived exercise of power in a manner which goes beyond the power of an institution, transgressing into the powers of the other institution. In doing so, constitutional counterbalancing mechanisms help to act as a safety valve as well as indirectly facilitating constitutional collaboration. Moreover, institutions should pay attention to the perceived reaction of the other institution, in addition to the reaction of the public, when thinking about exercising a mechanism of inter-institutional interaction which is more likely to facilitate constitutional counter-balancing than constitutional collaboration.

This chapter has also argued that each institution should ensure that it uses first-order and second-order reasoning, thinking not just about the reasons for or against preferring a particular determination of a right, but in addition assessing whether, in terms of relative institutional and constitutional competence, each institution should give weight to the reasoning of the other. Moreover, we have argued that each institution should exercise its powers in a manner which provides reasoned justifications, both for the conclusion each reaches as to the determination of a right and also for the reasons either institution has given weight to the reasoning of the other when reaching its determination. Finally, in order to ensure that democratic dialogue does not undermine the separation of powers or the independence of the judiciary, the type of second-order reasoning each institution should use depends upon the precise constitutional structure in any legal system. This determines whether an institution should exercise its powers by checking the determinations of the other, when it has specific knowledge and expertise that may help it to find and correct an error, or when it normally has more expertise, but is acting in response to the specific expertise and knowledge of the other in a particular area, or respecting the relative constitutional authority of the other.

Although this chapter has moved further in determining an account of democratic dialogue, it is still given at a fairly abstract level. This is understandable given that the account provided so far is designed to be broad enough to be adopted in a range of constitutions—be they ones adopting a commonwealth model of rights protections or those with a constitutional or a parliamentary protection of rights. If we are to evaluate democratic dialogue further, we need to apply it to a specific constitution. This takes place in the following three chapters through an analysis of the UK constitution. The UK constitution was chosen for two reasons. First, it is the constitution that I have studied the most. Second, the UK constitution provides an interesting testing ground for theories of democratic dialogue because it requires not only an assessment of the extent to which dialogue between the legislature and the court can provide a better means of protecting human rights, but also provides the opportunity to assess whether dialogue between the UK and European courts can achieve some of the values of democratic dialogue.

6

Democratic Dialogue and the UK Constitution

The previous chapters have redefined democratic dialogue. However, they have done so at a fairly abstract level, providing a general account of dialogue which can then be refined through its application to a particular legal system. In doing so we have described different forms of inter-institutional interaction and examined the relationship between democratic dialogue and the commonwealth model of rights protections. Democratic dialogue has also been described as a model. In order to assess how well this can be applied in the UK legal system, we need first to briefly explain what this means, before evaluating the extent to which democratic dialogue applies in the United Kingdom.

In their account of political constitutionalism, Gee and Webber point out that advocates of political constitutionalism often refer to models.[1] Political constitutionalism is seen as a model opposed to the alternative model of legal constitutionalism. However, there is very little attention paid to providing a precise account of what it means to refer to an account of the constitution as a model. Gee and Webber argue that most theorists use models to provide a simplified account of the constitution, whilst appealing to a particular ideal.[2] The reference to models is not limited to advocates of political constitutionalism, or to normative accounts of constitutions. Examples can be found of the use of models when providing rival accounts of the justification of judicial review and of various approaches to public law more generally. In addition, models are referred to for the purposes of comparing different legal systems and for giving an account of different approaches to constitutionalism over time. However, as with the reference to models by advocates of political constitutionalism, there is often little, if any, explanation provided as to why a particular academic uses the term model as opposed to a different term, or of what is added to their account by reference being made to models.

Broadly understood, a model is an idealized abstraction of reality. It operates both as a map and as a simplification, choosing to highlight particular characteristics. For example, a model of the city of Oxford may map the streets of Oxford, aiming to provide a simplified account of the streets and their connections with one another. The model of Oxford may choose to highlight various features to help providing a more simplified account of the city—for example, it may highlight colleges, churches, university institutions, public houses, or interesting artistic features. Whilst the maps highlighting these different features may all be potential models of the city of Oxford, they would serve different purposes. A map highlighting public houses would be of greater utility to a person wishing to complete the Oxford pub crawl than one highlighting the colleges and university buildings.[3] Each of these models would be evaluated according

[1] G Gee and GCN Webber, 'What is a Political Constitution?' (2010) 20 Oxford Journal of Legal Studies 273.

[2] ibid, 291–92.

[3] As a jaded Oxford academic, I refuse to comment on which of these is, in reality, of more use to Oxford undergraduate students.

to its ability to represent the real world, and according to the extent to which it fulfils its purpose. A map of the Oxford Colleges that missed out Hertford College would be less accurate than one that included the college. A map of Oxford public houses that included information on opening times, relative reception of landlords to students, and the price of various alcoholic beverages would better serve a student wanting to undertake a pub crawl and, in that sense, would be a better map than one that merely showed the location of public houses.

We normally think of models in one of two ways. First, we may be referring to a model in a descriptive sense, where a model aims to provide a simplified description of reality. For example, we use models to explain how atoms work. Models of atoms are often depicted as a series of circles, with electrons orbiting the neutron in a similar manner to the way in which planets orbit the sun. The model is deliberately simplified in order to provide a clear account of a more complex reality. The success of a purely descriptive model depends upon the extent to which it provides an accurate account of the real world, albeit a more simplified account in order to aid understanding. The value of the model depends upon this balance between accuracy and its ability to explain. Descriptive models are modified as we discover more about the world, such that the model is no longer accurate. However, models can never be completely accurate, being limited by our discoveries and our understanding as well as requiring simplification to aid understanding. The value of the model stems from its ability to depict the world as accurately as possible without losing its ability to explain a complicated reality in an understandable manner.

Second, we may refer to a model in a normative sense—where a model provides for an ideal that may or may not be able to be achieved in the real world. An example of a model in this sense is the model of perfect competition used in micro-economic theory. The model of perfect competition is a hypothetical model, resting on assumptions that are impossible to achieve in the real world. It is proposed as an ideal, providing an account of a market where allocative and productive efficiency are achieved. The model is not used to reflect reality. Rather, it is used as a normative goal, providing a justification for regulating markets in order to bring them closer to the ideal of perfect competition. The success of a normative model depends upon the value of the norms that it proposes, and the ability of the model to achieve these norms. The model of perfect competition is of value because it achieves allocative and productive efficiency, ensuring that goods are produced as cheaply as possible and that they are distributed to all those demanding the goods, with firms making normal profits in the long-term. If it were discovered that the model of perfect competition no longer achieved these aims, perhaps because we discovered that the mathematics underpinning the model was incorrect, or that producers did not always act so as to maximize profits, then the model would lose its value. In a similar way, the model could be criticized if we no longer valued allocative and productive efficiency. If these are not valuable, then the model of perfect competition has no value either—it aims to promote something we no longer consider valuable.

Democratic dialogue is a model with both descriptive and normative dimensions. It is presented as a normatively justifiable ideal. There is a normative justification for adopting democratic dialogue as it aims to promote things we value—a good protection of rights, deliberation, public participation, and a means of smoothing relationships between institutions. However, unlike purely normative models and in common with descriptive models, democratic dialogue is also designed to reflect reality. It is not a hypothetical model that cannot be achieved in the real world. Rather it rests on real facts and assumptions. But, as a normative model, its ideas may be achieved to a greater or lesser degree in different constitutions. Democratic dialogue, therefore, should be evaluated in terms of the values it promotes and its ability to achieve these values. It is also important to ensure that any assumptions on which democratic dialogue rests are reflected in reality. To apply democratic dialogue to the UK constitution, we need first to set out the assumptions on which democratic dialogue is based, evaluating the extent to which they are met in the UK constitution and, to the extent to which they are not, assessing how far this undermines the ability of democratic dialogue to achieve its normative objectives.

We have already discussed assumptions underpinning constitutional theories in Chapter 3. Democratic dialogue shares the general assumptions found in Waldron's argument against a strong legal protection of human rights. However, it does not accept Fallon's further assumption that society is better off when there is an over-protection as opposed to an under-protection of rights. Instead, it requires two further assumptions. First, democratic dialogue assumes that courts and legislatures protect rights in different ways and that society is better if institutions can work together to protect rights. Second, democratic dialogue assumes that legislatures and the courts are able to work together, without it being the case that one institution will always dominate the other institution such that one institution can predominantly override the rights-determinations of the other institution. Third, in order to facilitate deliberation, dialogue requires both the legislature and the courts to provide reasons for their determinations. Fourth, if citizens are to be engaged there needs to be a sufficient protection of freedom of expression and freedom of information. This chapter will argue that there is enough evidence to conclude that the UK constitution satisfies these assumptions, such that the model democratic dialogue can be applied to the UK constitution.

I. General Assumptions

Waldron's argument against a strong, legal protection of human rights rests on four basic assumptions: that a constitution has democratic law-making institutions that are in reasonably good working order; that the constitution has a set of judicial institutions in reasonably good working order; that there is a commitment of most members of society and most of its officials to the protection of human rights; and that there is persistent, substantial, and good faith disagreement about rights.[4]

When determining whether a constitution has democratic law-making institutions that are in reasonably good working order, Waldron expects such institutions to have a representative legislature, with universal suffrage, electing a reasonably large representative body on a fair and regular basis. In addition, this legislative body must enact legislation through a fairly elaborate and responsible process, with some form of safeguards over this process through bicameralism and scrutiny through committees, in addition to ensuring that debates connect with wider issues in society. In particular, there is a need for the legislative body to be kept in check to ensure political equality. There is no requirement that a legislative body be perfect, and Waldron's assumptions can be fulfilled even when there are clear examples of bad legislation, or legislation that has been enacted in a far from ideal manner. Rather, a legislative body needs to fulfil these criteria to a reasonable degree.

[4] J Waldron, 'The Core of the Case Against Judicial Review' (2006) 115 Yale Law Journal, 1346, 1359–69.

Given the flexibility inherent in the satisfaction of these criteria, it seems hard to argue that these are not met by the UK legislature. The UK Parliament is a reasonably large body, composed currently of 650 Members of Parliament in the House of Commons and 789 currently eligible members of the House of Lords. In addition to the Westminster Parliament, the United Kingdom has three further Parliaments or Assemblies in the devolved nations, including 129 members of the Scottish Parliament, sixty members of the Welsh Assembly, and 108 members of the Northern Ireland Assembly. Each of these legislatures is elected through a form of universal suffrage. The Westminster Parliament is elected through the first-past-the-post system, with the candidate with the majority of votes in a particular constituency being elected to the seat in that constituency. The Scottish Parliament and the Welsh and Northern Ireland Assemblies elect members through the Additional Member system. Each voter has two votes, one for their constituency MP elected on a 'first-past-the-post' basis and the second for a regional or list member, where the electorate votes for a party as opposed to a candidate, with the seats in the region being allocated in proportion to the number of votes cast for the particular political party. There is general universal suffrage, with the possible exception of the current blanket ban on prisoners, all of whom are currently ineligible to vote for the UK Parliament and the devolved legislatures.

The Westminster Parliament and the devolved legislatures also have a fairly robust structure of scrutiny over legislation, through committee structures and, in the case of the Westminster Parliament, through bicameralism. All of the four institutions debate issues that reflect wider issues in society. In the Westminster Parliament this is mostly achieved through the lobbying process and through the way in which constituents can raise issues with their constituency MP which can then be raised in Parliament through questions or debates, as well as each having a system through which members of the public can raise a public petition for the attention of the legislature or assembly. All four legislatures or assemblies also have organized political parties. The Electoral Commission and the Electoral Office in Northern Ireland, both independent organizations, play a role in ensuring the protection of political equality through its work scrutinizing elections and regulating party and electoral finances. This is supplemented by the internally enforced rules and regulations, for example relating to expenses and to the standards and conduct of the members of each assembly or Parliament.

If there is an issue that can potentially undermine the conclusion that the UK constitution meets Waldron's first assumption, it is the role of the House of Lords and the Monarch in the enactment of legislation in the United Kingdom. The members of the House of Lords are unelected. The House is composed of peers and life peers. The House of Lords Act 1999 reduced the number of hereditary peers to ninety-two,[5] with the rest of the House being composed of the twenty-six Church of England Bishops and life peers nominated either by the Prime Minister, with oversight from the House of Lords Appointment Commission, or non-political life peers nominated by the House of Lords Appointment Commission. There are now provisions for peers to resign from the House of Lords,[6] in addition to a means through which peers may cease to be a member of the House of Lords for non-attendance.[7] Both the Monarch and the House of Lords are normally required to approve legislation, unless the Parliament Acts 1911–49 are used to enact legislation without the consent of the House of Lords. By convention, known as the Salisbury Doctrine, the House of Lords does not vote against government-proposed legislation at its second or third reading

[5] House of Lords Act 1999, ss 1 and 2.
[6] House of Lords Reform Act 2014, s 1.
[7] House of Lords Reform Act 2014, s 2.

when this legislation stems from a manifesto commitment, thus giving it the mandate of the nation. Similarly, by convention, the Monarch does not refuse royal assent to legislation, unless advised by her Ministers to do so. Despite the Salisbury Doctrine, there is still evidence of defeats of legislation in the House of Lords, which can lead to legislation being later amended in the House of Commons.[8] The existence of these conventions means that, in general, the law-making process for the United Kingdom broadly satisfies Waldron's assumptions as to reasonably functioning legislature.

A similar conclusion is reached when we examine Waldron's second assumption regarding the need for a reasonably well-functioning judicial system. This assumption is satisfied when the legal system has an independent judiciary, which can uphold the rule of law through reviewing decisions of the executive in addition to hearing disputes between individuals, a binary judicial process and a hierarchy of courts. All of these conditions are satisfied to a reasonable degree in the United Kingdom. Section 63 of the Constitutional Reform Act 2005 requires that appointments to the judiciary are on merit only,[9] subject to the ability, when faced with two equally appointable candidates, to recommend the candidate most likely to improve diversity on the bench.[10] Appointments to the judiciary and to the Upper Tribunal in England and Wales are made through the Judicial Appointments Commission, who pass on their nomination to the appropriate appointing authority.[11] Similar provisions apply as regards appointments to the Scottish judiciary, through the Judicial Appointments Board in Scotland and to the Northern Irish judiciary through the Judicial Appointments Commission for Northern Ireland. Appointments to the Supreme Court are made through a selection committee convened by the Lord Chancellor which includes the President and Deputy President of the Supreme Court and members of the Judicial Appointments Commission for England and Wales, the Judicial Appointments Board in Scotland, and the Judicial Appointments Commission for Northern Ireland.[12] There is a clear hierarchy of courts, presided over by the Supreme Court and, although problems arise from the issues surrounding the use of closed material proceedings,[13] the fact that these provisions have been subject to such criticism and judicial scrutiny is suggestive of a healthy as opposed to an unhealthy judicial system.

There is also evidence to demonstrate the existence of a serious commitment to rights within the United Kingdom, coupled with genuine disagreement about central issues of human rights, including disagreement about the way in which rights are protected and disagreement about watershed issues of human rights. The Human Rights Act 1998 is clear evidence of a commitment to rights in the United Kingdom. Although there is currently a proposal from the Conservative Government to repeal the Human Rights Act, this is coupled with a commitment to enact a British Bill of Rights, as well as a strong assertion that Britain has long been committed to human rights through its protection of rights by the common law.[14] The work of the Joint Committee on Human Rights has also raised the profile of human rights and added to the general political commitment to the protection of rights in the United Kingdom. There is also

[8] http://www.ucl.ac.uk/constitution-unit/research/parliament/house-of-lords/lords-defeats.

[9] Constitutional Reform Act 2005, s 63(2).

[10] Crime and Courts Act 2013, Sch 13, ss 9–10.

[11] Constitutional Reform Act 2005, Sch 14.

[12] Constitutional Reform Act, ss 25–31 and Sch 8.

[13] See in particular the Justice and Security Act 2013, ss 6–11.

[14] See S Dimelow and AL Young, 'Common Sense or Confusion? The Human Rights Act and the Conservative party' http://www.consoc.org.uk/2015/06/common-sense-or-confusion-the-human-rights-act-and-the-conservative-party/.

a continuing trend in the reduction of cases in which the European Court of Human Rights has held the United Kingdom to be in breach of the Convention, and a growing tendency in the government to respond quickly to adverse human rights judgments.[15] In addition to the Human Rights Act, there is a growing recognition by the judiciary of the way in which the common law protects human rights.[16] The commitment to the protection of human right is reflected in the proportion of cases before the Supreme Court which concern human rights—eleven of the 115 judgments delivered by the Supreme Court in its 2013–14 sitting concerned human rights, with a further fourteen concerning immigration and five raising issues of judicial review.[17] In 2014–15, 269 applications for appeal cases were referred to the Supreme Court, with six concerning human rights, twenty-nine raising issues of immigration, and thirty-seven issues of judicial review.[18] Of the eighty-one judgments delivered in 2014–15, ten concerned human rights, four concerned immigration, and four raised issues of judicial review.[19]

The existence of disagreement about key human rights issues has already been seen with regard to the debate concerning prisoner voting in the United Kingdom, not to mention the continuing debate as to the desirability of the Human Rights Act, particularly concerning its connection to the European Court of Human Rights and the extent to which it empowers the judiciary to protect human rights. Divergence also arises between the different nations of the United Kingdom. For example, there is evidence of delays in the implementation of some decisions of the European Court of Human Rights by the Northern Ireland Assembly,[20] as well as areas where the devolved legislatures provide a stronger protection of rights, for example with regard to the protection of children's rights in Wales.[21]

II. Specific Assumptions

In addition to the general assumptions adumbrated above, there are further specific assumptions on which democratic dialogue is based. This section will assess the extent to which these are satisfied in the UK constitution. There are three further main assumptions underpinning theories of democratic dialogue. First, there needs to be sufficient balance between the actors taking part in democratic dialogue. This does not require that the participants have complete parity, with equal authority to determine a rights-issue. Rather, it requires that neither participant is able to continually override the wishes of the other participant. Second, it needs to be the case that both the

[15] House of Lords and House of Commons, Joint Committee on Human Rights 'Human Rights Judgments' 7th Report of Session 2014–15, HL Paper 130, HC 1088, 7–8. http://www.publications.parliament.uk/pa/jt201415/jtselect/jtrights/130/130.pdf.

[16] R Clayton, 'The Empire Strikes Back' [2015] Public Law 3; R Masterman and S Wheatle, 'A Common Law Resurgence in Rights Protection?' [2015] European Human Rights Law Review 57.

[17] The Supreme Court *Annual Report and Accounts 2013–14* HC 36 https://www.supremecourt.uk/docs/annual-report-2013-14.pdf.

[18] The Supreme Court *Annual Report and Accounts 2014–15* HC 50 https://www.gov.uk/government/uploads/system/uploads/attachment_data/file/434409/supreme-court-annual-report-2014-2015.pdf.

[19] ibid.

[20] House of Lords and House of Commons, Joint Committee on Human Rights 'Human Rights Judgments' 7th Report of Session 2014–15, HL Paper 130, HC 1088, 11–12 http://www.publications.parliament.uk/pa/jt201415/jtselect/jtrights/130/130.pdf.

[21] Rights of Children and Young Persons (Wales) Measure 2011 http://www.legislation.gov.uk/mwa/2010/1/contents and the Children's Rights Scheme 2014 http://gov.wales/docs/dsjlg/publications/cyp/140501-childrens-rights-scheme-2014-en.pdf.

legislature and the judiciary play different and complementary roles such that their participation is better able to ensure that democratic dialogue combines the advantages and minimizes the disadvantages of predominantly political and predominantly legal controls of human rights and over the executive. Third, if democratic dialogue is to facilitate deliberation, inter-institutional interactions should be reasoned, with both institutions paying attention to and engaging with the deliberations of the other institution. In addition, for this deliberation to engage citizens, there needs to be a sufficient protection of freedom of expression and freedom of information, as well as sufficient evidence of participation in democratic debate by the electorate.

I will argue that each of these assumptions is met to a sufficient degree in the UK constitution, but that there are nevertheless problems which may undermine the extent to which democratic dialogue will achieve all of its benefits when applied to the UK constitution. In particular, it is more likely to be the case that the UK constitution facilitates a form of inter-institutional interaction that is better able to operate as an effective check and balance and a safety valve, but where constitutional collaboration may arise more as a by-product, undermining the extent to which democratic dialogue facilitates constitutional collaboration and thereby challenging the extent to which democratic dialogue is able to arrive at better, more legitimate outcomes to rights-issues which engage citizens as well as the institutions of the constitution.

A. Constitutional balance

The requirement of constitutional balance has two sources. First, constitutional balance is needed to ensure democratic dialogue operates as a distinct model. If it were the case that either the legislature or the judiciary always had the ability to authoritatively resolve all determinations of rights-issues, or to control all actions of the executive, then, even if described as a model of dialogue, the model would be merely replicating the inter-institutional interaction found in theories of political or legal constitutionalism. All constitutional balance requires to satisfy this requirement is that neither the legislature nor the judiciary predominantly have the ability to authoritatively resolve a rights-issue. This assessment is difficult to ascertain precisely as it is a matter of degree. Second, constitutional balance helps to facilitate checks and balances and to ensure that democratic dialogue can act as a pressure valve, mediating between constitutional stability and constitutional flexibility. In the previous two chapters, we concluded that dialogue requires constitutional counter-balancing mechanisms, ensuring that both the legislature and the court recognize the right of the other institution to participate in the determination of rights-issues.[22] Moreover, each institution needed to use first-order and second-order reasons, paying attention to the relative expertise of the other institution when reasoning about rights.

Most of these requirements of constitutional balance do not pose problems for the application of democratic dialogue to the United Kingdom. Neither the legislature nor the courts are excluded from institutional interactions and neither imposes by fiat where those interactions should lead. However, the requirements of constitutional balance may not be fully met. Although both the legislature and the courts play a role in determining human rights decisions, it is not the case that both play the same role. In particular, there are two ways in which the judiciary may find that it plays a more limited role. First, in terms of its ability to put forward its own account of rights, the

[22] LB Tremblay, 'The Legitimacy of Judicial Review: The Limits of Dialogue Between Courts and Legislatures' (2005) 3 International Journal of Constitutional Law 617.

UK courts are limited in terms of their ability to present their own arguments, due to restrictions inherent to the performance of a judicial function and the extent to which section 2 of the Human Rights Act 1998 requires UK courts to follow judgments of the European Court of Human Rights. Second, parliamentary privilege may operate so as to exclude relevant information from the UK courts to enable the courts to engage effectively with arguments from the UK legislature concerning human rights determinations. Although related to concerns of constitutional balance, these arguments are more relevant to the determination of whether the judiciary and the legislature are able to effectively perform distinct roles. As such, they will be discussed in a later section. Of greater concern is the need to ensure there is no hierarchy between the legislature and the judiciary. This is difficult to reconcile with the characterization of the UK constitution as one adhering to the principle of parliamentary sovereignty. This section will evaluate this challenge to the suitability of applying democratic dialogue to the United Kingdom.

The traditional conception of parliamentary sovereignty appears to completely undermine any form of constitutional balance between the legislature and the judiciary. Traditionally understood, parliamentary sovereignty means that Parliament is supreme and has ultimate authority in a particular legal system. It would appear to imply, therefore, that there can never be a balance between the legislature and the judiciary as the Westminster Parliament has the power to overturn any measure of the judiciary. This supreme power of Parliament exists regardless of whether you accept the traditional views of sovereignty, found in the seminal work of Dicey, or other versions of sovereignty which empower Parliament to bind its successors. Recent discussions of bipolar sovereignty, however, cast doubt on this assessment, arguing that sovereignty is shared between the legislature and the judiciary. This section will argue in favour of a specific form of bipolar sovereignty, explaining how this means that sovereignty is shared between the legislature and the courts. As such, there is sufficient support for constitutional balance to support the application of democratic dialogue to the UK constitution. I will first discuss the traditional conception of parliamentary sovereignty, before explaining the particular version of bipolar sovereignty required to support a democratic dialogue account, before analysing recent key cases to demonstrate that this account of bipolar sovereignty is a feasible interpretation of the UK constitution.

(i) The traditional understanding of parliamentary sovereignty

It is almost impossible to start a discussion of parliamentary sovereignty without providing an account of Dicey's theory. Dicey asserted that

> [t]he principle of Parliamentary sovereignty means neither more nor less than this, namely, that Parliament thus defined has, under the English constitution, the right to make or unmake any law whatever; and, further, that no person or body is recognised by the law of England as having a right to override or set aside the legislation of Parliament.[23]

This is commonly referred to as the old or traditional view of parliamentary sovereignty. Although Parliament can legislate on any matter it wishes, without its provisions being set aside by a court, it cannot legislate so as to bind its successors. To do so would not only limit the sovereign powers of a future incarnation of Parliament,

[23] AV Dicey, *Introduction to the Study of the Law of the Constitution* (10th edn, London, Macmillan 1959) 39–40.

but would also lead to a situation where a court could declare legislation invalid as the actions of a future Parliament failed to comply with the requirements of an earlier Parliament. Understood in this manner, it is hard to see how we can argue for any form of constitutional balance when inter-institutional interactions take place between the legislature and the courts. If Parliament can make any law it likes, and courts cannot override or set aside such legislation, then any potential for dialogue between the two institutions would appear to take place on unequal terms. The Westminster Parliament will always have the final word.

Dicey's conception of sovereignty is in turn contrasted with the new view—broadly understood as meaning that Parliament can bind its successors as to the manner and form in which legislation is enacted. The new view is found in the work of Jennings[24] and Heuston,[25] who relied upon two cases to support their views: *Harris v Minister for the Interior*,[26] a decision of the Supreme Court of South Africa and *Attorney-General for New South Wales v Trethowan*,[27] a decision of the Privy Council on appeal from the High Court of Australia. In both of these cases, legislation proscribed a special process for its own modification. Legislation that was enacted without adhering to this special procedure was declared invalid—it had not been enacted in the manner prescribed by earlier legislation and, therefore, was not recognized as valid legislation.

This conception of parliamentary sovereignty may appear to provide for greater balance. After all, if courts are able to strike down legislation, it may not be the case that courts are subservient to Parliament, such that Parliament always succeeds in ensuring that its view prevails whenever the two institutions interact. By striking down legislation, courts would appear to play a more equal role, ensuring that they are able to prevail on some occasions. However, it is important to recognize that even the new view is a form of parliamentary sovereignty. It is Parliament who enacts legislation to bind its successors. When courts strike down legislation, they do so because they are enforcing the will of Parliament. If Parliament were to modify the Human Rights Act 1998, for example, stating that a two-thirds majority was required to enact legislation which contravened Convention rights, this would empower courts to strike down legislation that was contrary to Convention rights. However, they would only be able to do so when Parliament failed to obtain a two-thirds majority. Moreover, in doing so, they would be enforcing Parliament's will both to entrench Convention rights and to achieve this entrenchment through the requirement that legislation be enacted by a two-thirds majority.

This becomes apparent when we examine Goldsworthy's most recent account of sovereignty, which I have described elsewhere as a modified version of the new view.[28] Goldsworthy also concludes that Parliament can bind its successors. However, his argument does not propose that Parliament can bind its successors as to the manner and form in which legislation is enacted. Instead Parliament can only bind its successors as to the procedures through which legislation is enacted,[29] provided that (i) the substantive power of Parliament to legislate is not restricted and (ii) the process through which legislation is enacted does not make it so difficult for Parliament to legislate that it effectively restricts the substantive power of Parliament to enact legislation.[30]

[24] WI Jennings, *The Law and the Constitution* (5th edn, University of London Press 1959).

[25] RFV Heuston, *Essays in Constitutional Law* (2nd edn, Stevens and Sons 1964).

[26] [1952] (2) SA 428. [27] [1932] AC 526.

[28] AL Young, 'Parliamentary Sovereignty Re-defined' in R Rawlings, P Leyland, and AL Young (eds), *Sovereignty and the Law* (Oxford University Press 2013) 68.

[29] J Goldsworthy, *Parliamentary Sovereignty: Contemporary Debates* (Cambridge University Press 2010) 181.

[30] ibid, 174.

Goldsworthy argues that this restriction is needed to ensure the internal coherence of any account of sovereignty. Sovereignty is assessed in terms of power, specifically in terms of the power to enact legislation. Under both the old and the new view of sovereignty, Parliament has, at least theoretically, limits on its law-making power. Under Dicey's conception of sovereignty, Parliament is limited as it cannot bind its successors as to the manner and form under which to enact legislation. Under Goldsworthy's account, and the new view, Parliament has different potential restrictions on its law-making power. It may find that a predecessor Parliament has imposed a manner and form or a procedural restriction requirement on its ability to enact legislation. Goldsworthy prefers his account of sovereignty as it empowers Parliament to make long-standing commitments. The potential procedural restraint on Parliament is a small price to pay to further enhance Parliament's substantive law-making abilities by enabling it to enact legislation as and when it chooses, and also to empower it to make a long-standing commitment to certain values or principles, protecting these long-standing commitments from accidental erosion or a careless short-term desire to free oneself from a long-standing commitment.

What is common to all three of these conceptions of sovereignty is the understanding of sovereignty in terms of law-making power. If we understand sovereignty in this manner, and then conclude that Parliament is sovereign, then parliamentary sovereignty will indeed undermine any application of democratic dialogue to the UK constitution. However, it is important to recognize that these conceptions of sovereignty, although frequently referred to, are not the only conceptions. Others argue that to understand sovereignty in this manner is to misunderstand its nature. Martin Loughlin, for example, argues that to understand sovereignty in terms of power, law-making or otherwise, is to conflate sovereignty with the sovereign, confusing the ability to govern with the right to govern.[31] For Loughlin, sovereignty is 'an essential characteristic of a State. Every State possesses supreme, unlimited, and indivisible authority. There can be no limitations on a State's authority to rule by means of law.'[32] However, it is important to recognize that this does not mean that any one institution, such as Parliament, possesses this ultimate law-making power. Rather, sovereign authority is an abstract entity. Either the nation or the people, as bearers of constituent power, are sovereign.[33] Understood in this manner, sovereignty is not determined in terms of law-making power per se. It is an abstract quality possessed by the nation as a whole. Any form of distribution of power between the legislature and the courts would not detract from the ability of the institutions of government, however understood and composed, to assert their sovereign authority both internally, in terms of law-making power, and externally as a state playing its role in the international community.

Any choice between these competing conceptions of sovereignty needs to be made through an evaluation of their normative appeal, the validity of the conception's claims to achieve these normative values and the extent to which the factual assumptions on which these claims of normative value are based are reflected in reality. Merely recognizing that there are conceptions of sovereignty other than that advocated by Dicey, which would enable sufficient constitutional balance between the legislature and the judiciary to support the application of democratic dialogue in the UK constitution, is not enough to defeat the challenge that democratic dialogue is not possible in a constitutional system which rests upon a principle of parliamentary sovereignty. We need to explore conceptions of sovereignty further. In earlier work, I have argued that

[31] M Loughlin, 'Why Sovereignty' in Rawlings, Leyland, and Young (n 28) 34.
[32] ibid, 44. [33] ibid, 44–45.

the difference between Dicey's conception and other later conceptions of sovereignty is best understood not in terms of whether Parliament may bind its successors, but rather through an assessment of how sovereignty can be applied to different types of rule or of law-making.[34] An understanding of these two different applications of sovereignty can help to further our understanding of the conception of parliamentary sovereignty that is compatible with an account of democratic dialogue, before assessing whether this is a plausible account of the UK constitution.

First, sovereignty could be understood in terms of the power to enact primary legislation—that is rules that regulate the actions of individuals. This is often how we understand sovereignty when we ascribe sovereignty to the Westminster Parliament. Parliament is sovereign as Parliament can enact law which can govern every form of action of particular individuals, from regulating contracts to determining rights to assisted-suicide or the precise limits of freedom of expression. I will refer to this as sovereignty over primary rules. Second, sovereignty can be understood in terms of the power to enact specific rules regarding the definition of Parliament, the enactment of legislation and the ability to change the definition of Parliament and how legislation is enacted. I will refer to this as the power to enact secondary rules. Both are relevant to an assessment of whether democratic dialogue can apply to the UK constitution. In order to ensure constitutional balance, both Parliament and the courts need to play a role in determining secondary rules. This, in turn, entails that Parliament, acting alone, is unable to bind its successors. To understand this, we need to return to our earlier discussion of the old and the new view of sovereignty.

We argued above that both the old and the new versions of traditional conceptions of sovereignty would undermine the effective application of democratic dialogue to the UK constitution as, regardless of whether one adopted the view that Parliament could or could not bind its successors, Parliament retained the last word. Under Dicey's conception of parliamentary sovereignty, Parliament had the final word over the content of the law—primary rules—given that Parliament can enact law on any subject matter it wishes which cannot be questioned or overturned by the courts. Under the new conceptions of parliamentary sovereignty, Parliament had the final say over specific rules concerning how law is enacted—secondary rules. Although courts could strike down legislation, they could only do so as a means of enforcing the will of Parliament as to which provisions required a specific law-making process and the precise form of process required.

However, even though Parliament may have the final say over the content of the law, this does not mean that the courts are unable to play a role in developing primary rules, both in terms of the development of principles of the common law and in terms of the extent to which courts can interpret legislative provisions. We can see this, for example, in Dicey's account of the relationship between parliamentary sovereignty and the rule of law. Courts are able to draw on principles of the rule of law both when developing the common law and when interpreting legislation. For Dicey:

> Parliament is supreme legislator, but from the moment Parliament has uttered its will as lawgiver, that will becomes subject to the interpretation put upon it by the judges of the land, and the judges, who are influenced by the feelings of magistrates no less than by the general spirit of the common law, are disposed to construe statutory exceptions to common law principles

[34] I have argued elsewhere that this is to simplify the distinction between the two theories. See AL Young, *Parliamentary Sovereignty and the Human Rights Act 1998* (Oxford, Hart Publishing 2009); AL Young, 'Sovereignty: Demise, Afterlife or Partial Resurrection?' (2011) 9 International Journal of Constitutional Law 163.

in a mode which would not commend itself either to a body of officials, or to the Houses of Parliament, if the Houses were called upon to interpret their own enactments … By every path we come round to the same conclusion, that Parliamentary sovereignty has favoured the rule of law, and that the supremacy of the law both calls forth the exertion of Parliamentary sovereignty, and leads to its being exercised in a spirit of legality.[35]

This ability of the courts to interpret legislation by drawing on principles of the rule of law helps to facilitate constitutional collaboration, enabling both the courts and the legislatures to play a role in the development of the content of primary rules. However, in order for this collaboration to be effective, there also needs to be the element of mechanisms to ensure constitutional counter-balancing between the legislature and the courts. This occurs when both the legislature and the judiciary share sovereignty as to second-order rules. To understand this further, we need to re-examine the arguments for new views of parliamentary sovereignty.

Both Jennings and Heuston advocated that Parliament was able to bind its successors as to the manner and form of future legislation. Jennings's account relied on his assessment that the rules regarding the definition of Parliament, and ascertaining valid legislation, were provisions of the common law. This may appear, at first sight, to place sovereignty over secondary rules in the hands of the courts, as courts develop the common law. However, Jennings argued to the contrary that these rules could be modified by Parliament. This was because Parliament has the power to modify the content of the common law. When Parliament enacts legislation, if such provisions contradict provisions of the common law, then legislation overrides provisions of the common law. Therefore, Parliament could bind its successors through enacting legislation to modify the common law rules regarding the recognition of valid legislation.[36]

In a similar manner, RTE Latham argued that the rules determining the identification of Parliament and the means through which Parliament enacts valid legislation are logically prior to parliamentary sovereignty. Without these rules, it is impossible to have parliamentary sovereignty as you would be unable to identify the body which possessed sovereignty or to identify whether it had acted in the correct manner to enact legislation. Latham identified these rules regarding the definition of Parliament and of legislation as conventions that lie in the hands of the courts.[37] As such, courts can modify the definition of law and enable Parliament to bind its successors. However, courts would do so through recognizing a shift in convention as opposed to changing the common law.[38] Goldsworthy's account of how Parliament may bind its successors whilst still retaining sovereignty classifies the rules which determine the procedures through which legislation is enacted as a Hartian rule of recognition—a conventional rule that can only be modified through the officials of the legal system accepting such modification.[39]

All of these theories can be used to support the argument that neither the legislature nor the judiciary is sovereign as regards secondary rules, sovereignty over secondary

[35] Dicey (n 23) 413–14.

[36] Although, arguably, this is unstable. If the rule that 'legislative provisions override the common law' is also a principle of the common law, then it may be open to the courts to modify this provision, such that any purported legislative amendment to the manner and form in which legislation is enacted can be overturned by the courts through a modification of the common law.

[37] RTE Latham, 'The Law and the Commonwealth' in WK Hancock (ed), *Survey of British Commonwealth Affairs* Vol 1, *Problems of Nationality 1918-1936* (Oxford University Press 1937) 510–630; P Oliver, 'Law, Politics, the Commonwealth and the Constitution: Remembering RTE Latham, 1909–1943' (2000) King's College Law Journal 153.

[38] Goldsworthy (n 29) 175. [39] ibid, Ch 3.

rules being, in some sense, shared by both institutions. Understood in this manner sovereignty does not undermine the application of democratic dialogue to the United Kingdom. In previous work, I have argued for a conception of parliamentary sovereignty which advocates that Parliament should not bind its successors in order to ensure that sovereignty over secondary rules is shared between the legislature and the courts. I argued that these secondary rules were best understood as a Hartian rule of recognition, a conventional rule whose content, although reflected in the law, is determined and modified through acceptance of the change by officials administering the legal system. When courts recognize a shift in the rule of recognition, they do so through exercising a political as opposed to a purely legal function.[40] I also argued that Parliament did not have the power to authoritatively determine the manner in which its legislative provisions are to be interpreted, as the courts had wide interpretative powers, albeit that the courts are constrained and cannot overturn legislation. This does not place Parliament under a legally enforced limit as to the legislation that it can enact, given that Parliament is free to use clear and express words in legislation that can overturn an interpretation of legislation with which it disagrees.[41]

This reading of parliamentary sovereignty is similar to theories of bipolar sovereignty. In order to explain more clearly how the existence of parliamentary sovereignty in the UK constitution does not undermine the need for parity between the legislature and the judiciary, we need to examine accounts of bipolar sovereignty more closely, both in order to clarify the requirements of an account of sovereignty which is compatible with democratic dialogue and to assess the extent to which this theory can reflect our understanding of the UK constitution.

(ii) Bipolar sovereignty

Sir Stephen Sedley first coined the phrase 'bi-polar sovereignty' in 1995, concluding that the UK constitution was no longer best described as one where the 'rule of law must finally bend' to 'Dicey's supreme parliament' but rather was one of 'bi-polar sovereignty of the Crown in Parliament and the Crown in its courts, to each of which the Crown's ministers are answerable—politically to Parliament, legally to the courts'.[42] Sedley presented his argument as a more accurate description of the UK constitution, focusing in particular on administrative law. When analysing administrative law decisions, he concluded that the UK courts were willing to fill gaps in constitutional protection, developing principles of judicial review through the development of the common law as well as through creative interpretation of legislative provisions, drawing on the rule of law and other constitutional principles.[43] For Sedley, Parliament and the courts exercise 'discrete and interdependent functions' with each respecting the constitutional role of the other.[44] Sedley also provides examples of where, when the legislature and the courts do not respect each other's roles this may give rise to a

[40] See J Finnis, 'Revolutions and the Continuity of Law' in Simpson (ed), *Oxford Essays in Jurisprudence* (2nd edn, Clarendon Press 1973); NW Barber, 'Sovereignty Re-examined: The Courts, Parliament and Statutes' (2000) 20 Oxford Journal of Legal Studies 131.

[41] See Young, 'Sovereignty: Demise, Afterlife or Partial Resurrection?' (n 34) and Young 'Parliamentary Sovereignty Re-defined' (n 28).

[42] S Sedley, 'Human Rights a Twenty-First Century Agenda' [1995] Public Law 386, 389.

[43] ibid; S Sedley, 'The Sound of Silence: Constitutional Law without a Constitution' (1994) 110 LQR 270 and S Sedley, 'The Common law and the Constitution' in Nolan and Sedley (eds), *The Making and Remaking of the British Constitution* (Blackstone Press 1997) 26.

[44] Sedley, 'The Common law and the Constitution' (n 43) 26.

constitutional stand-off—for example in *Ashby v White*,[45] where the Speaker's threat of holding the judiciary in contempt of the House was met with the rejoinder that the court could hold the Speaker in contempt of court.[46]

Sedley is not alone in pointing to the way in which courts interpret legislative provisions as a means of demonstrating shared sovereignty between the legislature and the courts. Trevor Allan argues that there is no clear delineation between interpretation and repeal, using this to challenge accounts of parliamentary sovereignty. He argues that courts are not the mere servants of Parliament, interpreting legislation according to Parliament's will. Rather, judges make normative conclusions when interpreting legislation, drawing on the general presumed intention of Parliament to act according to the requirements of the rule of law.[47] Allan also asserts that 'the interpretative power of the superior courts is as fundamental as Parliament's legislative supremacy: shared sovereignty is intrinsic to constitutional government'.[48] Similar arguments are also found in the extra-judicial writings of Sir John Laws, in particular in his recent Hamlyn lectures where he criticizes the polarized debate as to whether Parliament is or is not sovereign. Rather, he regards the common law as placing practical limits on sovereignty, 'accepted in the name of reason, fairness and the presumption of liberty'.[49] This occurs, again, because statutory interpretation is not a matter of grammar, but of the elaboration of principles. Philip Joseph draws on similar evidence to argue that the relationship between the legislature and the courts is best understood as a collaborative enterprise.[50]

Christopher Knight draws on the work of WJ Rees to demonstrate how the recognition of the relative powers of the legislature and the courts can be classified as a sharing of sovereignty. Rees argued for two aspects of sovereignty—legal sovereignty and coercive sovereignty—where legal sovereignty occurs where the sovereign determines the actions of individuals through enacting authoritative law and coercive sovereignty occurs where the sovereign determines the actions of individuals through the use of force or the threat of force. Knight argues that coercive sovereignty is now understood in terms of the enforcement of the law. Both the legislature and the courts play a role in making authoritative legal determinations and in enforcing the law. Courts make law through developing the common law, in contrast to the broader law-making powers of the legislature. Although courts play the predominant role in the enforcement of the law through deciding legal cases, where their determinations are the final word as to the meaning of the law, the Westminster Parliament is also a court of law, albeit with a more limited jurisdiction. It is this connection of 'sovereignty' to law-making and law-enforcement which explains why the relative power of the courts to develop the common law and to interpret legislation according to principles of the common law

[45] (1705) 2 Ld Raym 938.

[46] Sedley, 'The Common law and the Constitution' (n 43) 26.

[47] For the most recent account of this argument, see TRS Allan, *The Sovereignty of Law* (Oxford University Press 2014) especially Ch 1 and Ch 5. See also TRS Allan, 'Legislative Supremacy and Legislative Intention: Interpretation, Meaning and Authority' (2004) Cambridge Law Journal 685; and TRS Allan 'Parliament's Will and the Justice of the Common Law: The Human Rights Act in Constitutional Perspective' (2006) Current Legal Problems 27.

[48] Allan, 'Parliament's Will and the Justice of the Common Law: The Human Rights Act in Constitutional Perspective' (n 47) 35.

[49] J Laws, *The Common Law Constitution* (Cambridge University Press 2014) 27–28. See also J Laws, 'The Good Constitution' (2012) 71 Cambridge Law Journal 567.

[50] P Joseph, 'The Demise of Ultra Vires—Judicial Review in the New Zealand Courts' [2001] Public Law 354; P Joseph 'Parliament, the Courts, and the Collaborative Enterprise' (2004) King's College Law Journal 321.

gives rise to the classification of the legislature and the courts as sharing sovereignty, to the exclusion of the executive.[51]

The references to bi-polar sovereignty in the literature help to make a prima facie case in favour of the application of democratic dialogue to the UK constitution, despite the long-standing recognition of the principle of parliamentary sovereignty which would appear to undermine the assumption of constitutional balance. However, it is important to recognize that this literature only provides a prima facie account. First, it is important to ensure that the requirements of democratic dialogue are underpinned by accurate accounts of the UK constitution and not merely that there is literature which asserts that this is the case. Second, there are differences between the accounts of bi-polar or shared sovereignty found in the literature, both as between each of the theories and also as concerns the way in which sovereignty is to be shared to satisfy the assumptions of democratic dialogue. Third, there are criticisms of this literature whose arguments need to be evaluated. We need to refine our account of shared sovereignty before assessing the extent to which this can provide a viable account of the UK constitution.

In order to support a theory of democratic dialogue, parliamentary sovereignty needs to operate to facilitate constitutional collaboration and maintain constitutional counter-balancing between the legislature and the courts. The constitutional collaboration required by democratic dialogue can occur either when the courts and Parliament perform their own distinct functions, drawing on their own process of reasoning towards conclusions about rights and the constitutional principles governing the extent to which the executive should exercise its powers. This does not mean that courts should not draw on constitutional principles when developing the common law or when interpreting legislation. However, it does argue that when doing so, courts and legislatures need to be sensitive to the scope of their constitutional authority and their distinct institutional features.

All of the theories discussed above recognize an aspect of constitutional collaboration between the legislature and the courts, particularly the account of Joseph which focuses predominantly on demonstrating how the legislature and the courts work together as a collaborative enterprise. Joseph and Sedley focus on how collaboration can occur through comity—that is where both the legislature and judiciary perform their own distinctive role under the Constitution, whilst respecting the role of the other. Joseph recognizes that courts have inherent jurisdiction, having a long history of developing principles of judicial review through developing the common law.[52] This inherent power of the courts means that courts, by definition, have the final authority to determine the content of the law.[53] Sedley refers to the way in which Parliament and the courts perform a discrete function, with each being required to respect the territory of the other.[54] However, as we discussed in the previous chapter, comity alone may not facilitate constitutional collaboration. Sedley's account may be more likely to facilitate constitutional collaboration, when each institution not only respects the decision-making authority of the other, but also explains clearly the weight to be given to each institution when considering rights-deliberations.

Laws and Allan go further, drawing not just on the element of each institution performing their own separate function, but linking this to fundamental principles or reasoning about rights. As discussed earlier, Allan's theory is underpinned by his

[51] CJS Knight, 'Bi-Polar Sovereignty Re-stated' (2009) 68 Cambridge Law Journal 361.
[52] Joseph, 'The Demise of Ultra Vires' (n 50) 358 and 363–65.
[53] Joseph, 'Parliament, the Courts and the Collaborative Enterprise' (n 50) 330–42.
[54] Sedley, 'The Common Law and the Constitution' (n 43) 26.

understanding of the rule of law. When interpreting legislation or developing the common law, courts should draw on normative arguments based on the rule of law as understood in the particular society in which the judge is operating. Laws regards the legislature and the judiciary as reflecting a conflict between two forms of morality—the morality of law and the morality of government, which in turn are based upon the conflict between protecting the autonomy of the individual and the interests of society as a whole. There is a need for both of these moralities in the constitution. Both the morality of law and the morality of government have weaknesses. The morality of law on its own may protect rights too strongly, limiting the ability of the government to administer policies for the good of all, whereas too strong a protection of the morality of government may lead to might overpowering the right. There is a need for both moralities, the tension between the two helping to form the principles of a good constitution.[55] Allan's account of shared sovereignty goes beyond the requirements of democratic dialogue and collapses into an account of legal constitutionalism, where the morality of law is ultimately more important than the morality of government.

Democratic dialogue also requires mechanisms of constitutional counter-balancing. The literature on bipolar sovereignty differs in its account of the nature of the relationship between the legislature and the courts. These differences help to identify the type of bipolar sovereignty required to support democratic dialogue. Constitutional counter-balancing requires not just that the legislature and the courts work together to produce principles of constitutional good government, controlling the executive and protecting human rights, but also that it is not the case that one institution always overrides the other institution. When we examine accounts of bipolar sovereignty, these theories advocate different relationships between the legislature and the courts which may undermine this balance.

The clearest example of this can be found in the accounts of Allan and Knight. Allan focuses not on the extent to which Parliament and the courts may conflict, but on the perceived tension between the rule of law and parliamentary sovereignty, where the rule of law is traditionally regarded as being in the purview of the courts and parliamentary sovereignty being ascribed to the actions of Parliament. Allan argues against viewing these principles as conflicting with one another. This is because both the rule of law and parliamentary sovereignty are grounded in reasons from political morality which underpin the sovereignty of parliament. Allan argues that parliamentary sovereignty, understood as a general principle of law, 'expresses a commitment to honour the reasonable decisions of elected representatives, in accordance with the proper demands of democratic equality'.[56] It is the role of the court to determine the limits of reasonable decisions, these limits being quite broad, determined by the application of general principles of the rule of law to the particular situation. This can normally be achieved through the reading of legislative provisions to ensure legislation is in line with general principles of the rule of law.[57]

Although Allan does not argue that, in UK law, there is a general principle that the rule of law will always override parliamentary sovereignty, or that, when faced with a conflict, courts will always strike down or disapply legislation, nevertheless Allan leaves open the possibility that courts could strike down legislation as invalid because of its breach of the reasonable limits imposed on legislative power by the rule of law. This possibility of courts overturning legislation under an account of bipolar sovereignty is expressed more clearly and specifically by Knight. He proposes that substantive limits

[55] Laws, *The Common Law Constitution* (n 49) 27–28.
[56] Allan *The Sovereignty of Law* (n 47) 33. [57] ibid, 35.

can be imposed on parliamentary sovereignty, drawing in particular on principles of the common law and on normative values derived from *jus cogens* in international law. Again, Knight does not specifically advocate that courts should be able to strike down legislation in all circumstances and his argument is made most strongly as regards the protection of common law rights of access to justice.[58]

The possibility of the judiciary striking down legislation is not, in and of itself, incompatible with democratic dialogue. Indeed, this potential for striking down legislation may be an effective means of ensuring constitutional balance, such that it is not the case that Parliament is always able to enforce its will over the courts. Both Knight and Allan are also clear to refrain from presenting a general principle that courts should always strike down legislation which breaches requirements of the rule of law. Therefore, it is not the case that the rule of law, as interpreted by the courts, will always override legislation which breaches its provisions. As such, it would appear that the necessary constitutional balance required for democratic dialogue could exist in the UK constitution—neither the legislature nor the courts would automatically be able to enforce its determination of a rights-issue over the other. Nevertheless, there is a problem with this account of bipolar sovereignty in terms of its ability to support democratic dialogue. It is clear that the content of the rule of law, and its application to a particular legal situation, determines both how legislation will be interpreted by the courts and also whether, in any one situation, courts should strike down legislation for breaching fundamental common law values or the rule of law. Although Allan explains this in terms of the superiority of reason justifying both legislative enactments and judicial decisions, it is the courts who are tasked with performing this reasoning process and reaching ultimate determinations on the content of the rule of law; the common law; the interpretation of legislation; and whether common law principles should override a particular legislative enactment. This undermines the constitutional balance needed for democratic dialogue.

This problem is not evident in the work of Laws, Joseph, and Sedley. Nevertheless, a further issue arises when we examine Laws' account of shared sovereignty. Laws recognizes the need to maintain a balance between the morality of law and the morality of government, the former being institutionally suited to the courts and the latter to the legislature. Whilst recognizing that both may invade the territory of the other, Laws advocates that there is a need to diminish these interventions, through a process of judicial restraint when the judiciary is called upon to balance issues of policy, and judicial activism when called upon to protect freedom of expression and freedom of conscience to ensure the maintenance of pluralism in society.[59] He therefore advocates a balance between the legislature and the courts. However, Laws also argues that sovereignty is a construct of the common law, being capable of being modified by the courts through their modification of the principles of the common law.[60] This causes problems for constitutional counter-balancing as it places sovereignty over the rules governing the composition of Parliament and the way in which law is enacted into the hands of the courts.

In *Thoburn*, for example, Laws LJ modified the common law to create a separate category of constitutional statutes which he argued were not subject to the doctrine of implied repeal.[61] As such, the courts modified the doctrine of parliamentary sovereignty.

[58] CJS Knight, 'Striking Down Legislation under Bi-polar Sovereignty' [2011] Public Law 90, 106–07.

[59] Laws, 'The Good Constitution' (n 49) 578–82.

[60] See Laws, *The Common Law Constitution* (n 49) 2–6 and 18–25.

[61] *Thoburn v Sunderland City Council* [2002] EWHC 195 (Admin), [2003] QB 151.

This modification looks, at first glance, to be similar to a change to the new view of sovereignty—that Parliament can bind its successors as to the manner and form of legislation. However, the new view refers to the situation which occurs when Parliament binds it successors as Parliament enacts legislation requiring that future legislation be enacted in a particular manner. For example, the new view would recognize the creation of constitutional statutes, which were not subject to the doctrine of implied repeal, because Parliament had enacted, for example, the Constitutional Statutes Act, setting out which current statutes were constitutional, explaining how future statutes could be recognized as constitutional and specifying that these statutes could only be expressly and not impliedly repealed. In *Thoburn*, however, it is the judiciary who have recognized this subcategory of statutes and determined that these statutes are not subject to implied repeal, in addition to establishing the criteria according to which the judiciary can add to the list of constitutional statutes in the future, or add to the differences between constitutional and other statutes. Just as there are problems for constitutional counter-balancing when we argue that Parliament alone can determine the content of parliamentary sovereignty, similar issues arise as regards the ability of the courts to determine the content of parliamentary sovereignty through acting alone to modify the content of the common law. This may enable the courts to always have the upper hand in any conflict, undermining the requirement of constitutional balance.

This analysis of theories of bipolar sovereignty helps to refine the account of sovereignty required to sustain an application of democratic dialogue in the UK constitution. First, it requires an acceptance of parliamentary legislative supremacy. This is not the same as parliamentary sovereignty. Rather, it requires the acceptance that Parliament alone is incapable of binding its successors, in the same way that courts are unable to modify parliamentary sovereignty merely by modifying provisions of the common law. Rather, sovereignty over the rules determining the composition of Parliament and the manner in which it enacts legislation needs to be shared between the legislature and the courts. It does not matter whether we classify these provisions as the rule of recognition, a constitutional convention, a Grundnorm, or as constitutional principles. What is important is that the modification of these rules cannot occur merely through the actions of either the legislature or the judiciary acting alone. The officials of both need to accept a modification to these rules. As a modification of a Hartian rule of recognition can only be made in these terms, I have previously referred to the requirements determining the composition of Parliament and the way in which it enacts legislation as a rule of recognition. However, this need not entail that I am asserting that these are facts about the legal system that are determining externally, or that their modification or acceptance must be divorced from a consideration of principles underpinning the legal system. What is important for the application of democratic dialogue is that neither the legislature nor the judiciary can modify these rules on their own, ensuring that it is never the case that one institution can always have the upper hand over the other.

Second, it requires that both institutions respect the relative constitutional and institutional roles of the other. This can be through the exercise of comity and, on the part of the courts, through the use of deference. As regards the legislature, this requires both that the legislature respects the principle of judicial independence, as recognized by Sedley,[62] and that the legislature does not remove or seriously undermine the constitutional role of the court—the performance of judicial review, as

[62] Sedley, 'The Common Law and the Constitution' (n 43) 26.

recognized by Knight.[63] In a similar manner to the account of Allan and Knight, this may require that the courts should, in certain circumstances, strike down legislation which either removes or seriously undermines the principle of judicial independence or which removes the power of judicial review from the courts. However, as with the theory of Allan and Knight, this does not amount to a general principle that the court should automatically strike down these provisions. First, courts should seek to use statutory interpretation and the development of the common law to prevent the erosion of these principles. Second, the court should use rhetoric to threaten to use its constitutional role as the institution which effectively recognizes valid law, and predominantly enforces the law, in a manner which would fail to recognize such legislation as legally valid. In doing so, the court is defending its constitutional position. In a similar manner, the legislature can threaten to undermine the position of the judiciary should the court have gone too far. Neither institution is sufficiently able to make good on these threats. Although the judiciary could strike down legislation, Parliament is then in a position to act so as to undermine the constitutional powers of the court. In a similar manner, if Parliament acts so as to undermine the constitutional position of the judiciary, courts are able to strike down, refuse to recognize, or refuse to enforce such legislation. It is this tension between the two institutions which helps to maintain constitutional counter-balancing. Both institutions have sufficient sovereignty understood in terms of enforcement and law-making power to cross the threshold of a claim to sovereignty, but, as sovereignty is shared, neither has the ability to fully make good on this claim, effectively enforcing its will over the other.[64]

Having clarified the specific nature of bipolar sovereignty required to apply democratic dialogue to the UK constitution, we now need to examine whether these assumptions are valid. This does not mean that an argument needs to be made that this is the only or the best account of facts about the UK constitution. The argument needs to be made that this is a viable account—that is that it is possible to make this argument when applied against the backdrop of the UK constitution.

(iii) A valid assumption?

To support the application of democratic dialogue to the UK constitution, we need to provide sufficient evidence that both the legislature and the courts play a role in the interpretation of legislation, with no one institution always having the definitive say over the meaning of legislation. Also, we need to demonstrate that, although both the legislature and the court may assert the ability to definitively determine how we identify valid legislation, and whether legislation is limited by constitutional principles, both institutions need to accept any changes in these rules.

It is easier to provide evidence to support the first assumption. Although theories of bipolar sovereignty differ from one another, one common feature is the recognition that, whilst the Westminster Parliament enacts legislation, it is the courts who interpret legislative provisions, drawing on principles of the common law, or the rule of law, when doing so. The clearest evidence of this is found in the 'principle of legality'. The principle of legality is a principle of statutory interpretation. It states that broad legislative terms are to be interpreted so as to comply with common law principles.

63 Knight (n 58).

64 For a discussion of how sovereignty can be understood as a threshold concept, see N Walker, 'Sovereignty and Differentiated Integration in the European Union' (1998) 4 European Law Journal 355.

Parliament would have understood, when legislating, that it was legislating against a backdrop of common law principles and so is not to have been taken to have intended to legislate in a manner that contradicts these principles unless it clearly and specifically expresses its intention to do so. The most cited statement of the principle of legality is found in Lord Hoffmann's judgment in *Simms*:

> Parliamentary sovereignty means that Parliament can, if it chooses, legislate contrary to fundamental principles of human rights. The Human Rights Act 1998 will not detract from this power. The constraints upon its exercise by Parliament are ultimately political, not legal. But the principle of legality means that Parliament must squarely confront what it is doing and accept the political cost. Fundamental rights cannot be overridden by general or ambiguous words. This is because there is too great a risk that the full implications of their unqualified meaning may have passed unnoticed in the democratic process. In the absence of express language or necessary implication to the contrary, the courts therefore presume that even the most general words were intended to be subject to the basic rights of the individual. In this way the courts of the United Kingdom, though acknowledging the sovereignty of Parliament, apply principles of constitutionality little different from those which exist in countries where the power of the legislature is expressly limited by a constitutional document.[65]

Lord Hoffmann's account also makes it clear that the intention of the principle of legality is not to provide courts with the ability to override parliamentary legislation. Rather, it refers to a shared intention of the courts and Parliament that legislation should normally be interpreted so as to ensure it does not contradict fundamental rights. It is still possible for Parliament to legislate contrary to human rights. But it must do so clearly and specifically. The judiciary determine when, and how far, the principle of legality applies.

The claim that both the courts and the legislature play a role in the interpretation of legislation is further illustrated by section 3(1) of the Human Rights Act 1998. The section does require courts to interpret legislation in a manner compatible with Convention rights, but only 'so far as it is possible to do so'. The limits of possibility are established in the seminal case of *Ghaidan v Godin-Mendoza*.[66] It is not possible to interpret legislation in a manner compatible with Convention rights where to do so contradicts a fundamental feature of the legislation. Courts have also shown reluctance to provide a Convention-compatible interpretation where to do so requires the choice between competing Convention-compatible interpretations which, given the complex social and moral implications of such a choice, is best left to the legislature, or where rendering legislation Convention-compatible would require the creation of particular procedures, again something more suited to the legislature than the courts. This, again, provides support for the application of democratic dialogue. Courts play a key role in interpreting legislation so as to ensure its compatibility with Convention rights. But it is not able to ensure that all legislation is compatible with the Convention, refraining from undermining fundamental features of legislation.

There is also evidence of inter-institutional interaction between the legislature and the judiciary. A clear example of this as regards the application of the principle of legality is the inter-institutional exchanges arising from *R (Ahmed) v Her Majesty's Treasury*,[67] which was followed by the Terrorist Asset-Freezing (Temporary Provisions) Act 2010 and the Terrorist Asset-Freezing etc Act 2010. In *Ahmed* the Supreme Court applied the principle of legality to strike down the Terrorism (United Nations Measures) Order

[65] *R v Secretary of State for the Home Department ex parte Simms* [2000] 2 AC 115, 131 paragraphs E-G.

[66] [2004] UKHL 30, [2004] 2 AC 557.

[67] [2010] UKSC 2, [2010] 2 AC 534.

2006. The Order was enacted under section 1 of the United Nations Act 1946, which just required the measure to be laid before Parliament, in order to implement a UN Security Council Resolution. The UN Security Council Resolution required states to 'freeze without delay funds and other financial assets or economic resources of persons who commit, or attempt to commit, terrorist acts or participate in or facilitate the commission of terrorist acts'.[68] The Terrorism (United Nations Measures) Order 2006 included the power to freeze the assets of individuals where there were 'reasonable grounds to suspect that the person is or may be' connected to terrorist activity. Section 1 of the United Nations Act 1946 empowered the government to 'make such provision as appears' to be 'necessary or expedient for enabling' measures of the UN Security Council 'to be effectively applied'. As the measures interfered with fundamental rights—the freezing of assets having severe consequences for freedom of movement and private life, as well as interfering with property rights—the Supreme Court applied the principle of legality. The UN Security Resolution required the freezing of assets of those involved in funding terrorism or terrorist activities. The UK Regulations went beyond this requirement, also enabling the freezing of assets of individuals where there were reasonable grounds to suspect that they were funding terrorist activities. As such, the measure went beyond the power granted by section 1 of the 1946 Act and was struck down as *ultra vires*. The Terrorist Asset-Freezing (Temporary Provisions) Act 2010 was enacted to provide temporary validity, until 31 December 2010, for the Orders in Council struck down by the Supreme Court. The Terrorist Asset-Freezing etc Act 2010 then provided statutory authority for the freezing of assets of anyone whom the Treasury reasonably believed is or has been involved in terrorist activity, or is owned or controlled by, or is acting on behalf of someone reasonably believed to be or have been involved in terrorist activity. Their assets can be frozen where the Treasury considers this is necessary to protect the members of the public from terrorism.

Although courts do use background constitutional principles when interpreting legislation, they have, to date, stopped short of using the principle of legality to strike down or disapply legislative provisions. This may appear to give the legislature the upper hand, challenging constitutional balance as Parliament can always override judicial interpretations. However, as the lack of evidence of engagement in this manner from Parliament as regards section 3 may suggest, it is not easy for Parliament to find the time to do so and it is likely that this will only occur when the interpretation of the courts undermines an important policy objective. In addition, there is a need to ensure that Parliament is not able to bind its successors to ensure the maintenance of constitutional balance between the legislature and the courts. This brings us to the second component of bipolar sovereignty required to support the application of democratic dialogue in the UK constitution.

There has been a number of recent perceived challenges to the traditional model of parliamentary sovereignty, particularly as regards the United Kingdom's membership of the European Union. First, there are examples of where the United Kingdom has suspended the application of legislation through the granting of an interim injunction and has disapplied legislation which breaches provisions of the EU Charter of Fundamental Rights. Are these examples of where the legislature has bound its successors through the enactment of the European Communities Act 1972? Second, the courts have also asserted that parliamentary sovereignty is a principle of the common law and therefore can be modified by the courts alone. Both of these sets of examples appear to challenge

[68] SCR 1373 (2001).

the application of a model of democratic dialogue in the UK constitution. However, I will argue that both of these examples are compatible with democratic dialogue. First, although legislation has been suspended or disapplied, to date the courts have stopped short of striking down legislation as unlawful due to its incompatibility with directly effective EU law. Moreover, any change that has been affected can be argued to be due to the shift in the definition of valid law occurring through an acceptance of a change in political facts by the courts and the legislature. This interpretation casts doubt on the extent to which this change has occurred as regards the EU Charter, given the current tension between Parliament and the courts as to the legal effect of the Charter. Second, cases relying on the common law are best understood as situations where courts are asserting their right to modify the common law, in a narrow range of circumstances. They can be understood as examples of judicial rhetoric, with evidence of the legislature responding to this rhetoric. Moreover, any change has to be examined in the light of the legal consequences of the referendum result in favour of leaving the EU.

(a) The disapplication of UK legislation

The most famous instance in which UK courts suspended the application of UK legislation occurred in the *Factortame* series of cases, concerning the validity of the Merchant Shipping Act 1988. The Act required fishing vessels to be registered in order to fish in British waters, making such registration contingent on demonstrating British nationality, domicile, and residency requirements. This prevented a cohort of Spanish fishing vessels from fishing in UK waters, contrary to their directly effective EU rights of freedom of establishment, which would allow them to fish in UK waters. In *Factortame (No 2)* the House of Lords granted an interim injunction, suspending the application of the Merchant Shipping Act pending the conclusion of the preliminary reference sent by the United Kingdom to the then European Court of Justice to determine whether the provisions of the Merchant Shipping Act breached directly effective EU law.[69] When reaching this conclusion, Lord Bridge made the seminal statement that

> whatever limitation of its sovereignty Parliament accepted when it enacted the European Communities Act 1972 was entirely voluntary. Under the terms of the Act of 1972 it has always been clear that it was the duty of a United Kingdom court, when delivering final judgment, to override any rule of national law found to be in conflict with any directly enforceable rule of Community law.[70]

Factortame (No 2) only suspended the application of the Merchant Shipping Act. Since then, directly effective EU law has been used to disapply legislation in a series of recent cases involving the application of the EU Charter of Fundamental Rights and Freedoms. The Court of Appeal in *Benkharbouche*, for example, disapplied section 1 of the State Immunity Act 1978 as contrary to Article 47 of the EU Charter.[71] The High Court in *Davis* issued a declaration of incompatibility as regards section 1 of the Data Retention and Investigatory Powers Act 2014, as contravening Articles 7 and 8 of the Charter, suspending an order to disapply this section until 31 March 2016 in order to enable Parliament to enact legislation to replace the Act.[72] The Court of Appeal referred the matter to the European Court of Justice, to determine whether

[69] *R v Secretary of State for Transport ex parte Factortame Ltd (No 2)* [1991] 1 AC 603.

[70] ibid, 659.

[71] *Benkharbouche v Embassy of the Republic of Sudan* [2015] EWCA Civ 33, [2016] QB 347.

[72] *Davis v Secretary of State for the Home Department* [2015] EWHC 2092 (Admin); [2016] 1 CMLR 443.

the provisions of the Act contravened European Union law.[73] Also in *Google v Vidal-Hall* the Court of Appeal disapplied section 31(2) of the Data Protection Act 1988, which prevented claimants from obtaining damages for emotional distress caused by the breach of the protection of personal data.[74] All of these cases can be seen as creating problems for parliamentary sovereignty as they suspended the application of legislation enacted after the European Communities Act 1972.

There has been a lot of academic ink spilt over the meaning of Lord Bridge's statement in *Factortame (No 2)* and the way in which this has undermined, or can be reconciled with, parliamentary sovereignty. It is not the place of this section to re-engage with this debate. Rather, what is needed is an assessment of whether it is possible to reconcile this statement with a model of democratic dialogue. Problems arise if the only possible explanation of the decision in *Factortame* is that Parliament bound its successors as to the manner and form of future legislation through enacting the European Communities Act 1972. However, although there are academics who support this view,[75] this is difficult to reconcile with the traditional understanding of the new view of parliamentary sovereignty.

The claim is made that the European Communities Act 1972 bound future Parliaments in that Parliament can no longer impliedly repeal the 1972 Act. Rather, any repeal of the Act would need to be express. This is because, in *Factortame* the provisions of the 1972 Act, which would have required that Spanish fishermen be able to fish, directly contradicted the provisions of the 1988 Act, which would have prevented them from fishing as they did not satisfy nationality requirements to register their fishing vessel. If we apply the doctrine of implied repeal, then the later legislation should repeal the earlier legislation. Therefore the 1988 Act should prevail, preventing Factortame from fishing in British waters. However, in *Factortame (No 2)* the 1988 Act was suspended because of the rights of the Spanish fishermen under the 1972 Act. This means the doctrine of implied repeal did not apply. From this, it is asserted that a new manner and form is required to overturn the 1972 Act—it must be overturned by express provisions. Implied repeal will not suffice.

However, there is a difficulty with this interpretation. Manner and form theories argue that Parliament can bind its successors as to the manner and form of future legislation, through enacting provisions establishing the way in which legislation can be amended. For this to apply, therefore, we would expect a provision in the 1972 Act setting out the way in which its provisions can be amended—for example a section clearly stating that the 1972 Act could only be expressly and not impliedly repealed. The 1972 Act does not contain any section specifically stating that its provisions can only be expressly repealed and cannot be impliedly repealed. The closest provision is found in section 2(4) of the Act which requires that 'any enactment passed or to be passed, other than one contained in this part of this Act, shall be construed and have effect subject to the foregoing provisions of this section'. The 'foregoing provisions of this section' include section 2(1) incorporating EU law into UK law, including the principle of the supremacy of directly effective EU law. This does require the courts to ensure that directly effective provisions of EU law are applied in the United Kingdom, even when they conflict with UK law, but they do not require that the 1972 Act can only be expressly repealed. Indeed, the principle of direct effect would require

[73] *Davis v Secretary of State for the Home Department* [2015] EWCA Civ 1185, [2016] 1 CMLR 1515.

[74] *Google v Vidal-Hall* [2015] EWCA Civ 311, [2016] 2 All ER 337.

[75] HWR Wade, 'Sovereignty-Revolution or Evolution?' (1996) 112 Law Quarterly Review 568.

the application of directly effective EU law even when this conflicted with legislation which had expressly stated that its provisions were to take effect regardless of EU law.

Even if we accept that *Factortame (No 2)* did modify parliamentary sovereignty, such that a special procedure is required to modify the European Communities Act 1972, it is clear that this special procedure stems from a combination of the provisions of the 1972 Act and how these provisions have been interpreted by the courts. It is at least plausible that the case law reflects a growing acceptance by the UK courts of the impact of directly effective EU law, itself having been incorporated into English law through the enactment of sections 2(1) and 2(4) of the European Communities Act 1972. The most recent cases show how this acceptance of direct effect has expanded to include the provisions of the Charter, which have been given the same legal effect as the Treaties following the Lisbon Treaty. If this is the case, then this perceived threat to parliamentary sovereignty will be removed as and when the United Kingdom leaves the EU. Of course, the nature of the relationship between EU law and UK law will depend upon the nature of the withdrawal agreement, particularly as concerns any vested rights of EU citizens and whether the United Kingdom becomes a member of the European Free Trade Association. Nevertheless, this does not mean that, following the United Kingdom leaving the EU, parliamentary sovereignty will be regained, given that other challenges persist to parliamentary sovereignty, particularly the challenge found in the next sub-section.

(b) Parliamentary sovereignty as a principle of the common law

The assertion that parliamentary sovereignty is a principle of the common law, which can therefore be modified solely by the courts, was first made definitively by Laws LJ in *Thoburn*.[76] The case concerned the validity of the Units of Measurement Regulations 1994, which incorporated the Matriculation Directive[77] of the EU into English law. The 1994 Regulations were enacted under section 2(2) of the European Communities Act 1972, a Henry VIII clause empowering the government to enact secondary legislation to implement its EU obligations, including using secondary legislation to overturn or amend primary legislation. The question arose as to the potential conflict between section 2(2) of the 1972 Act and the Weights and Measures Act 1985. The 1985 Act permitted both metric and imperial measurements of weight. The 1994 Regulations provided that only metric measurements of weight were legal. The argument was made that the 1985 Act had impliedly repealed the 1972 Act, placing a substantive restriction on the power to make secondary legislation under section 2(2) of the 1972 Act. This argument was rejected by Laws LJ. He concluded that there was no conflict between the 1985 and the 1972 Acts. Rather, section 2(2) of the 1972 Act empowered the government to enact secondary legislation to amend or repeal Acts of Parliament enacted both prior to and after the 1972 Act. As such, the 1985 Act was merely an example of primary legislation which could be modified or amended using the powers granted to the government by section 2(2) of the 1972 Act.[78]

After reaching this conclusion, Laws LJ then discussed the inter-relationship between directly effective provisions of EU law and UK legislation more generally, concluding that

> The common law has in recent years allowed, or rather created, exceptions to the doctrine of implied repeal: a doctrine which was always the common law's own creature. There are now

[76] *Thoburn v Sunderland City Council* (n 61). [77] Directive 89/617, as amended.
[78] *Thoburn v Sunderland City Council* (n 61) [50]–[52].

classes or types of legislative provision which cannot be repealed by mere implication. These instances are given, and can only be given, by our own courts, to which the scope and nature of parliamentary sovereignty are ultimately confided. The courts may say—have said—that there are certain circumstances in which the legislature may only enact what it desires to enact if it does so by express, or at any rate specific, provision. The courts have in effect so held in the field of European law itself, in the *Factortame* case, and this is critical for the present discussion. By this means, as I shall seek to explain, the courts have found their way through the impasse seemingly created by two supremacies, the supremacy of European law and the supremacy of Parliament.[79]

The European Communities Act 1972 was recognized in *Thoburn* as a constitutional statute. The common law was used to make this designation. The common law also determined that constitutional statutes could not be impliedly repealed. Instead:

[f]or the repeal of a constitutional Act or the abrogation of a fundamental right to be effected by statute, the court would apply this test: is it shown that the legislature's *actual* – not imputed, constructive or presumed – intention was to effect the repeal or abrogation? I think the test could only be met by express words in the later statute, or by words so specific that the interference to effect the result contended for was irresistible.[80]

It is important to recognize that, although the conflict between directly effective EU law and UK law was the catalyst for the recognition of parliamentary sovereignty as a principle of the common law, the European Communities Act was not the only act recognized as a constitutional statute. Laws LJ also referred to the Human Rights Act 1998 and the devolution statutes. Moreover, *Thoburn* is not the only example of courts proclaiming parliamentary sovereignty as a principle of the common law. In *Jackson* Lord Steyn referred to the supremacy of Parliament as a 'construct of the common law. The judges created this principle.'[81] In the same case, Lord Hope refers to '[t]he principle of parliamentary sovereignty which in the absence of higher authority, has been created by the common law'.[82] As such, as and when Britain leaves the European Union, the challenge posed to parliamentary sovereignty through its recognition as a principle of the common law still remains.

If parliamentary sovereignty is a principle of the common law, such that it is clear that the courts acting alone may modify the content of parliamentary sovereignty and Parliament is legally bound to adhere to this modification, then this undermines the account of bipolar sovereignty needed to support the application of democratic dialogue to the UK constitution. It is important to recognize, however, that although there are clear statements in *Jackson* that parliamentary sovereignty is a principle of the common law, these statements are not made by all of the members of the Supreme Court who discussed parliamentary sovereignty, including those who accepted that there may be occasions when the courts would not apply an Act of Parliament. Lady Hale recognized in her judgment that parliamentary sovereignty meant that 'Parliament can do anything'.[83] Nevertheless, she also stated that '[t]he courts will treat with particular suspicion (and might even reject) any attempt to subvert the rule of law by removing governmental action affecting the rights of the individual from all judicial scrutiny'.[84] But she did not refer to parliamentary sovereignty as a principle of the common law, preferring to classify it as a 'concept'.[85] In addition, her arguments as to the judgment in *Jackson* rested on whether

[79] ibid, [62]. [80] ibid, [63].
[81] *Jackson v Attorney General* [2005] UKHL 56,[2005] 4 All ER 1253, [102].
[82] ibid, [126]. [83] ibid, [159]. [84] ibid. [85] ibid.

Parliament had redesigned itself through enacting the Parliament Acts 1911 and 1949. In her words:

> If Parliament can do anything, there is no reason why Parliament should not decide to redesign itself, either in general or for a particular purpose. The body which was Parliament in 1911 could decide, by the decision-making procedure of the day, to redesign itself.[86]

Lady Hale's account is best understood as an acceptance of a version of the new view of parliamentary sovereignty. Parliament can bind its successors by enacting legislation to redefine itself, which future incarnations of Parliament will need to follow in order to enact valid legislation. Nor is Lady Hale alone in her recital of this account of parliamentary sovereignty. Before Lord Steyn's statement that parliamentary sovereignty is a principle of the common law, he too examined the new view of sovereignty, referring to *AG for New South Wales v Trethowan*, and *Harris v Minister of Interior*, two of the cases cited most frequently to support the manner and form theory of parliamentary sovereignty.[87] Drawing on this account of parliamentary sovereignty, Lord Steyn concluded that the 1949 Parliament Act was valid as it was enacted through the 1911 Parliament Act, which had redefined Parliament. This conclusion fits with an understanding that it is Parliament which redefined itself, giving Parliament at least some role in the determination of parliamentary sovereignty.

Moreover, when we examine Lord Hope's statement that parliamentary sovereignty is a principle of the common law, he is careful to qualify this assertion—if the principle of parliamentary sovereignty has been created by the common law, it was done so 'in the absence of higher authority'.[88] Earlier in his judgment, Lord Hope refers to the courts having a 'part to play in defining the limits of Parliament's legislative sovereignty'.[89] He also refers to Sir William Wade's observation that 'sovereignty is a political fact for which no purely legal authority can be constituted',[90] regarding the 1949 Parliament Act as valid as '[p]olitical reality is that of a general acceptance by all the main parties and by both Houses of the amended timetable which the 1949 Act introduced. I do not think that it is open to a court of law to ignore that reality'.[91] Lord Hope's analysis is compatible with the form of bipolar sovereignty required to apply democratic dialogue to the UK constitution. The definition of the sovereign legislature, how it enacts legislation, and the scope of its law-making powers is regarded as a political fact. Merely enacting the 1949 Parliament Act was insufficient to change this political fact. The new manner of enacting legislation became an established political fact due to its acceptance by political actors in Parliament and then by the courts. This is compatible with the argument that courts, due to the lack of a higher authority, proclaim parliamentary sovereignty as a principle of the common law. Courts have inherent jurisdiction to enforce the law. Courts are the last authority to determine the nature of sovereignty. But they do so not merely by modifying the common law; but by analysing political facts. Courts may assert their authority to modify sovereignty through the common law. But they are unable to fully make good on this claim. Just as Parliament asserts its authority to redefine itself, but is not able to make good on that claim. Parliament is not redefined unless and until this modification is recognized by the courts and the legislature.

Lord Hope re-asserts his assessment of parliamentary sovereignty in *AXA*, drawing on the extra-judicial writings of Lord Bingham and Lord Neuberger.[92] He concludes:

[86] ibid, [160]. [87] ibid, [81]–[84]. [88] ibid, [126]. [89] ibid, [107].
[90] ibid, [120]. [91] ibid, [124].
[92] *AXA General Insurance v Lord Advocate* [2011] UKSC 46, [2012] 1 AC 868, [2014] 2 All ER 109.

The question whether the principle of the sovereignty of the United Kingdom Parliament is absolute or may be subject to limitation in exceptional circumstances is still under discussion. For Lord Bingham, writing extra-judicially, the principle is fundamental and in his opinion, as the judges did not by themselves establish the principle, it was not open to them to change it: *The Rule of Law*, p 167. Lord Neuberger of Abbotsbury, in his Lord Alexander of Weedon lecture, *Who are the Masters Now?* (6 April 2011), said at para 73 that, although the judges had a vital role to play in protecting individuals against the abuses and excess of an increasingly powerful executive, the judges could not go against the will of Parliament as expressed through a statute. Lord Steyn on the other hand recalled at the outset of his speech in *Jackson*, para 71, the warning that Lord Hailsham of St Marylebone gave in *The Dilemma of Democracy* (1978), p 126 about the dominance of a government elected with a large majority over Parliament. This process, he said, had continued and strengthened inexorably since Lord Hailsham warned of its dangers. This was the context in which he said in para 102 that the Supreme Court might have to consider whether judicial review or the ordinary role of the courts was a constitutional fundamental which even a sovereign Parliament acting at the behest of a complaisant House of Commons could not abolish.[93]

This does not mean that Lord Hope does not think that it is the case that the courts would never strike down legislation. Nor does he assert that parliamentary sovereignty is the ultimate principle in the UK constitution. Rather, he goes on to state, as he did in *Jackson*, that 'the rule of law enforced by the courts is the ultimate controlling factor on which our constitution is based'.[94] As such:

It is not entirely unthinkable that a government which has that power may seek to use it to abolish judicial review or to diminish the role of the courts in protecting the interests of the individual. Whether this is likely to happen is not the point. It is enough that it might conceivably do so. The rule of law requires that the judges must retain the power to insist that legislation of that extreme kind is not law which the courts will recognise.[95]

It is important to recognize here the limit upon the ability of the courts to refrain from recognizing Acts of Parliament as valid legislation. Lord Hope regards Parliament as enjoying a general principle of parliamentary sovereignty because it is a democratic institution and through recognizing the balance between the role of the courts in protecting individual rights and the role of the legislature in protecting democracy. It is when democracy is threatened—through executive dominance—that he can imagine a potential threat to the rule of law. This threat to the rule of law stems from the threat to remove the power of the court to review decisions of the executive to protect individual rights—that is the removal of the court's constitutional power of judicial review. This is not regarded as a regular occurrence, but a measure preserved for extreme circumstances. A final back stop to be used in extreme circumstances to protect the necessary powers of the court, when other means fail.

This reading of Lord Hope's judgment also fits with Lord Steyn and Baroness Hale's statements. In *Jackson*, Lord Steyn refers to a similar restraint as to when courts may fail to recognize an Act of Parliament as legislation:

In exceptional circumstances involving an attempt to abolish judicial review or the ordinary role of the courts, the Appellate Committee of the House of Lords or a new Supreme Court may have to consider whether this is a constitutional fundamental which even a sovereign Parliament acting at the behest of a complaisant House of Commons cannot abolish.[96]

Lord Steyn also sees this as occurring only in exceptional circumstances, and again focuses on the removal of the constitutional role of the court to hold the executive to

[93] ibid, [50]. [94] ibid, [51]. [95] ibid. [96] *Jackson v AG* (n 98) [102].

account for its actions. Lady Hale also focuses on the power of the court to challenge legislation removing the power of the courts to scrutinize decisions of the executive to protect individual rights. Their statements, therefore, can also be read in a manner that supports bipolar sovereignty as required for the application of democratic dialogue. First, courts should only contemplate striking down legislation in extreme circumstances. Second, this should occur only when there is a threat to the constitutional role of the court; when its power to scrutinize the executive in order to protect individual rights is threatened. This can be seen as a situation in which the legislature is attempting to remove the power of the court, thus necessitating the response of the courts to threaten to strike down such legislation.

This is not to belittle the statements made by the judiciary asserting their claim to determine sovereignty as a principle of the common law. Rather, it is to reclassify these statements as necessary assertions of sovereignty to ensure that constitutional balance is maintained. These assertions have not gone unnoticed by Parliament. In particular, they appear to have motivated, at least in part, the 'sovereignty' clause found in section 18 of the European Union Act 2011 that

> [d]irectly applicable or directly effective EU law (that is, the rights, powers, liabilities, obligations, restrictions, remedies and procedures referred to in section 2(1) of the European Communities Act 1972) falls to be recognised and available in law in the United Kingdom only by virtue of that Act or where it is required to be recognised and available in law by virtue of any other Act.

When closing the debate on clause 18 of the then European Union Bill, David Lidington, the Minister for Europe, explained that the clause 'addresses the concern that the principle of parliamentary sovereignty, as it relates to European Union law, might in future be eroded by decisions of the United Kingdom's domestic courts'.[97] This erosion might occur if the courts were to regard EU law as entrenched in our legal system as part of the common law, rather than deriving its authority from a statute, where parliamentary sovereignty is regarded as a principle of the common law. David Lidington argued that there were three sources for this fear: (i) the judgment of Laws LJ in the 'Metric Martyrs' case;[98] (ii) statements from Lord Steyn in *Jackson*;[99] and (iii) the risk of further future challenges in the court to the claim that EU law gains direct effect in the United Kingdom through the operation of a UK statute.[100] For Sir William Cash, the fear was not limited to EU law, but to the relative importance of parliamentary sovereignty and the rule of law. When asserting that parliamentary sovereignty is a principle of the common law, the courts are claiming their authority over the content of parliamentary sovereignty itself, empowering themselves to strike down legislation that is contrary to principles of the rule of law.[101] By enacting section 18, Parliament were not merely aiming to assert that it was the United Kingdom, and not Europe, that determined the nature of the relationship between directly effective EU law and UK law, but also that it was Parliament and not the courts which made this decision. Parliament was re-asserting its role to determine the nature of its own sovereignty.[102]

The aim of this section is not to argue that this assessment is the only, or indeed the best, interpretation of sovereignty. Rather, it aims to argue that this reading of the

[97] Hansard, HC Deb vol 607, col 243–44, 11 January 2011.

[98] *Thoburn v Sunderland City Council* (n 61). [99] *Jackson v Attorney General* (n 80).

[100] Hansard, HC Deb vol 607, col 244, 11 January 2011.

[101] Hansard, HC Deb vol 607, col 248, 11 January 2011.

[102] See G Gee and AL Young, 'Regaining Sovereignty? Brexit, the UK Parliament and the Common Law' (2016) 22 European Public Law 131.

current position of the UK constitution is possible and plausible, thus satisfying one of the specific assumptions required for the feasibility of applying a model of democratic dialogue to the UK constitution more generally. This interpretation is at least as plausible, if not more plausible, than the assertion either that the UK Parliament is not supreme, or that its supremacy remains as it was in Dicey's day. As such, it is capable of demonstrating that the United Kingdom can satisfy the specific requirement of constitutional counter-balancing for the application of a model of democratic dialogue. Moreover, it is clear that this interpretation remains feasible even after the United Kingdom leaves the EU, regardless of the terms of any withdrawal agreement governing the UK's future relationship with the European Union.

B. Distinct and complementary roles

The legislature and the court do play distinct and complementary roles in the UK constitution. Nevertheless, there are some legal doctrines which may challenge the ability of both to fulfil their distinct roles. Although these difficulties may restrict the extent to which democratic dialogue may be facilitated in the United Kingdom, they are not sufficient to demonstrate that the United Kingdom does not fulfil the specific assumptions required for the application of democratic dialogue.

(i) Section 2(1) and the Ullah principle

Section 2(1) of the Human Rights Act 1998 may restrict the extent to which the judiciary is able to play a distinct and complementary role in human rights adjudication, potentially challenging the suitability of democratic dialogue to the Human Rights Act 1998. This section requires that '[a] court or tribunal determining a question which has arisen in connection with a Convention right must take into account' decisions of the European Court of Human Rights. This section was interpreted by Lord Bingham in *Ullah* such that '[the duty of national courts is to keep pace with Strasbourg jurisprudence as it evolves over time: no more but certainly no less'.[103] This is referred to as the 'mirror principle'; where judgments of the European Court of Human Rights act as both a ceiling and a floor. UK courts should ensure both that they protect rights as far as required by decisions of the Strasbourg court and that they go no further than required by that court. Lord Brown in *Al Skeini* appeared to go even further, rewording the mirror principle as 'no less but certainly no more'—albeit in a decision concerning the extra-territorial application of Convention rights as opposed to the content of Convention rights.[104]

Interpreted strictly, it could be argued that section 2(1) prevents the UK courts from performing their distinct role. First, it may prevent the courts from ensuring that legislation does not harm long-standing principles of the common law. If UK courts are only looking at cases from the European Court of Human Rights, this may mean that the specific, teleological interpretations of rights, recognizing the extent to which earlier decisions of the common law courts reflect a cultural commitment to a particular interpretation of a right, or a particular way in which to balance conflicting rights, or rights and other interests, is ignored and replaced with the decision of the European Court of Human Rights. It may also prevent UK courts from developing the common

[103] *R (Ullah) v Special Adjudicator* [2004] UKHL 26, [2004] 2 AC 323 [20].
[104] *R (Al Skeini) v Ministry of Defence* [2007] UKHL 26, [2008] 1 AC 153, [106].

law so as to reflect these values where this would go beyond the protection currently found in decisions of the European Court of Human Rights.[105] Second, courts may not reason as fully when they are directed to rely on prior judgments of the European Court of Human Rights as opposed to applying their own judgment. This may detract from the courts' ability to provide their form of judicial reasoning, damaging the extent to which democratic dialogue may facilitate a better protection of human rights.

These concerns do not undermine the extent to which democratic dialogue can be achieved under the Human Rights Act. First, although the *Ullah* principle has not been overturned by the UK Supreme Court, it is important to recognize the way in which this principle is applied, as well as the extent to which its application has been limited. First, the *Ullah* obligation only applies when there is a clear and consistent line of cases from the Strasbourg court for the UK courts to follow. This provides the UK courts with more flexibility than may be thought to exist on a strict reading of the *Ullah* principle. In particular, it can provide the UK courts with the ability to distinguish decisions of the Strasbourg court in order to enable the judiciary to perform its distinct role of preserving long-standing human rights principles.

For example, in *Animal Defenders International*, a question was raised as to the compatibility of section 321(3)(b) of the Communications Act 2003, which prohibited the broadcasting of political advertising, with the right to freedom of expression found in article 10 ECHR.[106] The general prohibition appeared to contradict the decision of the European Court of Human Rights in *Verein gegen Tierfabriken (VgT)*, which concluded that a blanket ban on political advertising in print media and broadcasting media was contrary to article 10 ECHR for failing to provide a strong enough protection of political speech.[107] The Joint Committee on Human Rights had recognized that this section of the Act was likely to be incompatible with Convention rights.[108] The Minister introducing the Bill had issued a section 19(1)(b) statement, explaining that the government wished to proceed with the legislation even though there were clear indications that this section would be incompatible with Convention rights.

Nevertheless, the House of Lords concluded that the section did not contravene Convention rights. Lord Bingham, giving the judgment for the majority, argued that the *VgT* case had not fully responded to arguments regarding the justification of a blanket ban, particularly with regard to the extent that permitting political advertising may allow those with deeper pockets to influence political arguments, particularly given the mischief of political advertising where constant repetition of an argument may mean that individuals are conditioned to accept that argument. Moreover, Lord Bingham concluded that later case law, where the Strasbourg Court had paid particular attention to the greater impact of broadcast over print media, as well as the failure in *VgT* to examine the extent to which individuals had the ability to access the media market through other means, had over-estimated the impact of a general ban as well as under-estimating the harm of broadcasted political advertising.[109] As such, Lord

[105] For a similar criticism, see Laws, *The Common Law Constitution* (n 49) Ch 3.

[106] *R (Animal Defenders International) v Secretary of State for Culture, Media and Sport* [2008] UKHL 15, [2008] 1 AC 1312.

[107] *VgT Verein gegen Tierfabriken v Switzerland* Application number 24699/94, (2001) 10 BHRC 473.

[108] Joint Committee on Human Rights '19th Report of the Session 2001-2002', HL Paper 149, HC 1102 (19 July 2002) and 'First Report of the Session 2002-2003' HL Paper 24, HC Paper 191 (20 December 2002); Joint Committee on Human Rights 'Fourth Report of the Session 2002–2003' HL Paper 50, HC Paper 397 (10 February 2003).

[109] *R (Animal Defenders International) v Secretary of State for Culture, Media and Sport* (n 105) [30]–[32].

Bingham did not conclude that the *VgT* decision compelled him to hold that the 2003 Act breached Convention rights, being also influenced by Parliament reaching a similar conclusion.[110] *Animal Defenders International*, therefore, illustrates how the UK judiciary are still able to perform their own role in protecting human rights decisions, despite the potential limiting influence of section 2(1) of the Human Rights Act 1998.

Second, there are some limits on the extent to which the *Ullah* principle applies. Although there is disagreement as to the extent to which these exceptions challenge the *Ullah* principle, nevertheless examples can be given both of when the UK courts will not follow a decision of the Strasbourg court and when the UK courts are prepared to protect rights further than is currently required by Strasbourg jurisprudence. UK courts have not followed decisions of Strasbourg when the decision appears to misunderstand elements of English law. For example, in *Horncastle*,[111] the Supreme Court did not follow *Al Khawaja*, a decision of the European Court of Human Rights that was on appeal to the Grand Chamber, which had concluded that article 6 ECHR had been breached as regards convictions where the sole and decisive evidence was hearsay evidence.[112] The House of Lords concluded that the Strasbourg decision had failed to recognize common law safeguards surrounding the exceptional circumstances in which hearsay evidence was admitted—in this case because the witness had died before the case came to trial.

There are also examples of cases where the UK courts have been willing to go beyond current Strasbourg decisions, particularly when this is seen to be in line with a chain of case law from the court, indicating possible future developments of Convention case law. In *Re P*, for example, the issue arose as to the compatibility of Northern Irish regulations, which prevented adoption by unmarried couples, with article 8 ECHR.[113] Although there had been no case examining whether such a provision would contravene Convention rights, the House of Lords concluded that they were free to go beyond the current Strasbourg case law. Although *Ullah* is clear that UK courts are not required to provide interpretations of Convention rights beyond the current case law, nevertheless UK courts may go beyond the protection of Convention rights currently provided in decisions of the European Court of Human Rights.

Third, the UK courts continue to protect human rights through the provisions of the common law. In *Osborn*, for example, the Supreme Court considered whether the requirements of procedural fairness required the holding of an oral hearing by the Parole Board.[114] The Supreme Court answered this question by looking first at the provisions of the common law, before concluding that the court would have reached the same conclusion had they applied the provisions of article 6 ECHR.[115] Again, this provides the UK courts with the requisite flexibility to perform their specific role as required by the model of democratic dialogue. UK courts can look to their own previous case law, as well as drawing on the reasoning of cases before the European Court of Human Rights. They are frequently able to exercise discretion when determining a clear and consistent line of cases from the European Court of Human Rights, in addition to rejecting decisions which contravene fundamental principles of the common law, or which fail to apply human rights precisely in the context of the provisions of UK law. Section 2(1), therefore, does not prevent the UK courts from performing their distinct constitutional function.

[110] ibid, [33]–[34]. [111] *R v Horncastle* [2009] UKHL 14, [2010] 2 AC 373.
[112] *Al-Khawaja and Another v United Kingdom* 49 EHRR 1.
[113] *Re P (and others) AP* [2008] UKHL 38, [2009] AC 173.
[114] *Osborn v Parole Board* [2013] UKSC 61, [2014] AC 1115. [115] bid, [101]–[113].

(ii) Parliamentary privilege

Parliamentary privilege may also restrict the ability of the courts to play a distinct role in democratic dialogue. Article 9 of the Bill of Rights 1689 requires that proceedings in Parliament ought not to be questioned in any court. Parliamentary privilege may pose two possible restrictions on democratic dialogue. First, if interpreted broadly, this provision will prevent courts from referring to parliamentary material. Such a broad interpretation would hinder democratic dialogue as courts would not be able to refer to materials which might help the courts to understand the mischief of legislation, in order to assess whether the legislation pursued a legitimate aim, as well as preventing the courts from understanding why the legislature defined human rights, or balanced human rights and policy consideration, in the specific way found in legislation. Second, even if interpreted narrowly, so as to permit courts to have access to such material, democratic dialogue may also be hindered if courts are not in a position to question parliamentary material. This may mean that courts are unable to scrutinize legislation effectively, or to apply second order reasons when determining the degree of weight to give to the opinion of the legislature on the basis of whether the legislature has taken into account a wide range of views and carried out an effective legislative process. Both may hinder the ability to achieve constitutional collaboration.

The leading case on the extent to which parliamentary privilege prevents the courts from having access to and scrutinizing parliamentary proceedings when carrying out human rights scrutiny under sections 3 and 4 of the Human Rights Act 1998 is *Wilson v First County Trust*.[116] Tom Lewis concludes that parliamentary privilege, as interpreted in *Wilson*, undermines democratic dialogue, as 'in any truly candid dialogue the courts would not be precluded from looking at and assessing the adequacy of reasons given by the legislature for measures interfering with fundamental rights'.[117] However, it will be argued below that a closer examination of *Wilson* negates this conclusion. Although parliamentary privilege may prevent some forms of scrutiny, courts are still able to scrutinize legislation effectively in order to participate in democratic dialogue. In addition, the restrictions placed upon the courts are best understood as means to ensure the relative constitutional positions of the legislature and the courts, including helping to establish their relative constitutional balance more generally. As such, the existence of parliamentary privilege does not undermine the suitability of democratic dialogue for the United Kingdom either when applied more generally or when applied to the Human Rights Act 1998.

In *Wilson*, the House of Lords criticized the way in which the Court of Appeal used Hansard when determining whether legislation contravened Convention rights. The Court of Appeal had looked at parliamentary debates not to determine the meaning of an ambiguous term, as permitted in *Pepper v Hart*, but to provide evidence of the aim and purposes of the legislation and the justification for restricting the Convention right to property, found in Article 1 of the First Protocol, scrutinizing and evaluating the reasons found in parliamentary debates. Jonathan Sumption QC, as he then was, argued that the court was wrong to use Hansard in this manner, given that it breached article 9 of the Bill of Rights. He advocated that courts should not have regard to Hansard at all when scrutinizing legislation for Convention-compatibility, limiting

[116] *Wilson v First County Trust (2)* [2003] UKHL 40, [2004] 1 AC 816.

[117] T Lewis, '"Difficult and Slippery Terrain": Hansard, Human Rights and *Hirst v UK*' [2006] Public Law 209, 218.

the use of Hansard to references to aid legislative interpretation. The House of Lords agreed that the Court of Appeal had gone too far when scrutinizing the reasoning found in parliamentary debates, but nevertheless concluded that courts could have regard to Hansard when applying sections 3 and 4 of the Human Rights Act 1998.[118] Hansard could be referred to as background evidence to ascertain the practical effect of legislation in order to determine the social purpose,[119] the mischief,[120] or the aim of the legislation.[121] However, courts should exercise caution when referring to parliamentary materials.[122] Courts should not question the reasoning found in parliamentary materials;[123] nor should they determine if the reasons justified the conclusions reached by Parliament;[124] nor should they use these materials to determine the weight to be given to the conclusions reached by the legislature.[125] Courts need to take care to ensure that their scrutiny is of the intention of Parliament, which is found in the words of legislative provisions.[126]

Although *Wilson* may limit the extent to which the judiciary can scrutinize legislative proposals, it does not unduly restrict it from performing its distinctive role so as to facilitate democratic dialogue. Although courts cannot scrutinize the reasoning provided in legislative debates, they can nevertheless evaluate whether legislative provisions comply with Convention rights. Also, although courts rarely look at Hansard, they do frequently examine other external resources—for example reports of committees, particularly the reports of the Joint Committee on Human Rights, White Papers, Green Papers, and governmental reports more generally—as background evidence.[127] This information can then be used by the court to help them to determine the Convention-compatibility of legislation, scrutinizing whether legislative provisions comply with Convention rights without questioning or criticizing proceedings in Parliament. For example in *Quila*, Lord Wilson referred to: data from the Forced Marriage Unit, set up by the Foreign and Commonwealth Office;[128] a report of the Home Office Select Committee of the House of Commons on 'Domestic Violence, Forced Marriage and "Honour"-based Violence';[129] the report of the Secretary of State for the Home Department, 'Marriage Visas: The Way Forward' setting out her proposals for reform;[130] and the report of the Home Affairs Select Committee of the House of Commons entitled 'Forced Marriage'[131] when determining whether a decision to increase the age for marriage visas from eighteen to twenty-one was compatible with Convention rights. Although Lord Wilson never questioned the veracity of any of the reports, he did use information in these reports effectively to argue that the change in the Immigration Rules was contrary to Convention rights. In particular, he was able to point to the fact that the Home Secretary had failed to fully define the mischief the change in the rules was designed to remedy—pointing out that most forced marriages take place between the ages of eighteen and twenty-one was not sufficient to

[118] *Wilson v First County Trust (2)* (n 115), [52]–[53] (Nicholls); [116] (Hope); and [143] (Hobhouse).
[119] ibid, [60] (Nicholls).
[120] ibid, (Nicholls); [142] (Hobhouse).
[121] ibid, [118] (Hope).
[122] ibid, [117] (Hope).
[123] ibid, [60] (Nicholls); [143] (Hobhouse).
[124] ibid, [115] (Hope).
[125] ibid, [66] (Nicholls).
[126] ibid, [53] and [67] (Nicholls); [111] (Hope); [139] and [142] (Hobhouse).
[127] See A Kavanagh, 'Proportionality and Parliamentary Debates: Exploring Some Forbidden Territory' (2014) 34 OJLS 443, 454–63.
[128] *R (Quila) v Secretary of State for the Home Department* [2011] UKSC 45; [2012] 1 AC 621, [10]–[11].
[129] ibid, [26].
[130] ibid, [27]–[29] and [48].
[131] ibid, [55].

demonstrate that most marriages that took place between a UK national and a non-UK national between the ages of eighteen and twenty-one were forced marriages.[132]

Aileen Kavanagh's recent extensive research on this issue concludes that courts do look at parliamentary material to examine whether there was a legislative focus on human rights, whether there was active parliamentary deliberation on an issue and whether opposing views were fully represented in such deliberations.[133] In addition, Kavanagh concludes that the current approach of the courts is normatively justified. In looking at external and parliamentary materials, courts are able to assess the extent to which legislation took account of a range of viewpoints and the extent to which the legislature took these views into account in a considered manner. This information is relevant to the degree of deference, or weight, to be accorded by the judiciary to legislation. The greater the detailed consideration of a wide range of viewpoints the more likely it is that the legislature will have reached a better conclusion, both in terms of the outcome and in terms of the democratic legitimacy of the legislative solution.[134] The same arguments are relevant to democratic dialogue. By looking to external materials as background information, using these to question legislative solutions, courts are able to effectively scrutinize legislation in order to perform their distinct institutional role in democratic dialogue. Moreover, by looking at that background information to determine the extent to which the legislature has taken account of a range of views, courts can ensure their reasoning about rights supplements parliamentary reasoning about rights, scrutinizing legislation more carefully to ensure mistakes are not made whilst giving sufficient weight to legislation which has taken account of the relative strengths of reasoning about rights by the legislature.

Moreover, protecting parliamentary privilege in this manner helps to ensure constitutional counter-balance between the legislature and the judiciary. Parliamentary privilege is justified not merely because it helps to facilitate democratic debate, but also because of its connection to parliamentary sovereignty.[135] Parliament determines its own privileges, whilst courts also play a role in determining the scope of parliamentary privilege through determining how the law interprets proceedings in Parliament and what it means to question such proceedings. This power of Parliament is devised to support parliamentary sovereignty. It can be understood as a constitutional self-defence mechanism,[136] ensuring Parliament's constitutional powers are not undermined by the courts questioning legislative debate. Maintaining this essential check and balance, therefore, helps to facilitate dialogue through providing a means of protecting constitutional balance. As such, it provides a means of facilitating as opposed to restricting democratic dialogue.

(iii) Executive dominance

Our discussion of democratic dialogue focuses on the extent to which the legislature and the judiciary can work together in order to provide a better protection of human rights. However, although we have identified the 'Queen-in-Parliament' as the UK legislature—consisting of the House of Commons, the House of Lords, and the Monarch—the composition of the 'Queen-in-Parliament' may challenge this

[132] ibid, [58]. [133] See Kavanagh (n 126) 463–64. [134] ibid, 467–72.

[135] See P Joseph, 'Parliament's Attenuated Privilege of Freedom of Speech' (2010) 126 LQR 568.

[136] NW Barber and AL Young, 'The Rise of Prospective Henry VIII Clauses and their Implications for Sovereignty' [2003] Public Law 112.

designation. We have already examined the extent to which the presence of the House of Lords and the Monarch may undermine the general assumption as to whether the United Kingdom provides a sufficiently strong protection of democracy. The challenge in this section is posed by the first-past-the-post electoral system combined with the way in which the UK Government is formed from the party—or parties—with the most seats. Not only is it possible that the government is formed from a political party that does not have the most votes cast, but this is frequently the case. And, as recently illustrated starkly by the resignation of David Cameron following the result of the EU referendum, a future Prime Minister can be determined by one political party—in this instance the Conservative Party—with no further say by the electorate.

In the 2015 general election, for example, the Conservatives obtained 331 seats, the Labour party 232 seats, the Scottish Nationalist Party 56 seats, the Liberal Democrats 8 seats, the Democratic Union Party 8 seats and others 15 seats. This provides the Conservative Government with a majority of 12 seats in the House of Commons, with a 36.9 per cent share of the votes cast. The Labour Party obtained 20.4 per cent, the Scottish Nationalist Party 4.7 per cent, the Liberal Democrats 7.9 per cent, and the Green Party 3.8 per cent. The United Kingdom Independence Party obtained 12.6 per cent of the votes cast, but were only able to achieve 1 seat in the House of Commons. In the 2010 general election, a Coalition Government was formed by the Conservative and the Liberal Democrat parties. The Conservative Party won 306 and the Liberal Democrats 57 seats, providing them with a combined total of 363 of the 650 seats. The Labour Party formed the main opposition party, with 258 of the 650 seats. However, the Conservative Party had 36.05 per cent, the Labour Party 28.99 per cent, and the Liberal Democrat Party 23.03 per cent of the votes cast. Although the Coalition Government had a combined total of 59.08 per cent of the votes cast, it could be argued that this is not representative of the majority wishes of votes cast, given that those voting would not have contemplated a Coalition Government in this manner, given the lack of a general history of Coalition Governments in the United Kingdom, and did not have the chance to vote on the coalition agreement agreed between the two parties after the election took place. Moreover, the Conservative Party obtained 23.47 per cent, the Labour Party 18.87 per cent, and the Liberal Democrat Party 14.99 per cent of support from the electorate as a whole. This would give the combined percentage of the Coalition Government as representing 38.46 per cent of the electorate. The figures for 2005 paint an even bleaker picture. A Labour Government was formed with 355 of the 650 seats, with 198 seats for the Conservative Party and 62 seats for the Liberal Democrat Party. However, the Labour Party received 35.19 per cent of the votes cast, compared to 32.36 per cent for the Conservative Party and 22.05 per cent for the Liberal Democrat Party. The Labour Party received 54.61 per cent of the seats of the House despite receiving 35.19 per cent of the votes cast. The 32.36 per cent of votes represented 30.46 per cent of the seats for the Conservative Party, with the Liberal Democrats receiving 9.54 per cent of the seats of the House of Commons with their 22.05 per cent share of votes cast. In terms of the percentage wishes of the electorate as a whole, the Labour Party represented 21.19 per cent of the electorate as a whole, with the Conservatives representing 19.85 per cent and the Liberal Democrats 13.53 per cent.

These figures challenge the UK Parliament's claim of democratic legitimacy. To this extent, they challenge how far legislative resolutions of human rights issues can lay claim to legitimacy. In particular, it may not be the case that the legislature represents the view of society as to the way in which different rights, or rights and interests should be balanced against each other. Although the legislature still represents a wider range of views than the judiciary, and may provide a better means of debating a wider range of issues, the executive dominance may also have an impact on the extent to which minority views are expressed and taken into account.

Executive dominance per se may not undermine the application of democratic dialogue to the United Kingdom. However, it is important to recognize that it should affect the extent to which the judiciary should give weight to legislative determinations of human rights. A more damaging impact of executive dominance relates to the extent to which the legislature performs its assigned role in accounts of democratic dialogue. Research by Hiebert and Kelly suggests that MPs may be more concerned with voting along party lines than on engaging in detailed human rights scrutiny, and that legal advice concerning whether legislative provisions will contravene human rights is often preferred to reports from the Joint Committee on Human Rights, with the government using risk-assessment strategies to achieve desirable policies despite potential restrictions on rights. They conclude that

> lower houses of parliament do not seem to be an effective venue for elected members to engage in independent, moral judgements about the scope of rights, or how rights-based or compatibility-based considerations should guide or constrain legislation. Instead, debating and voting in these parliamentary venues is heavily constrained by government domination, norms of party cohesion and an 'us v them' focus that emphasizes criticism of the government's legislative agenda rather than seeking the best way to ensure legislation is compliant with protected rights.[137]

This suggests a deeper problem for democratic dialogue. Not only does this suggest that legislative scrutiny of human rights does not fully match the requirements of democratic dialogue, but in addition it suggests further that the judiciary and the legislature may talk at cross purposes. Whilst the UK courts scrutinize legislative provisions as the expression of the will of Parliament, it may be better characterized as the will of the Government. Moreover, human rights scrutiny performed by the legislature may be focused predominantly on assessing the extent to which the government's legislative agenda can be achieved, minimizing the impact of human rights protections on achieving this agenda as opposed to focusing on strengthening human rights protections. This does not undermine the extent to which a democratic dialogue model is suited to the UK constitution. However, it does have implications for the appropriate mechanisms of dialogue and, in turn, the extent to which the UK can achieve the normative advantages of democratic dialogue models. In particular, it suggests that, in order to facilitate democracy, courts should pay more attention to anticipated reactions by the public as well as aiming to determine the intention of the legislature.

III. Conclusion

Having assessed the general and specific assumptions on which a model of democratic dialogue is based, this chapter has concluded that democratic dialogue is a suitable model for the UK constitution. However, it has also pointed to some of the ways in which the UK constitution may detract from the ability of democratic dialogue to

[137] J Hiebert and J Kelly, *Parliamentary Bills of Rights: The Experiences of New Zealand and the United Kingdom* (Cambridge University Press 2015) 411.

achieve its normative advantages. A more detailed evaluation of the extent to which democratic dialogue can achieve its normative advantages will be carried out in the next two chapters, when we assess the application of democratic dialogue to the protection of human rights in the United Kingdom, looking in particular at the impact on inter-institutional interactions between the legislature and the courts and inter-institutional interactions between the UK and European courts.

7

Democratic Dialogue and UK Human Rights Law

The previous chapter concluded that democratic dialogue can be applied to the United Kingdom. The aim of this chapter is to apply democratic dialogue more precisely, explaining how best to interpret the current provisions of the Human Rights Act 1998 in order to achieve the normative advantages of a democratic dialogue model.

The Human Rights Act is not the only means through which rights are protected. Human rights are also protected through the application of the common law, as well as European Union law, both through its protection of general principles of European Union law and the European Union's Charter of Fundamental Rights. This range of protections will be set out in order to provide an account of the range of inter-institutional interactions that occur in the field of human rights in the United Kingdom. We also need to be aware of the different ways in which human rights are protected as regards the Scottish, Welsh, and Northern Irish legislatures as opposed to as against the Westminster Parliament. This chapter will assess how far each of these protections of human rights may facilitate democratic dialogue, paying attention also to the protection of human rights found in the common law and through European Union law. Before embarking on this assessment, we need first to provide a comprehensive account of the way in which human rights are currently protected.

Given the uncertainty as to the relationship between UK law and EU law, following the decision in the referendum held on 23 June 2016 which decided in favour of leaving the European Union, in addition to the precarious future of the Human Rights Act 1998 and its proposed replacement by a British Bill of Rights, it is hard to predict how human rights will continue to be protected. However, as the United Kingdom will remain in the European Union unless and until a withdrawal agreement has been agreed and ratified, or the two-year time limit, with possible agreed extensions, has been concluded,[1] this chapter will provide an account of EU law as it is currently in force. It will also mention possible implications for the British Bill of Rights and the United Kingdom's exit from the European Union. These issues will be discussed in more depth in the conclusion.

I. Human Rights Protections in the United Kingdom

When discussing human rights protections in the United Kingdom, it is easy to focus just on the Human Rights Act 1998. The Act provides the main mechanism through which human rights are protected in the United Kingdom. However, it is important to recognize that human rights in the United Kingdom are also protected through provisions of the common law and European Union law. It is only by understanding

[1] Article 50 TEU.

this plethora of protection that we can fully understand the range of inter-institutional interactions to which democratic dialogue may apply.

A. Plethora of protection

The Human Rights Act 1998 remains the predominant means of protecting human rights. It does so through a variety of mechanisms. First, the Act provides a means of protecting human rights that may be harmed by legislation of the Westminster Parliament through a combination of sections 3, 4, 10, and 19 of the Act. Section 19 of the Act requires the Minister in charge of a Bill to make a statement regarding the compatibility of a Bill with Convention rights before its second reading. The provision provides for two possibilities. First, a Minister can issue a 'statement of compatibility' under section 19(1)(a) where, in the view of the Minister promoting the Bill, 'the provisions of the Bill are compatible with Convention rights'. Second, a Minister can issue a statement under section 19(1)(b) that despite being unable to make a statement of compatibility 'the government nevertheless wishes the House to proceed with the Bill'. Both of these statements are designed to facilitate democratic discussion of Convention rights during the legislative process, raising awareness of human rights issues and, particularly when a section 19(1)(b) statement is made, alerting the Westminster Parliament to the fact that legislation could be enacted that may contravene Convention rights, ensuring that any breach of Convention rights is either avoided, or fully justified before the House. Further protection of Convention rights can be achieved through sections 3 and 4 of the Act. Section 3 provides that courts must, so far as possible, read and give effect to legislation, so as to ensure its compatibility with Convention rights. Section 4 empowers courts of the level of the high court and above to issue a declaration of incompatibility when it is not possible to read and give effect to legislation so as to ensure compatibility with Convention rights. Section 10 of the Act empowers the government to enact remedial orders, enabling a quick and effective means of modifying primary legislation to ensure its compatibility with Convention rights.

Section 6 provides a means of protecting human rights from erosion by actions of the executive. The section provides that it is unlawful for a public authority to act in a manner that is incompatible with Convention rights. Section 6(2) provides that a public authority is not acting unlawfully when it is required by legislation to act in a way which breaches Convention rights, or where the public authority is acting to give effect to, or enforce a provision of, legislation which could not be interpreted in a manner compatible with Convention rights. Section 8 provides the court with a broad discretionary power to determine the appropriate remedy for a breach of Convention rights for a public authority. This includes the ability to strike down the act as unlawful, in addition to providing damages to those whose Convention rights were harmed.

Human rights also continue to be protected through the common law. Prior to the enactment of the Human Rights Act, the common law developed mechanisms for the protection of human rights which resemble those found under the Act. In *Brind*, the House of Lords confirmed that, when interpreting legislation, courts would apply a principle of statutory interpretation that Parliament would not wish to legislate contrary to its international obligations.[2] These included obligations under the European Convention of Human Rights. In *Brind*, the court examined whether

[2] *R v Secretary of State for the Home Department ex parte Brind* [1991] 1 AC 696.

a directive enacted under section 29(3) of the Broadcasting Act 1981 was beyond the scope of the powers of the 1981 Act. The directive prevented the broadcast of statements made by members of proscribed terrorist organizations, including the IRA, although it did permit such broadcasts if they contained a still photograph of a member of a proscribed organization accompanied by a voice-over reading out the statement. Counsel argued that this was contrary to Convention rights and that the 1981 Act should be interpreted so as to protect Convention rights. The House of Lords agreed that, when faced with ambiguous legislation, courts should adopt an interpretation of legislation which complies with Convention rights over one that does not. However, as the 1981 Act was not ambiguous, its clear words preventing the broadcast of these statements had to be applied.

The House of Lords in *Brind* specifically rejected the argument that this principle of statutory interpretation required that legislation could only grant the power to the executive to act in a manner which complied with Convention rights. However, the principle of legality, also developed by the common law, does operate so as to require specific and express words to empower the executive to act contrary to fundamental principles of the common law. The principle of legality recognizes that Parliament legislates against a backdrop of principles of the common law. Parliament would have understood, when legislating, the context of these principles. Therefore, its legislation is to be read in line with these principles, as Parliament clearly would not have intended to legislate contrary to these principles unless it clearly and specifically expressed its intention to do so.

The principle of legality operates in tandem with sections 3 and 6 of the Act. Were section 3 to be overturned and not replaced by a similar interpretative obligation, the courts could still use the principle of statutory interpretation in *Brind* if the United Kingdom were to remain a signatory to the ECHR. In addition, the principle of legality may protect common law rights which supplement Convention rights, providing a further means of striking down executive action. The principle of legality was used, for example, in *Her Majesty's Treasury v Ahmed*, concerning the United Kingdom's implementation of the UN Security Council resolution to freeze assets of those who were engaged in or were funding terrorist activity.[3] Section 1 of the United Nations Act 1946 empowered the executive to make provisions that were necessary or expedient for enabling the UN Security Council resolutions to be effectively applied. The Terrorism (United Nations Measures) Order 2006 enabled the freezing of assets of those where there were reasonable grounds to suspect that the individuals were engaged in or were funding terrorist activity. The Supreme Court concluded that the principle of legality should be applied given that the freezing of assets had an impact on fundamental rights, affecting not only property interests but the ability of those whose assets were frozen to lead a normal life. As such, the general words necessary and expedient had to be interpreted narrowly and would not empower the executive to enact measures which went beyond those strictly required to achieve the objectives of the UN Security Council resolution.

In addition to principles of interpretation, the common law recognizes the existence of fundamental principles of the common law which are used to shape the development of the common law and to influence the stringency with which the court reviews decisions of the executive. *Derbyshire County Council v Times* provides a clear example.[4] The *Sunday Times* printed two news stories which were critical of the financial dealings

[3] [2010] UKSC 5, [2010] 2 AC 534.

[4] [1993] AC 534.

of the Council. The County Council wished to bring an action for defamation and the preliminary issue was raised as to whether a democratically accountable public body had the capacity to sue for defamation. After examining authorities on this issue in the United Kingdom and the United States, Lord Keith, with whom the other Law Lords agreed, concluded that '[u]nder the common law of England a local authority does not have the right to maintain an action of damages for defamation'.[5] The Court of Appeal in *Derbyshire* had reached a similar conclusion through examining decisions of the European Court of Human Rights. The House of Lords, however, focused on the common law. The common law protected fundamental rights, including the right to freedom of expression. As such, the then common law tort of defamation was shaped by these fundamental principles of the common law, such that the tort could not be used by a local authority in order to protect the expression of political speech critical of democratically elected bodies.

The protection of human rights through the common law exists alongside the protection provided by the Human Rights Act 1998. Moreover, there has been a recent resurgence by the courts in the use of the common law as a means of protecting fundamental rights, particularly in those situations in which the common law appears to go further than Convention rights, or where the approach taken by the common law is more suited to the approach of domestic courts than the approach adopted by the European Court of Human Rights, even when the two would appear to reach the same solution. The use of the common law to protect rights in a manner that may go beyond the protection of the Convention is illustrated by the decision of the Supreme Court in *Kennedy v Charity Commission*.[6] The case concerned a request from Mr Kennedy, a journalist, for information from the Charity Commission about their investigation into a charity run by the then MP, George Galloway. Section 32 of the Freedom of Information Act 2000 provided for an exemption for requests for information where the information was used for the purposes of an inquiry or arbitration, or for the purposes of proceedings into a particular matter. Kennedy argued that this exemption should be interpreted so as to comply with his Convention rights, providing him with the ability to access information. The majority of the Supreme Court concluded that Convention rights, as interpreted by the Strasbourg Court, did not include a right of access to information in this manner. Nevertheless, section 78 of the Freedom of Information Act 2000 preserved the ability to access information where this would be granted by the common law. The common law included a principle of the right to open justice, which may require the granting of access in this case. The Supreme Court sent the case back for a decision on this issue.

When reaching this conclusion, Lord Mance stressed the close relationship between Convention rights and the common law, stating that '[i]n some areas the common law may go further than the Convention, and in some contexts it may also be inspired by the Convention rights and jurisprudence', explaining that 'the natural starting point in any dispute is to start with domestic law, and it is certainly not to focus exclusively on Convention rights, without surveying the wider common law scene'.[7] Lord Toulson added that

> [t]he growth of the State has presented the courts with new challenges to which they have responded by a process of gradual adaption and development of the common law to meet current needs. This has always been the way of the common law and it has not ceased on the enactment of the Human Rights Act 1998, although since then there has sometimes been a baleful

[5] ibid, 550. [6] [2014] UKSC 20, [2014] 2 All ER 847. [7] ibid, [46].

and unnecessary tendency to overlook the common law. It needs to be emphasised that it was not the purpose of the Human Rights Act that common law should become an ossuary.[8]

The importance of the common law in *Kennedy* rests on its ability to go beyond the protection found in Convention rights. Although the minority concluded that a right of open justice was in the direction of travel of current Strasbourg case law, this was not the conclusion reached by the majority. Also, the structure of the Freedom of Information Act made it easier to rely on a common law exemption than on reading section 32 of the Act so as to comply with Convention rights. The strong statements of Lord Mance and Lord Toulson make it clear that the common law continues to protect rights in tandem with the Human Rights Act.

Osborn v The Parole Board provides a further example of the use of the common law.[9] The issue arose as to whether oral hearings were required for certain parole board decisions. When determining the case, the Supreme Court focused predominantly on domestic law, even though counsel had pleaded the case in terms of the compatibility of domestic law with Convention rights. Lord Reed, when giving the judgment of the majority of the court, stressed the inter-relationship between Convention rights and domestic provisions. Whilst Convention rights establish general principles, it is domestic measures which provide a clear and detailed application of these principles. Although the importance of the Human Rights Act was 'unquestionable', as the means through which Convention rights are incorporated into domestic law, the Act 'does not supersede the protection of human rights under the common law or statute, or create a discrete body of law based upon the judgments of the European court. Human rights continue to be protected by our domestic law, interpreted and developed in accordance with the Act when appropriate.'[10] After analysing the principles of natural justice and fairness found in the common law, Lord Reed concluded that an oral hearing was required in the specific cases before the court. Having reached this conclusion, it was not necessary to use Convention rights to determine whether the decisions of the parole board in the cases before the court were valid. Nevertheless, the Convention was analysed in order to assess whether the common law protections were sufficient to protect Convention rights, or whether further protections were required. Lord Reed concluded that the common law fulfilled the requirements of the ECHR.

Developments in the common law also appear to be moving in the direction of eroding one of the distinctions between judicial review under the common law and judicial review under the Human Rights Act 1998. Section 6 of the Act states that it is unlawful for a public authority to act contrary to Convention rights. In order to assess whether a public authority has acted unlawfully, the court has to determine the content of a Convention right.[11] When determining the content of the Convention right, the court, in particular when examining the non-absolute rights found in Articles 8–11, has to determine whether any restriction on a Convention right is for a legitimate aim, is proscribed by law, and is necessary in a democratic society. This requires the application of a test of proportionality, which has been regarded as a more searching form of review than the traditional understanding of the *Wednesbury* test.[12]

[8] ibid, [133]. [9] [2013] UKSC 61, [2014] AC 1115. [10] ibid, [57].

[11] See *Huang v Secretary of State for the Home Department* [2007] UKHL 11, [2007] 2 AC 167; *Miss Behavin' Ltd v Belfast City Council* [2007] UKHL 19, [2007] NI 89; and *R (Lord Carlile of Berriew QC) v Secretary of State for the Home Department* [2014] UKSC 60, [2015] AC 945.

[12] See, for example, the criticisms of the judicial reasoning in *R v Ministry of Defence ex parte Smith* [1996] QB 517 by the European Court of Human Rights in *Smith and Grady v United Kingdom* [2000] ECHR 33985/96, (2000) 31 EHRR 620.

However, in addition to setting out the co-existence of both common law fundamental rights and the Human Rights Act, Lord Mance in *Kennedy* also made statements suggesting that there was little distinction between the unreasonableness and the proportionality test:

both reasonableness review and proportionality involve considerations of weight and balance, with the intensity of the scrutiny and the weight to be given to any primary decision maker's view depending on the context. The advantage of the terminology of proportionality is that it introduces an element of structure into the exercise, by directing attention to factors such as suitability or appropriateness, necessity and the balance or imbalance of benefits and disadvantages. There seems no reason why such factors should not be relevant in judicial review even outside the scope of Convention and EU law. Whatever the context, the court deploying them must be aware that they overlap potentially and the intensity with which they are applied is heavily dependent on the context. In the context of fundamental rights, it is a truism that the scrutiny is likely to be more intense than where other interests are involved.[13]

Lord Mance's statement was referred to in the Supreme Court decision of *Pham*, involving the deportation of a Vietnamese national.[14] Pham had Vietnamese nationality according to the laws of Vietnam, but had argued that, as he also had British nationality, the practice of the Vietnamese Government was to treat him as if he was not a Vietnamese national, meaning that a decision to deport him would have been unlawful as it would render him stateless. The Supreme Court concluded that there was no evidence that the Vietnamese Government would treat Mr Pham as a non-national by operation of its law, and that, therefore, the decision to deport him was lawful as it would not render him stateless by operation of the law. In reaching this conclusion, further statements were made as to the standard of review applicable in English law, with the justices of the Supreme Court referring to Lord Mance's statements in *Kennedy*.[15] Lord Mance specifically stated that, for a matter as serious as the loss of nationality, the court needed to apply a strict standard of review, concluding that 'the tool of proportionality is one which would, in my view and for the reasons explained in *Kennedy v Information Comr* [2014] 2 WLR 808, be both available and valuable for the purposes of such a review'.[16]

These statements in *Kennedy* and *Pham* recognize that neither proportionality nor unreasonableness are monolithic tests, where proportionality is always more stringent than the test of unreasonableness. Rather, both can be applied more or less stringently, depending on the circumstances of the particular decision to which they are applied. Second, it is clear that the recognition that the case involves fundamental rights or human rights is one which will influence the court in adopting a more stringent standard of review. Third, the courts are recognizing that, because of these similarities, it is often the case that there is little difference, if any, between the outcome that would be reached were the court to apply a proportionality test or a reasonableness test. Fourth, the real difference between the two tests is one of structure, with the proportionality test having a more structured approach, given the four stages of the test, than the test of reasonableness which is more fluid in its approach.

These remarks do not go so far as to conclusively demonstrate that proportionality is a general standard of review in English law. Indeed, the Supreme Court in *Keyu* refused

[13] *Kennedy v Charity Commission* [2014] UKSC 20, [2014] 2 All ER 847, [54].

[14] *Pham v Secretary of State for the Home Department* [2015] UKSC 19, [2015] 1 WLR 1591.

[15] See in particular, ibid, [59]–[60] (Lord Carnwath); [98] (Lord Mance); [108]–[110] (Lord Sumption); and [112]–[120] (Lord Reed).

[16] ibid, [98].

to take this step, considering that the constitutional ramifications of such a change were so great that it could not be undertaken by a court consisting of only five Justices of the Supreme Court.[17] Nevertheless, it is clear that, when fundamental rights are at stake, the courts will adopt a more stringent form of review that is highly unlikely to give rise to a different result from the application of a test of proportionality.[18] This significantly undermines any difference that may have appeared to exist between the protection of Convention rights through the application of section 6 of the Human Rights Act 1998 and the protection of fundamental rights in the common law through the application of judicial review.

In addition to the protection of human rights by the Human Rights Act and through the common law, human rights are also currently protected through the operation of EU law. There are two main sources of human rights protections in the European Union—the EU's Charter of Fundamental Rights[19] and the general principles of EU law.[20] Both are influenced by the European Convention of Human Rights (ECHR). The ECHR has long been recognized as a source of general principles of EU law, in addition to the constitutional traditions common to the member states. Titles I and II of the Charter contain rights that are similar to those found in the ECHR, with article 52(3) of the Charter clarifying that 'so far as this Charter contains rights which correspond to rights guaranteed by the Convention for the Protection of Human Rights and Fundamental Freedoms, the meaning and scope of these rights shall be the same as those laid down by the said Convention', whilst reserving the ability of the European Union to provide a more extensive protection than that provided by the ECHR.

The human rights protections in EU law currently apply to actions of the member states, in addition to their application to actions of institutions of the European Union. This occurs when member states are acting within the scope of EU law. Article 51(1) of the Charter states that the Charter applies to the 'Member States only when they are implementing Union law'. This appeared to provide a more restrictive application of the Charter to the actions of the member states than the application of general principles of EU law. However, the European Court of Justice in *Åkerberg Fransson* concluded that the Charter would also apply to member states when they were acting within the scope of EU law.[21]

It is difficult to determine with precision when a member state is acting within the scope of EU law. It is clear that a member state is within the scope of EU law when it is implementing EU law[22]—for example when enacting measures to implement a directive, or when it is acting as an agent of the European Union,[23] or when the member state acts in derogation of a provision of directly effective EU law in order to protect human rights—for example when enacting measures with may restrict the free movement of goods.[24] The scope of EU law was defined more broadly in two cases concerning the horizontal direct effect of a general principle of EU law which was reflected in a directive which had not yet been implemented into national law. In *Mangold*,

[17] *R (Keyu) v Secretary of State for Foreign and Commonwealth Affairs* [2015] UKSC 69, [2015] 3 WLR 1665.

[18] See, for example, statements to this effect in *R (Keyu) v Secretary of State for Foreign and Commonwealth Affairs* (n 17) and *Youssef v Secretary of State for Foreign and Commonwealth Affairs* [2016] UKSC 3, [2016] 2 WLR 509.

[19] C 362/391: 2012/C 326/02. This is referred to in art 6.1 TEU.

[20] Article 6.3 TEU.

[21] C-617/10 *Åklagaren v Hans Åkerberg Fransson*[2013] 2 CMLR 1273.

[22] C-260/89 *ERT* [1991] ECR I-2925.

[23] C-63/83 *R v Kent Kirk* [1984] ECR 2689.

[24] C-112/00 *Schmidberger v Austria* [2000] ECR I-5694.

Germany had not yet implemented the directive concerning equal treatment on the grounds of age, and the date of implementation for this directive had not yet passed. Nevertheless, Germany introduced legislation on fixed-term contracts of employment which contained provisions which made it easier to justify creating fixed-term contracts of employment for those aged over fifty-five. In enacting legislation which could have fundamentally undermined the main aims of the directive, Germany was acting within the scope of EU law and, therefore, the general principle of EU law could apply in this situation.[25] In *Kücükdeveci* the scope of EU law was pushed even further.[26] In this case, the date of implementation of the directive had passed and Germany had not implemented the directive. Nevertheless, it had legislative provisions which regulated the same subject matter as the directive. As such, this legislation was within the scope of EU law and, therefore, the general principle of EU law, in this case protecting the right against discrimination on the grounds of age, could apply.

The uncertainty surrounding the precise conditions when EU human rights law applies to the actions of the member states has meant that human rights have applied in situations which appear to be only indirectly connected to EU law. This was arguably the case in *Åkerberg Fransson*, which involved tax penalties and criminal proceedings against Mr Fransson for the non-payment of tax. Some of the taxes that Mr Fransson failed to pay related to breaches of his obligation to declare value added tax (VAT), a tax regulated through EU law directives, which imposed on the member states an obligation to 'take all legislative and administrative measures appropriate for ensuring collection of all the VAT due on its territory and for preventing evasion'.[27] This duty is also found in article 325 of the Treaty on the Functioning of the European Union (TFEU). Therefore, it followed that the national measures imposing tax penalties and criminal proceedings for tax evasion fell within the scope of EU law as they also extended to the non-payment of VAT, even though the legislation in question had not been implemented in order to fulfil the member state's obligation in EU law. However, it is important to recognize that the human rights obligations in EU law only applied to the non-payment of VAT and not to the non-payment of other taxes for which Mr Fransson was being prosecuted.

Moreover, as *Poclava* illustrates, there are also indications that the Court of Justice of the European Union will require a close connection between EU law and domestic law if the domestic law is to be regarded as within the scope of EU law.[28] Poclava was employed as a cook on a contract regulated by Spanish employment law designed to support entrepreneurs, which permitted the creation of contracts of indefinite duration with a one-year probationary period. The law enabled contracts to be terminated after one year should the candidate fail to meet the terms of their probationary period. EU directives and framework agreements regulated fixed-term contracts of employment—that is contracts of employment where there is a specified end of the contract determined by objective factors. As the contract of employment of Ms Poclava was for an indefinite period, save for the probationary period, the CJEU concluded that the contract was not a fixed-term contract within the scope of the directive. Therefore, the law was not within the scope of EU law and the Charter could not be applied.

[25] C-144/04 *Mangold v Helm* [2005] ECR I-9981.

[26] C-555/07 *Kücükdeveci v Swedex GmbH & Co KG* [2010] ECR I-365.

[27] *Åklagaren v Hans Åkerberg Fransson* (n 21) para 25.

[28] C-117/14 *Grima Janet Nisttahuz Poclava v Jose Maria Ariza Toledano* [2015] All ER (D) 104 (Feb).

The Charter has also been applied in English law. The Court of Appeal relied on the Charter to suspend the application of a statutory provision in *Benkharbouche v Embassy of the Republic of Sudan*.[29] Benkharbouche wished to be able to rely on the EU Working Time Directive and EU provisions relating to non-discrimination in an employment dispute with the Sudanese Embassy where she was employed as a chef. The Sudanese Embassy relied on provisions of the State Immunity Act 1978, which granted the Embassy immunity from legal proceedings with regard to the employment of Ms Benkharbouche. Benkharbouche argued that this general immunity was contrary to article 47 of the EU Charter, which protects the 'right to an effective remedy and to a fair trial', reflecting a general principle of Community law. This was because the general immunity provision effectively precluded her from pleading that the Working Time Directive would apply to her employment by the Embassy, meaning that it would prevent her from receiving a fair trial or an effective remedy of a breach of her rights under EU law. After concluding that the general immunity found under the 1978 Act precluded Benkharbouche from an effective remedy for a potential breach of her EU rights under the Working Time Directive, the Court exercised its discretion to suspend the application of the statutory provision, issuing a court order to disapply provisions of the 1978 Act 'to the extent necessary to enable employment claims … falling within the scope of EU law by members of the service staff, whose work does not relate to the sovereign functions of the mission staff, to proceed'.[30]

The Charter provisions were able to go beyond protections of Human Rights under the common law and under the Human Rights Act given the better remedies available. The Charter, following the Lisbon Treaty, has the same legal force as articles of the EU Treaty. As such, it is capable of having both vertical and horizontal direct effect, although not all of its provisions will have horizontal direct effect. Moreover, directly effective provisions of EU law override domestic law. Consequently, although in *Benkharbouche* the Court of Appeal concluded that the 1978 State Immunity Act also breached article 6 ECHR, the only remedy available to Ms Benkharbouche under the Human Rights Act was a declaration of incompatibility under section 4 of the Act. This declaration does not affect the validity, effectiveness, or legal force of the 1978 legislation. As such, if she were only able to rely on the Human Rights Act, Ms Benkharbouche would still be unable to plead that the actions of the Sudanese Embassy had breached her rights. However, as a directly effective provision of EU law, article 47 of the Charter was able to disapply the 1978 legislation, empowering Ms Benkharbouche to plead the Working Time Directive before the UK courts.

The Charter also protects a broader range of rights than those found in the ECHR. Both *Davis*[31] and *Google v Vidal-Hall*[32] illustrate how the Charter may supplement Convention rights. Both concerned invasions of privacy caused by breaches of data-retention rules. Article 7 of the Charter is similar to article 8 ECHR, providing a protection of the right of privacy. However, article 8 of the Charter includes a right of the protection of personal data, which goes beyond the protection found in article 8 ECHR. Moreover, article 47 of the Charter provides for the right to an effective remedy for those whose Charter rights have been breached. Although article 13 ECHR also includes the right to an effective remedy, this provision is not listed in the Convention rights protected by the Human Rights Act 1998. Article 47, therefore, can

[29] [2015] EWCA Civ 33, [2015] 2 CMLR 528. [30] ibid, [85].

[31] *Davis v Secretary of State for the Home Department* [2015] EWHC 2092 (Admin), [2016] 1 CMLR 443, [2015] ECWA Civ 1185, [2016] 1 CMLR 1515.

[32] *Google v Vidal-Hall* [2015] EWCA Civ 311, [2015] 3 WLR 409.

be used to further strengthen the remedy available to those whose Charter rights have been breached. In *Google v Vidal-Hall*, for example, the provision was used to disapply legislation which prevented the recovery of damages for the distress caused by the retention of personal data.

Although there is a plethora of human rights protections in the United Kingdom, this does not mean that individuals are faced with a random choice as to which form of human rights protection to apply in which circumstance. In most instances, the focus will be on a combination of the Human Rights Act and the common law, with some circumstances in which Convention rights are able to go further than the current provisions of the common law and other instances in which the common law provides for a stronger protection of rights than is currently found in the Strasbourg case law. Recourse can only be made to EU law when the case in question is within the scope of EU law. When this is the case, EU law can provide a much stronger remedy than the application of the Human Rights Act 1998 or the common law, as well as providing for a wider range of rights than those found under the European Convention of Human Rights. Clearly, the extent to which human rights can be protected in the future under EU law is hard to predict. Even if the United Kingdom were to withdraw from the EU Charter as part of its withdrawal agreement, the Charter and general principles of EU law would still be used as a means through which to interpret any EU legislation which continued to apply to the United Kingdom. To this extent, human rights, as interpreted in EU law, would continue to have an influence in UK law. However, it is unlikely that the Charter and general principles of EU law would continue to have direct effect and, even if this were the case, the scope of EU law in the United Kingdom is likely to be considerably reduced, minimizing the utility of the EU's protection of human rights in UK law.

B. A range of inter-institutional interactions

This variety of protections of human rights provides a range of inter-institutional interactions regarding the protection of human rights in UK law. There are inter-institutional interactions between the courts and the legislature, between the court and the executive and between domestic and other courts. This chapter will focus on the inter-institutional interactions between the legislature and the judiciary. The interactions between the UK courts and the European courts will be assessed in the following chapter.

Inter-institutional interactions between the legislature and the court can arise through the application of sections 3, 4, 10, and 19 of the Human Rights Act 1998 and from the application of the principle of legality and the presumption of statutory interpretation that legislation will not be interpreted contrary to obligations under international law. In addition, there is the further possible constitutional counter-balancing mechanism operating in the common law discussed in the previous chapter; the application of dicta in *Jackson v Attorney General*[33] and *AXA General Insurance v Lord Advocate*[34] that, when the legislature removes fundamental constitutional principles such as the right to judicial review, the courts may determine that this legislation should not be enforced. This chapter will examine both of these relationships in the same section. Although the same normative framework applies to both sections, the different forms of legal protection through the Human Rights Act and the common

[33] [2005] UKHL 56, [2006] 1 AC 262.

[34] [2011] UKSC 46, [2012] 1 AC 868.

law mean that the inter-institutional relationship is governed by different mechanisms. This affects, in particular, the extent to which the courts should use the mechanism of deference as a means of facilitating democratic dialogue.

With regards to the relationship between the executive and the courts, again the two types of inter-institutional interaction stem from the provisions of the Human Rights Act 1998 and the common law, with the former taking place through sections 6 and 8 of the Act and the latter through the principles of judicial review. Again, the difference between the two relates to the different mechanisms of dialogue available under the Act and under the common law. For example, it is easier to apply varying standards of review under the common law than it is under the Human Rights Act, where instead the courts will need to modify stringency of review as a means of facilitating democratic dialogue.

II. Inter-institutional Interactions between the Legislature and the Judiciary

This book has argued that, in order to provide a distinct account of how constitutions operate, or how they should protect human rights, democratic dialogue needs to explain how institutions need to work together in order to protect human rights. Our focus has predominantly been on the way in which the legislature and the judiciary work together. Democratic dialogue requires two distinct forms of interaction, constitutional collaboration and constitutional counter-balancing. These interactions occur because the legislature and the judiciary reason about human rights in a distinct manner. Given their institutional features, legislatures are better able to reason about rights which require a balancing of a series of interests, given that democratically representative bodies are better able to hear from a wider range of interest groups than courts who only hear the parties before them. Legislatures are also better able to provide practical solutions, being able to draft legislation and regulations. Courts are better able to ensure that broad legislative provisions do not harm individual rights, or inadvertently ignore or transgress long-standing principles. Moreover, courts can reason in a more abstract manner and do not need to be aware of appeasing different competing interest groups.

Given their constitutional positions, it is more legitimate for legislatures to balance competing interests or to determine the answers to watershed rights issues, that is those rights which arise to be determined for the first time in a particular society, where the determination of the relative weight to be given to competing values is legitimized as a reflection of the values adopted, or those which democratically elected individuals feel ought to be adopted in order to reflect the values of a particular community. Constitutionally, courts, as independent arbiters, lend legitimacy to the solution found to these threshold issues through their scrutiny to ensure that, in making this determination, the rights of any particularly group in society have not been inadvertently overlooked or that any group has been disproportionately burdened.

These differences need to be taken account of both as regards decisions as to the substance of a right—that is when determining whether an action of the legislature has transgressed a human right—and when assessing the appropriate remedy to be granted as regards this transgression. For example, recognizing that the legislature can often be better at practical reasoning is more relevant to an assessment of whether the legislature or the court is better able to remedy a breach of human rights by legislation as opposed to assessing whether legislation breaches human rights. As such, it should not play a role when determining whether legislation breaches human rights, but should play a role when assessing whether courts or the legislature are better placed to provide a remedy for a breach of human rights.

In addition to determining how legislatures and the judiciary should work together to facilitate democratic dialogue, we also need to determine the mechanism most suited to achieving this objective. The range of mechanisms available to the legislature and the court depends upon whether human rights are protected through the Human Rights Act or through provisions of the common law. Democratic dialogue is more likely to be achieved when there is transparency in inter-institutional interactions. The more the legislature and the judiciary provide reasons for their decisions, the easier it is for each institution to engage with the arguments of the other, using their relative strengths and weaknesses to provide better determinations of human rights. In assessing the means through which dialogue can be achieved we also need to take account of the institutional strengths and weaknesses of each institution and their constitutional role. For example, although the court could map out ways in which legislatures could avoid future human rights breaches, courts would be threatening their institutional independence and transgressing their proper constitutional role in the United Kingdom if they were to dictate solutions. Moreover, as discussed in the previous chapters, the benefits of democratic dialogue are better achieved through mechanisms that encourage constitutional collaboration, with constitutional counter-balancing mechanisms being reserved as a means of preventing one institution from transgressing its proper constitutional role and interfering with the role of the other.

Even this brief account of the analysis of the previous chapters illustrates the complexity of providing a complete normative framework for a range of possible human rights decisions. Space precludes a complete account of every form of reasoning about human rights in the UK constitution. Instead guidance will be provided as regards the nature of possible interactions between the legislature and the judiciary through the Human Rights Act and through the application of the common law. This will be illustrated through an evaluation of the different reasoning found in Supreme Court decisions, in addition to a more detailed illustration of how inter-institutional interactions may facilitate democratic dialogue using the Supreme Court decision in *Nicklinson*.[35]

A. Democratic dialogue and the Human Rights Act 1998

There are two mechanisms through which democratic dialogue can occur between the legislature and the judiciary under the Human Rights Act: through the use of sections 3 and 4 and through the use of deference when determining the content of the Convention right.

(i) Dialogue and sections 3 and 4 of the Human Rights Act 1998

In previous work, I advocated using sections 3 and 4 as the main means through which to facilitate democratic dialogue. That normative model focused on a similar, albeit less detailed account, of the relative rights-reasoning of the legislature and the judiciary. It recognized that section 3 and section 4 create different inter-institutional interactions between the legislature and the judiciary. Section 3 provides the court with a greater

[35] *R (Nicklinson) v Ministry of Justice* [2014] UKSC 38, [2015] AC 657.

role than section 4. The judiciary is empowered to determine the Convention right and provides the main remedy for a breach of Convention rights through reading and giving effect to legislation to ensure Convention-compatibility. The legislature may respond to the court decision by re-enacting legislation in a manner which makes the breach of a Convention right a fundamental feature of that legislation, effectively overturning the Convention-compatible interpretation of the judiciary. In section 4, the legislature has greater power than the judiciary. Following a declaration of incompatibility, it is for the legislature to decide if, and if so how, to respond to such a declaration, albeit that, should the European Court of Human Rights agree with the determination of the UK court, this political obligation is transformed into an obligation in international law under article 46 ECHR to comply with decisions addressed to the United Kingdom by the Strasbourg Court.

Given this difference between the inter-institutional interactions created by sections 3 and 4, I advocated that courts should apply section 4 when faced with a contestable or watershed rights-issue—a contestable issue being one where it is reasonable to disagree as to the resolution of the rights-issue. Democratic dialogue is facilitated when the courts provide a clear and detailed explanation for their conclusion that Convention rights have been breached. Moreover, democratic dialogue can be facilitated if the court provides a form of constitutional road-mapping, setting out possible ways in which Convention rights may not be breached whilst ensuring that the choice between these possible solutions remains that of the legislature. In response to a declaration of incompatibility, the legislature should engage in a detailed debate, proposing new or amended legislation in response to the decision of the court. Democratic dialogue is facilitated when the legislature engages in a wide consultation, and ensures that matters are fully discussed at the committee stage, including the Joint Committee on Human Rights. Democratic dialogue may not be facilitated where the government uses section 10 to remedy a declaration of incompatibility in these cases, given that this reduces democratic deliberation.

In contrast, the judiciary should use section 3 as opposed to section 4 when the court is faced with a non-contestable or non-watershed rights-issue, whose resolution can be resolved according to a clear application of long-standing principles of rights found in the UK constitution. Similarly, courts should favour the application of section 3 over section 4 when a breach of human rights occurs because legislation, which may generally comply with human rights, nevertheless harms human rights when applied to a particular individual in circumstances where modifying the legislation so as to protect that individual's human rights would not undermine the legislature's choice of balance between competing human rights, or require the courts to made sweeping changes to legislation beyond the scope of their powers.

This was the case, for example, in *R (on the application of M) v Secretary of State for Health* which concerned the compatibility of sections 26 and 29 of the Mental Health Act 1983 with article 8 ECHR.[36] The Act regulates the circumstances under which those suffering from serious mental health conditions can be detained. In order to ensure sufficient safeguards for those detained, the Act empowers the nearest relative to protect the rights of the person detained, providing a list of those designated as the nearest relative. However, the Act did not enable an individual detained to apply to remove or change the person identified under the Act as their nearest relative. This caused particular problems for M, where the criteria of the Act designated her adoptive

[36] [2003] EWHC 1094 (Admin), [2003] 3 All ER 672n.

father as her nearest relative, but where M alleged that her adoptive father had abused her as a child and therefore his role as her nearest relative caused considerable distress to M. It was clear from the European Court of Human Right's decision in *JT v United Kingdom*,[37] that the legislation was generally compatible with Convention rights, but that the legislative provision nevertheless harmed the rights of M in its specific application on the facts, as it would do to others in a similar position where there are concerns that the designated adult may not act in the best interests of the person detained, or their classification as a designated adult may harm the mental health of the person detained. The court is more suited to recognizing and, when there are no other difficulties, remedying these sorts of breaches of Convention rights through section 3. However, Convention-compatibility could only be achieved by providing a mechanism through which individuals subject to the provisions of the Act could apply to change or remove the person classified as their 'nearest relative' or by modifying the powers of the 'nearest relative' so as to remove its incompatibility with article 8 ECHR. Such modifications would have implications for other provisions of the Act.[38] As such, these problems would require the court to make a section 4 declaration of incompatibility, despite being faced with a non-contestable rights-issue. There were good practical reasons for the legislature to provide a suitable remedy for this breach of human rights.

In these circumstances, it should be rare for Parliament to enact new legislation to overturn the court's interpretation of the Convention right or, where section 3 is used, the statutory interpretation. The ability of Parliament to enact new legislation in response to the court's use of section 3 is best understood as a measure designed to ensure constitutional counter-balancing. As such, Parliament should only act in this manner if it is a facing a situation where it is clear that the courts have significantly contravened their constitutional role. This could occur, for example, if the courts blatantly contradicted a fundamental feature of the legislation in order to provide this Convention-compatible interpretation, or if the courts devised a practical solution that was more akin to creating judicial legislation, effectively creating secondary legislative measures in order to ensure Convention-compatibility. Moreover, in order to facilitate dialogue, Parliament should always provide a detailed justification of why it is acting to overturn legislation.

It can be difficult in practice to delineate between contestable rights-issues, watershed rights-issues, and rights-issues that are neither contestable nor raise watershed issues. To add to these complications, in earlier work I suggested three exceptions to this prima facie distinction between when democratic dialogue is facilitated through the inter-institutional interactions which occur through section 3 of the Human Rights Act and those occurring through section 4. First, when faced with a non-contestable constitutional rights issue that can only be made Convention-compatible through breaching a fundamental feature of the legislation in question, or directly contradicting the wording of legislation, courts should apply section 4 as opposed to section 3. This is necessary in order to preserve the different institutional roles of the legislature and the court as understood in the UK constitution. This relies upon an understanding of the separation of powers that it is the role of the court to interpret, not to legislate. Regardless of how one draws this distinction between interpretation and legislation, it is clearly required by section 3, which requires any reading of legislation to be

[37] Application number 26494/95, 26 February 1997, [2000] 1 FLR 909; [2000] Fam Law 533.
[38] *R (M) v Secretary of State for Health* (n 36) [11].

'possible'. It is also necessary to ensure constitutional balance between the legislature and the judiciary.

If dialogue is to be facilitated in these circumstances, when it is clear that legislation has breached Convention rights, we would expect both that the courts would issue a declaration of incompatibility and that the legislature would either use section 10 to enact remedial measures to ensure that the legislative provision in question is amended, or enact new legislation to remedy the incompatibility. Democratic dialogue would only be facilitated by the legislature not acting in this manner if, again, this were a means of exercising a constitutional counter-balancing mechanism. This would be the case, for example, if the legislature were convinced that, although the court may have good grounds for concluding that a rights-issue is not contestable, nevertheless Parliament has clear grounds for believing that it is, or Parliament had clear grounds for desiring to maintain this incompatibility. The latter may arise, for example, where the incompatibility derives from a clear decision of the Strasbourg Court which the legislature believes to contradict a clear understanding of the culture and values of the United Kingdom. In these cases, dialogue is only facilitated when the legislature provides clear, reasoned justifications for its conclusions that are open to more general, public debate.

Second, when faced with a non-contestable rights-issue that requires broad, sweeping legislative changes in order to make legislation compatible with human rights, courts should apply section 4 as opposed to section 3. This is an example of remedial deference, where the legislature rather than the courts is better able to remedy the breach of human rights caused by legislation. In *R (on the application of M) v Secretary of State for Health*, as discussed above, Convention-compatibility could only be achieved by providing a mechanism through which individuals subject to the provisions of the Act could apply to change or remove the person classified as their nearest relative or by modifying the powers of the nearest relative so as to remove its incompatibility with article 8 ECHR. Such modifications would have implications for other provisions of the Act and so are best left for Parliament. As such, these problems would require the court to make a section 4 declaration of incompatibility, despite being faced with a non-contestable rights-issue.[39] Once more, dialogue may be further facilitated where the court provides an account of factors that are relevant to remedying the breach of a human right, or outlines possible solutions to ensure legislation no longer breaches human rights. In these circumstances, the legislature should accept the definition of the right provided by the court, amending the legislation, again perhaps through the fast-track procedure, using its better ability to provide the broad sweeping changes required to make the legislation Convention-compatible. The legislature should only refuse to provide a remedy when there are clear reasons to demonstrate that the court has made an error in its assessment, or has transgressed the boundaries of its constitutional power. In these instances, dialogue is facilitated where the legislature provides clear justification for its actions which is able to further wider public debate.

Third, courts should use section 4 as opposed to section 3 when faced with a non-contestable rights issue where there is a range of possible modifications to legislation

[39] The complex history of the legislative response to this declaration of incompatibility provides further support for the conclusion that the judiciary were not suited to remedying this particular incompatibility. The government originally published a Bill in 2004, which was subsequently withdrawn in 2006, following substantial parliamentary opposition to its provisions. The incompatible provisions were finally replaced by ss 23–26 of the Mental Health Act 2007, which came into force on 3 November 2008.

that can be made to ensure it protects human rights, particularly where the precise definition of a right is contestable even when its application to a particular rights-issue is not. Again, this is an example of where the legislature is better able to provide a solution. This occurs not due to the better ability of the legislature to provide a practical solution to this issue, but because of the solution necessitating a weighing of competing interests, or choosing how to balance competing rights in a manner that best reflects the views of society. In these circumstances, the legislature should respond by accepting the conclusion of the court that the legislation in question breaches human rights when applied to the rights-issue in question, undertaking a debate as to how to modify the legislation so as to choose between a range of contestable definitions of the right in question. Democratic dialogue is facilitated when the courts provide an account of possible solutions, or issues arising in these cases, provided that their guidance does not dictate particular solutions.

(ii) Dialogue and deference

Deference can also be used to facilitate democratic dialogue. This is particularly true in those constitutions which provide the judiciary with the power to strike down legislation which contravenes constitutionally protected human rights. In such constitutions, deference can be used as a form of judicial minimalism by, for example, giving weight to legislative solutions, or through only striking down legislation which clearly contravenes a human right, or where, for example, the breach of a human right is unreasonable or manifest. Although the Human Rights Act does not provide courts with the ability to strike down legislation which contravenes Convention rights, deference also occurs under the Act when courts apply sections 3 and 4 of the Human Rights Act 1998, when courts determine the scope of a Convention right and whether this has been breached by the legislation in question.

As deference is applied when determining whether legislation breaches a Convention right, deference is more suited to facilitating dialogue related to substance as opposed to remedies—that is, it is most suited to facilitating dialogue through encouraging constitutional collaboration between the legislature and the judiciary to ascertain the content of human rights, rather than as regards the appropriate way of resolving a breach of human rights. Deference, therefore, could be used when courts are faced with contestable or watershed rights issues. When faced with these issues, courts should use deference in order to provide the legislature with a better ability to balance interests or rights, so as to respect the legislature's better constitutional legitimacy, in addition to its better institutional ability to hear arguments from a range of interest groups and to deal with complex factual issues.

As with the use of sections 3 and 4 of the Act, even when faced with a contestable rights-issue, there can be factors which would push towards exercising less deference, or no deference at all, even when the courts are faced with a contestable or watershed rights-issue. First, even when faced with a watershed or contestable rights-issue, courts may be able to correct a flaw in the reasoning process of the legislature, for example when it is clear that the purpose of the legislative provision is not achieved in practice, where the general legislative measure has an unintended consequence of harming rights when applied in an individual situation, or where there is a logical flaw in the reasoning process of the legislature. Second, even if the court is not faced with a contestable or watershed rights issue, nevertheless there may be a justification for the judiciary to defer to the legislature for institutional reasons. For example, it may be that the legislature has greater knowledge, due to its ability to look at a wider range of facts from a greater number of groups and individuals in society, or because the legislature has greater expertise at evaluating this information than the courts.

Deference is often referred to as giving weight to the conclusions of the legislature. This can be achieved in two main ways. First, courts can modify the stringency of the nature of the test used to determine whether a Convention right is breached through modifying the wording of the test. An example of this can be found in the Supreme Court decision of *R (SG) v Secretary of State for Work and Pensions* which assessed whether Regulations introduced to cap housing benefit for those whose income from other state benefits exceeded an amount equivalent to the net median earnings of working households contravened Convention rights.[40] It was argued that the benefit capping scheme was contrary to article 14 ECHR and article 1 of the First Protocol, as it had a greater impact on the income of women given its effect on single-parent families. As this concerned the assessment of a controversial area of social policy, the majority decision of the Supreme Court modified the standard of review, requiring the Regulations to be struck down if they were manifestly without reasonable foundation—that is, disproportionate in this context was interpreted to mean manifestly without foundation.

Second, weight can be given through a modification of the standard of proof required to demonstrate that a measure is disproportionate, or through a modification of the burdens of proof. A possible example of giving weight to the decision of the legislature in this manner can be found in the judgment of Lord Bingham in *Animal Defenders International Ltd*, concerning the Convention-compatibility of section 321 of the Broadcasting Act 2003 which included a blanket provision prohibiting the broadcast of political advertisements.[41] The government had issued a section 19(1)(b) statement when presenting the Communications Bill, given concerns that this provision was contrary to Convention rights and the issue was thoroughly discussed in Parliament and before the Joint Committee of Human Rights. Lord Bingham referred to the reports of the Joint Committee in his judgment. He concluded that 'great weight' should be given to the decision of Parliament for three reasons.[42] First, Parliament had greater expertise in determining the way in which to best preserve democracy than the judiciary.[43] Second, Parliament had taken account of the reasoning of the Strasbourg Court on this issue and nevertheless concluded that it was necessary to legislate for a blanket ban, recognizing that this may restrict forms of social advertising that may not damage the democratic process.[44] Third, Parliament has to legislate in broad terms through the making of general rules and Lord Bingham concluded that, if the general rule was on the whole justified, it was not for the court to strike down the rule as a whole because some political advertising which might not harm the democratic process may fall on the wrong side of the general rule.[45]

Lord Bingham recognized that, if a more specific case had been met where a social advertisement was proposed to counter the impact of commercial speech, then that applicant may have had 'strong grounds' to request the broadcast of that advertisement. However, this was not the case before the court.[46] This suggests that weight is given to the decision of the legislature by requiring stronger arguments from the applicant to satisfy that Convention rights have been breached. In this case, it required the applicant to present a very specific argument explaining how a precise form of social advertising in order to challenge commercial speech would have been wrongly

[40] [2015] UKSC 16, [2015] 1 WLR 1449.

[41] *R (Animal Defenders International Ltd) v Secretary of State for Culture, Media and Sport* [2008] UKHL 15, [2008] 1 AC 1312.

[42] ibid, [33]. [43] ibid. [44] ibid. [45] ibid. [46] ibid, [34].

excluded from being broadcast as opposed to bringing a general challenge that the legislation could infringe on social advertising and, therefore, should have been drafted so as to delineate between social advertising and political advertising as opposed to imposing a general ban.

Third, deference can occur through the way in which courts determine the scope of a Convention right. Less deference is paid when the court provides a very specific and detailed account of the scope of a Convention right, essentially providing fewer opportunities for a restriction on this right. More deference is paid when the court defines the right in a looser manner, such that there is a wider range of options of restricting the right in order to achieve a particular policy objective. This is often referred to as granting a greater discretionary area of judgment to the legislature. It gives more weight to the opinion of the legislature by providing a greater range of options for the legislature in which it can act to achieve its policy objectives without harming human rights. A possible example of this form of deference is found in the case of *Austin* concerned with the kettling of protestors in Oxford Circus on 1 May 2001.[47] Following previous anti-capitalist demonstrations which had resulted in severe disturbances of the peace in previous years, the police were present in the area given the expectation of a demonstration. In order to prevent a disturbance of the peace, when a procession arrived in Oxford Circus the police cordoned off the area, preventing people from entering or leaving an area around Oxford Circus for around seven hours, regardless of whether those individuals were members of the demonstration or other members of the public. It was argued that this was a breach of article 5 ECHR, an absolute right preventing the deprivation of liberty. However, although article 5 is absolute, the House of Lords concluded that, in order to determine whether the right was triggered, the court had to take into account the purpose of the deprivation of liberty and not merely assess the duration of the deprivation of liberty. As such, the court concluded that deprivations of liberty for the purposes of controlling crowds in the public interest would not fall within the scope of article 5 when these restrictions of liberty were proportionate and not arbitrary. Even though the deprivation of liberty for seven hours was greater in degree and intensity than shorter deprivations of liberty, nevertheless, given that it was not possible for the police to have released individuals earlier than this in order to control the crowd effectively, the restriction had not breached article 5.

In defining the right in this manner, a greater area of discretionary judgment is given to the police than if the court had, instead, used the amount of time alone to determine whether article 5 was breached, or if the court had used a stricter means of assessing the balance between individual rights than merely ensuring that a deprivation of liberty was not arbitrary. This conclusion was confirmed by the European Court of Human Rights in a close majority decision, with the majority focusing on the exceptional and specific nature of the facts in this case, despite the coercive nature of the detention, the physical discomfort of those detained and the inability of anyone to leave the cordon pointing towards a deprivation of liberty. Although the Strasbourg Court reached the same conclusion as the UK court, it defined article 5 in more precise terms. There is no mention in the decision of the trigger of an arbitrary detention, with a focus more on the duration of a deprivation of liberty and its effects on those detained, with the nature of the detention then being used to trigger a more precise scrutiny of the facts to nevertheless demonstrate that there had been no deprivation of liberty.[48]

[47] *Austin v Commissioner of Police of the Metropolis* [2009] UKHL 5, [2009] AC 564.

[48] *Austin v United Kingdom* Application Number 39692/09, (2012) 32 BHRC 618.

To facilitate democratic dialogue, deference needs to take account of subjective second-order reasoning. Courts should pay attention to the reasons for and against deferring to the legislature, focusing on reasons which would explain why the legislature is better-placed to reach a particular determination of rights. There are two forms of subjective second-order reasoning—weight adjustment and epistemically bounded second-order reasoning. The suitability of these forms of second-order reasoning depends upon the constitutional relationship between the legislature and the courts. Our discussion of deference so far appears to point to a use of weight-adjustment. This form of deference would advocate that the court determines for itself whether a legislative provision contravenes Convention rights, giving weight to the assessment of the legislature when determining whether legislation breaches human rights. This contrasts with the model of epistemically bounded second-order reasoning, which occurs when the judiciary conclude that the legislature should determine whether legislation is compatible with Convention rights, the courts agreeing with this conclusion unless the courts are better placed to, and are able to, find a flaw in the reasoning of the legislature. It can be difficult to differentiate between these two models in practice. It is clear from the line of cases from *Denbigh High School*[49] and *Miss Behavin' Ltd*,[50] culminating in the *Lord Carlile of Berriew* case, that the courts consider that it is their constitutional role to determine the content of Convention rights.[51] This does not mean that the court substitutes its assessment of the merits of a legislative provision for that of the legislature. However, it is the job of the court to determine the scope of a Convention right in order to determine whether the legislative provision breaches this Convention right. As such, weight-readjustment, through giving weight to the decisions of the legislature, is the most appropriate form of deference in the constitutional context of the Human Rights Act.

In order to facilitate democratic dialogue, the weight given to the decisions of the legislature must reflect the different constitutional and institutional roles of the legislature and courts. In addition, dialogue is facilitated when the court is transparent about its reasoning process, determining clearly why deference is granted to the legislature and evaluating clearly the extent to which deference should be granted. This requires the courts to assess whether democratic debate has taken place. Where there is evidence that the legislature has debated an issue, then there is a greater justification for giving weight to the democratic assessment of the legislature. In addition, democratic dialogue is facilitated when the courts are able to examine the reasoning provided by Parliament for reaching its conclusions. This is not to enable the judiciary to specifically question or criticize the reasoning, but in order to ensure that the courts can understand the aims and purpose of legislative enactments which potentially impinge on human rights, enabling the courts to use this information when applying the proportionality test.

(iii) Towards a detailed normative framework

Inter-institutional interactions between the legislature and the judiciary can occur both through the way in which the courts use sections 3 and 4 and through their use of deference. Both of these mechanisms of inter-institutional interaction may be used to

[49] *R (SB) v Governors of Denbigh High School* [2006] UKHL 15, [2007] 1 AC 100.

[50] *Miss Behavin' v Belfast City Council* [2007] UKHL 17, [2007] 1 WLR 1420.

[51] *R (Lord Carlile of Berriew) v Secretary of State for the Home Department* [2014] UKSC 60, [2014] 3 WLR 1404.

facilitate democratic dialogue when the inter-institutional interactions are based on the relative ability of the legislature and the judiciary to reason about rights, where there is transparency in the reasoning process of both institutions and when there is a focus on constitutional collaboration as opposed to a preference for constitutional counter-balancing mechanisms to facilitate democratic dialogue. An assessment of whether one mechanism is to be preferred to the other, or whether, and if so how, these mechanisms should inter-relate depends upon an assessment of their relative ability to facilitate dialogue and how effectively the normative model can be achieved given current legal provisions and the way in which the current members of the judiciary and the legislature behave.

Sections 3 and 4 would appear to have an advantage over the use of deference, as they provide a means of facilitating interactions concerning remedies as well as the content of rights. In addition, sections 3 and 4 are meant to provide for a commonwealth model of rights protections, which we have argued is more likely to facilitate constitutional collaboration, given that it provides for formal, legal constitutional counter-balancing mechanisms. Deference is predominantly used for inter-institutional interactions through a form of judicial minimalism, where courts empowered to strike down legislation nevertheless refrain from a full exercise of their powers in order to provide the legislature with a wider choice of discretionary action. This would appear to suggest that the application of sections 3 and 4, as discussed above, provides the best means through which to facilitate democratic dialogue in the United Kingdom.

However, although sections 3 and 4 can be applied in this manner, this is not how the UK courts have applied these sections. There is no clear evidence that the courts determine whether to apply section 3 or 4 of the Human Rights Act by examining whether an issue is contestable and, therefore, more suited to the inter-institutional interactions created through section 4 than through section 3. Rather, courts focus on whether it is possible to interpret legislation in a manner compatible with Convention rights by looking at linguistic features—for example where a Convention-compatible interpretation would require a direct contradiction of legislative provisions—or where it would undermine a fundamental feature of the legislation. In addition, courts approach cases under sections 3 and 4 of the Act by first examining whether the legislation is incompatible with Convention rights, before determining whether it would be possible to interpret legislation so as to achieve compatibility with Convention rights, as opposed to examining whether a rights-issue is contestable, or otherwise, in order to determine whether to apply section 3 or 4 of the Act. As discussed in earlier chapters, democratic dialogue is not achieved if this requires institutions to act differently from their accepted means of behaviour unless there is an incentive to change. This consistent practice in the courts suggests, therefore, that, if democratic dialogue is to be facilitated, both sections 3 and 4 and deference need to be combined. The best way in which this could facilitate democratic dialogue would be for deference to apply in a manner which reflects the different ways in which the legislature and the courts reason about the content of rights and for the application of sections 3 and 4 to take account of issues concerning the different ways in which the legislature and the courts can remedy breaches of human rights.

This combination could be achieved in the following manner. First, courts would determine the content of a Convention right, paying attention to whether the rights-issue raises contestable or watershed issues involving complex issues of weighing up competing rights, or whether the general legislation nevertheless contravened Convention rights in its specific application, or where it ignored long-standing principles. Where required, the judiciary should give weight to the reasoning of the legislature, through modifying the stringency with which the proportionality test is applied, either through shifting the standard of proof or through modifying the wording of the test of proportionality or, where proportionality is not used to determine the content of the Convention right, through providing a more or less specific definition of the Convention right. Second, courts should determine whether section 3 or 4 provides the best means through which to remedy the breach of a Convention right by legislation, examining both aspects of linguistic possibility and refraining from undermining a fundamental feature of legislation, as well as reflecting when there are good constitutional and institutional reasons for empowering the legislature to choose from a range of possible means of interpreting legislation so as to ensure Convention-compatibility—that is when this raises contestable or watershed rights-issues in addition to those instances in which Convention-compatibility requires the creation of complex administrative regulations better-suited to the legislature.

Care needs to be taken to ensure that the role of the judiciary is not undermined in those instances where deference is applied to the determination of the Convention right and section 4 is then the appropriate remedy through which to remedy the breach of Convention rights. In these cases, it may appear as if the judiciary are deferring twice over, relying on the contestable nature of the right both to define the Convention right in a manner which gives a greater discretionary area of judgment to the legislature and to use section 4 as opposed to section 3, despite there being no good grounds for rejecting the ability of the court to interpret legislation in a Convention-compatible manner. Were the court to act in this manner, it would thus fail to ensure that it performs its role when working with the legislature to determine the content of Convention rights. This difficulty can be alleviated by ensuring that courts distinguish clearly between substantive and remedial deference. In particular, issues concerning the relative contestability of a rights-issue are only relevant to sections 3 and 4 when there is the recognition of a number of ways in which legislation could be made compatible with Convention rights and that the legislature is better placed to determine from amongst those Convention rights. Second, in these instances, it is more justifiable for the court to provide its account of the range of ways in which legislation could be rendered compatible with Convention rights, providing explanations for these possibilities in order to provide the legislature with more information to help the legislature determine the best solution from a range of possible options.

As discussed above, the more transparent the reasoning of the court and the legislature, the more this will facilitate democratic dialogue by encouraging constitutional collaboration. Also, we argued above that, in order to facilitate democratic dialogue, the courts should determine whether the legislature has actually discussed the legislative provision in issue when assessing whether there are good constitutional and institutional reasons for granting weight to the legislature and to determine the extent to which such weight should be granted. This may be problematic in the UK constitution due to the protection of parliamentary privilege, found in article 9 of the Bill of Rights 1689, which prevents the courts from questioning proceedings in Parliament. In *Wilson v First Country Trust*, the House of Lords discussed the extent to which the courts could use parliamentary materials, particularly Hansard, when assessing the compatibility of legislation with Convention rights.[52] There are dicta in this case supporting the argument that the courts can refer to proceedings in Parliament in order to provide background information as to the purpose, or the practical impact of the

[52] [2003] UKHL 4; [2004] 1 AC 816.

legislation. In particular, this information can be helpful when ascertaining whether Convention rights have been breached, or when determining whether the restriction on a Convention right is proportionate. Consequently, this aspect of democratic dialogue can be achieved without breaching parliamentary privilege.

Wilson, however, states nothing as to the ability of the court to assess whether the legislature has examined an issue in order to ascertain the degree of weight to be given to the legislature's assessment that Convention rights have not been breached by legislation. As Aileen Kavanagh's work shows, there is evidence that courts do look to whether issues have been discussed in Parliament, particularly in order to give greater weight when it is clear that the legislature has carried out a comprehensive discussion.[53] Also, as Kavanagh argues, the use of Hansard and the reports of the Joint Committee on Human Rights in this manner does not breach parliamentary privilege if courts ensure that they are looking to see if debate has taken place and that human rights issues were discussed, without questioning the reasoning provided by MPs. Kavanagh argues that a similar analogy can be provided by the doctrine of relevant considerations in administrative law, where the courts are used to assessing which considerations have been taken into account by the administration, without going further and assessing the weight that should have been given to these considerations.[54] She also advocates that courts should take notice of parliamentary debates in this manner, in order to aid the court when exercising deference through giving weight to the reasoning of the legislature.[55] In addition, it is important for the courts to ensure that parliamentary privilege is not breached as parliamentary privilege provides a further way in which Parliament can maintain constitutional balance. The privilege ensures that Parliament can debate freely, without the potential of restriction from the courts as to the content of parliamentary debates. It also helps to prevent the courts from restricting the manner in which Parliament performs its functions.

A similar problem of the court exercising their powers in a way which may detract from democratic dialogue, is the argument that courts are being too deferential and, therefore, potentially harming constitutional collaboration. This has arisen in recent Supreme Court cases, where the court has been reluctant to exercise its discretionary power to grant a declaration of incompatibility. It is clear that section 4 grants the courts a power and not an obligation to grant a declaration of incompatibility. Nevertheless, in *Chester* the Supreme Court declined to issue a declaration of incompatibility, despite agreement that there was a clear breach of Convention rights given a clear and consistent line of cases from the Strasbourg court.[56] In *Nicklinson*, Lords Neuberger, Mance, and Wilson declined to issue a declaration of incompatibility, whilst reserving the possibility of issuing one in the near future if Parliament continued to decline to legislate on this matter. Lord Neuberger concluded that there were good reasons not to issue a declaration of incompatibility, even though he was prepared to accept that the legislation breached Convention rights.[57] Lord Mance and Lord Wilson were less persuaded that the legislation in question had breached Convention rights.

Mark Elliott is critical of the refusal to issue a declaration of incompatibility in *Nicklinson*. First, he recognizes that this can give rise to double deference, where issues

[53] A Kavanagh, 'Proportionality and Parliamentary Debate: Exploring Some Forbidden Territory' (2014) 34 Oxford Journal of Legal Studies 443, 456–64.

[54] ibid, 464–67. [55] ibid, 467–72.

[56] *R (Chester) v Secretary of State for Justice* [2013] UKSC 63, [2014] AC 271.

[57] *R (Nicklinson) v Ministry of Justice* [2014] UKSC 38, [2015] AC 657.

relating to substantive deference—which he refers to as adjudicative deference—are used to determine remedial deference.[58] Moreover, he argues that the justification given by Lord Neuberger in *Nicklinson* for not issuing a declaration of incompatibility had already been accommodated by the courts when they decided to issue a declaration of incompatibility as opposed to using section 3 to read legislation in a manner compatible with Convention rights.[59] Both of these criticisms show how a failure to issue a declaration of incompatibility could hinder democratic dialogue, either through double counting or through using an inappropriate mechanism of inter-institutional interaction.

Elliott's criticism is pertinent, particularly as regards Lord Neuberger's statement in *Nicklinson* suggesting that courts should be unwilling to issue a declaration of incompatibility when faced with a sensitive issue which involved complex assessments of ethics and morality.[60] If dialogue is to be facilitated, courts should look carefully at whether the legislature is better able to make these decisions, analysing their reasoning and assessing whether, despite the fact that there are good reasons for allowing the legislature to authoritatively resolve this issue, there are no errors in their assessment which the court is better able to spot and to correct. Moreover, if these concerns demonstrate that the legislature is better able to remedy the Convention incompatibility, then they are better accommodated by providing a reason for the courts to issue a declaration of incompatibility. For the same factors to then be used to justify an exercise of the court's discretion to nevertheless not issue a declaration of incompatibility may hinder as opposed to facilitate democratic dialogue.

Lord Mance in *Chester*[61] and Lord Neuberger in *Nicklinson*,[62] for example, declined to issue a declaration of incompatibility because of the existence of a range of possible solutions through which to remedy the potential breach of a Convention right. In *Chester*, although a blanket ban on prisoner voting clearly breached Convention rights, the legislature was left with a wide range of possibilities when determining which prisoners should and which should not be allowed to vote, depending, for example, on the seriousness of the nature of their offence, or the sentence given, or the length of sentence left to be served. In *Nicklinson*, a similar issue arose, with some of the Justices of the Supreme Court concluding that a blanket ban on assisted suicide breached Convention rights. Again, Parliament is then faced with a wide range of choices to ensure Convention-compatibility to ascertain when assisted suicide should be permitted and the circumstances in which this permission should be granted to ensure sufficient protection of the vulnerable. However, rather than using these justifications to decline to exercise a discretion as to whether to issue a declaration of incompatibility, these are justification for issuing a declaration of incompatibility rather than providing a Convention-compatible interpretation of the legislation. Democratic dialogue would have been furthered here if a declaration had been issued, with a clear explanation of the reasons for the declaration and an outline of the considerations the legislature should take into account when determining if, and how, to respond to this declaration of incompatibility.

However, Lord Neuberger is right to recognize that there may be some circumstances in which dialogue would be facilitated by the court's refusal to issue a

[58] http://publiclawforeveryone.com/2014/06/26/the-right-to-die-deference-dialogue-and-constitutional-authority/.

[59] ibid. [60] *R (Nicklinson) v Ministry of Justice* (n 57) [116].

[61] *R (Chester) v Secretary of State for Justice* (n 56) [40]–[42].

[62] *R (Nicklinson) v Ministry of Justice* (n 57) [116].

declaration of incompatibility.[63] Lord Neuberger was conscious of the fact that, for the court to conclude that the blanket ban on assisted suicide was now contrary to Convention rights marked a significant departure from the House of Lords decision in *Pretty v DPP*, which had concluded less than thirteen years earlier that the blanket ban on assisted suicide did not breach Convention rights.[64] This may appear to Parliament as quite a harsh reprimand. A subtler form of inter-institutional interaction, where the courts conclude that it may now be the case that the blanket ban does breach Convention rights, but recognizes that this area is difficult and problematic, so no declaration is made at this time, may be more likely to encourage Parliament to re-investigate this issue.

Similar concerns may have influenced Lord Mance's justification for not issuing a declaration of incompatibility in *Chester*. A declaration had already been issued concerning the blanket ban on prisoner voting, there had been a series of decisions of the Grand Chamber of the Strasbourg court concluding that the blanket ban on prisoner voting breached article 3 of the First Protocol and there had been debates in Parliament in response to this issue.[65] In those cases where Parliament is actively engaging with the Convention-incompatibility in question, Parliament may see the issue of a declaration of incompatibility in a more negative light, akin to the venting of scorn on Parliament's refusal to act, as advocated in certain situations by Tom Hickman,[66] rather than producing constitutional collaboration in order to further refine the definition of a Convention right. This may dissuade, as opposed to facilitate, democratic dialogue as it may detract from constitutional collaboration. This concern to facilitate constitutional collaboration as opposed to constitutional counter-balancing can be seen in Lord Neuberger's judgment in *Nicklinson*:

> Dialogue or collaboration, whether formal or informal, can be carried on with varying degrees of emphasis or firmness, and there are times when an indication, rather than firm words are more appropriate and can reasonably be expected to carry more credibility.[67]

Nevertheless, it is important that, when justified as a measure of constitutional counter-balancing, courts are willing to issue further declarations of incompatibility. It is at least arguable in *Chester* that the court would have been justified in issuing a further declaration of incompatibility given the consistent failure of the government to amend legislation to provide a right for some prisoners to vote, particularly given the debates which had focused less on arguments for and against prisoner voting and more on the emotional reaction of the government to a decision to allow any prisoner to vote.[68] Moreover, as Lord Mance and Lord Neuberger recognize, the situation may be different were the issue to arise again in the near future and for there to be no evidence of Parliament having engaged with the issues raised. Moreover, these cases may provide a clear example of when there are stronger reasons for the courts to engage in a form of constitutional road-mapping, setting out possible ways of remedying a breach of Convention rights, as can be found in the judgment of Lord Mance.[69]

63 ibid, [116]. 64 ibid, [116].

65 *R (Chester) v Secretary of State for Justice* (n 56) [39].

66 T Hickman, *Public Law After the Human Rights Act* (Hart 2010) Ch 3.

67 *R (Nicklinson) v Ministry of Justice* (n 57) [117].

68 See, for example, Hansard HC Deb vol 517, col 771 (2 November 2010), for the debate in Parliament and Hansard HC Deb vol 517, col 921 (3 November 2010) for the statement of David Cameron that it would make him 'physically ill even to contemplate having to give the vote to anyone who is in prison'.

69 *R (Nicklinson) v Ministry of Justice* (n 57) [205].

Moreover, democratic dialogue may not be hindered where the court exercises its discretion not to issue a declaration of incompatibility where, although legislation may generally breach Convention rights, nevertheless the legislative provision in question does not breach the Convention rights of the applicant before the Court. Lady Hale's judgment in *Chester*, for example, provides an example of this reason for not issuing a declaration of incompatibility.[70] Chester had been convicted of murder and sentenced to life imprisonment. Case law from Strasbourg indicated that, given the serious nature of Chester's offence and the length of his sentence, he was in the category of prisoners whose Convention right to vote would not be harmed were he to be prevented from voting whilst serving his sentence.[71] In *Chester* there was an awareness of the breach of Convention rights by the general ban on prisoner voting. In circumstances where Parliament was aware of this situation and was in the process of deliberating about the issue, a further declaration of incompatibility may not be required to further dialogue and is also not needed to provide the particular applicant before the court with a remedy.

B. Illustration

Two points can be gleaned from the above discussion. First, given the complex interaction between formal mechanisms of dialogue, found in sections 3 and 4 of the Human Rights Act 1998, and the informal mechanisms of dialogue which can apply through the use of deference, it can be difficult to determine a precise normative framework for how judicial reasoning under the Human Rights Act should operate in order to maximize democratic dialogue. Second, democratic dialogue is an ideal. Its benefits can be achieved to a greater or lesser degree and the ability of judicial approaches to facilitate democratic dialogue are influenced by, and need to take account of, judicial cultures and traditions, in addition to those of the legislature. It would help, therefore, to provide a detailed examination of one case to evaluate how far different judgments may facilitate or hinder democratic dialogue, as well as providing an account of how democratic dialogue could have been better facilitated.

Nicklinson provides a good case study to exemplify forms of inter-institutional interaction which may facilitate, or hinder, democratic dialogue. *Nicklinson* concerned the viability of section 2 of the Suicide Act 1961, as amended by section 59(2) of the Coroners and Justice Act 2009, which criminalizes 'encouraging or assisting the suicide or attempted suicide of another person',[72] as well as any act 'intended to encourage, or assist suicide or an attempt at suicide'.[73] The applicants in the case argued, inter alia, that this legislative provision was incompatible with Convention rights, in particular article 2, the right to life, and article 8, the right to respect for your private life. The case was decided by nine members of the Supreme Court, with seven of them deciding not to issue a declaration of incompatibility, and two deciding that a declaration of incompatibility should be made by the court.

The case illustrates a range of views as to the nature of the relationship between the legislature and the courts under the Human Rights Act, as well as illustrating arguments concerning when the courts should issue a declaration of incompatibility. As Baroness Hale points out in her judgment, although the Supreme Court appears to be split between a majority against a declaration and a minority in favour, the judgments

[70] *R (Chester) v Secretary of State for Justice* (n 56) [102] (Baroness Hale).
[71] See, for example, *Scoppola v Italy (No 3)* [2012] ECHR 126/05; 33 BHRC 126.
[72] Suicide Act 1961, s 2(1)(a). [73] Suicide Act 1961, s 2(1)(b).

of the Justices of the Supreme Court actually reflect four different viewpoints as to the relationship between the judiciary and the legislature: (i) the view of Lord Neuberger, Lord Wilson and Lord Mance that, although no declaration of incompatibility should be issued in this case, it may be the case that one should be issued in future cases (with Lord Mance's argument being weaker on this point, seeing this more as a possibility, whilst also recognizing that Parliament is the better institution to make any such decision); (ii) the view of Lady Hale and Lord Kerr that a declaration of incompatibility should be issued; (iii) the view of Lord Clarke and Lord Sumption that there is no need to issue a declaration of incompatibility, as it should be for Parliament to debate this matter, but that the court should intervene should Parliament refuse to debate the matter in future; and (iv) the view of Lord Reed and Lord Hughes that this is a matter solely for Parliament to decide.[74] This variety of viewpoints makes the case a useful means through which to illustrate both how the Human Rights Act can be used to facilitate dialogue between the legislature and the judiciary, as well as the potential ways in which it may produce inter-institutional interactions which may fail to encourage, dissuade, or even prevent democratic dialogue.

(i) How can we best facilitate democratic dialogue under the Human Rights Act 1998 as currently applied?

A helpful starting point is to discuss how the normative framework of democratic dialogue would have applied in this case. Before doing so, it is helpful to provide as clear a précis as possible of the above discussion of the general normative framework of democratic dialogue and how this should apply to the Human Rights Act 1998, taking account of how both the judiciary and the legislature have been applying the Act in practice.

(a) Democratic dialogue is an ideal. It aims to maximize the benefits of inter-institutional interactions, drawing on the relative strengths and weaknesses of judicial and legislative reasoning about rights. These benefits are more likely to be achieved through mechanisms which encourage constitutional collaboration, with emphasis being placed on transparency and the provision of reasons explaining why either the legislature or the judiciary conclude that rights have not been transgressed by legislation.

(b) When applied to the Human Rights Act 1998, given the way in which the judiciary has developed its approach to the Act, and the need to avoid possible over-complication, it is better for courts to use deference as a means of facilitating dialogue, using factors relevant to the different ways in which courts and legislatures reason about rights. This is not the ideal mechanism through which democratic dialogue can be facilitated. It would be better if sections 3 and 4 were used in this manner. However, as discussed earlier, democratic dialogue is a constitutional model and, as such, needs to ensure that it applies in a manner which reflects how constitutions operate in practice, recognizing that ideals may not be fully realized, but that nevertheless some of the benefits of democratic dialogue can be achieved.

(c) When exercising dialogue, courts should grant more weight to the legislature when dealing with contestable as opposed to non-contestable rights-issues—that

[74] *R (Nicklinson) v Ministry of Justice* (n 57) [299].

is, those issues about which it is reasonable to disagree. The line between contestable and non-contestable rights-issues is difficult to draw, but it nevertheless influences the degree of deference to be granted. When applying deference, courts need to be sensitive to those situations in which legislation is the result of a complex balance of competing rights and interests, in addition to taking care to ensure that any such balancing does not harm long-standing understandings of rights, or harms individual rights in its application.

(d) When exercising deference, democratic dialogue is more likely to be facilitated when courts give weight to the reasoning of the legislature, rather than assuming that the assessment of the legislature is correct and only correcting the decision of the legislature when the courts are able to recognize that the legislature has made a mistake and be in a better position to remedy this mistake—for example when the courts can recognize and correct a mistake made in the reasoning process of the legislature. Courts should ensure that they only grant weight to the decision of the legislature when there are good reasons to do so—for example when there is evidence that the legislature has consulted widely and has taken account of competing rights and interests.

(e) Democratic deference is also more likely to be facilitated when courts provide a clear outline of their reasons for exercising deference, in addition to their justification for concluding that rights have or have not been breached.

(f) Sections 3 and 4 are then used predominantly as a means through which to exercise remedial deference. Courts should use section 3 when there is a clear ability of the court to remedy a breach of a Convention right without having to choose from a range of competing solutions, or to devise procedural mechanisms to protect rights, or where there would be knock-on consequences for other legislative provisions when providing a Convention-compatible interpretation. In addition, courts should not use section 3 where to do so would transgress linguistic restrictions. In these situations, courts should use section 4 as opposed to section 3.

(g) When courts use section 3, legislatures should only use their ability to enact new legislation to change the Convention-compatible interpretation of the court when it is clear that the court has transgressed its proper constitutional role.

(h) When courts use section 4, legislatures should pay attention to the reasoning of the court, recognizing that the courts will have given weight to the legislature's analysis and nevertheless has concluded that Convention rights have been breached. When section 4 has been used because of linguistic constraints, legislatures should normally follow the reasoning of the courts, unless it is clear that the courts have transgressed the constitutional limits of their power. When responding to declarations of incompatibility where the legislature is faced with a choice of possible Convention-compatible solutions, or which require a range of procedural mechanisms, or have consequences for other legislative provisions, democratic dialogue is better facilitated when courts provide an account of possible Convention-compatible solutions, with reasons, and the legislature engages effectively with these reasons, providing justifications for its actions.

(i) Courts should only exercise their discretion to refuse to grant a section 4 declaration of incompatibility in exceptional circumstances. This may occur when section 4 is not required as a means of providing a remedy for the individual applicant before the court, given that even though legislation is generally incompatible with Convention rights (perhaps because this imposes a blanket ban) nevertheless, the specific Convention rights of the applicant before the court have not been breached. In addition, this may occur when issuing a declaration of incompatibility which may be perceived by the legislature as a breach of the proper constitutional role of the courts, meaning that democratic dialogue is better able to be facilitated informally as opposed to formally.

(ii) *How would this apply to Nicklinson?*

It is clear that the issue which arises—whether there should be a blanket ban on assisted suicide—is contestable. As was recognized in the case, this issue raises complex issues of morality, religion, and ethics. It is reasonable to disagree as to whether the right to life is designed to protect the sanctity of life, or whether it also includes, or predominantly protects, the right to choose how to live one's life, including the choice as to when to end that life. In addition, it can be reasonable to disagree as to whether the right to assist another to take their own life should be limited to the assistance of those who are not in a position to commit suicide, or whether this should extend to others. It can also be reasonable to disagree as to whether those who encourage others to take their own life—perhaps by designing machines which may equip others to take their own life, or by providing literature in support of the right to euthanasia—are breaching the right to life in the same way, or to the same extent, as an individual who helps someone travel to another country whose laws allow for voluntary euthanasia, or as a member of the medical profession who initiates a lethal injection at the request of a patient. This also raises a watershed issue. The balancing of these competing interests and rights represents a statement by a particular society about the relative weight it assigns to these values. This may well fluctuate over time. As such, there are good reasons for deference when determining whether the legislation is incompatible with Convention rights.

Democratic dialogue under the Human Rights Act is facilitated when the courts assign weight to the judgment of the legislature, based on its relative institutional and constitutional ability to reason about a particular rights-issue. Here, there are good reasons for the court assigning weight to the legislature given that, institutionally, the legislature is better able to take account of a wide range of views on this issue, helping to ensure that any position taken reflects the views of society as to how to balance these competing rights and interests. In addition, there are good constitutional reasons for preferring a democratic resolution of this contestable issue. However, in order to ensure that deference facilitates dialogue, courts should still engage with the issue and not merely regard this as purely for the resolution of Parliament. In addition, where there has been legislative discussion of this issue, courts should examine Hansard to discover the reasons for the wording of the legislative provision and the purpose it was meant to achieve, as well as providing information as to whether the legislature believed this was a proportionate solution. Here, this would require an assessment of whether there is information as to the choice for a blanket ban as opposed to other measures which may have allowed for some forms of assisted suicide. Courts should also determine whether the issue has been discussed in Parliament and whether this discussion took account of a wide variety of views, as well as whether there was any consultation on this issue. This evidence can help to determine the degree of weight to be given to the opinion of the legislature.

If the court does conclude that the Convention right is breached, the normative framework of democratic dialogue proposed in this book then requires courts to assess whether this should be remedied by an application of section 3 or section 4. First, the court needs to assess whether there are linguistic difficulties in reading section 2 of the Suicide Act in a manner which would render the legislation compatible with Convention rights. Section 2 criminalizes assisted suicide. It would be hard to read this general prohibition in a manner that allows for certain forms of assisted suicide in order to protect Convention rights. Even if this were possible, by creating a new exception to be read into the legislation, there are good reasons for not using section 3. There is a range of possible ways of rendering this legislation Convention-compatible, especially given the contestable nature of the rights-issue. Moreover, any modification to the legislation to render it Convention-compatible would require complex administrative mechanisms, involving the establishment of procedures regulating those forms of assisted suicide that should be permitted under the Convention, or which the legislature believes should be permitted to reflect the opinion of UK society on this issue. Therefore, there are good reasons for exercising remedial deference and courts should use section 4 as opposed to section 3 in order to facilitate democratic dialogue.

Second, as the courts are faced in *Nicklinson* with a highly contestable, watershed rights-issue, democratic dialogue would be facilitated here if the court were to provide some guidelines as to the factors influencing why the Convention right has been breached, as well as indications of factors to be taken into account by the legislature to aid it when determining whether, and if so how, to modify the legislation. The court needs to ensure that it does not dictate a legislative solution, or overly influence the legislature in its choice of solutions, as to do so would harm judicial independence as well as damaging constitutional collaboration. Moreover, if there is evidence of the legislature having discussed this issue recently, engaging with other decisions of the UK and Strasbourg courts, where the earlier recent court decisions suggested that the blanket ban on assisted suicide did not breach the Convention, then this could provide reasons for facilitating a more indirect form of democratic dialogue in order to facilitate constitutional collaboration. As such, there may be reasons for not issuing a declaration of incompatibility, even if the Convention right has been breached. This is particularly the case when it is suspected that Parliament may regard a declaration of incompatibility as a requirement to modify legislation, as opposed to an invitation to re-open the issue to see if, following a full democratic debate and wide consultation, there are good reasons to change the blanket ban.

(iii) Analysing the judgments in Nicklinson

There are statements by the Justices of the Supreme Court in *Nicklinson* which describe possible inter-institutional interactions between the legislature and the judiciary which may both facilitate or dissuade democratic dialogue. Before analysing these statements, it is important to recognize that they arise in response to a specific issue put before the Supreme Court—the argument of the Secretary of State that the UK courts did not have the constitutional authority to determine whether the legislation had breached Convention rights. All of the Justices of the Supreme Court recognize that the issue before the court is contestable, pointing out that it raises complex issues of religion, ethics, and morality as well as requiring the courts to balance the sanctity of life and personal autonomy.[75] However, they vary in response to their assessment of how this contestability affects the nature of the constitutional relationship between the legislature and the courts and this in turn influences the extent to which their approach facilitates or dissuades democratic dialogue.

Support for a democratic dialogue approach can be found in most of the judgments, albeit there are differences between their views. All of the judgments, with the possible exception of Lord Hughes, accept that both Parliament and the courts can collaborate to determine a contestable human rights issue. Lord Hughes states that it is for Parliament alone to decide whether to change the law, given that the blanket ban is within the margin of appreciation:

> It is true that Strasbourg thus regards the question as one to be resolved by individual States within their margin of appreciation. But in this country, this is very clearly a decision which falls to be made by Parliament ... A change, whether desirable or not, must be for Parliament to make.[76]

If interpreted as a general approach to the role of the judiciary under the Human Rights Act as regards provisions on assisted suicide, then this fails to facilitate inter-institutional interactions as it prevents the UK courts from playing their role in determining whether, despite being within the margin of appreciation, there may nevertheless be a good case for arguing that UK law should be changed to permit some forms of assisted suicide. Lord Hughes reinforces his argument by explaining that any change in the law should be one for Parliament alone as 'a change would be likely to call for an infrastructure of safeguards which a court decision could not create'.[77] However, the development of the necessary infrastructure is relevant to remedial as opposed to substantive deference. This may provide a justification for issuing a section 4 declaration of incompatibility as opposed to using section 3 to read legislation to render it compatible with Convention rights. It does not provide a justification for the courts to refuse to determine whether Convention rights are breached on constitutional grounds. It is important to recognize, however, that Lord Hughes' statements can also be interpreted as a specific response to the precise issue before the court. In *Nicklinson*, the legislation relating to assisted suicide had been frequently debated in Parliament and there was no clear case law from the European Court of Human Rights concluding that the law was contrary to Convention rights. Rather, the court was being asked to determine whether, given the wide margin of appreciation, the courts had the constitutional power to issue a declaration of incompatibility. Lord Hughes' remarks that this is for Parliament alone to decide could be restricted to this situation. It is not clear that Lord Hughes would argue that there was no role for the courts if Parliament had decided to change the law on assisted suicide, the courts then being asked to determine whether this new legislation was compatible with Convention rights.

All of the other judgments can be used to exemplify inter-institutional interaction. However, each advocates a different role for the legislature and the judiciary, giving rise in turn to inter-institutional interactions that could facilitate, or detract from, democratic dialogue. Lord Kerr and Baroness Hale give greater emphasis to the role of the court. Both would have issued a declaration of incompatibility. However, Baroness

[75] *R (Nicklinson) v Ministry of Justice* (n 57), [49]–[54] (Lord Neuberger); [160]–[162] (Lord Mance); [207]–[210] (Lord Sumption); [297] (Lord Reed); [267] (Lord Hughes); [292] (Lord Clarke); [300] (Baroness Hale).
[76] ibid, [267]. [77] ibid.

Hale's judgment gives rise to inter-institutional interactions which are more likely to facilitate democratic dialogue than Lord Kerr.

Baroness Hale recognizes that, given the contestable nature of the rights-issue and the wide margin of appreciation, 'Parliament is much the preferable forum in which the issue should be decided'.[78] Nevertheless, there is still a role for the court in determining the compatibility of section 2 of the Suicide Act 1962 with Convention rights. Her justification for concluding that the legislative provision is incompatible with Convention rights focuses on the lack of exceptions to a blanket criminalization of assisted suicide, even when coupled with a policy issued by the DPP concerning the exercise of the discretion to prosecute. Baroness Hale recognizes the problem of ensuring that any relaxation of the law does not undermine the necessary protection of the vulnerable. Nevertheless, she believes that this does not justify 'a *universal* ban, a ban which forces people like Mr Nicklinson, Mr Lamb and Martin to stay alive, not for the sake of protecting themselves, but for the sake of protecting other people'.[79]

In reaching her conclusion, Baroness Hale is focusing on arguments that the judiciary are better-equipped to make, recognizing in particular that a universal prohibition could impede the rights of some individuals, such as those before the court. Baroness Hale is not balancing rights and interests in her judgment. Rather, her arguments are based on the institutional ability of the court to recognize how legislation, which is generally compatible with Convention rights, may nevertheless harm the rights of an individual before the court.[80] Her approach can also be understood in terms of deference—if not expressed in those terms. Baroness Hale recognizes that Parliament should generally decide these issues. Her scrutiny of the legislation can be regarded as pointing out a potential flaw in the legislative policy, questioning the justification of a blanket ban given that this may harm the rights of some individuals. Baroness Hale's approach can facilitate democratic dialogue. Her judgment decides in favour of making a section 4 declaration of incompatibility, whilst recognizing that Parliament is the '*only* forum in which a solution can be found which will render our law compatible with the Convention rights'.[81] Baroness Hale also sets out what she regards as the essential requirements needed to devise a policy which would allow for exceptions, providing an outline of a constitutional roadmap to help the legislature determine how to resolve the potential mistake arising from the specific application of a general law.[82] The legislature has the ability to respond to this judgment, taking account of the reasoning of Baroness Hale and her suggestions. The legislature is then in a good position to determine whether Baroness Hale's arguments provide a justification for creating specific exceptions to the blanket ban. In addition, Baroness Hale's clear statement that Parliament 'may do nothing', recognizes that the court is faced with a contestable, watershed issue of human rights and is designed to ease the perception that the legislature must always respond to court decisions by complying with judicial determinations of rights and modifying legislation accordingly. Her statement helps to facilitate constitutional collaboration, empowering the legislature to determine whether, on the strength of her reasoning, there are justifications for adopting exceptions. There is no suggestion in Baroness Hale's judgment that she is confronting Parliament for failing to protect Convention rights.

Lord Reed's judgment also has elements that facilitate democratic dialogue. He concludes that, even within an area where there is a greater margin of appreciation, it is still the role of the court to determine the content of Convention rights. He recognizes

[78] ibid, [300]. [79] ibid, [313]. [80] ibid, [325]. [81] ibid, [300].
[82] ibid, [314].

that the issue 'raises highly controversial questions of social policy and, in the view of many, moral and religious questions of which there is no consensus', concluding that Parliament should be 'allowed a wide margin of judgment' such that 'the courts should attach very considerable weight to Parliament's assessment'.[83] However, as Lord Reed does not think that the legislation's assessment is unjustifiable under the Convention, he is not prepared to issue a declaration of incompatibility, whilst recognizing that this situation may change in the future as society's attitudes evolve. Lord Reed's approach may facilitate dialogue given that he allows for both the court and the legislature to play a role in determining the content of Convention rights, using factors concerning the relative ability of the legislature and the court to reason about rights-issues to determine the amount of weight to give to the legislature. He is also conscious of the attitudes of society as a whole, such that his judgment indirectly engages citizens, with the courts being aware of the need to assess when legislative provisions may fail to continue to reflect the views of society. Lord Reed's judgment, therefore, is more likely to facilitate informal dialogue, where the views of citizens are more likely to be engaged when discussing this watershed rights-issue.

Lord Kerr's judgment, however, is less likely to facilitate democratic dialogue. Although he does recognize that, following a section 4 declaration of incompatibility 'it is open to Parliament to decide to do nothing',[84] Lord Kerr regards the role of the court to be that of determining the law and the role of Parliament to make a 'political decision, informed by the court's view of the law'.[85] Rather than viewing the court and the legislature as working together to determine a complex area of Convention rights, Lord Kerr regards it as the role of the court to determine rights, with the scheme of section 4 allowing Parliament to ignore this determination if it so wished. Although his approach does allow inter-institutional interaction, this interaction is more confrontational and less likely to facilitate constitutional collaboration, focusing instead on constitutional counter-balancing. It is also based on allocating distinct areas to either the legislature or the courts, failing to recognize how both the legislature and the courts may play a role in the determination of policy and of rights, especially as the line between these two is difficult to draw with precision.

Lord Kerr is also unwilling to grant deference on institutional grounds. He recognizes that the 'court's approach in these difficult areas may call for a less exacting examination of the proffered justification', however:

> this more generous attitude is not based on the view that Parliament is better placed to make a judgment on the need for the measure than is the court or that the court should therefore regard itself as inept to conduct an assessment of the incompatibility of the measure. Rather, it reflects the reality that choices in these areas are difficult to make and that it may not be easy to prove that the right choice has been made.[86]

In other words, Lord Kerr is defining Convention rights so as to include a wider range of possible ways of balancing the right to life in article 2 and the right to a private life, including self-determination, in article 8. However, this may be less likely to facilitate democratic dialogue, as the courts are not using second-order reasoning and determining how much weight to give to legislative determinations. Constitutional collaboration may occur, but this may only be through indirect as opposed to direct means.

At the opposite end of the scale are those judgments which place greater emphasis on the role of Parliament. Again, although similar in the nature of inter-institutional interactions that may occur following the judgment of the court, some of the judgments

[83] ibid, [297]. [84] ibid, [343]. [85] ibid, [344]. [86] ibid, [348].

are more likely to facilitate democratic dialogue than others. Lord Sumption's judgment focuses on those instances in which, like the present, the court is dealing with an issue of social policy, within the margin of appreciation, where there is more than one rational choice. He concludes that

> the question whether relaxing or qualifying the current absolute prohibition on assisted suicide would involve unacceptable risks to vulnerable people is in my view a classic example of the kind of issue which should be decided by Parliament.[87]

This is for three reasons. First, because the issue 'involves a choice between two fundamental but mutually inconsistent moral values' and there are strong constitutional reasons for allowing this choice to be made by the legislature.[88] Second, because Parliament has already acted by debating the issue recently, deciding not to modify the law. As Parliament has been active in this area, it would be wrong for the courts to subvert this democratically mandated choice.[89] Third, there are good institutional reasons for leaving this decision to Parliament, given that Parliament is better able to hear the views of a wider range of people in society and 'where firm factual conclusions are elusive, Parliament can legitimately act on an instinctive judgment about what the facts are likely to be in a case where the evidence is inconclusive or slight'.[90] Lord Sumption was also of the opinion that, even if it were the case that Nicklinson, Lamb, and Martin had suffered or would suffer 'a painful and degrading death for the sake of others' it was nevertheless for Parliament to decide whether this was the correct general balance as a means of protecting Convention rights; 'the social and moral dimensions of the issue, its inherent difficulty, and the fact that there is much to be said on both sides make Parliament the proper organ for deciding it'.[91]

It is important to recognize here that Baroness Hale and Lord Sumption are not disagreeing about the contestable nature of the rights-issue before the court; or that there may be evidence that the Convention rights of those before the court are being harmed for the sake of providing a general rule based on the prevention of harm to the vulnerable; or that ultimately it is for Parliament to determine whether the rule should be changed. However, their difference in approach means that the inter-institutional interactions between the legislature and the court that derive from the approach of Lord Sumption are less likely to give rise to dialogue than those which may arise from the approach of Baroness Hale. Lord Sumption is unwilling to express a view on whether the individual rights of those before the court have been harmed. Moreover, he would not issue a declaration of incompatibility, given that this issue is for the legislature to resolve. The only possible instance in which he might issue a declaration would be if:

> it were possible to say that Parliament had abdicated the task of addressing the question at all, so that none of the constitutional organs of the state had determined where the United Kingdom stood on the question.[92]

The inter-institutional interactions envisaged by the approach of Lord Sumption in *Nicklinson* focus more on constitutional counter-balancing. The court should intervene only if Parliament has abdicated its responsibility to decide, with the courts prompting the legislature to act by then issuing a declaration of incompatibility. Lord Clarke's approach is similar to that of Lord Sumption, expecting the court to intervene if 'Parliament chooses not to debate these issues', whilst choosing not to make a declaration of incompatibility if Parliament 'does debate them and, after mature

[87] ibid, [230]. [88] ibid. [89] ibid, [231]. [90] ibid, [232].
[91] ibid, [233]. [92] ibid, [233].

consideration, concludes that there should be no change in the law as it stands, as at present advised and save perhaps in exceptional circumstances'.[93]

Lord Neuberger and Lord Wilson adopt a position in between these extremes, with Lord Wilson's approach being one which is more likely to facilitate dialogue than that of Lord Neuberger. Both recognize the complexities over determining whether the general prohibition on assisted suicide is contrary to Convention rights. Nevertheless, even if they were to conclude that there had been a breach, both believe that the court should refrain from exercising its power to issue a declaration of incompatibility. The previous section examined Lord Neuberger's justification for refusing to exercise this discretion: the contestable nature of the rights-issue; the difficulty in determining how to remedy the rights-issue in question; the recent and frequent debates of Parliament on this issue; and the dramatic change in direction that a declaration of incompatibility would be as this would mark a change in the recent decision of the House of Lords in *DPP v Pretty* that there was no breach of Convention rights.[94] We argued above that there were problems with Lord Neuberger's reasons for refusing to issue a declaration of incompatibility which may damage democratic dialogue. In particular, the contestable rights-issue is more relevant to the determination of whether legislation has breached Convention rights, it being an indication that greater weight should be given to the opinion of the legislature when there was evidence of political debate on the issue. The fact that there may be a choice of remedies, or the need for administrative structures to achieve Convention-compatibility, is relevant to remedial deference, providing evidence for the courts to issue a declaration of incompatibility rather than read legislation so as to ensure Convention-compatibility for the purposes of section 3.

However, Lord Neuberger recognizes the need for informal as well as formal collaboration. The *Nicklinson* case may provide an example of an exceptional situation in which not issuing a declaration of incompatibility may be more likely to facilitate constitutional collaboration than if the courts were to issue a declaration of incompatibility. First, as Lord Neuberger indicates in his judgment, this is not an issue on which the law has stood still or on which Parliament has not acted. The House of Lords Committee on Medical Ethics looked at issues of assisted suicide following the decision of the House of Lords in *Bland*,[95] and the issues surrounding changing the laws on assisted suicide 'have been debated in the House of Lords and House of Commons on at least six occasions' in the nine years leading up to the *Nicklinson* decision in 2014, in addition to the Falconer Report, published in 2012, produced by Lord Falconer as chair of a Commission on Assisted-Dying. Following the *Purdy* decision,[96] the DPP issued guidelines determining when individuals would be prosecuted for assisted suicide. As Lord Neuberger indicates, to reach the conclusion that Convention rights are now breached by this general prohibition may dissuade as opposed to encourage constitutional collaboration, given that the Convention grants a wide margin of appreciation, there is no clear Strasbourg authority concluding that the blanket ban breaches Convention rights, and given that this conclusion would mark a drastic change from quite recent case law.

Lord Wilson's judgment goes further than that of Lord Neuberger, in that he is willing to provide guidance to Parliament, asserting that 'a court will be of maximum assistance to Parliament in this regard if it not only identifies the factors which precipitate infringement but articulates options for its elimination'.[97] He then proceeds to provide

[93] ibid, [293]. [94] ibid, [116]. [95] ibid, [50].

[96] *R (Purdy) v Director of Public Prosecutions* [2009] HL 45, [2010] 1 AC 345.

[97] *R (Nicklinson) v Ministry of Justice* (n 57), [204].

a list of factors which may be relevant to help determine whether an individual is one who genuinely wishes to be assisted to end their own life, whose rights may be harmed were this not to be allowed, as opposed to a vulnerable individual whose rights would be harmed were permission for assisted-suicide to be granted.[98] Lord Neuberger, however, believes that the expression of these factors is premature, preferring to judge this later if a further application for a declaration of incompatibility is applied for either following Parliament's lack of future engagement with the issue, or following a legislative decision not to amend the legislation in question.[99]

Lord Wilson's account of possible considerations can help to facilitate constitutional collaboration if, as discussed above, these are presented as possible factors or options, with explanations, but there is no preference expressed for a specific solution. This may furnish the legislature with more information to help facilitate parliamentary debate. Moreover, there is no threat to judicial independence when the courts draw on their own expertise—as Lady Hale and Lord Wilson do in *Nicklinson*—drawing on examples from similar cases to explain the individual factors which would be relevant from the perspective of the court. Nor is there a threat to the separation of powers if the legislature responds to these suggestions by examining them according to their own merit, without giving weight to the fact that these suggestions came from the judiciary.

What our analysis of *Nicklinson* demonstrates is that democratic dialogue does not dictate one particular solution in any case. Nor does it require the courts to reach specific decisions on rights-issues. Rather, it focuses on the way in which the judiciary approaches each case, requiring the courts to draw on their own expertise when reasoning about rights, whilst being sensitive to instances where the legislature may be better-placed to reason about rights. In addition, it favours reasoned decisions, and evidence-based justifications for granting weight to the opinion of the legislature as opposed to a strict division of power between the legislature and the judiciary based on the subject matter of the right, or the relative contestability of the rights-issue. In addition, it is sensitive to approaching ways in which the legislature and the judiciary can co-operate in order to provide a better protection of human rights.

C. Dialogue and the common law

Inter-institutional interactions about human rights can occur through the common law as well as through the Human Rights Act 1998. The same normative framework applies, based on the relative ability of the courts and the legislature to reason about the content of human rights and to provide a remedy for breaches of human rights. However, there are three ways in which these inter-institutional interactions differ through the common law and the Human Rights Act which, in turn, give rise to different mechanisms regulating these interactions.

First, instead of referring to section 3 to read and give effect to legislation in a manner compatible with Convention rights, so far as it is possible to do so, courts use the principle of legality. Here, courts examine whether legislative provisions are general or specific. General legislative words cannot be used to restrict human rights. In other words, their general provisions can be read down so as not to harm human rights. A general power to regulate the advertisement of political broadcasts, for example, could be read down so as not to restrict those broadcasts that would be needed in order to provide a strong enough protection of freedom of expression. However, when there

[98] ibid, [205]. [99] ibid, [118].

is specific legislative authority to act in a manner which breaches human rights, the courts are unable to read the legislation to ensure it complies with human rights.

Second, when interpreting the scope of Convention rights, courts refer to the European Convention of Human Rights and its application of the principle of proportionality. This is not the case when courts determine the content of the common law. Here, courts determine the scope of common law rights, but there is, as yet, no requirement to apply the principle of proportionality to determine whether legislation is a proportionate restriction on a common law right. Although there is dicta that it is now at least arguable that the standard of review in common law human rights cases would require the application of the principle of proportionality.[100] This means that deference, if required, may need to apply in a different manner, through modifying the definition of the common law right rather than applying a more or less stringent form of the test of proportionality.

Third, there is no equivalent of a section 4 declaration of incompatibility. As such, the common law only gives rise to one form of inter-institutional interaction where the courts read legislation so as to comply with common law rights and the legislature can respond to this either through enacting legislation to reverse the decision of the courts—even retrospectively—or by tacitly accepting this interpretation by not reversing it through legislative means. There are two implications of this different form of inter-institutional interaction. First, it means that there is no specific mechanism to deal with remedial deference, for example where there may be a clear breach of human rights, but where interpretation is not able to deal with this breach, it being better remedied through practical mechanisms that are better suited to the legislature, or where a remedy requires the courts to make a choice between possible interpretations which would comply with human rights. Second, inter-institutional interactions occur only when courts are able to interpret legislation, providing a remedy which then places the legislature in a more difficult position to overturn this human-rights compatible interpretation.

The principle of legality can facilitate dialogue in a manner similar to that under section 3 of the Human Rights Act. When applying the principle of legality, courts are looking to long-standing principles of the common law, ensuring that legislation does not inadvertently—through the use of general words—remove a principle of the common law. Courts are better able to reason about rights in this manner than the legislature. Moreover, as Lord Hoffmann illustrates in his seminal recital of the justification of the principle of legality, the distinction between general and specific words preserves the ability of the legislation to act contrary to human rights, provided that the legislature does so by clear and specific words.[101] This helps to facilitate democratic dialogue. The respect for parliamentary sovereignty helps to ensure that the constitutional counter-balancing mechanisms are maintained. Also, the court is focusing on its relative strength and preventing rights from being accidentally eroded, whilst preserving the ability of the legislature to reach different conclusions from courts on human rights, provided that this is done clearly.

Nevertheless, there are potential problems as to the extent to which democratic dialogue can be facilitated by this form of inter-institutional interaction. First, care needs to be taken over the way in which the courts identify the principles of the common law which cannot be restricted by general legislative provisions. Given that the principle of

[100] See *R (Keyu) v Secretary of State for Foreign and Commonwealth Affairs* (n 17) and *Youssef v Secretary of State for Foreign and Commonwealth Affairs* (n 18).

[101] [2000] 2 AC 115, 131, at paras [E]–[G].

legality only facilitates dialogue akin to that which may be facilitated through section 3 of the Human Rights Act, care needs to be taken over the identification of common law principles. Dialogue is more likely to be facilitated where the courts draw on a clear and consistent line of case law to determine the content of a long-existing common law right. Difficulties may arise where courts identify newly emerging rights of the common law, or when they provide too precise a definition of a common law right where the courts are dealing with a contestable rights-issue.

These difficulties can be illustrated by the issue which arose in *Moohan*, concerning whether prisoners should be given the right to vote in the Scottish independence referendum.[102] The majority concluded that the right to vote in the referendum was neither a Convention right, nor a right under EU law, nor a right in the common law, despite its clear constitutional importance. Lord Hodge had 'no difficulty in recognising the right to vote as a basic or constitutional right'.[103] He also recognized that the court could adapt and develop the common law 'through the reasoned application of established common law principles to keep it abreast of current social conditions' taking account of binding rules of international law whilst developing the common law in this manner.[104] Nevertheless, Lord Hodge could not regard the common law as including a 'right of universal and equal suffrage from which any derogation must be provided for by law and must be proportionate' given that the right to vote is not found in a consistent line of common law case law, but through legislative intervention.[105] Baroness Hale reached a similar conclusion, asserting that 'it would be wonderful if the common law had recognised a right of universal suffrage', however the right to vote was not a creation of the common law, but 'has been the creation of Parliament' through increasing legislative intervention.[106]

This approach to the identification of a common law right can be contrasted with the dissenting judgment of Lord Kerr. Lord Kerr's remarks are *obiter dicta*, as he concluded that the right to vote in a referendum was a Convention right. He also stated that 'it was at least arguable' that the common law included the right to vote,[107] given that the 'common law can certainty evolve alongside statutory developments without necessarily being entirely eclipsed by the latter, and democracy is a concept which the common law has sought to protect by the incremental development of a system of safeguarding fundamental rights'.[108] Lord Kerr's approach appears to suggest that the courts can go further than recognizing long-standing principles of the common law. Under his approach, it may be possible for the courts to transform a constitutional principle into a principle of the common law, even when there is no previous line of case law and even when there is a series of legislative interventions establishing how a constitutional principle is to be applied in the common law. This is to go beyond the area in which courts are more institutionally suited to reason about rights than the legislature. This may help to facilitate dialogue where the courts are acting in response to the wishes of the public. However, when this strays too far from the traditional constitutional role of the courts, it may give rise to constitutional conflict between the legislature and the courts.

Although the recognition of democracy as a fundamental constitutional principle is not controversial, nevertheless the question of whether prisoners should be able to vote in the Scottish independence referendum is a contestable rights-issue. In a similar manner, there is a range of ways in which the constitutional principle of democracy

[102] *Moohan v Lord Advocate* [2014] UKSC 67, [2015] 2 WLR 141. [103] ibid, [33].
[104] ibid. [105] ibid, [34]. [106] ibid, [56]. [107] ibid, [87].
[108] ibid, [86].

can be translated into a series of rights protected by legislation or the common law. Given that the inter-institutional interactions which may operate in the common law do not specifically include the equivalent of a section 4 declaration of incompatibility, democratic dialogue is more likely to be facilitated when courts are relying on their better ability to protect long-standing principles of the common law, or when recognizing how general provisions which are in line with human rights may nevertheless harm the human rights of the individual before the court without this questioning the overall balance between competing rights. This is because the inter-institutional interactions which take place under the common law give relatively more power to the courts than the legislature, as courts have the ability to provide a remedy for an individual whose rights have been harmed, making it more difficult for the legislature to overturn this provision.

A further potential way in which these inter-institutional interactions may detract from democratic dialogue is the manner in which the principle of legality requires courts to provide a specific iteration of how a right applies in a particular situation. This may make it harder to exercise deference through giving the legislature a wider range of options through which to ensure its legislation complies with Convention rights. This can be illustrated through the way in which the principle of legality was applied in *Simms*.[109] The issue arose as to the interpretation of the prison rules, which included a general prohibition on visits to inmates by journalists when this visit by the journalist was in their professional capacity. The argument was made that this breached the common law right of freedom of expression. More specifically, the argument was made that this restricted the ability of journalists to have access to prisoners for professional purposes in order to investigate potential miscarriages of justice. In order to decide the case, the court had to determine whether the common law right to freedom of expression included this specific right of journalists to visit prisoners in order to facilitate an investigation into a potential miscarriage of justice. Having concluded that the common law did include this specific right, the prison rules were interpreted so as to permit of an exception to the general prohibition for journalists seeking access to prisoners in order to investigate a miscarriage of justice.

It is important to recognize that *Simms* involves the relationship between the executive and the legislature, in that the prison rules were enacted by the administration and not the legislature. Nevertheless, the case serves to illustrate how the principle of legality can be quite a blunt tool when it comes to facilitating democratic dialogue. Where courts are faced with a contestable rights issue, there is the need either to provide a very specific account of the nature of a common law human right, in order to conclude that the right has not been specifically restricted by a general legislative provision, or to reach the conclusion that there is no specific iteration of this common law right. This latter conclusion would leave the courts in a position where they would not be able to conclude that a general provision had breached a specific common law right. There is less scope for constitutional collaboration, with the court being able to provide an outline of the content of the common law rights and the confines of where rights may or may not be restricted by legislation. The principle of legality, therefore, may serve to facilitate democratic dialogue where courts are able to protect the specific rights of individuals from intrusion by general provisions, but it is less able to facilitate democratic dialogue between the legislature and the courts when dealing with contestable human rights.

[109] *R v Secretary of State for the Home Department, ex parte Simms* [2000] 2 AC 115.

A further way in which the inter-institutional interactions which can arise through the application of the principle of legality may detract from democratic dialogue arises from the lack of accommodation of remedial deference given the lack of an express ability of the courts to issue a declaration of incompatibility. This can be illustrated by the application of the principle of legality in *Ahmed* concerning the legality of the Terrorism (United Nations Measures) Order 2006 which was designed to implement the UN Security council resolution on terrorist asset-freezing.[110] As discussed above,[111] the Supreme Court concluded that the measures were unlawful, following an application of the principle of legality when interpreting section 1 of the United Nations Act 1946. Once the court had concluded that the measures were unlawful, the orders were quashed. This left a gap in the law, meaning in turn that the United Kingdom was no longer complying with its obligation under international law to implement the UN Security council resolution. This problem could provide an explanation for the retrospective validity given to these measures, on a temporary basis, in order to plug this potential gap in the law.[112]

This is not to criticize the actions of the court in *Ahmed* per se. Rather, it is to recognize that this blunt mechanism is less able to enable collaborative constitutionalism and, therefore, less able to facilitate democratic dialogue. This problem may be remedied through courts recognizing the ability to suspend the implementation of a quashing order in order to provide the legislature with the time to respond to a breach of human rights without an ensuing gap in the law. This occurred, for example in *Davis* where the High Court, concluded that section 1 of the Data Retention and Investigatory Powers Act 2014 was contrary to EU law.[113] The High Court suspended the application of its order to disapply the legislation, issued on 17 July 2015, until 31 March 2016, giving the legislature the time to respond to this court order without leaving a gap in the law. Moreover, as the judgment provided a detailed account for its conclusions as to why the Charter was breached, these reasons can provide the legislature with information to help modify legislative provisions to ensure future compatibility. This provides a better means through which the courts and the legislature can work together to protect human rights than through the blunt mechanism of either providing an interpretation of legislation which complies with the court's specific interpretation of the common law right, which may fail to recognize the legislature's better ability to remedy a potential breach of a human right, or where the court, instead, accommodates issues of remedial deference by modifying the content of the common law right.

The above discussion suggests that courts should be more cautious when applying the principle of legality as opposed to when applying sections 3 and 4 of the Human Rights Act. If the principle of legality is to encourage democratic dialogue, courts should focus on providing clear protections of common law rights when they are certain that broad legislative provisions are infringing long-held principles of common law rights, or where there is clear evidence that general legislative provisions infringe common law rights when applied to a specific individual. Courts should be more cautious about applying the principle of legality when faced with contestable common law rights, or when faced with a situation in which there are good reasons to exercise remedial discretion. One exception to this cautious approach arises when courts are using the principle of legality as a means of protecting their constitutional role from erosion

110 *Her Majesty's Treasury v Ahmed* [2010] UKSC 2; [2010] 2 AC 534.

111 See Chapters 4 and 6.

112 Terrorist Asset Freezing (Temporary Provisions Act) 2010.

113 *Davis v Secretary of State for the Home Department* (n 31).

by the legislature—that is when giving rise to inter-institutional interactions designed to protect constitutional counter-balance when courts are faced with a potential erosion of their constitutional position, or when acting to bring the law in line with their perception of the changing views of society.

This can be illustrated by the different applications of the principle of legality in the first *Bank Mellat* case, concerning whether it was possible to hear closed material proceedings in the Supreme Court.[114] The case concerned a challenge to the Financial Restrictions (Iran) Order 2009, made under Schedule 7 to the Counter-Terrorism Act 2008, which directed institutions in the financial sector not to enter into, or to continue to pursue, financial transactions or other business with, inter alia, Bank Mellat. Bank Mellat issued proceedings under section 68 of the 2008 Act to set aside the Order. Due to the sensitive nature of the material involved in the case, the government applied for and was granted permission for the hearing to be conducted as a closed material proceeding. As such, sensitive information would not be given to Bank Mellat, being given instead to a Special Advocate who was required to give the gist of the information to Bank Mellat in order to enable it to challenge the order. The Bank was unsuccessful in overturning the order and appealed to the Court of Appeal and then to the Supreme Court. As the appeal would concern an examination of aspects of the judgment reached in closed proceedings, the issue arose as to whether the Supreme Court would be able to conduct a closed material proceeding.

The Supreme Court concluded that it did have the power to hear closed material proceedings, with Lords Hope, Kerr, and Reed dissenting. In reaching their conclusions, the minority, and the leading majority judgment of Lord Neuberger, all referred to the principle of legality. The principle of legality was relevant because of the earlier Supreme Court decision of *Al Rawi v Security Service*[115] which had concluded that closed material proceedings were contrary to the principle of open justice—a fundamental principle of the common law—that could not be eroded unless there were compelling reasons to do so and, preferably, by statute. As such, only Parliament should have the power to introduce closed material proceedings through detailed legislative provisions. Moreover, when applying the principle of legality, any general legislative provisions could not be interpreted so as to contravene the common law right of open justice.

The minority concluded that, when applying the principle of legality, neither the broad legislative provisions of the Counter-Terrorism Act, nor the broad provisions of section 40 of the Constitutional Reform Act 2005 could be interpreted so as to empower the Supreme Court to hold closed material proceedings given that these proceedings breached the common law right of open justice. Lord Kerr argued that the power to hold closed material proceedings could only be granted 'in the most unambiguous and forthright terms or by unmistakeably necessary implication'.[116] It is difficult to find this express grant of power in either the Counter-Terrorism Act or the Constitutional Reform Act. The Counter-Terrorism Act empowered courts to develop 'rules of court' to hear closed material proceedings. However, section 68 of the Act defined 'rules of court' as 'rules for regulating the practice and procedure to be followed in the High Court or the Court of Appeal or in the Court of Session'. No express mention was made of the power to develop rules of court for the Supreme Court. The Constitutional Reform Act empowers the Supreme Court to 'determine any question

[114] *Bank Mellat v Her Majesty's Treasury (No 1)* [2013] UKSC 38, [2014] AC 700.
[115] *Al Rawi v Security Service* [2011] UKSC 34, [2012] 1 AC 531.
[116] *Bank Mellat v Her Majesty's Treasury (No 1)* (n 114) [105] (Lord Kerr).

necessary to be determined for the purposes of doing justice to an appeal to it under any enactment'.[117] Section 45(1) of the Act empowers the President of the Supreme Court to enact the 'Supreme Court Rules' which govern 'the practice and procedure to be followed by the Court'. The Supreme Court Rules enacted under this section state that the Supreme Court has all the powers of the court below,[118] as well as having the ability to conduct hearings in private, provided there is a prior public announcement of its reasons for doing so.[119] These general words would not empower the Supreme Court to create rules which contravened the common law right of open justice given that no specific empowerment was given to the Supreme Court to act in this manner. Both Lord Reed and Lord Hope referred to Lord Hoffmann's judgment in *Simms* to argue that the Constitutional Reform Act would only have been able to empower the Supreme Court to create closed material proceedings if it did so by express words, the broad words in the Act being insufficient.[120]

Lord Neuberger, however, giving the majority judgment, concluded that there was a strong case for enabling the Supreme Court to hold closed material proceedings, focusing in particular upon the practical consequences that would arise were the Supreme Court to hear an appeal from the Court of Appeal where closed material proceedings had been used. If the Supreme Court were not able to hear closed material proceedings it could either: not hear the appeal; hear the appeal with the materials that were previously subjected to a closed material proceeding being heard in open court; hear the appeal with the Supreme Court being unable to consider the materials subject to the closed material proceedings; be bound to allow the appeal; or be bound to refuse the appeal.[121] In essence, the Supreme Court would not be able to do justice to the appeal if it were not able to hear a closed material proceeding.[122]

In reaching his conclusion, Lord Neuberger recognized the importance of the principle of legality, but he concluded that this principle had to be interpreted according to the context and the purpose of the statute before the court.[123] As regards section 40(2) of the Constitutional Reform Act 2005, the provision was best understood as 'broad' as opposed to 'general'. It provided that all decisions of the Court of Appeal could be appealed to the Supreme Court unless this was precluded by another statute. Given that the Court of Appeal can hold closed material proceedings, this purpose could only be achieved by the broad provision of the Constitutional Reform Act if the Supreme Court were empowered to hold closed material proceedings.[124]

These different approaches illustrate how the principle of legality can be applied in a manner which gives greater or smaller amounts of discretionary power to the legislature, in this case as regards the legislature's ability to create closed material proceedings, which breach the common law human right to open justice, in turn providing legislative authority for the Supreme Court to create this right. Lord Neuberger's approach provides a greater discretionary area of judgment to the legislature, both through his approach to the right to open justice and his distinction between 'general' and 'broad' legislative provisions, enabling him to interpret 'broad' legislative provisions in a way which recognizes the practical need for closed material proceedings in certain situations. The approach taken by the minority is less flexible. They are less willing to admit that the principle of open justice may require a different approach in order to take

[117] Constitutional Reform Act 2005, s 40(5).
[118] Rules of the Supreme Court, r 29(1).
[119] Rules of the Supreme Court, r 27(3).
[120] *Bank Mellat v Her Majesty's Treasury (No 1)* (n 114) (Lord Reed).
[121] ibid, [39]–[42] (Lord Neuberger).
[122] ibid, [43] (Lord Neuberger).
[123] ibid, [55] (Lord Neuberger).
[124] ibid, [56] (Lord Neuberger).

account of practical situations and are less willing to recognize legislative provisions as 'general' as opposed to 'broad'.

Lord Neuberger's approach is more deferential than that of Lords Kerr, Hope, and Reed. His approach is more suited to situations in which courts are faced with contestable rights-issues. Given the difficulty surrounding the application of the right of open justice in these circumstances, it is arguable that Lord Neuberger's approach is more in line with democratic dialogue. The refusal to recognize the right of the Supreme Court to hear closed material proceedings could give rise to a range of practical problems, potentially creating a gap in the law which, we argued above, may provide a justification for remedial deference. Moreover, it is arguable that, in not applying the principle of legality rigidly, Lord Neuberger was facilitating democratic dialogue as it was clear that Parliament had debated generally whether the courts should be granted the power to hold closed material proceedings. The lack of express inclusion of the Supreme Court to hold closed material proceedings was because, at the time of the enactment of the Counter-Terrorism legislation, the Supreme Court did not exist. There was no need for the court to apply the principle of legality so as to fail to recognize the power of the Supreme Court to hold closed material proceedings given that the legislature had debated this issue and had provided clear wording empowering courts generally to hold these proceedings.

Nevertheless, Lords Kerr, Hope, and Reed's approach could be justified given the context of constitutional counter-balancing. The holding of closed material proceedings erodes a constitutional safeguard that courts are designed to protect—judicial review over the executive. Moreover, the principle of legality itself can be understood as a constitutional safeguard which should be applied rigidly in order to protect the constitutional role of the court, as opposed to being open to a purposive interpretation in a manner which may erode common law rights. The approach of the dissent, therefore, could be understood as a means of asserting constitutional counter-balance, especially when this is placed against the background of a series of interactions between domestic courts, the European Court of Human Rights and the legislature concerning the use of closed material proceedings as a means of balancing article 6 and the right to a fair trial, the common law right of open justice and the need to protect national security.

The disparate possible readings of democratic dialogue illustrate how democratic dialogue is facilitated to a greater or lesser degree. The dispute between the minority and the majority stems from their different interpretation of the constitutional role of the courts and whether this would be transgressed by the development of closed material proceedings for the Supreme Court. A more clear-cut example of the use of the common law as a means of protecting constitutional balance is found in the dicta of Lord Steyn in *Jackson v Attorney General*[125] and of Lord Hope in *AXA General Insurance Ltd v Lord Advocate*.[126] As discussed above,[127] in both of these cases dicta to the effect that courts may decide not to give effect to or would disapply legislation were made in the context of legislative provisions which were designed to remove the power of judicial review from the courts generally. Such a general threat to the power of the courts would justify a decision not to apply legislation as a means of constitutional counter-balancing.

The different form of inter-institutional interaction between the legislature and the judiciary also has an impact on how the legislature should respond to the application of the principle of legality by the courts. If courts apply the principle of legality in order

[125] See n 33. [126] See n 34. [127] See the discussion in Chapter 6.

to ensure that general provisions of legislation do not erode long-standing principles of the common law, or to ensure that general provisions do not give rise to breaches of common law rights when applied to specific individuals, then, in these situations, there should be little need for the legislature to respond to these decisions by re-enacting new legislative provisions. When acting in this manner, the court is acting in areas where the court is more suited to determining rights-issues. Democratic dialogue would be enhanced if the legislature were only to respond to these decisions in situations where the legislature had good reasons to conclude that the courts had provided a clear and specific definition of a contestable rights-issue, such that the actions of the court in defining the common law right failed to provide the necessary legislative input to resolve a contestable rights-issue.

Second, given the lack of a clear means through which to deal with remedial deference when applying the principle of legality, the legislature would be justified in responding to a judicial decision by modifying the legislative interpretation of the court where the court's interpretation relied upon the creation of administrative measures through which to ensure the protection of common law rights, or where the court has made a choice between possible means of interpreting legislation so as to comply with a common law right when that choice should have also had legislative input as it required the balancing of contestable rights and interests.

Moreover, as illustrated in *Ahmed*,[128] there may even be a justification for the legislature to enact emergency legislative provisions to reverse judicial decisions in order to prevent gaps in the law which could seriously erode other human rights or other interests. This is possibly illustrated in *Ahmed*, where the annulment of executive measures meant that the United Kingdom would be in breach of its obligations in international law and where the removal of the ability of the power to freeze the assets of terrorist suspects could have seriously impeded national security and potentially undermined the ability of the legislature to protect the right to life. However, it is important to recognize that, given its implications for the rule of law and other rights, this power of the legislature should only be used in extreme circumstances. Democratic dialogue is better served where courts, instead, used their discretion over the nature of the remedy in administrative law to suspend orders disapplying or annulling legislative or administrative measures. Moreover, democratic dialogue is enhanced further where, in these cases, courts provide guidance to the legislature as to how this situation may be resolved and provides clear explanations for why common law rights have been breached.

III. Conclusion

In this chapter, we have explored how inter-institutional interactions under both the Human Rights Act 1998 and the common law may facilitate, and hinder democratic dialogue. Our analysis illustrates how the extent to which democratic dialogue is facilitated depends more on the manner in which the legislature and the judiciary exercise their relative constitutional powers, as opposed to depending upon whether inter-institutional interactions arise predominantly through legal or political mechanisms. Nevertheless, there is less scope for the institutional interactions between the legislature and the judiciary that are generated by the principle of legality to facilitate democratic dialogue than occurs through the inter-institutional interactions which arise under the

[128] See n 110.

Human Rights Act 1998. This chapter has also illustrated that there is no one approach that is required to facilitate democratic dialogue. Rather, dialogue may be facilitated to a greater or lesser degree depending on the nature of the interactions between the legislature and the courts. In addition, there can be disagreement both as to the extent to which rights are contestable and as to the proper constitutional role of the legislature and the court in any particular constitution. This conclusion does not undermine the claim that democratic dialogue has value as a constitutional model and can be used to evaluate rights protections. However, it is important to recognize that democratic dialogue is not a panacea. It will not provide a perfect protection of rights and it requires other normative values. Nevertheless, it provides a viable framework from which to evaluate inter-institutional interactions.

8

Dialogue between Courts

Our analysis of inter-institutional interactions so far has focused on the interactions between two different types of institution—the courts and the legislature. The normative framework developed for interactions between the legislature and the courts focused on their different institutional features and the constitutional role of these different institutions. This, in turn, influenced their ability to reason about rights. One of the normative claims of the constitutional model of democratic dialogue is that this interaction helps to produce a better protection of human rights. The interactions between courts, however, are of a different nature. Our analysis would suggest that courts reason about rights in a similar manner. It would appear odd, therefore, to suggest that the model of democratic dialogue can provide a framework from which to analyse the relationship between different courts. This oddity is exacerbated by the inclusion of the word 'democratic'—how can a model of democratic dialogue apply to the interactions between two institutions that are neither democratically composed nor democratically accountable?

Despite these concerns, it is hard to deny that dialogue has been regarded as playing a role when describing interactions between courts. There are suggestions that the relationship between the UK courts and the European Court of Human Rights, as well as those between the UK courts and the Court of Justice of the European Union, can best be described as an example of dialogue; or that they should be interpreted in a manner which facilitates dialogue between the UK courts and the European courts. The existence of such dialogue is also acknowledged in judicial decisions in the United Kingdom,[1] by members of the UK judiciary[2] and also by the European Court of Human Rights.[3] There are also claims that the field of human rights is particularly suited to these interchanges.[4] Clearly, in the light of the decision of the United Kingdom to leave the

[1] See, for example, *Manchester City Council v Pinnock* [2010] UKSC 45, [2010] 3 WLR 1441.

[2] See, for example, M Arden, 'The Changing Judicial Role: Human Rights, Community Law and the Intention of Parliament' (2008) 67 Cambridge Law Journal 487; Lord Kerr, 'The Conversation between Strasbourg and National Courts: Dialogue or Dictation?' John Maurice Kelly Memorial Lecture, Trinity College Dublin 20 November 2009; Lord Kerr, 'The UK Supreme Court: The Modest Underworker of Strasbourg?' Clifford Chance Lecture, 25 January 2012; and Lord Reed, 'EU Law and the Supreme Court' The Sir Thomas More Lecture 2014.

[3] See, for example, the series of seminars organized by the European Court of Human Rights, 'Dialogue between the Judges' http://www.echr.coe.int/Documents/Dialogue_2006_ENG.pdf; http://www.echr.coe.int/Documents/Dialogue_2007_ENG.pdf; http://www.echr.coe.int/Documents/Dialogue_2008_ENG.pdf; http://echr.coe.int/Documents/Dialogue_2009_ENG.pdf; http://www.echr.coe.int/Documents/Dialogue_2010_ENG.pdf; and the more recent specific seminars organized under that series: 'What are the Limits to Evolutive Interpretation of the Convention?' http://www.echr.coe.int/Documents/Dialogue_2011_ENG.pdf; 'How Can We Ensure Greater Involvement of National Courts in the Convention System?' http://www.echr.coe.int/Documents/Dialogue_2011_ENG.pdf; 'Implementing the European Convention of Human Rights in Times of Economic Crisis' http://www.echr.coe.int/Documents/Dialogue_2013_ENG.pdf; and 'Implementation of the Judgments of the European Court of Human Rights: A Shared Judicial Responsibility?' http://www.echr.coe.int/Documents/Dialogue_2014_ENG.pdf.

[4] See B-O Bryde, 'The Constitutional Judge and the International Constitutionalist Dialogue' (2005) 80 Tulane Law Review 203; and M Cartabia, 'Europe and Rights: Taking Dialogue Seriously' (2009) 5 European Constitutional Law Review 5.

European Union, discussion of dialogue taking place between the Court of Justice of the European Union (CJEU) and the UK courts may, in the future, have more of a historical than a current importance. Nevertheless, an understanding of these interactions may be useful for other countries remaining in the European Union, as well as providing a means of evaluating the extent to which these interactions casts light on the claim that, through leaving the European Union, the United Kingdom would regain the sovereignty it appeared to have lost through the impact of directly effective EU law and the nature of the relationship between the UK courts and the CJEU.

As with our analysis of other areas of inter-institutional interactions and discussions of democratic dialogue, there is a plethora of terminology in the literature, which can lead to confusion. Before analysing whether democratic dialogue can apply to interactions between courts, we need first to explore some of this terminology. Anne-Marie Slaughter's work on judicial dialogue provides a useful means of clarifying and explaining the range of interactions between courts. Slaughter recognizes that dialogue takes place between domestic courts; between transnational, international, and supranational courts and between transnational courts and domestic courts. She refers to dialogue between national or regional courts across borders as 'horizontal communication'. For example, if UK courts were to refer to decisions of the Canadian Supreme Court, this would be horizontal communication. This often takes place informally as a form of monologue, where the decisions of one national court are not addressed to other courts, but where nevertheless courts in other jurisdictions may refer to these decisions in order to lend weight to their own conclusions, or to seek guidance in the reasoning of other courts in the face of a similar problem.[5]

Slaughter classifies dialogue between domestic and supranational courts as 'vertical' dialogue, regarding the interactions between domestic courts and both the CJEU and the European Court of Human Rights (ECtHR) as exemplars of this form of dialogue.[6] This form of dialogue is more structured and direct, being facilitated either directly through the preliminary reference procedure of article 267 TFEU, or indirectly through the right of petition of an individual to the ECtHR, where often an assessment of whether Convention rights have been breached requires the ECtHR to assess the conclusions of a national court that there had been no breach of Convention rights, particularly in the United Kingdom where the protection of human rights is directly linked to Convention rights. Slaughter also recognizes that there are examples of 'mixed vertical and horizontal communication' giving rise to 'mediated dialogue' where the supranational court takes account of the views of domestic courts, and often can derive principles of supranational law by taking account of the decisions of national courts.[7]

This chapter will focus on vertical dialogue, between the UK courts and the ECtHR and the CJEU. It is not concerned predominantly with horizontal dialogue or other forms of informal 'trans-judicial communication',[8] 'transnational judicial conversation',[9] or 'transnational judicial dialogue'[10] which take place informally between national courts. However, the recognition of these interactions is relevant when assessing the way in which supranational courts refer to the decisions of national courts for

[5] A-M Slaughter, 'A Typology of Transjudicial Communication' (1994) 29 University of Richmond Law Review 99.

[6] ibid, 106–11. [7] ibid, 111 and 113. [8] Slaughter (n 5).

[9] C McCrudden, 'A Common Law of Human Rights? Transnational Conversations on Constitutional Rights' (2000) 20 Oxford Journal of Legal Studies 499.

[10] MA Waters, 'Meeting Norms and Identity: The Role of Transnational Judicial Dialogue in Creating and Enforcing International Law' (2005) 93 Georgetown Law Journal 487.

factual purposes. This occurs in particular when the CJEU refers to decisions and laws in the member states in order to determine the common constitutional traditions of the member states of the European Union, or when the ECtHR evaluates different interpretations of Convention rights across the signatory states to the ECHR. It will argue that interactions currently take place between the UK courts and both the CJEU and the ECtHR. It will provide a framework that helps to explain how these interactions may be used to facilitate the achievement of normative values underpinning democratic dialogue.

It is important to recognize the limits of this framework. First, there is insufficient awareness in these exchanges of the role of other institutions of the constitution. Although this chapter focuses on judicial interaction, nevertheless the model of democratic dialogue requires the judiciary to be aware of the constitutional role of the legislature and the executive. A failure to bear these concerns in mind can undermine the ability of interactions between courts to further democratic dialogue. Second, it is important to recognize that this chapter is not arguing that the current interactions which take place between the national courts and both European courts facilitate the achievement of the normative values of democratic dialogue perfectly. However, the chapter will argue that it is possible to propose a normative framework for inter-institutional interactions between courts which can facilitate democratic dialogue, but that these interactions are not sufficient to achieve these values without being supplemented by interactions between the judiciary and the domestic and European legislatures.

I. Institutional and Constitutional Differences

If we are to provide a normative framework for interactions between the UK courts and the CJEU and the ECtHR, we need to assess the institutional and constitutional differences between these courts to determine how far interactions may help to provide a better protection of rights, to facilitate deliberative democracy, with the possibility of citizen engagement in democratic deliberation, and to provide an effective check and balance between these two institutions. The starting point for this analysis is to recognize that there are institutional differences between the UK courts and the ECtHR and between the UK courts and the CJEU. The CJEU is a supra-national court. It is a general court which determines issues of EU law and its members develop greater expertise in EU law than the UK courts through applying EU law on a regular basis. The UK courts are domestic courts, focusing on analysing the law of England and Wales and of Scotland and Northern Ireland. The CJEU is also in a better position to understand rights-issues from a European as opposed to a domestic perspective than the UK courts. The CJEU hears cases predominantly through article 267 references, where domestic courts refer questions of EU law to the European Court of Justice which determines the issue of EU law. By receiving an array of applications, the CJEU is in a better position to take a pan-European view than the UK courts.

Similar institutional differences exist between the UK courts and the ECtHR. The ECtHR is an international court whose role is to apply the European Convention of Human Rights and to ensure that the signatory states to the Convention are not reneging on their obligation to uphold Convention rights. This means that, institutionally, the ECtHR has greater expertise as regards Convention rights, given that it specializes in analysing Convention rights as opposed to analysing more general issues of domestic law. In addition, in a similar manner to the CJEU, the ECtHR is more able to adopt a pan-European perspective. It hears cases from all of the signatory states across

Europe. Moreover, it can hear representations from other signatory states as to how a particular Convention right would be interpreted in their country both as these states represent themselves in cases brought against the states and when making representations in cases brought against other states. This places the ECtHR in a better position institutionally than the UK courts to take a pan-European view, being aware of how Convention rights are perceived across the states and also recognizing whether there is a European perspective on how to balance competing rights or interests.

These similar institutional differences between the UK courts and the ECtHR and the CJEU already suggest one way in which the UK courts and the European courts may be better placed to reason about rights. The UK courts will be better placed to assess the United Kingdom's perspective on how rights should be interpreted and be able to ascertain when a general right which is protected in Europe may nevertheless harm long-standing rights protected in the United Kingdom, or harm a delicate cultural balance between competing rights or competing interests. The ECtHR and the CJEU on the other hand, are better placed to assess when a domestic protection of rights nevertheless falls short of the protections regarded as providing a minimum European standard of rights or where, in the case of the CJEU, the way in which the UK protects rights may nevertheless harm the values of the European Union.

It is these institutional differences which underpin the concept of the 'margin of appreciation' in the ECtHR. Similar factors that influence whether the courts are more or less suited to resolving a rights issue as compared to the legislature also influence the degree of the margin of appreciation. When faced with a contestable or watershed rights-issue, there are good arguments for limiting the role of the ECtHR to that of ensuring that the core element of Convention rights has not been transgressed, granting a wider margin of appreciation to the UK courts in order to allow the United Kingdom to balance these competing interests in a way which is more likely to reflect the United Kingdom's views as to the relative merits of competing rights, or a weighing of competing interests. The margin of appreciation recognizes that the rights-issue may be better resolved at the domestic as opposed to the European level. However, this need not mean that the issue should be better resolved by the UK courts as opposed to the UK legislature or the UK executive. Although there is still a role for the UK courts when the ECtHR grants a wide margin of appreciation, the extent to which the UK courts should play this role depends upon the relative institutional and constitutional differences between the UK courts and the legislature and the executive. Similar arguments can be made as regards the inter-relationship between the UK courts and the CJEU. However, the CJEU does not accord a margin of appreciation in the same manner, due to the different constitutional relationship between the CJEU and the UK courts and between directly effective EU law and national law and between Convention rights and national law.

The institutional differences between the UK courts and the CJEU and the ECtHR provide one factor which should influence inter-institutional interactions between the two courts. Inter-institutional interactions may facilitate constitutional collaboration. This can occur when UK courts provide information to the European courts as to UK perspectives on the scope of human rights and the way in which the UK balances competing rights and interests. In addition, the European Courts can ensure that, when reaching these conclusions, the United Kingdom does not provide a weaker protection of rights than the pan-European consensus, providing an additional check to ensure that rights are effectively protected. This helps protections of rights to reflect community values, whilst also ensuring that national perspectives on how to balance competing rights and interests does not transgress a common consensus as to the core components of a particular human right. Moreover, by passing information to the European Courts about the consensus reached in the United Kingdom, this provides the European Courts with the ability to modify the understandings of the common core component of human rights, enabling the European Courts to modify the content of the core components of a right to reflect common European perspective as societies across Europe evolve. This latter form of exchange may provide for mutual checks, hopefully leading to better protections of rights both as a European standard and as regards domestic protections of rights.

Although these institutional differences are generally common to both the ECtHR and the CJEU, there are nevertheless differences as to the relative constitutional positions of the ECtHR and the CJEU to the UK courts. The ECtHR is a court in international law. Although the UK is bound by article 46 ECHR to ensure that it adheres to judgments of the ECtHR addressed to the United Kingdom, there is no obligation in international law for domestic courts to adhere to all of the decisions of the ECtHR. The ECtHR does not stand in a hierarchal relationship to national courts. In addition, it is clear that, subject to the requirements of article 46 ECHR, the United Kingdom determines the nature of the relationship between the UK courts and the ECtHR. Moreover, as a court of international law, the relationship between the ECtHR and the national courts, in a manner similar to the Convention rights themselves, is only governed by international law to the extent that this has been incorporated into national law. This is tempered by the constitutional position of the ECtHR, under the Convention, to provide authoritative determination of Convention rights.

In contrast, the CJEU is referred to as an institution of supra-national as opposed to international law.[11] This is due to the primacy of directly effective provisions of EU law, developed by the CJEU as a principle of EU law. From the perspective of EU law, whenever there is a conflict between directly effective principles of EU law and national law, including primary legislation and constitutional provisions, directly effective EU law is to be applied and not the national law. Moreover, EU law has extended the concept of state liability to domestic courts, such that, when national courts commit a sufficiently serious breach of EU law—if, for example, the Supreme Court were to fail to fulfil its obligation, where applicable, to refer a question of EU law to the CJEU under article 267—an action for damages may lie against the national court in EU law.[12] Moreover, the CJEU is not a specialist human rights court. Rather its specialization is EU law. As such, the court has to balance human rights against the other aims and values of the EU. This may mean that, on occasion, the national as opposed to the European courts may be better able to protect human rights. These differences affect both the way in which constitutional counter-balancing measures may operate between the CJEU and the UK courts and the ECtHR and the UK courts, in addition to giving rise to different mechanisms regulating the institutional interactions between the different European courts and the UK courts.

The different nature of the relationship between the UK courts and the CJEU also appears to raise the same problem for the application of the constitutional model of democratic dialogue as we encountered in Chapter 6 when we investigated whether democratic dialogue was suited to the UK constitution. In the UK constitution, we

[11] The difference between an international and a supra-national organization is a matter of degree. Slaughter, for example, refers to both the CJEU and the ECtHR as supra-national courts given the right of individual petition to the ECtHR. See Slaughter (n 5); and L Helfer and A-M Slaughter, 'Towards a Theory of Effective Supranational Adjudication' (1997) 107 Yale Law Journal 273.

[12] C-224/01 *Gerhard Köbler v Republik Österreich* [2003] ECR I-10239, [2004] QB 848.

were concerned about parliamentary sovereignty, which appeared to undermine the requirement of democratic dialogue that no one institution is always able to ensure that its will prevails in order to resolve institutional interactions. When applying the model of democratic dialogue to interactions between national courts and the CJEU, the primacy of EU law would appear to cause a similar problem. This principle asserts that directly effective EU law overrides all forms of national law, including constitutional protections of human rights. This would appear to imply that the CJEU will always be able to prevail over national courts, thus undermining the applicability of the model of democratic dialogue to interactions between the UK courts and the CJEU. How can there be interactions between equal institutions if, according to the primacy of directly effective EU law, the determinations of one—the CJEU—are always meant to prevail?

In order to provide a more detailed model of court-to-court dialogue therefore, we need to discuss the ECtHR and the CJEU separately. We will first examine the relationship between the UK courts and the ECtHR, before examining that between the UK courts and the CJEU. When discussing the latter, we will first have to explain how an application of the model of democratic dialogue can be possible given the challenge posed by the primacy of EU law. This will be answered by accepting as accurate some, but not all, of the accounts of constitutional pluralism as applied to the European Union. It is this evaluation which indirectly casts doubt on some of the claims that the United Kingdom lost sovereignty through joining the EU, which will be regained when the United Kingdom leaves the EU. This bare assertion misunderstands the more subtle nature of the relationship between directly effective EU law and national law, as well as the relationship between the UK courts and the CJEU.

II. Dialogue between the UK Courts and the European Court of Human Rights

As mentioned above, the European Court of Human Rights and the UK courts are not part of a hierarchical relationship where the ECtHR hears appeals from decisions of the UK courts, with the decision of the ECtHR replacing that of the UK court. Nor does the ECtHR determine the precise nature of the relationship between the ECtHR and national courts. Article 46 of the Convention does require that the United Kingdom, as a state, complies with decisions of the ECtHR to which the United Kingdom is a party. As an institution of the state, this obligation extends to the courts. However, there are no precise obligations as regards decisions of the ECtHR addressed to other countries on the same issue. As far as UK law is concerned, these are found in section 2(1) of the Human Rights Act 1998 which states that the UK courts must 'take into account' decisions of the ECtHR when applying Convention rights. Following Lord Bingham's seminal judgment in *Ullah* the UK courts generally follow a clear and constant line of case law of the ECtHR.[13] However, there are examples of where the national courts will refuse to follow a clear and constant line of case law, as well as examples of where the national courts are more willing to go beyond the current case law of the ECtHR.

Where the clear and constant line of the decisions of the ECtHR is inconsistent with 'some fundamental substantive or procedural aspect of our law' or when the reasoning of

[13] *R (Ullah) v Special Adjudicator* [2004] UKHL 26, [2004] 2 AC 323.

the Strasbourg court appears to 'overlook or misunderstand some argument or point of principle' of English law, then the UK courts may decide not to follow a decision of the ECtHR.[14] UK courts are less willing to refuse to follow a decision of the Grand Chamber of the ECtHR. This would appear to be possible only if the Grand Chamber were to 'ignore a truly fundamental principle of our law' or demonstrate a 'most egregious oversight or misunderstanding'.[15] On the other hand, where the ECtHR grants a large margin of appreciation, national courts enjoy a choice as to whether to interpret Convention rights beyond their interpretation in the current case law of the ECtHR.[16]

The approach taken to section 2 rests, at least in part, on the acknowledgement that the ECtHR has the requisite constitutional authority to determine the content of Convention rights. In *Ullah*, Lord Bingham justified the requirement of the national courts to 'follow any clear and constant jurisprudence of the ECtHR' as this 'reflects the fact that the European Convention is an international instrument, the correct interpretation of which can be authoritatively expounded only by the ECtHR'.[17] Even though there is no clear hierarchical relationship between the two courts, the recognition of the authoritative position of the ECtHR to determine the meaning of Convention rights does place the court in a form of quasi-hierarchical relationship. However, this relationship is one where the UK courts are also able, through their interpretation of section 2(1), to determine partly for themselves. This relationship helps to ensure that it is not the case that the ECtHR is always able to enforce its view of Convention rights on national courts. This is reinforced by the way in which some means of inter-institutional interaction between the UK courts and the ECtHR can be used as a means of exercising constitutional counter-balancing.

Merris Amos argues that the relationship between the UK courts and the ECtHR gives rise to three opportunities for inter-institutional interaction. First, this can occur when the UK courts refuse to follow a decision of the ECtHR because it considers that the judgment of the ECtHR is wrong. Second, interactions can occur when there is a greater margin of appreciation. Third, interactions can occur when there is a range of decisions by the ECtHR but, because the ECtHR is not bound by precedent in the same manner as the UK courts, there is no clear and constant line of case law.[18] Of these three examples, the first shares characteristics of mechanisms of constitutional counter-balancing as well as measures of constitutional collaboration. The other two forms of interaction have greater potential to facilitate constitutional collaboration. Given their different roles, democratic dialogue applies differently to these distinct forms of inter-institutional interaction. In addition to the interactions identified by Amos, we also need to recognize an extreme form of constitutional counter-balancing mechanism; where the UK courts consistently refuse to follow a decision of the ECtHR. Although there are no clear examples of this to date, it is arguable that the refusal of the Supreme Court to issue a declaration of incompatibility in prisoner voting cases comes close to an example of this form of constitutional counter-balancing. We will look first at how

[14] *Manchester City Council v Pinnock* [2010] UKSC 45, [2011] 1 All ER 285, [48] (Lord Neuberger).

[15] *R (Chester) v Secretary of State for Justice* [2013] UKSC 63, [2014] AC 271, [27] (Lord Mance).

[16] See, for example, *Moohan v Lord Advocate* [2014] UKSC 67, [2015] AC 901; *Rabone v Pennine Care NHS Foundation Trust* [2012] UKSC 2, [2012] 2 AC 72; and *R (Hicks) v Commissioner of the Police of the Metropolis* [2014] EWCA Civ 3, [2014] 1 WLR 2152.

[17] *R (Ullah) v Special Adjudicator* (n 13); *Manchester City Council v Pinnock* (n 14).

[18] M Amos, 'The Dialogue between the United Kingdom Courts and the European Court of Human Rights' (2010) 61 International and Comparative Law Quarterly 557.

interactions between the UK courts and the ECtHR can facilitate constitutional collaboration, before examining constitutional counter-balancing mechanisms.

A. Constitutional collaboration

The ECtHR's development of the margin of appreciation provides a good means of facilitating constitutional collaboration which reflects the relative institutional strengths of the ECtHR and the national courts. The margin of appreciation should apply to contestable rights-issues, recognizing that national courts, being better placed to assess how their community wishes to resolve this issue, are more institutionally suited to determining the precise way in which to resolve the human rights issue. The ECtHR's function is more of a checking role, ensuring that the resolution of the national court does not transgress a core understanding of the Convention right. Dialogue is able to take place because the ECtHR is exercising judicial restraint. Rather than using its position to provide a precise resolution of a rights-issue, determining the scope of the Convention right in question, the court instead grants a margin of appreciation, allowing the signatory states greater discretion to resolve a particular rights issue.

Slaughter refers to this form of democratic dialogue as intermediated mixed vertical and horizontal dialogue.[19] Her classification recognizes the role of the ECtHR in granting a margin of appreciation, allowing the national courts to develop their own resolution of contestable rights-issues. This designation also recognizes that dialogue occurs informally through the ECtHR referring to the decisions of the different national courts when they apply Convention rights in areas where there is a wide margin of appreciation. Dialogue is informal as the decisions of the national courts need not be addressed to Convention rights and are referred to as examples from other jurisdictions, often when these national courts were not intending to address the ECtHR or to discuss the content of Convention rights. Given the close correlation between the Human Rights Act 1998 and Convention rights, the UK courts are more likely to refer to the Convention when determining issues within the margin of appreciation. However, other constitutional courts may refer to their own constitutional protections of human rights. Constitutional collaboration is facilitated when the ECtHR is able to refer to these decisions as evidence of an emerging consensus across Europe, using this to determine the scope of the margin of appreciation. For constitutional collaboration to operate effectively, national courts need to determine the contestable rights-issue for themselves, taking account of reasons for when an issue may be more suited for resolution by democratic institutions as opposed to the courts. This then ensures that the ECtHR can obtain accurate information when it carries out legal research to determine whether there is a European consensus concerning the resolution of a contestable rights-issue. Also, by examining the reasoning provided in these judgments, the ECtHR and the national courts may be able to collaborate informally to help provide better resolutions of contestable rights issues. Collaboration does not occur here because either of the courts gives weight to the opinion of the other. Rather, each court evaluates the reasoning of the other according to the merits provided in the judgment.

One example of constitutional collaboration operating in this manner concerns the issue of adoption by unmarried couples, including, but not limited to, same-sex couples. The issue arose in the UK courts in *Re P*, a decision of the House of Lords concerning the inability of unmarried couples to apply to adopt a child, whereas married

[19] Slaughter (n 5).

couples were able to apply to adopt a child.[20] Although there was no case directly discussing this issue in the ECtHR case law, nevertheless there were other cases referring to adoption where the ECtHR had granted a wide margin of appreciation. In *Fretté v France,* for example, the Strasbourg court did not find a breach of a Convention right when a French court had refused to allow a single homosexual man to apply to adopt a child, even though it was clear that this decision was based on his sexual orientation.[21] In reaching this conclusion, by a narrow majority, the ECtHR granted a wide margin of appreciation to the signatory states, recognizing that there was, at the time, 'little common ground' regarding the prevention of discrimination on the grounds of sexual orientation, with the law appearing to be in a transitional phase.[22] As such, national authorities had a better ability to determine the extent to which article 8 ECHR included the right of non-married or homosexual couples to adopt. The granting of a wide margin of appreciation by the ECtHR can help to facilitate democratic dialogue, particularly as this wide margin of appreciation is provided to give national authorities a greater ability to determine a contestable issue.

Following the decision in *Fretté v France*, the ECtHR in *EB v France* concluded by a majority of ten votes to seven that articles 8 and 14 ECHR had been breached when a woman who was in a stable relationship with another woman had been refused permission to adopt predominantly on grounds of her sexual orientation.[23] In reaching this conclusion, the ECtHR stated that 'where sexual orientation is in issue, there is a need for particularly convincing and weighty reasons to justify a difference in treatment regarding rights falling within Article 8',[24] observing in addition that the Convention was a 'living instrument interpreted in the light of present-day conditions'.[25] Although the ECtHR was conscious of the need to grant a wide margin of appreciation in the face of contestable rights-issues, it also recognised the need to keep abreast of any emerging consensus of opinion across Europe which may require the margin of appreciation to be narrowed. The emerging consensus regarding differential treatment on the basis of sexual orientation led the ECtHR to reach a different conclusion from its earlier decision which granted a wider margin of appreciation. The ECtHR is acting in a manner which can facilitate informal constitutional collaboration, the decisions of courts across Europe helping to provide information as to an emerging consensus regarding the need for Convention rights to prevent sexual orientation discrimination.

Lord Hoffmann's judgment in *Re G* is sensitive to the modifications of the margin of appreciation in the ECtHR case law that is indirectly relevant to the issue before the House of Lords in that case. After recognizing the modification of the margin of appreciation, Lord Hoffmann concludes that the House of Lords should not be concerned about potentially moving beyond the decisions of the ECtHR when reaching the conclusion that the prevention of unmarried couples from applying for adoption is contrary to Convention rights. He goes on to recognize, in obiter dicta, that even if *EB v France* had not been decided, or if the ECtHR were to revert back to its decision in *Fretté v France,* nevertheless the UK courts should, when acting within a wide margin of appreciation from the ECtHR, decide the issue for themselves, including going beyond the current Convention case law. When dealing with an area where there is a wide margin of appreciation, Lord Hoffmann advocates that it is 'for the court in the United Kingdom to interpret arts 8 and 14 and to apply the division between the decision-making powers of courts and Parliament in the way which

[20] [2008] UKHL 38, [2009] AC 173.
[21] *Fretté v France* (2002) 38 EHRR 438.
[22] ibid, para 41.
[23] *EB v France* Application No 43546/02, [2007] ECHR 211.
[24] ibid, para 91.
[25] ibid, para 92.

appears appropriate for the United Kingdom'.[26] This ability of the national authorities to resolve a rights-issue within the margin of appreciation, thereby interpreting Convention rights under the Human Rights Act 1998 beyond the current case law at Strasbourg, was also recognized by the other judges in the House of Lords.[27] This can facilitate constitutional collaboration both by allowing the national courts to develop their own decisions, reflecting their better ability to reason about rights in a local situation, and through informal dialogue as the ECtHR takes account of the decisions of domestic courts, using this information to determine whether there is an emerging European consensus on rights.

Constitutional collaboration may arise in a similar manner when there is no clear and constant line of case law in the decisions of the ECtHR. However, it is important to recognize that the constitutional collaboration which may take place here is of a different type from that which may arise within the margin of appreciation. The inter-institutional interactions which take place here are not based on the different institutional features of the ECtHR and the national courts. Rather, as with horizontal dialogue between national or supranational courts,[28] or trans-judicial dialogue/conversation,[29] this occurs informally, with courts referring to judgments of other jurisdictions as they recognize they are engaged in the common purpose of interpreting Convention rights. Interactions occur informally as courts refer to the judgments of other jurisdictions in terms of the merits of the reasoning provided in the judgments referred to, rather than due to the recognition of any hierarchical relationship. This is tempered with regard to the interactions between the ECtHR and the national courts given the quasi-hierarchical relationship between these two courts and the recognition of the constitutional authority of the ECtHR to determine the content of Convention rights. Such interactions may allow the courts to generate better interpretations of Convention rights,[30] as well as providing additional legitimacy to the conclusions reached by any particular court.[31] These inter-institutional interactions may facilitate democratic dialogue where national courts are free to adopt their own interpretations of unclear decisions of the ECtHR, focusing on the reasoning of the ECtHR in the decisions it analyses as opposed to focusing on the relative institutional or constitutional authority of the national courts and the ECtHR. Moreover, in interacting in this manner, courts should focus on the reasoning process and the persuasive authority of legal judgments; both as regards the national courts looking at the decisions of the ECtHR and the ECtHR when it looks to the judgments of national courts in order to examine its own case law.[32]

It is harder to find examples of informal institutional interactions taking place between the UK courts and the ECtHR. Where the UK courts cannot find a clear and constant line of case law, the UK courts consider themselves free to develop Convention rights, taking account of the reasoning of the ECtHR but doing so in a way which enables them to develop their own interpretation of Convention rights. This lack of clear examples is understandable given that in some cases where the national court

[26] *Re P* (n 20) [37].

[27] ibid, [50] (Lord Hope); [118]–[119] (Lady Hale); [126]–[130] (Lord Mance). Lord Walker accepted the choice was for national authorities to determine rights within the margin of appreciation, but argued that this decision was more suited to the legislature than the courts [82].

[28] Slaughter (n 5).

[29] See McCrudden (n 9) and Waters (n 10).

[30] Waters (n 10) and L Helfer and A-M Slaughter, 'Towards a Theory of Effective Supranational Adjudication' (1997) 107 Yale Law Journal 273.

[31] McCrudden (n 9).

[32] See C Romano, 'Deciphering the Grammar of International Jurisprudential Dialogue' (2008–9) 41 New York University Journal of International Law and Politics 755.

develops its own interpretation of a Convention right, the court will develop the case law to conclude that the individual's Convention rights have been breached, using the provisions of the Human Rights Act 1998 to provide a remedy. This means that there will be no opportunity for this case to go before the ECtHR given that the state does not have a right to petition the ECtHR. The only exception would be where the UK courts issued a declaration of incompatibility, which would mean an individual will have exhausted her rights before the domestic courts, but would still have a right to petition the ECtHR given that her Convention rights will still be breached despite the declaration of incompatibility. This means, again, that interactions between the two courts tend to be formal as opposed to informal.

Formal interactions may occur in cases where the UK courts use the lack of a clear and constant line of case law as a justification to distinguish a case from the ECtHR which appears to favour the individual in favour of other cases from the ECtHR which do not. In this scenario, the individual whose Convention rights are not protected will have exhausted her domestic remedies and is therefore able to, and is likely to, exercise her right to petition the ECtHR. One example of this is *Animal Defenders International Ltd* which involved a challenge to the Broadcasting Act 2003 which prohibited the broadcasting of political advertisements.[33] However, the institutional interactions which took place between the domestic court and the ECtHR also illustrates how such interactions may fail to fully facilitate democratic dialogue.

When Parliament enacted the Broadcasting Act 2003, it issued a statement under section 19(1)(b) of the Human Rights Act, recognizing that the legislation might be contrary to Convention rights. In particular, as discussed in Parliament and in the Joint Committee on Human Rights, there was concern that the blanket ban on the broadcasting of political advertisements contravened the decision of the ECtHR in *Verein gegen Tierfabriken* (*VgT*).[34] In *VgT* the applicants wished to broadcast an advertisement dissuading the consumption of meat in reaction to television commercials for meat products which encouraged the consumption of meat. In a similar manner to the Broadcasting Act, Swiss legislation prohibited the broadcast of political advertisements on television and radio. The ECtHR recognized the need to protect public opinion from being swayed by those with more financial means than others, in this case from powerful financial groups with commercial influence. It also recognised the stronger impact of television as opposed to other advertising mediums. Nevertheless, as Swiss law could allow commercial entities to sway public opinion through selling goods, but would not allow campaign groups to advertise the alternative viewpoint, there were concerns that article 10, protecting the right to freedom of expression, had been breached. The ECtHR did not believe that the Swiss Government had provided sufficient justification for this differential impact and, therefore, concluded that article 10 ECHR had indeed been breached.

The facts of *VgT* were very similar to those in *Animal Defenders International*. Animal Defenders International wished to broadcast an advertisement to protect the rights of animals in their 'My Mate's a Primate' campaign. Nevertheless, Lord Bingham, giving the leading judgment in the House of Lords, concluded that there was no breach of Convention rights. He relied, in part, on observations in *Murphy v Ireland*, a case decided after *VgT* which concerned the ban on the broadcast of political and religious advertisements. Although the facts of *Murphy v Ireland* concerned religious expression,

[33] *R (Animal Defenders International Ltd) v Secretary of State for Culture, Media and Sport* [2008] UKHL 15, [2008] 1 AC 1312.

[34] *VgT Verein gegen Tierfabriken v Switzerland* [2001] EHRR 24699/94, (2001) 34 EHRR 159.

nevertheless Lord Bingham referred to the case to reinforce his assessment that there had been no breach of Convention rights in *Animal Defenders International*. In particular, he concluded that *VgT* had not taken account of the impact of permitting political advertising on the fairness of the democratic process in the run up to elections. In particular, he was concerned that viewers of advertisements advocating particular political opinions will accept these opinions through dint of repetition, rather than their persuasive force. This may mean that elections results were partially dependent upon whether political parties had sufficient resources to fund political advertising, or whether social advertisers who had a similar outlook to a particular political party were well-funded and therefore able to advertise indirectly in support of the views of that party.[35] The greater immediacy of television broadcasting in particular justified the pressing need for a blanket restriction on political advertising. Lord Scott and Lady Hale agreed with Lord Bingham, focusing in particular on the extent to which decisions of the ECtHR are fact-specific and recognizing the different facts in *VgT* and *Animal Defenders International Ltd*. The House of Lords were also influenced by the detailed parliamentary debate, and the scrutiny of the Joint Committee of Human Rights. In particular, they gave great weight to their assessment that it would be impossible to provide a precise rule which would prevent the damage to general elections from allowing for the broadcast of political advertisements, whilst allowing for social advertisements which advocated particular viewpoints.

Animal Defenders International petitioned the ECtHR, where the Grand Chamber of the ECtHR agreed with the conclusion of the House of Lords, by nine votes to eight, that there had been no violation of article 10 ECHR.[36] In reaching its conclusion, the ECtHR classified the measure as a 'general measure'. When determining whether a 'general measure' was a proportionate restriction, the task of the ECtHR was not to determine 'whether less restrictive rules should have been adopted' or 'whether the State could prove that, without the prohibition, the legitimate aim would not be achieved. Rather the core issue is whether, in adopting the general measure and striking the balance it did, the legislature acted within the margin of appreciation afforded to it.'[37] The ECtHR also recognized that the rule was designed to ensure equality in the electoral process, recognizing the breadth of approaches as each country determines its own version of the democratic process, such that the margin of appreciation in this area may be greater.[38] The ECtHR also recognized that the precise issue in this case concerned the need to balance the 'right to impart information and ideas of general interest which the public is entitled to receive with, on the other hand, the authorities' desire to protect the democratic debate and process from distortion by powerful financial groups with advantageous access to influential media'.[39] When carrying out its assessment of the proportionality of the restriction, the ECtHR referred to the judgment of the House of Lords, and the deliberations of Parliament and the report of the Joint Committee on Human Rights, as well as recognizing the access to other media available to Animal Defenders International.[40]

The decision of the ECtHR marks a move away from the approach in *VgT*. It is also possible to see influences of the approach of the House of Lords on the decision of the ECtHR, albeit that these influences are indirect as opposed to direct. Having

[35] *R (Animal Defenders International Ltd) v Secretary of State for Culture, Media and Sport* (n 33) [29].

[36] *Animal Defenders International Ltd v The United Kingdom* [2013] ECHR 48876/08.

[37] ibid, para 110. [38] ibid, para 111. [39] ibid, para 112.

[40] ibid, paras 114–16.

taken account of the reasoning in the House of Lords, the ECtHR focuses more clearly on the general need to regulate elections, and is also willing to grant a wider margin of appreciation in this regard than it did in *VgT*. Also, more attention is paid to the alternative means of advertising open to Animal Defenders International, in newspapers and on the internet. This assessment was also looked at by the House of Lords. Moreover, the ECtHR was more willing to regard the general measure as justified given the careful democratic debate of this issue during the enactment of the Broadcasting Act 2003. In addition, this is arguably influenced by the approach of the House of Lords where greater deference was paid to Parliament.

This interaction between the UK courts and the ECtHR, therefore, can be seen as an example of informal dialogue which can give rise to indirect constitutional collaboration, with the UK courts and the ECtHR working together to help clarify the meaning of a Convention right when faced with a lack of a clear and constant line of case law. The interaction is informal as the ECtHR is influenced by the reasoning of the House of Lords on the basis of its assessment of the argument found in the judgment. No weight is given to this conclusion because it stemmed from the House of Lords. Nevertheless, there are difficulties with the approach of the ECtHR and the UK courts in this case which detract from the ability of this interaction to facilitate democratic dialogue. First, as noted above, these interactions are only likely to arise directly when the UK courts are using the lack of a clear and constant line of case law to distinguish a decision of the ECtHR which appears to protect Convention rights when the UK courts believe that Convention rights have not been breached. In such examples, the national court is not just choosing between competing ways of interpreting what may appear to be contradictory case law. Rather, it is specifically choosing to ignore one decision or, in *Animal Defenders International* to distinguish a case before the ECtHR from the one before the domestic court. In these circumstances, the court needs a stronger reason for choosing to distinguish a case of the ECtHR than a mere disagreement with its conclusions. It could be argued that the House of Lords did have a good enough justification to reach this conclusion, given the good reasons to defer to Parliament on this issue and the concern that the *VgT* case had ignored the importance of the regulation of political speech and the need to ensure that it was not influenced by wealth. Nevertheless, care needs to be taken to ensure that these inter-institutional interactions facilitate as opposed to hinder democratic dialogue.

Second, even when inter-institutional interactions do occur in this manner, they take place informally. If these informal interactions are to lead to better definitions of Convention rights, it is important that each court focuses on evaluating the arguments found in other court decisions. Courts should not be influenced by the authority of the institution taking the decision, or on institutional features unless the decision also concerns areas where a greater margin of appreciation would be granted. Moreover, for dialogue to be facilitated, courts need to provide a clear account of their reasons for interpreting a Convention right in a particular manner. The decision of the ECtHR in *Animal Defenders International* can be criticized in this regard. As Tom Lewis argues, in classifying some measures as 'general measures' which can be justified in a different manner from 'blanket bans', the ECtHR created a new approach whose provenance is hard to discern from previous case law. It may also be hard to distinguish 'general measures' from 'blanket bans', despite the fact that the ECtHR applies proportionality differently in these two cases.[41] Whilst there may be good grounds for delineating

[41] T Lewis, '*Animal Defenders International v UK*: Sensible Dialogue or a Bad Case of Strasbourg Jitters' (2014) 77 Modern Law Review 460.

between 'blanket bans' and 'general measures', the difficulty of distinguishing between these two types of legislation, when no clarification is given, may undermine the ability of these informal interactions to improve the interpretation of Convention rights.

Lewis goes further in his criticism of the ECtHR in *Animal Defenders International*, suggesting a further problem that may prevent inter-institutional interactions from facilitating democratic dialogue. He argues that the ECtHR could possibly be accused of reacting to hostile pressures from the UK media as opposed to engaging in constructive dialogue. Whilst not wishing to cast doubt on the motives of the ECtHR, the ability to make such criticisms demonstrates the importance of providing clear reasons for judicial conclusions and of ensuring that courts engaging in these informal interactions focus on the persuasive force of judgments from other jurisdictions and not on other factors. If both courts in reaching their conclusions are influenced by public opinion, this can help to facilitate the engagement of citizens, enabling judgments to reflect the views of society. However, to ensure that this facilitates wider deliberative democracy, there needs to be greater transparency in the reasoning process and a need to evaluate and critically reflect on these opinions if they are to be used to reflect genuine societal preferences for a particular manner in which to balance human rights with other rights or interests.

B. Constitutional counter-balancing

There are two forms of inter-institutional interaction which are more suited as a means of exercising constitutional counter-balancing than as a means of facilitating constitutional collaboration. First, there are interactions which arise when the UK courts refuse to follow a decision of the ECtHR not because they are able to distinguish the decision from a clear and constant line of cases, or because it is not possible to determine a clear and constant line of cases, but because the UK courts consider that the decision is wrong. Second, constitutional counter-balancing may occur indirectly in situations where the UK courts accept a decision of the ECtHR and its definition of Convention rights, but nevertheless indirectly undermine the decision by exercising their discretion not to issue a declaration of incompatibility. These interactions are best understood as achieving constitutional counter-balancing as the interactions are neither an informal means of collaboration to determine the meaning of Convention rights, nor interactions based on the relative institutional competences of the courts. Rather, they are examples of the UK courts intervening on constitutional grounds, either because the ECtHR has made an error which questions the validity of the grounds for its decision, or because the ECtHR has transgressed the proper constitutional bounds of its power. As such, these mechanisms should be used sparingly if they are to facilitate democratic dialogue.

There would appear to be two circumstances in which the UK courts will refuse to follow a decision of the ECtHR. The clearest statement of these limits is found in the decision of Lord Neuberger in *Pinnock*, where he provides a summary of section 2(1) based on earlier case law, summarizing the law to explain that UK courts are not required to adhere to decisions of the ECtHR but:

> [w]here, however, there is a clear and constant line of decisions whose effect is not inconsistent with some fundamental substantive or procedural aspect of our law, and whose reasoning does not appear to overlook or misunderstand some argument or point of principle, we consider that it would be wrong for this Court not to follow that line.[42]

[42] *Manchester City Council v Pinnock* (n 1) [48].

Lord Neuberger's statement suggests two possible limits to the position that UK courts will normally follow a clear and constant line of cases. First, the clear and constant line of cases must not be 'inconsistent with some fundamental substantive or procedural aspect' of UK law. Second, the reasoning of the case law must not 'overlook or misunderstand some argument or point of principle' of UK law.

UK courts may decline to follow a decision of the ECtHR where the decision of the ECtHR contradicts a fundamental procedural or substantive provision of UK law. For these interactions to facilitate democratic dialogue, they need to be exercised sparingly. In this instance, the UK courts are best understood as acting to maintain constitutional balance. The UK courts are declining to follow decisions not because of a fundamental misunderstanding of domestic law, which the UK courts are institutionally best-placed to correct, but because they believe that the ECtHR has transgressed its constitutional role in a manner which harms the constitutional role of the UK courts to protect human rights. As such, it requires evidence of a clear and egregious breach of a sufficiently foundational principle of the UK constitution to merit the exercise by the United Kingdom of its refusal to adhere to the decision of the ECtHR. It should not be used merely because the UK courts disagree with the conclusions reached by the ECtHR.

Lord Neuberger's first limit may only facilitate the normative values underpinning democratic dialogue if used sparingly. There is no example of the UK courts refusing to adhere to a decision of the ECtHR on these grounds. The approach of the Supreme Court in *Chester*, however, demonstrates that the Supreme Court is aware of the extreme circumstances which need to exist in order to exercise this power to refuse to adhere to the decision of the ECtHR.[43] As discussed in the previous chapter, the Attorney General invited the Supreme Court to decline to follow the ECtHR in this case. He argued that the clear line of case law of the ECtHR, which had concluded that blanket bans on prisoner voting contravened Convention rights, had failed to pay sufficient regard to the margin of appreciation granted to the signatory states when determining arrangements for promoting democracy; had failed to take account of more recent democratic debate on the issue of prisoner voting; and had not recognized that the blanket ban was not indiscriminate in nature, given the high threshold of seriousness of criminal offences which led to custodial sentences. Lord Mance not only dismissed the reasoning of the Attorney General, but also refused to recognize that a blanket ban on prisoner voting was a fundamental aspect of UK law:

> deep though the 'philosophical differences of view between reasonable people' may be on this point, it would in my opinion exaggerate their legal and social importance to regard them as going to 'some fundamental substantive or procedural aspect of our law'.[44]

Lord Sumption was even more cautious. Despite his strong criticism of the approach of the ECtHR to this issue,[45] he regarded the idea that the 'disenfranchisement of convicted prisoners could be categorised as a fundamental feature of the law of the United Kingdom' as an 'extreme suggestion'.[46]

Lord Neuberger's second limit can give rise to inter-institutional interactions which enable the national courts to challenge decisions of the ECtHR which are based on errors which the national courts are better placed to understand. This limited form of institutional interaction recognizes that, normally, there are good reasons for the national courts to follow the decisions of the ECtHR given that the ECtHR is the

[43] *R (Chester) v Secretary of State for Justice* (n 15). [44] ibid, [35].
[45] ibid, [135]–[137]. [46] ibid, [137].

court with the constitutional power to authoritatively determine the interpretation of Convention rights. Nevertheless, national courts have good reason not to follow decisions of the ECtHR in those circumstances where it is clear that the ECtHR has made an error and when the national courts are better placed to recognize and to correct this error. National courts are experts in national law. The ECtHR are experts in the interpretation of the ECHR. The UK courts are therefore better able to identify when a decision of the ECtHR has overlooked, ignored, or misunderstood an aspect of English law. In these circumstances, democratic dialogue is facilitated when national courts focus on examining whether a legal error is made and provide a clear account of this legal error. If this results in the applicant not being granted a Convention right which they would appear to enjoy according to the 'incorrect' decision of the ECtHR, then the individual who believes her rights have been harmed can petition the ECtHR. The ECtHR can then refer to the decision of the national court, evaluating its reasoning on the merits of the case and also recognizing that, given the greater institutional expertise of the national court, weight needs to be given to the decision of the national court. The clearer the reasoning provided by the national court and the ECtHR, the more likely it is that this inter-institutional interaction will facilitate democratic dialogue.

This form of inter-institutional interaction is primarily a means of ensuring constitutional counter-balance. As such, for this to facilitate democratic dialogue, national courts need to ensure that this mechanism is used sparingly and only when there are good grounds for its exercise, being conscious of the relative expertise of the ECtHR to determine Convention rights, and also of the extent to which the ECtHR has developed a clear and constant line of cases and whether the decision of the ECtHR is one of the Grand Chamber. It is clear from the discussion in later cases that the Justices of the Supreme Court are cautious when deciding whether to exercise their power to refuse to follow a decision of the ECtHR, particularly when faced with a clear and constant line of cases from the Grand Chamber.

This reticence is illustrated by statements in *Chester* concerning the refusal to allow prisoners to vote in the elections for the European Parliament caused by the general legislative blanket ban on prisoner voting.[47] The ECtHR had consistently concluded that a blanket ban disenfranchising all prisoners was contrary to Convention rights. This conclusion was found in a series of decisions of the ECtHR, including by the Grand Chamber. Nevertheless, the Attorney General argued that, given that section 2(1) of the Human Rights Act 1998 only required the national courts to take decisions of the ECtHR into account, the Supreme Court was free not to follow decisions of the ECtHR and should not follow the clear and constant line of case law from the ECtHR in this case. The Supreme Court refused to accept the invitation of the Attorney General not to follow the decisions of the ECtHR. In reaching their conclusion, Lord Mance confirmed that, following Lord Phillips's account in *Horncastle* the Supreme Court should only refuse to follow decisions of the ECtHR on 'rare occasions', the need for extreme circumstances being particularly pertinent when the Supreme Court was considering decisions of the Grand Chamber.[48] He recognized the utility of dialogue between the national courts and the ECtHR, whilst also recognizing that there were limits to how this should operate:

> In relation to authority consisting of one or more simple Chamber decisions, dialogue with Strasbourg by national courts, including the Supreme Court, has proved valuable in recent years.

[47] ibid. [48] ibid, [25].

The process enables national courts to express their concerns and, in an appropriate case such as *R v Horncastle*, to refuse to follow Strasbourg case-law in the confidence that the reasoned expression of a diverging national viewpoint will lead to a serious review of the position in Strasbourg. But there are limits to this process, particularly where the matter has been already to the Grand Chamber once or, even more so, as in this case, twice. It would have then to involve some truly fundamental principle of our law or some more egregious oversight or misunderstanding before it could be appropriate for this Court to contemplate an outright refusal to follow Strasbourg authority at the Grand Chamber level.[49]

Lord Sumption also recognized that the Supreme Court should exercise its power to refuse to follow a decision of the ECtHR rarely, recognizing that although the Supreme Court could reject a decision of the ECtHR as 'wrong', 'this is not an approach that a United Kingdom court can adopt, save in altogether exceptional cases'.[50]

There are two examples of where a refusal to follow a decision of the ECtHR has given rise to inter-institutional interactions between the UK courts and the ECtHR which have facilitated democratic dialogue. In *Horncastle*, Lord Phillips, giving the judgment of the court, recognized for the first time that there may be 'rare occasions' where the court 'has concerns as to whether a decision of the Strasbourg court sufficiently appreciates or accommodates particular aspects of our domestic process' such that the national courts were free to 'decline to follow the Strasbourg decision', concluding that declining to follow the ECtHR 'is likely to give the Strasbourg court the opportunity to reconsider the particular aspect of the decision that is in issue, so that there takes place what may prove to be valuable dialogue between this court and the Strasbourg court'.[51] *Horncastle* concerned convictions which were based on hearsay evidence and the compatibility of these convictions with article 6 ECHR. In *Al-Khawaja v UK*, the ECtHR concluded that, where a conviction is based 'solely or to a decisive degree on depositions that have been made by a person whom the accused has had no opportunity to examine or have examined' then article 6 ECHR is breached.[52] The ECtHR did recognize that it may be possible for such convictions not to breach article 6 where there are special circumstances, citing the example of when a witness refused to testify in court because of fear induced by the defendant, or where there are counterbalancing factors which would ensure the protection of the rights of defence found in article 6 ECHR. However, the ECtHR concluded that this was not the case in *Al-Khawaja*.

Lord Phillips disagreed with the assessment, focusing on the extent to which the case law surrounding the 'sole and decisive' rule had been developed in response to criminal procedures found in civil law as opposed to common law systems. Lord Phillips was of the opinion that 'case law appears to have been developed without full consideration of the safeguards against an unfair trial that exist under the common law procedure'[53] and he suspected that the ECtHR had not 'given detailed consideration to the English law of admissibility of evidence, and the changes made to that law, after consideration by the Law Commission, intended to ensure that English law complies with the requirements of art 6(1) and (3)(d)'.[54] Lord Phillips reached this conclusion after taking 'careful account of the Strasbourg jurisprudence' and set out a clear and careful account both of why he felt that *Al Khawaja* was not in line with

[49] ibid, [27]. [50] ibid, [121].
[51] *R v Horncastle* [2009] UKSC 14, [2010] 2 AC 375, [11].
[52] *Al-Khawaja v UK* [2011] ECHR 26766/05, (2009) 49 EHRR 1, para 36.
[53] *R v Horncastle* (n 51), [107]. [54] ibid, [107].

earlier decisions and how it failed to take account of the protections for defendants found in English law.[55]

Al-Khawaja was on appeal before the Grand Chamber at the time that *Horncastle* was decided. The Grand Chamber of the ECtHR referred extensively to the decisions of both the Court of Appeal and the Supreme Court in *Horncastle*, looking carefully at the reasons provided in those courts both as regards the ability of the common law to provide sufficient safeguards to protect the defendant during the admission of hearsay evidence and the extent to which the 'sole and decisive' test may fail to take account of decisions of the ECtHR.[56] The Grand Chamber also examined the conclusions of the Supreme Court carefully when assessing whether it should modify the 'sole and decisive' test, again, looking carefully at the reasons provided by the Supreme Court and evaluating their validity on the strength of these reasons.[57] After taking these considerations into account, the Grand Chamber modified its approach, concluding that it would not automatically breach article 6 if hearsay evidence was the sole or decisive evidence on which a conviction was based, provided that this was subject to searching scrutiny, drawing on the reasoning of Lord Mance in UK decisions that the law would require 'sufficient counterbalancing factors' and 'strong procedural safeguards'.[58] The Grand Chamber then concluded that there were sufficient safeguards for Al Khawaja, but not for Tahery, whose article 6 rights had been breached. Here, the ECtHR was prepared to change its position on the admission of hearsay evidence given its reflection on the judgment of the UK Supreme Court in *Horncastle*, as well as its reference to other Supreme Court judgments.

A second example of institutional interactions following a refusal to follow a decision of the ECtHR involves the discussion of whether the imposition of automatic life sentences for murder contravened Convention rights. In *Vinter v UK* the Grand Chamber concluded that, although life sentences per se were not incompatible with article 3 ECHR, nevertheless for a mandatory life sentence to be compatible with article 3 there must be the prospect of a release and a possibility of review, where the review allows for the consideration of whether there have been such significant changes in the life prisoner, or such progress towards rehabilitation, that imprisonment can no longer be justified on penological grounds.[59] Although recognizing that UK law did include an ability for review, the Grand Chamber concluded that there was a 'lack of clarity as to the current law concerning the prospect of release of life prisoners'.[60] Although recognizing that the guidelines could be interpreted by the executive so as to comply with Convention rights, especially given the requirements of sections 3 and 6 of the Human Rights Act, nevertheless the Grand Chamber was concerned 'with the law as it presently stands on the published policies as well as in judicial dicta and as it is applied in practice to whole life prisoners'[61] and concluded that these published policies, which focused on compassionate grounds, were too restrictive. This, coupled with the lack of clarity of the law, led the Grand Chamber to conclude that there was a breach of article 3 ECHR.

Following this decision, the Attorney General referred the issue of the validity of life sentences to the Court of Appeal.[62] The Court of Appeal reviewed the decision in *Vinter* and disagreed with its conclusion that English law was insufficiently

[55] ibid. [56] *Al-Khawaja v UK* (n 52) [51]–[62]. [57] ibid, [129]–[132].
[58] ibid, [147]. [59] [2013] ECHR 66069/09. [60] ibid, [125].
[61] ibid, [126].
[62] *Attorney General's Reference (No 60 of 2013), R v McLoughlin; R v Newell* [2014] EWCA Crim 188, [2014] 3 All ER 73.

clear to provide a real hope and possibility of release. The Court of Appeal argued that it was clear in English law that the Secretary of State would have to act in line with Convention rights when exercising her discretion. Moreover, although the Lifer Manual referred to 'compassionate grounds', which may be read as too narrow as to provide any real hope or possibility of release, it was important to recognize that the Secretary of State was not able to fetter her discretion and, therefore, was not bound to merely follow the criteria set out in the Manual. Rather, she had to hear the exceptional circumstances of any application for release, ensuring that her assessment of whether this gave rise to compassionate grounds for release was determined in line with the requirements of Convention rights. In addition, any refusal of release would then be subject to judicial review, which would also take account of Convention-compatibility. When understood in this way, the Court of Appeal concluded that English law did provide a real hope and possibility of release that was sufficiently clear and certain, thus satisfying the requirements of article 3 ECHR as established in *Vinter v UK*.[63]

The issue of the compatibility of life sentences with article 3 ECHR then returned to the ECtHR in *Hutchinson v UK*.[64] Here the attention of the ECtHR was drawn to the decision of the Court of Appeal in *R v Newell*. The ECtHR concluded that

> Where, following the Grand Chamber's judgment in which it expressed doubts about the clarity of domestic law, the national court has specifically addressed those doubts and set out an unequivocal statement of the legal position, the Court must accept the national court's interpretation of domestic law ... Further, as the Grand Chamber observed in *Vinter and Others*, the power to release under section 30 of the 2003 Act, exercised in the manner delineated in the Court of Appeal's judgment in *Bieber* and *Oakes*, and now *R v Newell; R v McLoughlin*, is sufficient to comply with the requirements of Article 3.[65]

As such, the ECtHR concluded that there had been no breach of Convention rights.

Both of these examples illustrate how inter-institutional interactions which occur following a refusal to follow a decision of the ECtHR can facilitate democratic dialogue. In each of these examples the UK courts demonstrated general reluctance to refuse to follow a decision of the ECtHR, doing so where there were clear examples of the ECtHR failing to understand English law. The UK courts are better placed to recognize these errors and to correct them. Moreover, in reaching their conclusions, the UK courts exercised comity, showing respect for the decisions of the ECtHR and adhering to the legal principles underpinning these decisions, if disagreeing with their application to English law. The ECtHR also exercised comity, paying attention to the reasoning found in the UK judgments and recognizing the better institutional ability of the UK courts to understand and apply domestic law. As such, the interactions between the two courts were able to facilitate a better application of Convention rights, albeit indirectly. These measures of constitutional counter-balancing were able to indirectly facilitate constitutional collaboration.

In addition, it could be argued that inter-institutional interactions may arise indirectly when the UK courts recognize a clear and constant line of decisions of the Strasbourg court, which they do not decline to follow, but where nevertheless the Supreme Court exercises its discretion to refuse to issue a declaration of incompatibility. This is a less extreme form of constitutional counter-balancing mechanism. *Chester* provides a possible example of this indirect form of constitutional counter-balancing. Despite concluding that the blanket ban on prisoner voting did indeed contravene Convention rights, nevertheless the Supreme Court declined to issue a declaration of

[63] ibid, [29]–[36]. [64] [2015] ECHR 57592/08. [65] ibid, [25].

incompatibility under section 4 of the Human Rights Act 1998. Lord Mance, with whom Lord Hope and Lord Kerr agreed, declined to issue a declaration of incompatibility as he did not believe that the declaration would serve any useful purpose. A declaration of incompatibility had already been issued by the Scottish courts and the Attorney General was aware of the incompatibility given a series of high profile decisions of the Strasbourg court. The government had, therefore, been given the opportunity to issue a remedial order, but had chosen not to do so.[66] In addition he recognized that, although the blanket ban on prisoner voting contravened the Convention, nevertheless it was clear that the Convention rights of the individual applicants had not been breached.[67] Lord Mance was also influenced by the fact that it was clearly for Parliament to decide how to render the legislation Convention-compatible.[68] Baroness Hale, however, justified the refusal to issue a declaration of incompatibility on narrower grounds, focusing on the fact that no purpose would be served here as the applicants before the court—who were serving life sentences—were within the category of prisoners that the ECtHR had accepted could have their right to vote revoked. As such, the Convention rights of the applicants had not been breached even though the blanket ban on voting did breach Convention rights.[69]

Baroness Hale's more cautious approach is more likely to facilitate democratic dialogue. It is clear here that her decision to decline to issue a declaration of incompatibility carries no connotations of inherent criticism of the decision of the ECtHR. Rather, she is recognizing that, in situations where the rights of the applicant are not harmed, there is no need to issue a remedy. As such, there is a justification for declining to issue a declaration of incompatibility. The broad approach of Lord Mance, however, could give rise to problems if this were to enable the Supreme Court to refuse to issue declarations of incompatibility whenever it strongly disagreed with a clear and constant line of case law. Even though the government was aware of the breach, this does not provide sufficient justification for refusing to issue a declaration of incompatibility. This may be misconstrued as indirectly condoning the breach of Convention rights. Moreover, further pressure on the government through the issue of a further declaration of incompatibility may serve as a reminder to the UK Government and legislature of the need to respond to a clear breach of Convention rights. Even if this is deemed a matter for Parliament, a declaration of incompatibility does not create problems in this regard. Parliament has the opportunity to respond to a declaration of incompatibility, providing its reasons for modifying or declining to modify legislation. Care needs to be taken to ensure that a decision to decline to issue a declaration of incompatibility is not inadvertently construed as a means of challenging the constitutional position of the ECtHR when there are no grounds for doing so, thereby indirectly undermining the aims of democratic dialogue through an inappropriate exercise of a constitutional counter-balancing mechanism.

III. Dialogue between the UK Courts and the Court of Justice of the European Union

In contrast to the interactions between the national courts and the ECtHR, EU law provides for a formal means for national courts to interact with the CJEU through

[66] *R (Chester) v Secretary of State for Justice* (n 15) [39]. [67] ibid, [40]–[41].
[68] ibid, [42]. [69] ibid, [99]–[102].

the preliminary reference procedure. Article 267 TFEU empowers the CJEU to hear preliminary references both as to the validity of EU law and as to its interpretation. Any national court which is not the final court of appeal enjoys a discretionary power to refer a question to the CJEU. Final courts of appeal are required to make a reference when an issue as to the validity of EU law or its interpretation is raised before it, unless the question has been determined by the CJEU before, or where the answer to the question is clear given previous decisions of the CJEU.[70] Although this may be at the request of the parties, it need not be. National law may empower national courts to make a preliminary reference of their own volition. It is the national court who determines the phrasing of the question to the CJEU, although the CJEU has some power to modify the question. When hearing the preliminary reference, it is the job of the CJEU to provide a judgment on the legal issue—that is to explain how a provision of EU law should be interpreted or to determine the validity of EU law. Only the CJEU has the power to determine that EU law is invalid.[71] This formal means of facilitating inter-institutional interactions is supplemented by informal interactions, where the CJEU refers to decisions of courts across the member states and where national courts refer to decisions of the CJEU even when deciding not to make an article 267 reference, or where determining issues of national as opposed to EU law.[72]

Moreover, these interactions have played a role in developing the protection of human rights in the European Union. The original EU Treaties did not provide a protection of human rights. Nevertheless, the then European Court of Justice developed its protection of human rights through general principles of European Community/EU law. The elaboration of these principles arose in case law where national courts—in particular in Germany—indirectly questioned the extent to which directly effective EU law should override national law, especially when faced with an apparent conflict between directly effective EU law and constitutionally protected human rights. These challenges were indirect as they arose in cases before the German Federal Constitutional Court, but no article 267 reference was made. When deciding cases on human rights, the European Court of Justice developed the concept of general principles drawn, inter alia, from the constitutional traditions common to the member states and from Treaties—such as the ECHR—which had been ratified by all of the member states.[73] By recognizing these general principles the European Court of Justice was not only able to remove a possible source of tension between the court and the national courts which could have undermined the primacy of EU law, but also the court increased the legitimacy of EU law through its incorporation of general principles. The recognition of these general principles of EU law by the court initiated a process of growing recognition of the importance of human rights by the other institutions of the EU, culminating in the adoption of the EU's Charter of Fundamental Rights and its recognition by the Lisbon Treaty.[74]

The existence of these interactions, both formal and informal, and particularly the way in which there is evidence of interactions in the field of human rights, would suggest that a model of democratic dialogue could cast light on developing a normative

[70] C-283/81 *CILFIT v Ministry of Health* [1982] ECR 3415.

[71] C-318/85 *Foto-Frost v Hauptzollamt Lübeck-Ost* [1987] ECR 2811.

[72] See F Jacobs, 'Judicial Dialogue and the Cross-Fertilisation of Legal Systems: The European Court of Justice' (2003) Texas International Law Journal 547.

[73] See C-29/69 *Stauder v City of Ulm* [1969] ECR 419 and C-11/70 *Internationale Handelsgesellschaft v Einfuhr-und Vorratstelle für Getreide und Futtermittel* [1970] ECR 1125.

[74] Article 6 TEU.

framework for interactions between the national courts and the CJEU. However, the constitutional relationship between the UK courts and the CJEU casts doubt on this assertion. First, although the relationship between the CJEU and the national courts is not hierarchical, nevertheless the principle of the primacy of directly effective EU law, coupled with the way in which decisions taken by the CJEU as to the validity or interpretation of EU law against one member state may act as a precedent for the courts in other member states of the European Union,[75] appears to undermine the requisite element of balance between the national courts and the CJEU. Although democratic dialogue does not require an equal distribution of relative decision-making power between institutions, nevertheless it does require that it cannot be the case that one institution is able to authoritatively determine the outcome of inter-institutional interactions. This would appear to be contradicted by the primacy of EU law, where national courts of the member states are required to disapply national laws, including legislation and constitutional provisions, which contradict directly effective provisions of EU law.[76] The first section will reject this possible objection to the application of the constitutional model of democratic dialogue to develop a framework of inter-institutional interactions between the national courts and the CJEU by drawing on arguments from constitutional pluralism, although it is important to recognize that adopting a framework of democratic dialogue does not entail an acceptance of all of the elements of constitutional pluralism. It will also explain how interactions can still arise between the national courts and the CJEU in the field of human rights protections, despite the lack of an equivalent of the margin of appreciation in EU law, as well as recognizing that the application of democratic dialogue is not undermined by the fact that the CJEU is not a specialist human rights court. This discussion also has importance in the light of the recent UK referendum decision to leave the EU, some of the arguments being based on the perception of a loss of sovereignty due to the impact of directly effective EU law. The assessment of constitutional pluralism, and its application to the United Kingdom, recognizes that the relationship between directly effective EU law and national law is far more complex, recognizing the more subtle ways in which national courts interact with the CJEU.

A. Democratic dialogue and the EU

(i) Constitutional pluralism

The principle of the primacy of directly effective EU law would appear to provide little means for national courts to enter into any constructive debate. The principle requires that directly effective EU law overrides national law, including provisions of constitutional law. Understood in this manner, the CJEU has effective authority to determine the content of EU law and, once its determination is made, as a matter of EU law the national courts are to apply the CJEU's determination of EU law. There would appear to be little room for dialogue in this relationship. Whilst the national courts refer matters to the CJEU under article 267, the CJEU determines EU law, and the role of the national courts is then to apply EU law, as determined by the CJEU. Moreover, by establishing the principle of the primacy of directly effective EU law, the CJEU is

[75] See C-283/81 *CILFIT v Ministry of Health* (n 70).

[76] C-26/62 *Van Gen den Loos v Nederlandse Administratie der Belastingen* [1963] ECR 1 and C-106/77 *Amminstrazione delle Finanze dello Stato v Simmenthal SpA* [1978] ECR 629.

asserting its ability to authoritatively determine the nature of the relationship between directly effective EU law and national law; directly effective EU law overrides national law because the CJEU has determined that it will.

However, as discussed earlier, UK law also asserts its ability to determine the nature of the relationship between directly effective EU law and national law.[77] This provides the UK courts with a mechanism of inter-institutional interaction which can provide the requisite ability of the UK courts to ensure that it is not the case that all interactions are authoritatively resolved by the CJEU, thus providing a platform for inter-institutional interactions which can facilitate democratic dialogue. This can occur in two ways. First, the UK courts can place limits on the extent to which directly effective provisions of EU law can disapply national law, giving rise to the possibility that the UK courts will refuse to apply directly effective EU law. Second, the UK courts could refuse to adhere to a decision of the CJEU sent back to the UK courts following an article 267 reference. To understand the relationship between the national courts and the CJEU in this manner requires an adoption of some, but not all, of the elements of constitutional pluralism, a term used by some academics to describe the nature of the relationship between the European Union and the member states. However, as with our discussion of bipolar sovereignty, it is important to understand more precisely the extent to which applying a model of democratic dialogue to the relationship between the UK courts and the CJEU requires an acceptance of constitutional pluralism, as well as a further understanding of what is meant by this term in the account in this chapter and whether this can stand in the face of criticisms of constitutional pluralism.

Constitutional pluralism in the European Union finds its origins in the work of Neil MacCormick.[78] MacCormick's analysis was originally written in response to the decision of the German Federal Constitutional Court on the compatibility of the Maastricht Treaty with the German Constitution.[79] The Court did not make an article 267 reference, but nevertheless remarked upon the status of the relationship between German Constitutional law and EU law. In particular, the German Federal Constitutional Court asserted its ability to authoritatively determine the nature of the relationship between German law and directly effective EU law. If EU law were to override German law, for example, this would be because of the provisions of German law and not purely because of the provisions of EU law. MacCormick argued that a better understanding of the relationship between the European Union and the member states was not to regard the European Union, and its member states, as belonging to one legal system, where the decisions of the CJEU are hierarchically superior to the decisions of the member states, overriding national law. Rather, MacCormick argued that 'the most appropriate analysis of the relations of legal systems is pluralistic, rather than monistic, and interactive rather than hierarchical'.[80] It was not the case that either national law or EU law was definitively superior to the other. Rather, the CJEU was the superior court which made authoritative determinations within the EU legal

[77] See, for example, *Thoburn v Sunderland City Council* [2002] EWHC 195 (Admin), [2003] QB 151; *R (HS2) v Secretary of State for Transport* [2014] UKSC 3, [2014] 1 WLR 324; and European Union Act 2011, s 18.

[78] N MacCormick, 'The Maastrichts Urteil: Sovereignty Now' (1995) 1 European Law Journal 259; and N MacCormick, *Questioning Sovereignty: Law State and Nation in the European Commonwealth* (Oxford University Press 1999).

[79] Case 2 BvR 2134, 2159/92 *Maastricht* [1993] BVerfGE 89, [1994] 1 CMLR 57.

[80] MacCormick, 'The Maastrichts Urteil: Sovereignty Now' (n 78) 264.

system and the national domestic courts were the superior courts which made authoritative determinations as regards their own domestic legal system. The legal systems of national law and EU law were separate, but overlapping, interacting with each other in this area of overlap.[81]

If we are to adopt MacCormick's original analysis of a plurality of legal systems, then we can begin to understand both how a constitutional model of democratic dialogue can apply to the relationship between the national courts and the CJEU, as well as how a model of democratic dialogue may add value. If it is the case that the UK courts authoritatively determine UK law, including the nature of the relationship between directly effective EU law and UK law, and that the CJEU authoritatively determines EU law, including the nature of its relationship between EU law and UK law, then it is easy to argue that there is sufficient equality between these institutions in order to apply a model of democratic dialogue. Both, on this analysis, appear to have equal authority—the authority to determine the nature of the relationship between directly effective EU law and UK law. Moreover, MacCormick argued that the relationship between the UK courts and the CJEU was best understood as interactive as opposed to hierarchical. An account of democratic dialogue may provide a means of explaining how the two institutions can interact so as to facilitate the values of a better protection of human rights, in addition to whether these interactions can facilitate deliberative democracy, involving both institutions and the people, and provide a means of stabilizing what might otherwise be a potentially difficult relationship between two institutions, both of which assert the authority to determine the nature of the relationship between directly effective EU law and UK law.

However, it is important to recognize that accounts of constitutional pluralism have evolved since MacCormick's early analysis of pluralistic legal systems.[82] In their introduction to a recent collection of essays on constitutional pluralism, Jan Komárek and Matej Avbelj provide an account of six varieties of constitutional pluralism, which they describe as socio-telelogical constitutionalism, epistemic meta-constitutionalism, best-fit universal constitutionalism/cosmopolitan constitutionalism, harmonious discursive constitutionalism, multi-level constitutionalism, and pragmatic constitutionalism.[83] Models of constitutional pluralism are also criticized, some of these criticisms mirroring those which have been used to undermine claims of democratic dialogue. To adopt a model of pluralism set out by MacCormick is to accept that there can be two overlapping, competing legal systems, each providing a potentially different answer to the question as to whether directly effective EU law has primacy over UK law and each asserting its right to authoritatively determine the nature of the relationship between directly effective EU law and national law. It is easy to see how this analysis appears to be an unstable, temporary situation. As such, we would expect that the temporary situation will be resolved, with either the national courts or the CJEU establishing hierarchical superiority over the other. If this is not possible, then we may have to accept

[81] ibid, 264–65.

[82] See, for example, N Walker, 'The Idea of Constitutional Pluralism' (2002) 65 Modern Law Review 317; JHH Weiler, 'In Defence of the Status Quo: Europe's Constitutional *Sonderweg*' in JHH Weiler and M Wind (eds), *European Constitutionalism Beyond the State* (Cambridge University Press 2003) 23; M Paoires Maduro, 'Contrapunctual Law: Europe's Constitutional Pluralism in Action' in N Walker (ed), *Sovereignty in Transition* (Oxford University Press 2003) 501; and M Kumm, 'The Jurisprudence of Constitutional Conflict: Constitutional Supremacy in Europe Before and After the Constitutional Treaty' (2005) 11 European Law Journal 262.

[83] J Komárek and M Avbelj, 'Introduction' in J Komárek and M Avbelj (eds), *Constitutional Pluralism in the European Union and Beyond* (Hart 2012) 1, 4–7.

that the two are distinct legal systems, with each asserting authority in its own area, ignoring the potential interactions or overlap between the systems, or accept that there is plurality, but that this has nothing to do with constitutionalism, it being merely an example of competing entities, the relationship between the two being ultimately determined as a power struggle.

Neil Walker refers to these scepticisms as the potential collapse to unitarism, the collapse into constitutional plurality, or the rejection of the constitutional element of constitutional pluralism.[84] The collapse into unitarism occurs when theorists resolve the potential tension between the national courts and the CJEU through recognition of underlying legal principles that can be used by both the national courts and the CJEU when determining whether directly effective EU law should override national law, in addition to determining which institution should authoritatively determine this issue. The collapse into constitutional plurality occurs when we recognize that the two systems overlap, but that there are no rules as to how to resolve the potential clash. Any resolution would appear to be resolved either through chance, through might, or a series of unreasoned compromises. The latter would appear to suggest that there is no constitutionalism in constitutional pluralism. Understood in this manner, the scepticism appears to resemble the difficulties we found when examining democratic dialogue—is there no middle ground for constitutional pluralism, these competing claims either being resolved through underlying legal principles (similar to seeing democratic dialogue collapsing into accounts of legal constitutionalism) or through a resolution of weighing up competing interests (similar to regarding democratic dialogue as collapsing into a model of political constitutionalism)? If we are to avoid these similar difficulties, we need to be careful as to the precise nature of the assumptions on which an application of the model of democratic dialogue to the relationship between the UK courts and the CJEU rests and the extent to which it requires an acceptance of an account of constitutional pluralism.

Miguel Poiares Maduro argues that constitutional pluralism makes three claims: the empirical claim, the normative claim, and the thick normative claim.[85] The empirical claim of constitutional pluralism is that there exists a 'plurality of constitutional sources and claims of final authority which creates a context for potential constitutional conflicts that are not hierarchically regulated'.[86] Maduro analyses this in terms of a plurality of legal systems within the EU legal order, defining a legal order as symbolic and normative, with legal systems representing the legal practices and institutions where the legal order is reproduced. The EU legal order is best understood as a series of normative values and principles accepted across the European legal systems, these values been applied by the UK courts in the UK legal system and the CJEU in the European legal system. The normative claim of legal pluralism advocates that the question of whether the final authority to resolve issues of the relationship between EU law and the domestic laws of the member states should be left open and unresolved.[87] For Maduro, this ensures a minimal level of equality of the competing claims of the domestic courts and the CJEU to authoritatively determine the nature of the relationship between EU law and national law, enabling these competing claims to be balanced against each other. The thick normative claim asserts that constitutional

[84] N Walker, 'Constitutionalism and Pluralism in Global Context' in Komárek and Avbelj (n 83) 17, 18–20. See also M Kumm, 'Re-Thinking Constitutional Authority: On the Structure and Limits of Constitutional Pluralism' in Komárek and Avbelj (n 83) 39, 39–43.

[85] M Poiares Maduro, 'Three Claims of Constitutional Pluralism' in Komárek and Avbelj (n 83) 67.

[86] ibid, 69–70. [87] ibid, 75–77.

pluralism provides a better ability to achieve the ideas of constitutionalism than either an insistence on purely national constitutionalism, where national constitutional law is hierarchically superior, or through the adoption of a form of EU constitutionalism, with the CJEU being hierarchically superior to national courts.[88] The application of a model of democratic dialogue only requires an acceptance of the empirical claim and a partial acceptance of the normative claim. It does not require acceptance of the thick normative claim.

The empirical claim recognizes the existence of constitutional conflicts coupled with the lack of any hierarchical resolution of these conflicts. This is required for the application of a model of democratic dialogue between the UK courts and the CJEU in order to ensure that effective dialogue can take place when these conflicts arise. If it were the case that these conflicts were always resolved hierarchically, then there could be no effective dialogue. The empirical claim appears easy to satisfy, especially in the light of our earlier discussion of *HS2.* The CJEU has long asserted the principle of the autonomy of the EU legal order, coupled with the primacy of directly effective EU law over national law, including national constitutional law.[89] In addition to the *HS2* decision, the House of Lords decision in the seminal *Factortame (No 2)* case contains the statement of Lord Bridge that, in giving effect to directly effective EU law, the courts were merely ensuring that they complied with the intentions of Parliament as expressed in the European Communities Act 1972.[90] Although Laws LJ in *Thoburn* concluded that any change had occurred through the modification of the common law,[91] the theme common to both decisions is the reference to English law—be it common law or Act of Parliament—to determine the extent to which, and how, the primacy of directly effective EU law was to be accommodated into English law. It is also clear that there are differences between the assertions of the CJEU and of English courts as to the extent to which directly effective EU law can disapply national law. Regardless of how one interprets *Factortame II* and *Thoburn*, this is evident from the statements in *HS2* that

> [i]t is, putting the point at its lowest, certainly arguable (and it is for the United Kingdom law and courts to determine) that there may be fundamental principles, whether contained in other constitutional instruments or recognised at common law, of which Parliament when it enacted the European Communities Act 1972 did not either contemplate or authorise the abrogation.[92]

Alexander Somek, however, would disagree with this empirical claim. Somek does recognize the existence of these conflicts, acknowledging both that EU law and national law may conflict in terms of the content of the law and in terms of their assertions of relative constitutional authority to resolve these conflicts.[93] Nevertheless, he argues that, to regard this as providing evidence of legal pluralism, supporting the existence of two legal orders, is to ask the wrong question. Were such a conflict to arise in a national court, the question that would arise is as to the legal solution which would be adopted by the domestic court. The national court is essentially faced with two arguable solutions to this conflict: (i) that a decision of the CJEU declaring national law contrary to EU law is invalid as the CJEU has failed to recognize that the EU can only act within

[88] ibid, 77–84.

[89] C-26/62 *Van Gend en Loos v Nederlandse Administratie der Belastingen* (n 76) and C-106/77 *Amminstrazione delle Finanze dello Stato v Simmenthal SpA* [1978] ECR 629.

[90] *R v Secretary of State for Transport ex parte Factortame Ltd (No 2)* [1991] 1 AC 603.

[91] *Thoburn v Sunderland City Council* (n 77).

[92] *R (HS2 Action Alliance Ltd) v The Secretary of State for Transport* [2014] UKSC 3, [207] (Lord Neuberger and Lord Mance).

[93] A Somek, 'Monism: A Take of the Undead' in Komárek and Avbelj (n 83) 343, 356–57.

the powers conferred to it by the member states and the member states did not confer on the EU the power to act contrary to the constitutional principles found in that member state; or (ii) that EU law overrides national law, even national constitutional law principles. Courts will, de facto, choose one solution over the other. Both of these solutions are compatible with Somek's monist account of the nature of the relationship between EU law and national law. If the national court followed the EU, then this would be compatible with EU law. If the national courts failed to adhere to EU law, then although the CJEU could require that national courts pay damages to the individual whose human rights are harmed by that decision, it could not force the national courts to adhere to EU law. As such, national courts are free to determine, according to a principle of legal effectiveness, the extent to which EU law overrides national law; 'the overarching legal system vests the power to adjudicate supremacy conflicts in the national system'.[94]

Even if we accept Somek's interpretation,[95] it need not challenge the application of the model of democratic dialogue to the relationship between the national courts and the CJEU. Somek's interpretation may vest the power to determine the nature of the relationship between domestic law and the EU law in the hands of the domestic courts. However, it is at least arguable that Somek is only recognizing that, given the nature of the article 267 reference procedure, any real conflict would have to be resolved by the domestic courts as it is the domestic courts who have to determine how to apply the decisions of the CJEU in their national systems following an article 267 reference. In practice, this means they have the final say when applying both domestic law in domestic courts and directly effective provisions of EU law in domestic courts. Moreover, Somek argues that the domestic courts should resolve this issue according to a principle of legal effectiveness. As such, it is open for domestic courts either to follow national law or EU law. In making this decision, issues as to the relative authority of the CJEU and the national courts may help to determine whether legal effectiveness is better served by adhering to national law or by adhering to directly effective EU law. As such, even Somek's interpretation admits of the possibility of interactions between domestic courts and the CJEU, on a sufficiently equal basis. The difference between Somek's view and the model of democratic dialogue would be that Somek would look for interactions which facilitated legal effectiveness, or would reject the need for interactions, whereas a model of democratic dialogue would require different interactions between the two courts in order to facilitate different normative values.

Accepting Maduro's normative claim of constitutional pluralism is more controversial. However, it is important to recognize the minimal nature of this assumption. Maduro argues that the normative claim of constitutional pluralism merely advocates that the final authority to determine the nature of the relationship between EU law and domestic law should be left open and unresolved. The model of democratic dialogue need not go so far. Democratic dialogue does not require that the issue should remain unresolved. Rather, democratic dialogue merely assumes that a framework can be provided for inter-institutional interactions which can have value and that these interactions can provide a means of minimizing conflict between domestic courts and the CJEU, thus promoting constitutional stability balanced against the necessary constitutional flexibility, in addition to facilitating deliberative democracy and a better protection of human rights. For democratic dialogue to apply to the interactions between

[94] ibid, 360.

[95] For a criticism of this argument, see M Poiares Maduro 'Three Claims of Constitutional Pluralism' in Komárek and Avbelj (n 83) 71–73.

the UK courts and the CJEU, it merely requires that there can be value in leaving the question of the final authority unresolved. This value is found in the normative values which can be achieved through a model of democratic dialogue. These values are less likely to be facilitated in a system where inter-institutional interactions are always authoritatively resolved by either the national courts or the CJEU. The adoption of a model of democratic dialogue need not accept Maduro's deep normative claim as applied to the relationship between domestic law and EU law.

(ii) No margin of appreciation

A second difference between the constitutional relationship between the UK courts and the ECtHR and the UK courts and the CJEU is that the CJEU has not adopted a concept of the margin of appreciation. The margin of appreciation helps to facilitate dialogue between the ECtHR and the national courts by providing a means of facilitating constitutional collaboration which focuses on the relative institutional features of the national and the supranational court. It recognizes that the national courts are more institutionally suited to determining contestable or watershed human rights issues, being better placed to assess how their national culture will develop human rights. However, although the CJEU has not adopted a margin of appreciation, it nevertheless can exercise comity when it recognizes that the determination of a human rights issue may be better suited to the national court.[96]

In *Omega Spielhallen*, for example, the CJEU recognized the constitutional importance of human dignity in the German Constitution.[97] Omega Spielhallen provided laser tag games, where individuals could use laser guns to fire at targets worn by other players in the game. It received its equipment to run these games from a British company. It was prohibited from running these games in Germany because it was deemed to breach the constitutional protection of the right to human dignity. Omega challenged this decision, claiming that this was a restriction on the freedom to provide services and on the free movement of goods, both of which are directly effective provisions of EU law. When determining whether this was a proportionate restriction on the free movement of goods and services, the CJEU recognized the importance of the protection of human dignity to the German constitution and concluded that this was a proportionate restriction, given that it only prevented the use of the equipment when the guns were used to fire at targets worn by other humans, essentially enabling people to 'play at killing'. It did not matter that other member states of the European Union did not protect human rights in the same manner and did allow laser tag games of this nature to take place in their own countries. In reaching this decision, the CJEU is exercising comity through recognizing the importance of this right to the German constitution. The CJEU can exercise this form of comity by modifying the standard of proportionality, requiring less proof that the measure is a proportionate restriction of the free movement of goods or the free movement of services.

This ability to modify the standard of proportionality provides one means through which formal dialogue under article 267 may take place between the UK courts and the CJEU. This is supplemented by the ability of the member states to intervene in

[96] See, for example, G Davies, 'Constitutional Disagreement in Europe and the Search for Pluralism' in Komárek and Avbelj (n 83) 269; and X Groussot, 'Constitutional Dialogues, Pluralism and Conflicting Identities' in Komárek and Avbelj (n 83) 319.

[97] C-36/02 *Omega Spielhallen- under Automatenaufstellungs-GmbH v Oberbürgermesiterin der Bundesstadt Bonn* [2004] ECR I-9609.

decisions of the CJEU and informal dialogue which takes place when the national courts and the CJEU refer to decisions of other jurisdictions. This may provide a means of facilitating constitutional collaboration, enabling the CJEU and the UK courts to work together to refine human rights. In a manner similar to constitutional collaboration with the ECtHR, the national courts can provide information to the CJEU concerning the constitutional protections of rights in their national constitutions, providing the CJEU with information to help it to develop an EU perspective on rights, whilst also enabling the CJEU to respect the constitutional traditions of the member states. However, the lack of a conception of the margin of appreciation may mean that any constitutional collaboration which occurs in this manner may undermine the ability of inter-institutional interactions to facilitate democratic dialogue. The margin of appreciation draws attention to the need to evaluate not only arguments relating to the content of the right, but also issues as to whether the national or the supra-national court is better-placed to determine a rights-issue. The lack of a margin of appreciation means that this issue may arise indirectly as opposed to directly. This may, in turn, mean that the relative roles of the national courts and the CJEU in this form of inter-institutional interaction are not always based upon their different institutional features.

(iii) Insufficient human rights expertise?

A further difference between the CJEU and the ECtHR which also has the potential to undermine democratic dialogue between the UK courts and the CJEU is that the CJEU, unlike the ECtHR, is not a specialized human rights court. The CJEU hears all issues of EU law, not just those concerning human rights. The CJEU is also concerned to ensure the effectiveness of EU law. This objective may restrict the extent to which formal and informal interactions between the UK courts and the CJEU are able to give rise to the better resolution of human rights issues. Concerns for the efficiency of EU law and the objectives of the EU may mean that the CJEU focuses less on protecting human rights and may fail to recognize situations in which the national courts may be better placed to resolve rights-issues. Despite these differences, it is still possible that inter-institutional interactions occurring either through article 267, or informally through judicial references to decisions of either the national courts or the CJEU, may be able to facilitate democratic dialogue in a manner similar to that found in the interactions between the UK courts and the ECtHR.

B. Constitutional collaboration

As with our discussion of constitutional collaboration between the national courts and the ECtHR, interactions are more likely to facilitate democratic dialogue when they are focused on the different institutional features of the domestic and the supranational court, when interactions are more informal, with the weight of the reasoning found in different human rights decisions determining the extent to which any one court will rely on the decisions of another or when supranational courts refer to the decisions of national courts to provide information regarding a common consensus of rights across Europe. Space precludes a detailed examination of all of the interactions between the CJEU and the national courts. Rather, examples will be used in this section to illustrate the ways in which these interactions can facilitate and also undermine democratic dialogue.

Omega Spielhallen, discussed above, provides an example of how interactions between national courts and the CJEU may facilitate the achievement of the normative values underlying the constitutional model of democratic dialogue. Here, the CJEU can provide greater decision-making authority to the national court, recognizing, if not explicitly, the better ability of the national court to resolve a contestable rights issue concerning the extent to which the protection of human dignity is harmed by laser tag games where other players may be identified as targets.[98] The CJEU recognized that individual member states were not required to adopt a uniform conception of a particular human right in order to justify a restriction on the free movement of services,[99] and concluded that the measure was a proportionate restriction as it was limited to what was necessary to protect human dignity as understood in German law. However, there are limits to the extent to which this case can generate democratic dialogue. The decision of the CJEU is short and there is no explicit mention either of the better institutional capacity of the German courts to decide this issue, or a detailed analysis of the reasoning for resolving the rights-issue in a particular manner. This lack of transparency and detailed analysis may undermine the extent to which national courts and the CJEU may collaborate effectively to resolve human rights issues according to their relative institutionally based abilities.[100] It also calls into question the extent to which the CJEU is willing to engage in constitutional collaboration, suggesting that constitutional collaboration may be more likely to be inadvertent than advertent.[101]

There is also a lack of clarity in the decisions of the CJEU as to when the court is willing to grant greater decision-making power to the national courts. This can be illustrated through a comparison of the role of the CJEU in the *Viking Line*[102] and *Laval* cases.[103] In *Viking Line* a potential conflict arose between the right to strike and the right to freedom of establishment. Viking Line ran a ferry service between Finland and Estonia. Its ferry service was running at a loss in the face of competition from Estonian ferry services, which could operate more cheaply due to lower labour costs. Viking Line wished to re-register its vessel under an Estonian flag, allowing it to employ cheaper labour. The International Transport Union had a general policy against 'flags of convenience' which would be transgressed by registering a Finnish-owned vessel under an Estonian flag. Its members went on strike in response to the decision of Viking Line to re-register its vessel. Viking Line argued that this strike contravened EU law—specifically the free movement of workers[104] and the freedom to provide services.[105] In *Laval* the issue arose as to the legality of a strike by Swedish builders blockading a Latvian building firm who had posted workers to Sweden, but who did not comply with the agreed terms as to wage payments made in a collective bargaining agreement between the unions and Swedish building firms.

Greater express authority was given to the national courts to determine the rights-issue in *Viking Line*, where the CJEU stressed that it was for the national court to determine whether the restriction on freedom of establishment was pursuing a legitimate aim,[106] whether the strike was suited to pursuing this aim[107] and whether the strike did not go beyond what was necessary to achieve this aim.[108] However, although

[98] ibid. [99] ibid, para 37.

[100] For a similar criticism, see M Cartabia, 'Europe and Rights: Taking Dialogue Seriously' (2009) 5 European Constitutional Law Review 5.

[101] See, for example, JHH Weiler, 'Prologue: Global and Pluralist Constitutionalism—Some Doubts' in G de Búrca and JHH Weiler (eds), *The Worlds of European Constitutionalism* (Cambridge University Press 2011) 8; and JHH Weiler, 'Dialogical Epilogue' in G de Búrca and JHH Weiler (eds), *The Worlds of European Constitutionalism* (Cambridge University Press 2011) 266.

[102] C-434/08 *International Transport Workers Federation v Viking Line ABP* [2007] ECR I-10779.

[103] C-341/05 *Laval un Partneri Ltd v Svenskabyggnadsarbetareförbundet* [2007] ECR I-11767.

[104] Article 45 TFEU. [105] Article 56 TFEU.

[106] See *International Transport Workers Federation v Viking Line ABP* (n 102) para 80.

[107] ibid, paras 81–82. [108] ibid, paras 84–85.

the CJEU made it clear that it was for the national court to determine whether, on the facts, the strike action was a proportionate restriction, the court nevertheless provided clear guidelines. In particular, the CJEU made it clear that the national court had to establish whether there was a serious threat to national jobs in order to justify the strike.[109] Moreover, the national court had to determine whether the union's policy really did endorse strike action for any form of re-flagging of ships and not merely where this would threaten national jobs. If that were the case, then the strike would be a disproportionate restriction on freedom of establishment.[110] By defining the legitimate interest more specifically—as strike action designed to protect the rights of national workers facing a serious threat to their jobs—the CJEU narrowed down the circumstances under which the action of the unions would be justified. This gives less discretion to the national courts when applying the law to the facts, in practice giving the CJEU more decision-making power over the rights-issue than the national courts.

Even less decision-making authority was given to the national authorities in *Laval*, where the CJEU determined as a matter of law that the strike action was contrary to the freedom to provide services. Again, this occurred because of the more specific definition given of the legitimate aim that could be pursued by the strike—a matter of law to be determined by the CJEU as opposed to an issue of fact to be determined by the national courts. The CJEU concluded that the strike and the blockades would only serve a legitimate objective were the action designed to ensure that posted workers received the same minimum wage as provided to Swedish workers. However, as there was no minimum wage in Sweden, wages being determined by a series of collective bargaining agreements between unions and different work sectors, it was impossible to determine if the building firm, in refusing to accept the terms of the Unions, was refusing to provide the Swedish minimum wage to its workers.[111] This led to the conclusion that the strike was not pursuing a legitimate objective.

Viking Line and *Laval* illustrate a lack of clarity concerning when greater decision-making authority will be given to national courts. This can undermine the ability of the interactions between the national courts and the CJEU to facilitate constitutional collaboration and thereby to facilitate democratic dialogue. Moreover, these cases are criticized for exemplifying a further difficulty which arises because the CJEU is not a human rights court, being concerned more generally with ensuring the efficient application of EU law. *Viking Line* and *Laval* are criticized for placing too much emphasis on the free movement of services and the freedom of establishment—both key aims of the EU—to the detriment of the protection of the right to strike.[112] The concern to promote the aims of the EU over the protection of human rights is also illustrated by the opinion of the CJEU that accession to the ECHR, as established in the agreement between the EU and the Council of Europe, would undermine the aims and autonomy of EU law.[113]

The primacy of EU law may also undermine the extent to which the normative values underpinning democratic dialogue can be facilitated through constitutional collaboration between the national courts and the CJEU. The primacy of EU law can require national courts to disapply constitutionally protected human rights which contradict

[109] ibid, paras 81–82. [110] ibid, para 88.

[111] See *Laval un Partneri Ltd v Svenskabyggnadsarbetareförbundet* (n 103) paras 106–11.

[112] See, for example, ACL Davies, 'One Step Forward, Two Steps Back? The *Viking* and *Laval* Cases in the ECJ' (2008) 37 Industrial Law Journal 126–48 and the contributions to M Freedland and J Prassl (eds), *Viking, Laval and Beyond* (Oxford, Hart 2015).

[113] *Opinion 2/2013 on EU Accession to the ECHR* EU:C:2014:245 (18 December 2014).

directly effective EU law. This may detract from the ability of national courts and the CJEU to work together to protect human rights, particularly if national courts find that their constitutionally protected right is overridden by European law which provides a weaker protection of human rights. This arguably occurred in *Melloni*, concerning the validity of a European Arrest Warrant to a Spanish resident who had been convicted of a criminal offence *in absentia* in Italy.[114] Melloni argued that the European Arrest Warrant was contrary to his human rights, specifically the rights of defence guaranteed under the Spanish Constitution, which would require that the arrest only be executed if there was a guarantee of a re-trial in Italy where Melloni was present to provide a defence. The Spanish Constitutional Court referred three questions to the CJEU, regarding the interpretation of the provisions of the Framework Directive implementing the European Arrest Warrant, whether the Framework Directive was contrary to human rights and whether article 53 of the Charter permitted Spain to apply a higher standard of human rights than that found in EU law.

The CJEU concluded that the Framework Directive required compliance with a European Arrest Warrant, even when this arrest was made against an individual who had been tried *in absentia*, if the criteria of the Framework Directive had been met. Article 4 of the original Framework Directive, enacted in 2002[115] had made the execution of a European Arrest Warrant when an individual had been tried *in absentia* subject to a guarantee that the individual would be re-tried and would be present at this re-trial. However, this had been replaced in 2009 by new provisions which provided a detailed account of the circumstances in which a European Arrest Warrant was to be executed when a person was tried *in absentia*, including the circumstances that had occurred in Melloni's case—where the individual was aware of the trial, had instructed lawyers to provide his defence and these lawyers had attended the trial on the individual's behalf and provided a defence.[116] As such, the Framework Directive required that the European Arrest Warrant be executed, even without the guarantee of a re-trial.[117] In reaching this conclusion, the CJEU protected human rights to a lesser degree than they appeared to be protected under the Spanish Constitution, despite article 53 of the Charter which specifically empowers member states to provide stronger human rights protections than those found in EU law.

Following the decision of the CJEU, the Spanish Constitutional Court then had to apply the outcome of that decision, applying this to the facts of *Melloni*. The Spanish Constitutional Court accommodated the decision of the CJEU by revisiting its interpretation of article 24 of the Spanish Constitution. It reinterpreted the provision to conclude that, in situations governed by international law, it was not the case that all of the elements of article 24 would apply. Rather, the essence of article 24 would apply, with the content of the additional elements beyond the essence of article 24 being determined by the application of the relevant international law.[118]

It is, to put it mildly, difficult to see the series of exchanges between the CJEU and the Spanish Constitutional court as a paragon of constitutional collaboration.

[114] C-399/11 *Stefano Melloni v Ministerio Fiscal* [2013] QB 1067.

[115] Framework Directive 2002/584/JHA of 13 June 2002.

[116] Framework Directive 2009/584 Amendment of 26 February 2009.

[117] *Stefano Melloni v Ministerio Fiscal* (n 114) paras 35–46.

[118] STC 26/2014 (Spanish Constitutional Court), http://boe.es/boe/dias/2014/03/11/pdfs/BOE-A-2014-2650.pdf. See K Leonarts, 'EU Values and Constitutional Pluralism: The EU System of Fundamental Rights Protection' (2014) 24 Polish Yearbook of International Law 135; and A Torres Perez, '*Melloni* in Three Acts: From Dialogue to Monologue' [2014] European Constitutional Law Review 308.

Criticism can be levelled at both the Spanish Constitutional Court and the CJEU. The CJEU's strong stance on promoting the supremacy of directly effective EU law here does not facilitate constitutional collaboration. Torres Perez, for example, argues that the CJEU should have been more accommodating to the arguments of the Spanish Constitutional Court regarding the ability of interpreting the Charter to provide for a stronger protection of rights, thereby using the Charter to override provisions of the European Arrest Warrant. Although Bot AG was willing to engage with, albeit ultimately rejecting, this argument, the CJEU did not refer to this possibility in its judgment.[119] Nor did the CJEU refer to article 53 of the Charter, which provides that 'nothing in this Charter shall be interpreted as restricting or adversely affecting human rights and fundamental freedoms as recognised by ... the Member States' constitutions'. Torres Perez concludes that, by failing to discuss these issues, the CJEU cut off effective dialogue between the CJEU and the Spanish Constitutional Court.[120] Criticisms may also be levelled at the original decision of the Spanish Constitutional court. As Besselink recognizes, the Spanish Constitutional Court's conclusion that the European Arrest Warrant provisions breached the Spanish constitution was reached despite the opposite conclusion being reached in lower courts and, presumably by the Spanish Government when it agreed to the provisions and signed the Framework Decision incorporating the ability to execute an arrest warrant when an individual had been tried *in absentia*, but where this individual had been represented in court by a legal representative.[121] Constitutional collaboration could have operated better here if the Constitutional Court had been more willing to interpret the Spanish Constitution in a manner which reduced the potential conflict with the Framework Directive, as it did following the decision of the CJEU.

In *Melloni* the CJEU took a strong line on the supremacy of EU law in the face of a conflict with national constitutional provisions, contrary to other case law, such as *Omega Spielhallen*, where the CJEU appears to be more willing to encourage dialogue between itself and national courts. However, despite the fact that this decision may undermine constitutional collaboration, nevertheless there are indications that the CJEU is conscious of the value of encouraging dialogue between national courts and the CJEU, referring to the need for judicial co-operation and uniformity of application of the European Arrest Warrant if this measure is to achieve its purpose.[122] However, it is less clear how far the CJEU wishes to consciously encourage dialogue between the national courts and the CJEU.[123] Moreover, the modification of the Framework Directive could be interpreted as the product of a form of inter-institutional interaction between the national courts and the CJEU. The detailed list of criteria established in the 2009 Amendment to the 2002 Framework Directive was designed specifically to respond to difficulties that arose with the original 2002 solution. The 2002 Directive relied on the need for guarantees between member states as to the possibility of a retrial. This solution was unsatisfactory, particularly as it led to uncertainty as to the assessment of whether this guarantee was sufficient to ensure the protection of the rights of defence. It was also criticized by national courts. The legislation in 2009 aimed to provide a detailed list of criteria, to which the different member states had contributed

[119] Torres Perez n 118. [120] ibid.

[121] LMF Besselink, 'The Parameters of Constitutional Conflict After *Melloni*' [2014] European Public Law Review 541, 547.

[122] *Stefano Melloni v Ministerio Fiscal* (n 114) paras 43–44, 51, and 62–63.

[123] See, for example, Weiler, 'Prologue: Global and Pluralist Constitutionalism—Some Doubts' (n 101); and Weiler, 'Dialogical Epilogue' (n 101).

and agreed, to ensure an improvement in legal certainty, judicial co-operation, mutual trust amongst the judiciary, and to ensure a good protection of the rights of defence drawing on the problems faced in earlier case law and the constitutional protections found in different member states.[124] In addition, the decision to insist on the enforcement of EU law here, limiting the role of the national courts, can be justified because of the use of the democratic process to determine a solution, a means of ensuring inter-institutional interactions between the EU legislature and the courts. Although, as Besselink recognizes, we may be critical as to the extent to which this process satisfies the requirements of a democratic agreement between the member states.[125]

C. Constitutional counter-balancing

In a similar manner to the interactions between the national courts and the CJEU, there are two mechanisms of constitutional counter-balancing which can be weighed against the CJEU's assertion of the primacy of EU law, where the UK courts place limits on the extent to which directly effective EU law overrides national law and either refuses to follow, or indicates a potential refusal to give primacy to directly effective EU law and where the UK courts refuse to implement a decision of the CJEU following an article 267 reference from the UK courts. As with all measures of constitutional counter-balancing, if these mechanisms are to facilitate democratic dialogue they should be used sparingly to counteract situations where the CJEU has transgressed its constitutional powers, or where the UK courts have a better ability to recognize and correct a mistake made by the CJEU. The examples of constitutional counter-balancing interactions between the UK courts and the CJEU illustrate that the national courts are conscious of these restrictions, exercising constitutional counter-balancing in a manner which may facilitate democratic dialogue.

The clearest example of an indirect interaction used to enforce constitutional counter-balancing is the *HS2* decision of the UK Supreme Court, which concerned the legality of the government's decision to use a hybrid Bill process to provide a legal basis for the high speed rail link from London to the north of England.[126] The issue arose as to whether the decision to use a hybrid Bill breached requirements under EU law, specifically relating to whether there was a need for a strategic environmental assessment and whether the hybrid Bill procedure would satisfy the procedural requirements relating to decision-making in areas which have an impact on the environment. The case is not an example of one where the Supreme Court refused to follow directly effective EU law. Nevertheless, there are three aspects of the case which illustrate the potential for inter-institutional interactions between the UK Supreme Court and the CJEU which may help to provide mechanisms of constitutional balance.

First, there is evidence of the UK courts interpreting EU law in a manner which aims to reduce possible tensions between directly effective EU law and national law, whilst also paying attention to common principles of both EU and national law. The applicants argued that, in order to comply with the provisions of the Environmental Impact Assessment Directive there would need to be elements of public participation in the decision.[127] Article 1(4) of the Directive provided an exemption from these

[124] *Stefano Melloni v Ministerio Fiscal* (n 114) paras 65–71 of the opinion of Bot AG and paras 44 and 62 of the judgment.

[125] Besselink (n 121) 547.

[126] *R (HS2 Alliance Ltd) v Secretary State for Transport* (n 92).

[127] Directive 2011/92; [2012] OJ L26/1.

requirements with regard to 'projects the details of which are adopted by a specific action of national legislation', recognizing that the legislative process fulfilled the objectives of the Directive. When interpreting this provision, the CJEU concluded that this only applied when there was evidence that the legislative process did indeed satisfy the requirements of the Directive, doing so by ensuring that the legislative process actually had taken place and that there was no evidence that the legislative enactment was merely a ratification of an executive decision. However, this had been added to by statements by Advocate Generals which required a more detailed analysis, looking at whether the legislature had respected the appropriate procedure and whether information on the environmental project had been circulated to and read by the participants in the legislative debate, enabling the participants to debate and examine these issues effectively. To adopt this interpretation of the requirements of the Directive, as advocated by the applicants, would give rise to problems in UK law given the principle of parliamentary privilege, specifically the parliamentary privilege of freedom of expression, found in article 9 of the Bill of Rights 1689, preventing the questioning of proceedings in Parliament by the courts.

When interpreting EU law, the Supreme Court took account of the principle of parliamentary privilege, conscious of the fact that this rested on the separation of powers which was a constitutional principle common to the member states of the EU and also formed part of EU law. Therefore, there were good grounds for adopting the narrower interpretation of article 1(4) of the Directive, such that the courts would check that debate had taken place and there was no mere ratification, but would stop short of questioning proceedings in Parliament. Lord Reed, for example, stated that, given the separation of powers, and the extent to which a detailed analysis of the legislative process could cause problems in most EU member states, 'it appears unlikely that the Court of Justice intended to require national courts to exercise a supervisory jurisdiction over the internal proceedings of national legislatures'.[128] This approach facilitates democratic dialogue as the UK Supreme Court refers to constitutional principles common to the EU when reaching this conclusion. This indirect form of dialogue can indirectly facilitate constitutional collaboration, reinforcing common constitutional principles and helping inform the CJEU as to the nature of a consensus of constitutional principles across the EU. Moreover, by adopting this interpretation, the national court removes the potential for conflict. The Supreme Court tries first to reduce conflict, reserving its power to refuse to apply directly effective provisions of EU law for extreme circumstances.

Second, the *HS2* case illustrates how the normative values underpinning the model of democratic dialogue can be enhanced through constitutional counter-balancing mechanisms through the clear assertion of the UK Supreme Court that the nature of the relationship between directly effective provisions of EU law and UK law is, as far as the UK courts are concerned, regulated by UK as opposed to EU law. Lord Reed, for example, asserts that the nature of the relationship between directly effective EU law and national law 'cannot be resolved simply by applying the doctrine developed by the Court of Justice of the supremacy of EU law, since the application of that doctrine in our law itself depends upon the 1972 Act', the 1972 Act being the European Communities Act 1972.[129] Moreover, Lord Reed states that '[i]f there is a conflict between a constitutional principle ... and EU law, that conflict has to be resolved by our courts as an issue arising under the constitutional law of the United Kingdom'.[130]

[128] *R (HS2 Alliance Ltd) v Secretary State for Transport* (n 92) [110].
[129] ibid, [79].
[130] ibid.

Lord Neuberger and Lord Mance conclude that '[u]nder the European Communities Act 1972, United Kingdom courts have also acknowledged that European law now requires them to treat domestic statutes, whether passed before or after the 1972 Act, as invalid if and to the extent that they cannot be interpreted consistently with European law'.[131] In other words, UK courts look to UK legislation, as interpreted by UK courts, to determine the nature of the relationship between EU law and UK law.

These statements can be interpreted as an indirect exercise of a constitutional counter-balancing mechanism. The UK Supreme Court is not refusing to follow directly effective EU law. Nevertheless, it is making it clear that, to the extent that the UK courts disapply national legislation which contravenes the provisions of directly effective EU law, this is due to their application of national law. The UK courts are asserting their ability to determine the nature of this relationship. The expression of this authority, coupled with measures to adhere to directly effective EU law in this case, is in line with the provisions for constitutional balance found in the model of democratic dialogue. The constitutional counter-balancing measure is kept in reserve, to be used only in situations in which it is not possible to interpret directly effective EU law in a manner which removes the possibility of its conflict with a fundamental principle of the UK constitution.

Third, the Justices of the Supreme Court in *HS2* make it clear that they would only refuse to adhere to the primacy of directly effective EU law when this conflicted with fundamental constitutional statutes, constitutional instruments, or fundamental constitutional principles of the common law. In the words of Lord Neuberger and Lord Mance:

> [i]t is, putting the point at its lowest, certainly arguable (and it is for the United Kingdom law and courts to determine) that there may be fundamental principles, whether contained in other constitutional instruments or recognised at common law, of which Parliament when it enacted the European Communities Act 1972 did not either contemplate or authorise the abrogation.[132]

Not only is it clear that it is only fundamental constitutional principles which may trigger a refusal to comply with directly effective EU law, but also it is clear that this statement is expressed cautiously. First, it is clearly obiter dicta from Lord Neuberger and Lord Mance. Second, the Justices of the Supreme Court do not clearly assert a limit to the primacy of directly effective EU law, but instead state that it is arguable that such a limit may arise. Third, further caution and limits arise from the way in which the courts look to whether the principles are so fundamental that Parliament would not have intended their abrogation. All of these factors illustrate a cautionary approach to the use of a constitutional counter-balancing mechanism, using this as a last resort as required for these mechanisms to facilitate democratic dialogue. The statements in *HS2*, therefore, illustrate how constitutional counter-balancing mechanisms may be used in a manner which facilitates democratic dialogue between the UK courts and the CJEU. It also illustrates the more subtle relationship between directly effective EU law and national law, particularly pertinent when evaluating the extent to which leaving the EU will restore sovereignty to the UK. The UK Supreme Court was willing to recognize that there may be some aspects of sovereign power which would not be disapplied by directly effective provisions of EU law. Moreover, Michael Gove, when presenting evidence before the Justice Sub-Committee of the House of Lords' EU Committee, recognized the potential of the then proposed British Bill of Rights to

[131] ibid, [206]. [132] ibid, [207].

provide a list of these principles, specifically referring to the decision of the Supreme Court in *HS2*.[133]

The UK Supreme Court has also shown that it is sensitive to the problems which may arise should they be in a position where they are required to provide a remedy to a potential breach of directly effective EU law by legislation, where the amendment of the legislation so as to comply with these provisions may be best left to the legislature. This illustrates how constitutional counter-balancing mechanisms can facilitate democratic dialogue by being sensitive to the constitutional distribution of power between the legislature and the courts. In *Chester*, for example, the issue arose as to whether the blanket ban on prisoner voting, extending to votes in municipal elections, breached EU law.[134] Although the court concluded that the blanket ban did not breach EU law, nevertheless Lord Mance discussed the potential implications should such a breach have been established, stating that

> the only relief that could be considered under domestic law would be a generally phrased declaration that the legislative provisions governing eligibility to vote in European Parliamentary and municipal elections in the United Kingdom were inconsistent with European Union law. Thereafter, it would be for the United Kingdom Parliament to address the position and make such legislative changes as were considered appropriate.[135]

This dicta recognizes the difficulties which arise with blanket bans which may breach rights, but where the choice as to how the blanket ban should be modified so as to ensure rights are adequately protected can require the balancing of complex policy issues and may also include specific regulation or implementation. There are therefore good reasons for using a remedy which would facilitate democratic resolution made by the legislature. This is particularly the case when it would be unclear as to whether the specific rights of the individual before the court had been breached by this blanket ban.

Finally, constitutional counter-balancing may occur indirectly when UK courts refuse to implement a decision of the CJEU following an article 267 reference from the national court to the CJEU. For this to be exercised in a manner which facilitates democratic dialogue it should only occur rarely when the UK court is better placed to recognize and correct a mistake made by the CJEU, in particular when the CJEU misunderstand an issue of national law. In this regard it is similar to the democratic dialogue which may occur when the UK courts refuse to follow a clear and constant line of case law from the ECtHR. The only instance in which the UK Supreme Court did not follow the decision of the CJEU following an article 267 preliminary reference is *HMRC v Aimia Coalition Loyalty Limited*, concerning VAT payments on the nectar card reward scheme.[136]

The case had been referred to the CJEU under article 267 TFEU by the House of Lords in 2008. When hearing the reference, the CJEU had joined the case with another that also concerned VAT issues from loyalty card schemes—*Baxi v HMRC*. The CJEU concluded that payments from companies like Aimia, who facilitated loyalty schemes, were consideration payments as regards contracts to which they were third parties and, as such, VAT could not be deducted. When determining whether to adhere to the decision of the CJEU following this article 267 reference, the majority

[133] M Gove, giving evidence to the Justice Sub-Committee of House of Lords' European Union Committee on 2 February 2016. A transcript of the evidence is available here: http://data.parliament.uk/writtenevidence/committeeevidence.svc/evidencedocument/eu-justice-subcommittee/potential-impact-of-repealing-the-human-rights-act-on-eu-law/oral/28347.html.

[134] *R (Chester) v Secretary of State for Justice* (n 15).

[135] ibid, [72].

[136] [2013] UKSC 15, [2013] 2 All ER 719.

of the Supreme Court examined closely the different responsibilities of the national courts and the CJEU under the article 267 reference procedure, recognizing the role of the CJEU to determine the law and the national courts to apply these legal determinations to the facts. The majority in *Aimia* concluded that the law was fairly clear and that the real issue here was how the law applied to the distinct factual arrangements in the nectar card loyalty scheme. Although the preliminary reference in *Aimia* was joined to that in *Baxi*, the majority felt that the two schemes differed on their facts. *Baxi* involved schemes where A contracted with B to administer loyalty schemes by B to its customers. In effect, customers received points from B and redeemed them for goods and services from B, the scheme being administered by A. The nectar card scheme in *Aimia* was different, relying on a series of transactions. If company B wished to join the scheme, it would contract with Aimia to supply points to customers, C, buying goods and services from B. Aimia would agree to redeem these points to C. In order to do so, Aimia contracted with other companies supplying goods and services, D, to pay for the goods and services supplied by D to C when C used their points rewarded to them from buying goods from B. B would pay Aimia for the points it issued and Aimia would pay VAT on this transaction. In addition, Aimia paid D an amount per point to enable D to supply the goods and services to C using their points. In other words, C received points from B and redeemed them to obtain goods and services from a range of companies, sometimes this would be B, but it need not be from B and could be from D, E, F etc. This difference in facts meant that the Supreme Court was not bound by the conclusion of the CJEU that VAT could not be deducted.

The approach of the Supreme Court in *Aimia* illustrates the reluctance of the UK Supreme court to defy the CJEU, reserving this as a possible means of last resort. Also, it reflects the relative institutional competences of the national courts and the CJEU. National courts are better placed to determine factual issues, whereas the CJEU is better placed to resolve issues of the law, being an expert in European Union law. Exercising constitutional counter-balancing mechanisms in this way, as well as exercising them in a manner which reflects the different institutional competences of national and supranational courts is a better means of ensuring that constitutional counter-balancing mechanisms facilitate democratic dialogue.

IV. Conclusion

Inter-institutional interactions can and do arise between the UK courts and the ECtHR and between the UK courts and the CJEU. Although the formal mechanisms through which these interactions arise may differ, in addition to the different constitutional relationships, nevertheless it is possible for both of these forms of inter-institutional interaction to facilitate democratic dialogue. This is more likely to occur when these interactions facilitate constitutional collaboration, through both formal and informal dialogue, with mechanisms of constitutional counter-balancing reserved for those situations in which one court appears to have transgressed its constitutional authority, or where there are good reasons for challenging the factual basis on which the decision of the court is based. There is less evidence of inter-institutional interactions facilitating deliberative democracy. This may be the case where the courts give weight to democratic decision-makers and may also occur informally when decisions of the courts are reported on by the media and discussed more broadly in society.

The inter-institutional interactions between the UK courts and the ECtHR cast doubt on the extent to which the Human Rights Act 1998 needs to be modified due to concerns of the strong influence of the ECtHR. There is evidence that both the UK courts and the ECtHR are sensitive to those instances where the relative institutional features of the courts mean that the rights-issue is better suited for determination by either the ECtHR or the national courts. There is also evidence of informal dialogue, where both courts play a role in the development of human rights, in addition to instances where the UK courts are willing to use constitutional counter-balancing mechanisms where the ECtHR has taken decisions which have failed to take account of English law. These mechanisms of inter-institutional interaction may provide a better means of regulating the relationship between the UK courts and the ECtHR than the current proposals to make decisions of the ECtHR advisory only.

The inter-institutional interactions between the CJEU and the UK courts also cast doubt on the extent to which directly effective EU law overrides national law. First, these interactions suggest that there are constitutional limits on the extent to which UK transferred sovereignty to the EU and second, they suggest that there are clear indications that UK courts regard UK law as determining the nature of the relationship between directly effective EU law and national law. An understanding of the more subtle interactions between the UK courts and the CJEU questions the portrayal of some that the CJEU is clearly hierarchically superior to the UK Supreme Court and that the UK courts accepted this hierarchy through their acceptance of directly effective EU law in the *Factortame* series of decisions.

Conclusion

This book has argued that there are many misunderstandings about democratic dialogue. It is not the case that accounts of democratic dialogue are able to provide a new and distinct method of protecting human rights, providing the perfect balance between legal and political protections of human rights. Accounts of legal and political constitutionalism already provide for a combination of political and legal protections of rights and if we search for a middle ground between these two accounts, we find that there is no stable middle ground for democratic dialogue to occupy. Nor is it the case that democratic dialogue is different because it is dynamic, drawing on the way in which institutions interact. We can find accounts of legal and political constitutionalism which have the same dynamic element, drawing on how interactions between institutions of the constitution can generate definitions of rights. Moreover, it is not the case that democratic dialogue can only take place in those legal systems which have adopted a commonwealth model of rights protection. Dialogue can take place in a variety of constitutional protections of rights, including those with constitutionally protected rights, where courts are empowered to strike down legislation which contravenes human rights. Commonwealth models establish formal or legal means of institutional interactions and it may well be that democratic dialogue is more likely to be facilitated through these mechanisms of inter-institutional interaction. However, it can equally be the case that a commonwealth model does not facilitate democratic dialogue given the way in which the legislature and the court exercise their powers under any particular commonwealth model.

Given the inherent difficulty of finding a clear middle ground for democratic dialogue to occupy, and the many ways in which democratic dialogue appears to merge with, or collapse into, arguments for a legal or a political protection of rights, there is a danger that democratic dialogue is dismissed as either non-existent or ubiquitous. This book argues that the better interpretation is to embrace dialogue's apparent ubiquitous nature, recognizing that this can be regarded as a strength as opposed to a weakness. If we are to understand democratic dialogue, we need to recognize that its value lies in investigating and evaluating inter-institutional interactions. The dialogue model is useful both in terms of understanding how institutions interact and determining the value of these interactions. We argued that inter-institutional interactions can help to provide for a better protection of rights by drawing on the relative strengths and weaknesses of the way in which the legislature and the courts reason about rights respectively. In addition, these interactions can facilitate deliberation, both in the institutions of the constitution and more widely in society by facilitating democratic debate. Interactions may also provide a good set of checks and balances, helping institutions to resolve potential constitutional crises before they arise.

We then applied democratic dialogue to the UK constitution, in terms of its general application and its specific application to the protection of human rights in the United Kingdom through the Human Rights Act 1998, European Union law, and the common law. We also examined how far democratic dialogue can apply to interactions between the UK courts and both the European Court of Human Rights and the

Democratic Dialogue and the Constitution. First Edition. Alison L Young. © Alison L Young 2017. Published 2017 by Oxford University Press.

European Court of Justice. Our analysis demonstrated that democratic dialogue is an ideal. Its achievement is based on assumptions which may be satisfied to a greater or lesser degree in different constitutional settings. Moreover, we recognized that democratic dialogue can be facilitated, or frustrated, by a range of different interactions. Rather than adopt democratic dialogue as an ideal means of protecting human rights, we must recognize that a better protection of rights may be facilitated to a greater or lesser degree through the means in which institutions of the constitution interact with each other. We also need to recognize other values which may be facilitated, which may require interactions of a different nature from those which aim to provide for a better protection of rights. Moreover, any form of interaction has to take account of the division of power in a particular constitution, ensuring that interactions do not undermine the independence of the judiciary. We also noted that interactions will be tempered by the traditional manner in which institutions behave. Institutions will not change their behaviour in order to facilitate democratic dialogue unless there is an incentive to do so.

Constitutional law does not stand still. It sometimes evolves slowly and sometimes moves in sudden bursts, responding to political tensions and crises. This has been blatantly and dramatically demonstrated by recent events in the UK constitution. During the writing of this book, the law has changed significantly in terms of the protection of human rights. The Conservative Party came into power in 2015 having made two manifesto commitments which, if and when they are implemented, will have a vivid impact on the way in which the United Kingdom protects human rights. First, there was the promise to 'scrap' the Human Rights Act 1998 and replace this with a British Bill of Rights and Responsibilities—later a British Bill of Rights—with an outline of the possible direction of change being found in an earlier document produced by the Conservative Party.[1] Although the Queen's Speech of 2015 mentioned that the government 'will bring forth proposals for a British Bill of Rights',[2] this being repeated in the Queen's Speech for 2016,[3] to date no specific proposals have been brought forth. Second, the Queen's Speech in 2015 stated that the government would 'renegotiate the United Kingdom's relationship with the European Union' and introduce legislation 'to provide for an in-out referendum on membership of the European Union before the end of 2017'.[4] The promise of a referendum was repeated in the Queen's Speech of 2016.[5] On 23 June 2016 the referendum was held and a majority of the electorate voted in favour of leaving the European Union. In the meantime, a series of cases before the Court of Appeal used the EU's Charter of Fundamental Rights to disapply legislation which contravened human rights protected by the Charter. The conclusion will draw on these recent developments to help further illustrate the argument presented in this book.

I. The British Bill of Rights

It is difficult to predict when the proposals for a British Bill of Rights will appear, in addition to the difficulty of predicting the possible content of these proposals given the

[1] The Conservative Party, *Protecting Human Rights in the UK: The Conservative Party's Proposals for Changing Britain's Human Rights Laws* https://www.conservatives.com/~/media/files/downloadable%20Files/human_rights.pdf.

[2] https://www.gov.uk/government/speeches/queens-speech-2015.

[3] https://www.gov.uk/government/speeches/queens-speech-2016.

[4] See n 2.

[5] See n 3.

potential impact of the Referendum vote to leave the European Union. What appeared at first to be rather dramatic statements concerning the desire to 'scrap' the Human Rights Act 1998, now appear to have been watered down to a set of proposals that may make little difference to the protection of human rights in the United Kingdom. According to a recent report of the House of Lords European Union Committee:

[t]he principal motives for a British Bill of Rights are to restore national faith in human rights and to give human rights greater national identity, rather than to enhance human rights protections in the UK.[6]

The proposals, therefore, are likely to focus on this aim of repatriating human rights, seeking to reduce the impact of decisions of the European Court of Human Rights (ECtHR) on UK courts and to redress the balance between competing rights where the United Kingdom would balance rights differently from the ECtHR. The most oft-cited example being the need to redress the perceived imbalance caused by the ECHR giving greater protection to privacy over and above the interests of freedom of expression.[7] There are also concerns about the extra-territorial scope accorded to the Convention by the Strasbourg courts, and advocates of repatriating rights seek derogations from the application of the Convention to British troops serving abroad.[8]

There are two main themes found in the reform proposals which are relevant to the discussion of democratic dialogue. These themes can be gleaned from the Conservative Party's manifesto,[9] its policy paper 'Protecting Rights in the UK: The Conservatives' Proposals for Changing Britain's Human Rights Laws'[10] published in October 2014, and ministerial statements. First, there is a desire to limit the role of the ECtHR, particularly to restrict what the Conservative Government regards as 'mission creep', where the decisions of the ECtHR are seen to go beyond the original intentions of the initial signatories to the Convention. Second, there is a desire to redress the balance between Parliament and the courts, reducing the powers of the court to read and give effect to legislation to ensure its compatibility with Convention rights. Both of these aims will have an impact on the inter-institutional interactions between the legislature and the court and between the UK courts and the ECtHR. The proposal to make decisions of the ECtHR advisory only may alter the interactions between the UK courts and the ECtHR. The proposal to modify section 3(1) would alter the relationship between the courts and the legislature. Democratic dialogue casts doubt on the justification for modifying the impact of judgments of the ECtHR and of reducing the powers of the court. The assumptions on which these proposed reforms are based fail to take account of the impact of inter-institutional interactions between the legislature and the judiciary, and between the UK courts and the ECtHR. Of greater concern, both proposals have potentially deleterious consequences for the facilitation of democratic dialogue in the United Kingdom.

At the date of writing, it is possible to point to two means through which a proposed British Bill of Rights could reduce the influence of the ECtHR. First, it appears that the British Bill of Rights will set out specific human rights in sections of primary legislation, these provisions mirroring Convention rights. This replaces the current system

[6] See European Union Committee, *The UK, the EU and a British Bill of Rights* 12th Report of Session 2015-16, HL paper 139, 9 May 2016, http://www.publications.parliament.uk/pa/ld201516/ldselect/ldeucom/139/139.pdf, para 44.

[7] ibid, para 41. [8] ibid, para 40.

[9] The Conservative Party, *Strong Leadership, a clear economic plan, a brighter more secure future: The Conservative Party Manifesto 2015*, https://www.conservatives.com/manifesto.

[10] See n 1.

in the Human Rights Act 1998 where the primary provisions of legislation refer to Convention rights, with a Schedule to the Act setting out the Convention rights the Human Rights Act 1998 incorporates into UK law. Second, it would appear that there is a desire to modify section 2(1) of the Human Rights Act 1998. As discussed above, section 2 requires the UK courts to 'take into account' decisions of the Strasbourg Court. It would appear that the British Bill of Rights may intend to make decisions of the ECtHR advisory only, as a means of reducing the influence of the ECtHR over domestic decisions on human rights. The aim is to reverse what the Conservative Government refers to as 'mission creep' on the part of the ECtHR.[11] In addition, the British Bill of Rights is likely to modify section 3(1) of the Human Rights Act 1998. The government appears to be concerned that section 3(1) has given too much power to the courts, empowering the courts to read legislation in a way which contradicts the clear wording of legislation. Although there is no clear statement in the Conservative Party's manifesto setting out a precise modification to the provisions of section 3(1), the Conservative Party's earlier proposals suggested that section 3(1) would be modified such that courts would be unable to interpret legislation so as to comply with human rights where to do so would contradict the ordinary meaning of legislation.

The proposals are motivated by a desire to reduce the impact of the judgments of the ECtHR, which stands accused of mission creep by taking decisions which are beyond the scope of its competences. This concern appears to arise in particular where the ECtHR uses its judgments not to ensure that each signatory state remains a stable democracy, but to challenge the protection of human rights found in countries with stable democracies. In addition, there is concern that the ECtHR fails to grant a sufficiently large margin of appreciation when applying proportionality to determine whether a restriction on a right is necessary in a democratic society. However, as our analysis of section 2 and the inter-institutional interactions between the UK courts and the ECtHR demonstrated, there are examples of where UK courts have declined to follow decisions of the ECtHR. Moreover, we argued that these examples helped to facilitate constitutional collaboration between the two courts, as well as providing a means of maintaining constitutional balance. This was demonstrated most clearly in the inter-institutional interactions over life sentences. Here, the UK courts believed that the ECtHR had failed to understand an issue of English law. The UK courts then declined to follow the decision of the ECtHR, pointing out clearly the way in which this decision had failed to fully understand the application of English law. In turn, the ECtHR took account of the decision of the UK court, modifying its conclusion as to the compatibility of UK law with the ECHR in the light of the reasoning of the UK court. Both courts recognize that, although the ECtHR has the relative constitutional authority to determine Convention rights, domestic courts have more expertise in the field of national law.[12]

In addition, UK courts have clarified that, should a decision of the European Court of Human Rights breach a fundamental feature of English law, then the UK courts may not adhere to that decision of the European Court of Human Rights, although to date this has not occurred. This provides another means of constitutional balance, providing the United Kingdom with a means of responding when it is felt that the ECtHR has transgressed the proper bounds of its constitutional power. These mechanisms not

[11] See n 9, 73.

[12] *Vinter v UK* [2013] ECHR 66069/09; *Attorney General's Reference (No 60 of 2013), R v McLoughlin; R v Newell* [2014] EWCA Crim 188, [2014] 3 All ER 73; and *Hutchinson v UK* [2015] ECHR 57592/08.

only question the conclusion that the ECtHR has engaged in mission creep, but they also provide a different means of dealing with a perception of mission creep. This book has argued that mechanisms of constitutional counter-balancing provide a better way of responding to specific examples of where the ECtHR is believed to have transgressed the proper bounds of its constitutional power, aiming to find a solution where both courts can collaborate and learn from each other, rather than taking a more drastic measure which may harm the relationship between the UK courts and the ECtHR. It has also argued that these mechanisms should be seen as a form of constitutional back stop, used only in those situations where an institution has transgressed its constitutional role.

This conclusion is reinforced when we reflect on the way in which constitutional collaboration takes place between the UK courts and the ECtHR. Where there is no clear and constant line of case law, or where there is a wide margin of appreciation, the UK courts have no specific decision of the ECtHR to follow. In addition, they may distinguish a case of the ECtHR from the case before the UK courts, or from a previous clear and constant line of cases from the ECtHR. In these circumstances, informal dialogue may occur between the two courts. The ECtHR refers to and takes account of decisions of national courts, both as regards their arguments concerning the definition of Convention rights as well as providing information regarding an emerging European consensus which may influence the scope of the margin of appreciation.

The current inter-institutional interactions focus on the relative institutional features of the ECtHR and the national courts. Each court gives weight to the decisions of the other as regards their expertise. This helps to facilitate reasoning about rights, allowing a combination of the relative strengths of rights-reasoning in the UK courts and the ECtHR. By seeing decisions as 'advisory only', the UK courts may conclude that they can only examine the decision of the ECtHR in the same way they would regard decisions of courts in other jurisdictions—that is, that no weight should be given to the relative expertise of the ECtHR, its decisions being accepted only on the merits of the reasons the court provides for reaching a particular conclusion. This may reduce the ability of constitutional collaboration to reach better resolutions of rights-issues, drawing on the relative institutional expertise of both courts and giving weight to these conclusions accordingly.

Second, making decisions of the ECtHR advisory only alters the way in which constitutional counter-balancing mechanisms operate. The current interpretation of section 2 of the Human Rights Act 1998 means that constitutional counter-balancing mechanisms operate more as a back-stop rather than as the first port of call. UK courts only refuse to follow a clear and constant line of cases from the ECtHR when there are good reasons to do so—correcting legal errors which the UK courts are better placed to correct and as a last resort if the ECtHR were to override a fundamental feature of the UK constitution. If decisions were advisory only, the UK courts may refuse to follow decisions of the ECtHR more frequently. This may undermine one of the advantages of democratic dialogue; its ability to facilitate comity and allow for fluctuations in rights over time whilst minimizing conflict between the two courts.

Similar conclusions arise when we reflect on the proposals to modify section 3(1). There is a concern that the courts have more power than the legislature through the way in which the UK courts have interpreted 'so far as possible'. However, when we examine the way in which the UK courts have exercised their powers, they have been reluctant to contravene a fundamental feature of legislation, in addition to recognizing those circumstances in which the legislature is better placed to provide a remedy for a breach of Convention rights. The legislature has the ability to respond to any interpretation of legislation with which it disagrees—and there is evidence of the legislature doing so with regard to other court decisions—but the legislature has been reluctant to do so with regard to section 3.

The move to restrict the power of the courts to interpret legislation to comply with Convention rights may also harm the constitutional balance between the legislature and the judiciary. The proposals appear to be motivated to restrict the power of the courts by ensuring that the courts exercise interpretation so as to comply with the will of Parliament, rather than providing a means of protecting rights in situations where courts may be better able to reason about rights than the legislature. This threatens to remove a constitutional counter-balancing mechanism, as well as damaging constitutional collaboration. There are three possible consequences of this proposed reform. First, it may make little difference to how the courts use their powers to interpret legislation. Courts may interpret 'ordinary meaning' as including the same linguistic constraint as is currently found in their interpretation of section 3 of the Human Rights Act 1998, ensuring that legislation does not stretch the meaning of legislation and that it does not contradict a fundamental feature of the legislation in question. If this is the case, then the proposed reforms will have no impact on the extent to which human rights protections in the United Kingdom facilitate democratic dialogue.

Second, courts may perceive the reforms to the Human Rights Act as a challenge to their constitutional role to interpret legislation so as to ensure it does not contravene common law rights. This may have the effect of converting a mechanism of constitutional collaboration into a mechanism of constitutional counter-balancing. Instead of interpreting legislation so as to protect human rights, courts may feel that their only option to reason effectively about human rights would be to build on the dicta found in *Jackson*,[13] and *AXA*,[14] issuing court orders to disapply legislation which breaches not only the constitutional power of the court but also what the courts perceive to be fundamental constitutional principles of human rights. Human rights may be protected more through constitutional counter-balancing as opposed to constitutional collaboration, potentially undermining democratic dialogue and reducing its ability to operate as a pressure valve. It may also damage the rule of law through giving rise to greater legal uncertainty and instability.

Third, courts may read the proposed reforms as restricting their ability to interpret legislation in a manner which complies with Convention rights and, instead, refer more frequently to common law rights to provide a strong protection of human rights, applying the principle of legality. However, the inter-institutional interactions which occur through the application of the principle of legality are less likely to facilitate democratic dialogue than those occurring through the Human Rights Act 1998, particularly given the lack of an equivalent of section 4. Inter-institutional interactions under the common law would occur through courts refraining from exercising their powers, or from legislation overturning judicial interpretations of common law rights. These mechanisms may be more likely to facilitate constitutional counter-balancing, to the detriment of constitutional collaboration, potentially undermining the ability of inter-institutional interactions to facilitate democratic dialogue and provide a better protection of rights through maximizing the advantages and minimizing the disadvantages of predominantly legal or political protections of rights.

[13] *Jackson v Attorney General* [2005] UKHL 56, [2005] 4 All ER 1253, [102].

[14] *AXA General Insurance v Lord Advocate* [2011] UKSC 46, [2012] 1 AC 868.

II. Brexit

The consequences of the United Kingdom's exit from the European Union are even harder to predict. First, despite the referendum vote in favour of leaving the EU, it is not completely beyond the realms of possibility that the United Kingdom may end up remaining in the EU. However, given the new Prime Minister Theresa May's statement that 'Brexit means Brexit' this seems now like a very distant possibility indeed. Second, any speculation as to the impact of the referendum depends upon the terms of the withdrawal agreement. However, as with our discussion of the potential changes from the British Bill of Rights, democratic dialogue casts doubt on the justifications for Brexit. Moreover, the consequences of Brexit may reduce the ability of the UK constitution to facilitate democratic dialogue.

The possibility that, despite 'Brexit meaning Brexit', the United Kingdom may nevertheless remain in the EU, is reinforced by the wording of article 50 TEU, in addition to the constitutional requirements of the United Kingdom. Article 50 empowers the United Kingdom, and any other member state, to initiate the process of leaving the European Union, making this conditional on the United Kingdom satisfying its own constitutional requirements for doing so. There is considerable speculation as to what these requirements may entail[15]—ranging from a mere use of the prerogative power by the Prime Minister, to its being politically expedient, or constitutionally necessary through the adoption of a new convention, for the exercise of article 50 to be subject to parliamentary debate or a parliamentary resolution, or the need for an Act of Parliament.[16]

At the time of proofreading, the High Court had concluded in *Miller* that the Crown could not use prerogative power alone to trigger article 50.[17] The Government has already announced its intention to appeal the decision, which will be heard by the Supreme Court in December 2016. Given that part of the legal argument for the requirement of an Act of Parliament relies on a specific interpretation of article 50, it is not beyond the realms of possibility that an article 267 TFEU preliminary reference will be requested, although in the High Court, both parties conceded that article 50 was irrevocable. Even if the legal case were to succeed, and the Supreme Court were to conclude that an exercise of prerogative power could not be used to trigger article 50, a declaratory order will only determine the legal position. It would still be up to Parliament to determine how to respond in the light of this declaration of the legal position—although it would be a brave Parliament that ignored a declaratory order of the Supreme Court. It would be an equally brave Parliament that, in the face of a referendum decision, would refuse to pass an Act of Parliament granting the power to the Prime Minister to trigger article 50. However, were public opinion to shift drastically in favour of remain during the hiatus in which this legal issue is decided, Parliament may believe that the wisest course of action may be to prevent the triggering of article 50 to reflect this change.

To add to the complications, in the opinion of the author article 50 TEU would allow the United Kingdom to stop the article 50 procedure once triggered. This is

[15] AL Young, 'Brexit, Article 50 and the "Joys" of a Flexible, Evolving, Un-codified Constitution' UK Const L Blog (1 July 2016), available at https://ukconstitutionallaw.org.

[16] N Barber, T Hickman, and J King, 'Pulling the Article 50 "Trigger": Parliament's Indispensable Role' UK Const L Blog (27 June 2016), available at https://ukconstitutionallaw.org.

[17] *R(Miller) v Secretary of State for Exiting the European Union* [2016] EWHC 2768 (Admin).

supported by the relationship of article 50 to the Vienna Convention on the Law of Treaties, the wording of article 50, and teleological justifications. Article 54 of the Vienna Convention on the Law of Treaties allows a state to withdraw from a Treaty either through the consent of all of the parties to the Treaty following negotiations, or through the procedures set out in a particular international Treaty. Article 50 TEU provides the procedures through which member states can withdraw from the European Union. In international law, therefore, the United Kingdom remains a member of the EU unless and until the procedures of article 50 are completed. Moreover, paragraph 3 of article 50 states that:

> The Treaties shall cease to apply to the State in question from the date of entry into force of the withdrawal agreement or, failing that, two years after the notification referred to in paragraph 2, unless the European Council, in agreement with the Member State concerned, unanimously decides to extend this period.

In other words, the United Kingdom remains part of the EU unless and until a withdrawal agreement is determined, or the two-year period, subject to agreed extensions, comes to an end. It is clearly possible, therefore, for the United Kingdom to change its mind and remain a member of the EU, withdrawing from article 50 before the period of negotiations is over or the withdrawal agreement has come into force. This is particularly pertinent in the light of section 20 of the Constitutional Reform and Governance Act 2010 requiring, subject to narrow exceptions, Treaties to be laid before Parliament before ratification, with the ability of Parliament to vote against the ratification of the Treaty. In other words, it is possible that a parliamentary resolution may prevent the coming into force of the withdrawal agreement in the United Kingdom. In those circumstances, the United Kingdom would be forced either to withdraw its initial request, or to find itself being forced to completely leave the EU, with no withdrawal agreement. When this provision is interpreted teleologically, the functioning of the EU, and the relationship between the EU and the United Kingdom, are more likely to run smoothly if the United Kingdom has the option to stop the article 50 procedure and remain in the European Union in such a situation. Any possibility that the United Kingdom could use this flexibility abusively, to continue lengthening the negotiation period without the consent of the rest of the members of the EU, would be checked by a potential legal action, where the CJEU is likely to interpret that article 50 TEU cannot be used in this manner.[18]

Unless and until any withdrawal agreement is concluded, it is hard to determine the nature of the future relationship between the United Kingdom and the EU. However, it is clear that those advocating that the United Kingdom leave the EU were concerned by perceived increases in regulation by the EU (which some believe to be an encroachment upon parliamentary sovereignty), and by a desire to reduce immigration through modifying provisions relating to the free movement of workers. In the light of these concerns, it is likely that any withdrawal agreement will remove the United Kingdom from the EU Charter of Fundamental Rights, and that the United Kingdom will no longer be subject to the directly effective provisions of EU law, including general principles, which can disapply national law. Nevertheless, EU human rights may continue to have an indirect influence over United Kingdom law following a withdrawal agreement. All of EU law will continue to be interpreted in the light of the general principles and the Charter, including those provisions to which the United Kingdom will continue to adhere regulating any form of free trade agreement between the United Kingdom and the EU.

[18] See P Craig, 'Brexit: A Drama in Six Acts' (2016) 41 European Law Review 447.

Democratic dialogue casts doubt on some of the assumptions underpinning the Brexit debate. Our analysis of recent decisions of the Court of Appeal illustrated that directly effective provisions of EU law can be used to disapply legislation. However, we also recognized that the Supreme Court in *HS2* stated that directly effective EU law may not override constitutional statutes, constitutional instruments, or constitutional principles.[19] This constitutional counter-balancing mechanism provided an effective mechanism of allowing the UK courts to push back against a perceived transgression by the CJEU of its constitutional powers. Moreover, as Michael Gove, then the Minister of Justice, indicated when questioned by the Justice Sub Committee of the EU Committee of the House of Lords, the provisions of the British Bill of Rights would have provided parliamentary input into the definition of these constitutional provisions which could override directly effective EU law.[20] This mechanism, properly understood, could have provided a better means of regulating the constitutional balance between the United Kingdom and the EU than the potential constitutional crisis created by the decision to withdraw from the EU. In addition, it is important to recognize that although the UK's membership of the EU, with the need to accommodate the primacy of directly effective EU law, may have been the catalyst for the modification of parliamentary sovereignty, however understood, any modification did not occur through the operation of EU law alone. It occurred (in the first place) through the explicit recognition and acceptance by domestic courts that membership of the EU had altered the nature of parliamentary sovereignty in specific contexts. It is perfectly feasible, therefore, for the courts to modify parliamentary sovereignty in the future, such that other constitutional principles can be used to disapply legislation. The UK Parliament may regain sovereignty in the sense of being able to legislate in areas in which EU law currently places restrictions, but it may lose sovereignty in comparison to the UK courts, in addition to losing its power to influence the content of EU law to which it may still be bound under the withdrawal agreement.

This can be clearly illustrated by dicta in *Moohan v Lord Advocate*.[21] In *Moohan*, the applicants were arguing that the decision not to include prisoners in the franchise for the Scottish independence referendum contravened a Convention right or a fundamental common law right. The Supreme Court, with Lord Kerr dissenting, concluded that the Convention did not extend to include a right to vote in a referendum, as the referendum was not the equivalent of the election of a democratic legislative body. The Court also concluded that, although democracy was a fundamental principle of the common law, the common law did not extend to include a right to vote, such that this right could only be restricted by proportionate measures. Nevertheless, Lord Hodge, with whom Lord Neuberger, Baroness Hale, Lord Clarke, and Lord Reed concurred, stated in dicta that:

> [w]hile the common law cannot extend the franchise beyond that provided by parliamentary legislation, I do not exclude the possibility that in the very unlikely event that a parliamentary majority abusively sought to entrench its power by a curtailment of the franchise or similar device, the common law, informed by principles of democracy and the rule of law and international norms, would be able to declare such legislation unlawful.[22]

[19] *R (HS2 Action Alliance Ltd) v The Secretary of State for Transport* [2014] UKSC 3, [2014] 2 All ER 109.

[20] M Gove, giving evidence to the Justice Sub-Committee of House of Lords' European Union Committee on 2 February 2016. A transcript of the evidence is available here: http://data.parliament.uk/writtenevidence/committeeevidence.svc/evidencedocument/eu-justice-subcommittee/potential-impact-of-repealing-the-human-rights-act-on-eu-law/oral/28347.html.

[21] [2014] UKSC 67, [2015] AC 901.

[22] ibid, [35].

It is important to understand the context of this dicta. It illustrates the potential for the Supreme Court to use a constitutional counter-balancing mechanism in situations where it is felt that the UK legislature has transgressed the proper confines of its powers. This may have also been partly motivated by the lack of the ability to use constitutional collaboration mechanisms in *Moohan*. Section 3 of the Human Rights Act 1998 could not be used because article 3 of the First Protocol only applied to the right to vote for a democratic law-making body. Moreover, there was no fundamental right to vote in the common law. Extensions to the franchise in the United Kingdom had arisen from a series of legislative provisions, and could not be seen to derive from a set of decisions of the common law courts. Nor could the applicants resort to the EU Charter given that the referendum on Scottish independence was outside the scope of EU law. The only means left to the court to protect rights in these circumstances is to do so indirectly through the use of a mechanism of constitutional counter-balancing. That the courts may be prepared to do this when faced with extreme situations that may threaten their constitutional role was recently reinforced by the dicta of Lord Neuberger, with which Lady Hale, Lord Mance, Lord Reed, Lord Carnwath, Lord Hughes, and Lord Toulson all agreed, that:

> In our system of parliamentary supremacy (subject to arguable extreme exceptions which I hope and expect will never have to be tested in practice), it is not open to a court to challenge or refuse to apply a statute, save to the extent that Parliament authorises or requires a court to do so.[23]

This confirms that the measure of disapplying legislation, mentioned in *Jackson* and *AXA*, is an extreme mechanism, designed as a last resort, with courts first seeking to protect rights through statutory interpretation, or where legislation empowers the courts to do so. This is precisely how mechanisms of constitutional counter-balancing should apply. The worry which arises is, if there is a reduction in the means through which courts can protect fundamental rights in UK law, coupled with the removal of the means of disapplying legislation through EU law, will the courts be tempted to find more 'extreme circumstances' in which to disapply legislation in order to protect fundamental rights and not just as a means of preserving the constitutional position of the court?

The situation which arose in *Moohan* demonstrates that, even if the United Kingdom were to fully withdraw from the EU, there would still be sufficient evidence of bipolar sovereignty in the UK constitution to support an application of democratic dialogue. It also illustrates that human rights may continue to be protected in the United Kingdom following its withdrawal from the EU, and potentially the overturning of the Human Rights Act and its replacement by a British Bill of Rights, even one which severs the connection between human rights and the European Convention on Human Rights. However, the ability of the UK constitution to facilitate democratic dialogue through constitutional collaboration may be reduced. There may also be an impact on the ability of constitutional counter-balancing mechanisms being used to provide a pressure valve, smoothing potential conflicts between the legislature and the courts. Inter-institutional interactions in the United Kingdom may be more likely to protect rights through constitutional friction and attrition rather than through constitutional collaboration. Constitutional counter-balancing mechanisms should only be used in extreme circumstances, reducing the current formal and legal mechanisms which can apply as a better means of facilitating inter-institutional comity and collaboration.

[23] *R (on the application of the Public Law Project) v Lord Chancellor* [2016] UKSC 39.

III. Conclusion

This book has argued that democratic dialogue is a viable constitutional model which may have normative benefits. It has recognized that democratic dialogue depends as much on how powers are exercised as it does on the legal powers given to different institutions of the constitution. However, it is important to recognize the modest nature of the argument presented. First, this book has not carried out an extensive empirical analysis of whether the institutions of the constitution do act in the manner required of democratic dialogue. Rather, it has provided a normative framework and pointed out some of the features which may hinder the application of democratic dialogue. This does not undermine the argument made in the book. However, it may challenge the extent to which any constitution can and does adhere to the model of democratic dialogue by questioning the extent to which the assumptions on which democratic dialogue are based are met in any particular constitution, in addition to questioning whether institutions are prepared to act in the manner required to facilitate democratic dialogue. This, in turn, questions the extent to which normative benefits of democratic dialogue may be achieved. Second, we have argued that democratic dialogue can facilitate deliberative democracy, allowing a process of rights-determination which engages citizens. However, more work needs to be done on the extent to which citizens are willing to engage in this process and whether this means that democratic dialogue would require voting rights and rights of freedom of expression and freedom of information to have a more foundational status than other human rights. Third, although we have proposed a model of democratic dialogue, we have not argued that democratic dialogue is better than legal or political constitutionalism. We have merely argued that it is a viable alternative which can achieve normative goals. Although more remains to be done, it is hoped that this book has set out the ground work and has provided a means of explaining how democratic dialogue can operate as an alternative model of constitutionalism.

It is hard not to conclude that the consequences of the UK's decision to withdraw from the European Union, combined with the proposed replacement of the Human Rights Act 1998 with a British Bill of Rights could provoke a sea change in the UK constitution. This conclusion has focused on the impact on the protection of rights in the United Kingdom and more specifically on the consequences for democratic dialogue. However, both also have the potential to threaten the stability of the Union. The Scottish First Minister has already indicated that, should the United Kingdom withdraw from the EU, she may well ask for a second independence referendum. The Northern Ireland Act 1998, section 1, also provides for a referendum for the people of Northern Ireland, to determine whether to remain as part of the United Kingdom or to join Ireland, with a legal obligation on the UK Parliament to respect the outcome of the referendum.

In addition, it seems hard to conclude anything other than that legislation to implement the withdrawal agreement, and probably to replace the Human Rights Act 1998, would require the consent of the devolved legislatures. Section 2 of the Scotland Act 2016 inserted a new provision into section 28 of the Scotland Act 1998, recognizing the Sewel Convention that the 'Parliament of the United Kingdom will not normally legislate with regard to devolved matters without the consent of the Scottish Parliament'. A similar provision is contained in clause 2 of the Draft Welsh Bill. It is possible to argue that these new provisions do not create a legally enforceable obligation, merely recognizing a convention. In addition, it is possible to argue that the replacement of the Human Rights Act and the withdrawal from the EU are both constitutional matters, and hence are matters for the Westminster Parliament and not the devolved Parliaments and Assembly. Despite these technicalities, such a strong statement recognizing the convention would make it difficult to ignore politically. It would also be wise to err on the side of consultation given the impact of the withdrawal from the EU and the modification of the Human Rights Act 1998 on the scope of the law-making powers of the devolved nations.

Given the confusion surrounding the interpretation of the constitutional requirements for triggering article 50 TEU, and the tension created by the lack of a provision in the Referendum Act requiring a specific majority in favour of leaving the EU—be that in terms of percentages or reflecting a majority in all of the component nations of the United Kingdom—there may be calls for the United Kingdom to adopt a codified constitution. Or we may see the meteoric rise of common law constitutionalism as the courts fill the legal gap potentially created by the modification of the Human Rights Act and the UK's withdrawal from the EU. Neither of these directions mean that democratic dialogue is no longer suited to application to the UK constitution. However, when considering future constitutional change, it would be wise to remember that collaboration through inter-institutional interactions may provide a better means of resolving these tensions than a series of constitutional crises. The ad hoc and inadvertent collaboration through the use of constitutional counter-balancing mechanisms generated by crisis-reaction may be a less effective means of charting our path through dangerous constitutional waters. It would also be wise to take account of the realities of the UK's relationship with both the Court of Justice of the European Union and the European Court of Human Rights.

Democratic dialogue may not be the panacea which provides a miraculous means of the ideal blend of political and legal protections of rights. Nor is it capable of smoothing all instances of potential constitutional tension, removing constitutional crises and battles and replacing them with sophisticated dialogue and calm and respectful collaboration. Nor can it stop divisions arising between the desires of the political elites and the citizens they govern. However, a better understanding of inter-institutional interactions and the benefits they may facilitate becomes all the more important if we are to steer ourselves safely through choppy constitutional waters.

Index

The manufacturer's authorised representative in the EU for product safety is Oxford University Press España S.A. of el Parque Empresarial San Fernando de Henares, Avenida de Castilla, 2 – 28830 Madrid (www.oup.es/en or product.safety@oup.com). OUP España S.A. also acts as importer into Spain of products made by the manufacturer.

www.ingramcontent.com/pod-product-compliance
Ingram Content Group UK Ltd.
Pitfield, Milton Keynes, MK11 3LW, UK
UKHW020906180926
475638UK00003B/28
* 9 7 8 0 1 9 8 7 8 3 7 4 9 *